NYSTCE®

Complete Preparation for the

LAST, ATS-W, & MULTI-SUBJECT CST

Sixth Edition

NYSTCE®

Complete Preparation for the

LAST, ATS-W, & MULTI-SUBJECT CST

(Liberal Arts and Sciences Test) **(Assessment of Teaching Skills–Written)** **(Multi-Subject Content Specialty Test)**

Sixth Edition

Sandra Luna McCune and Kim S. Truesdell

KAPLAN

PUBLISHING

New York

NYSTCE, New York State Teacher Certification Examinations, and the NYSTCE logo are trademarks, in the United States and/or other countries, of the New York State Education Department and Pearson Education, Inc. or its affiliate(s).

This publication is designed to provide accurate and authoritative information in regard to the subject matter covered. It is sold with the understanding that the publisher is not engaged in rendering legal, accounting, or other professional service. If legal advice or other expert assistance is required, the services of a competent professional should be sought.

Published by Kaplan Publishing, a division of Kaplan, Inc.
1 Liberty Plaza, 24th Floor
New York, NY 10006

Artwork in LAST Diagnostic and Practice Tests is from the EclectiCollections (SM).

Printed in the United States of America

10 9 8 7 6 5 4 3 2 1

ISBN 13: 978-1-4195-5072-0

TABLE OF CONTENTS

SECTION ONE: PREPARING FOR THE NYSTCE

KAPLAN

ABOUT THE AUTHORS

Sandra Luna McCune, PhD, is a professor of elementary education at Stephen F. Austin State University, Nacogdoches, Texas. She is a nationally known expert in the area of teacher testing.

Kim S. Truesdell, EdD, is the director of the Teacher Education Institute at the University at Buffalo, New York, where she has been involved in the development of the teacher education program, the administration of the teacher certification program, and the creation and instruction of several education courses.

ABOUT THIS BOOK

New York requires that all candidates seeking teacher certification in the state achieve a qualifying score on the New York State Teacher Certification Examinations (NYSTCE). The NYSTCE consists of the Liberal Arts and Sciences Test (LAST), the Assessments of Teaching Skills–Written (ATS-W), Content Specialty Tests (CSTs), Bilingual Education Assessments (BEAs), and the Assessment of Teaching Skills–Performance (ATS-P).

In order to receive an *initial* teaching certificate in New York, you must pass the LAST assessment, the appropriate ATS-W exam, and the appropriate CST exam. Before you receive a *professional* teaching certificate, you must pass the ATS-P (a video assessment)* and a CST in the subject(s) in which you wish to be certified. Achieving a qualifying score on the BEAs is required of all candidates seeking bilingual education certificates or extensions.

Kaplan's *NYSTCE: Complete Preparation for the LAST, ATS-W, & Multi-Subject CST* will help you tackle that first step—achieving a passing score on the LAST, the ATS-W, and the Multi-Subject CST. This book is designed to prepare you for these three important components of the NYSTCE by providing you with essential information such as test content and layout, proven test-taking strategies and tips, and valuable practice complete with detailed explanations. Once you are familiar with these three exams and the objectives they are designed to test, you will be on your way to an initial certification in the state of New York. Good luck with your studies!

*Candidates who are issued an initial certificate effective February, 2, 2004, are not required to take the ATS-P.

Available Online

For Any Test Changes or Late-Breaking Developments

kaptest.com/publishing

The material in this book is up-to-date at the time of publication. However, the New York State Education Department may have instituted changes in the test or test-registration process after this book was published. Be sure to read carefully the materials you receive when you register for the test. If there are any important late-breaking developments—or any changes or corrections to the Kaplan test preparation materials in this book—we will post that information online at **kaptest.com/publishing**.

To access our exclusive online review guides for the tests, log onto **kaptest.com/education/NYSTCE.**

For customer service, please contact us at **booksupport@kaplan.com.**

PREPARING FOR THE NYSTCE

CHAPTER 1: THE TESTS

The LAST, the ATS-W, and the Multi-Subject CST are part of a series of assessments called the New York State Teacher Certification Examinations (NYSTCE), which you must pass in order to be certified to teach in New York State. The NYSTCE and the program that goes with them are the results of requirements adopted by the New York State Board of Regents in 1989, effective September 2, 1993. To apply for an initial teaching certificate, you will have to submit evidence of having achieved a satisfactory level of performance on the LAST, the ATS-W, and the CST portions of the NYSTCE. Your provisional certificate will be valid for five years.

THE LAST

The Liberal Arts and Sciences Test (LAST) portion of the NYSTCE is required for all those seeking initial teacher certification in New York State. The test is the same for every certification area (unlike the ATS-W, which has an elementary and secondary component). The LAST comprises a series of 80 multiple-choice questions and 1 written assignment. The multiple-choice portion covers a broad spectrum of liberal arts objectives, assessing analytical skills, critical thinking, communication skills, and multicultural awareness. The LAST assesses introductory liberal arts knowledge.

There are four subareas of the LAST: scientific, mathematical, and technological processes; historical and social scientific awareness; artistic expression and the humanities; and communication and research skills. These are assessed through the 80 multiple-choice questions. The fifth subarea, written analysis and expression, is assessed through a written performance task in which you will be given two sides of an issue—unrelated to any of the subareas—and asked to defend one of the sides.

THE ATS-W

ATS-W stands for the Assessment of Teaching Skills–Written. There are two versions of this test: the Elementary and the Secondary. If you are seeking a PreK–6 common branch teaching certificate, you should take the Elementary ATS-W. If you are seeking a certificate for a secondary academic subject, you should take the Secondary ATS-W. If your goal is K–12 certification, you may elect to take either version of the ATS-W.

Each version of the test consists of approximately 80 multiple-choice questions and a written assignment. The ATS-W assesses knowledge of the learner, instructional planning and assessment, instructional delivery, and the professional environment. Each of these four subareas is defined by a set of objectives, which we will define and analyze in chapters 9 and 10.

THE CSTs

Each candidate wishing to acquire an initial teaching certification in New York must pass the Content Specialty Test in the specific subject required by his or her certification pathway. There are currently 38 different CSTs, assessing knowledge in subjects from Agriculture to Visual Arts. The CSTs typically consist of multiple-choice questions and a written assignment, but some also include taped listening and/or speaking components. To find out more about your required CST, be sure to visit www.highered.nysed.gov.

All candidates seeking initial certification in childhood education are required to take the Multi-Subject CST, which is covered by this book and is the most widely taken CST. The test consists of 90 multiple-choice questions and 1 written assignment.

The subareas covered on the Multi-Subject CST are English language arts, mathematics, science and technology, social studies, fine arts, health and fitness, family and consumer science, and career development. The written component focuses on foundations of reading. Each of these subareas is defined by a set of objectives, which we will define in chapter 15.

OTHER TESTS IN THE NYSTCE PROGRAM

BILINGUAL EDUCATION ASSESSMENTS (BEAs)

A candidate seeking a bilingual education extension to a certificate must pass the appropriate BEA. The tests are comprised of multiple-choice questions and constructed-response assignments and contain recorded listening and speaking components in English and listening, speaking, reading, and writing components in the tested language.

COMMUNICATION AND QUANTITATIVE SKILLS TEST (CQST)

The CQST is a multiple-choice-only test that is one of the requirements for a Transitional A certificate and an initial certificate in career and technical education subjects.

ASSESSMENT OF TEACHING SKILLS–PERFORMANCE (ATS-P) (VIDEO)

The ATS-P (video) requires a candidate to submit a 20- to 30-minute video-recorded sample of his or her teaching performance.

For more detailed information on these tests, be sure to visit the official NYSTCE site at www.nystce.nesinc.com.

HOW DO I REGISTER?

The New York State Teacher Certification Examination Program recommends that you take the LAST and the CST during your sophomore or junior year—after you have completed most of the basic liberal arts and sciences coursework. You should delay taking the ATS-W until you have had an opportunity to apply what you have learned in your pedagogical coursework to actual teaching situations, such as in student teaching. You will need to demonstrate this kind of thinking on the ATS-W.

Once you are certain when you want to take the exams, sign up as soon as possible. Application deadlines for the tests are very strict, and you will have to pay monetary penalties for registering late. The best thing for you to do is obtain a NYSTCE *Registration Bulletin* the semester *before* you want to take the tests so that you do not miss the deadline for regular registration.

You can find additional information, testing requirements, and the application form in the NYSTCE *Registration Bulletin*, available through most New York State institutions of higher education that have teacher education programs. Alternatively, you can obtain a copy from National Evaluation Systems (NES) or the Office of Teaching:

National Evaluation Systems, Inc.
Website: www.nystce.nesinc.com

Office of Teaching Initiatives
New York State Education Department
89 Washington Ave, 5N EB
Albany, NY 12234
Website: http://ohe33.nysed.gov/tcert/
Email: tcert@mail.nysed.gov
Telephone: (518) 474-3901
TTY for the deaf: 800-421-1220 (within NYS); 800-855-2880 (nationwide)

WHEN ARE THE TESTS GIVEN?

Candidates can take two of the exams on the same day (either the ATS-W or CST in the morning and the LAST in the afternoon) or take each test on a different day. You are allotted 4.5 hours for each test (4 hours of testing plus 30 minutes for instructions). The ATS-W and the Multi-Subject CST are administered from 8:00 A.M. to 12:30 P.M. (morning session); the LAST is given from 1:00 P.M. to 5:45 P.M. (afternoon session).

For the most up-to-date information on test dates, registering, and score report deadlines, visit the official NYSTCE website at www.nystce.nesinc.com.

HOW ARE THE TESTS SCORED?

There are two types of scores: raw scores and scaled scores. Raw scores represent the number of correctly answered items or the number of points earned on the written assignment. Scaled scores represent the raw score compared with everyone else who has taken the test.

You must attain a scaled score of 220 (of a maximum of 300) on each of the examinations to pass. Because the scoring formula is not made public, it is difficult to determine precisely how many items you must answer correctly to get a passing scaled score. Remember, a qualifying score on both exams is required for certification. So if you pass one exam but fail the other, you must retake the failed exam until a passing score is achieved.

CHAPTER 2: **THE STRATEGIES**

The key to success with the LAST, the ATS-W, and the CSTs is to *take control*. When you feel powerless and out of control, you cannot proceed with assurance. When you feel in control of a situation, you can perform at peak levels. Here are 10 powerful strategies to help you take control of these tests and achieve a maximum score.

KAPLAN'S TOP 10 STRATEGIES

1. **Know what to expect.** Don't go into the test cold.

2. **Practice.** You should complete at least one practice test before test day.

3. **Get ready.** Be in top mental and physical condition on the day of the test. Think in advance about what you'll need and have it all ready the night before the test.

4. **Pace yourself.** Your goal is to get as many correct answers as you can in the allotted time. Avoid getting bogged down on one question. Keep moving.

5. **Do easy questions first.** Focus first on the questions you know how to answer. You can skip the ones you're unsure of the first time through the test. Be sure to go back and answer the questions you skipped.

6. **Think first.** Think about the question stem for a few seconds before looking at the answer choices.

7. **Consider all options.** Don't choose an answer until you've read all the answer choices.

8. **Work by a process of elimination.** When you know a choice is wrong, eliminate it. If you can eliminate three choices, then the one that's left is the answer. If you can eliminate only one or two choices, you at least improve your chances of guessing correctly.

9. **Answer every question.** There is no penalty for choosing a wrong answer. When you're not sure what the answer is, you have nothing to lose and everything to gain by guessing. It is foolish to leave even a single question unanswered.

10. **Don't misgrid.** All your hard work and clear thinking can go to waste if you make a mistake in filling in the ovals on your answer sheet. Be careful.

Every piece of advice we have to offer in this chapter—every one of the 10 strategies and all their corollary tips—is a way of taking control of the LAST, the ATS-W, and the CST.

STRATEGY 1: KNOW WHAT TO EXPECT

Don't try to go in and take this test cold. The New York State Teacher Certification Exams are scary enough as it is. If you go into the test center hardly knowing what to expect, you're bound to be anxious, and you're bound to work at less than optimum efficiency and accuracy.

The LAST, the ATS-W, and the Multi-Subject CST are standardized exams, which means that each edition over the years is designed to measure the same knowledge and skills. That makes them predictable. You can't find out legitimately exactly what questions will be on the next test, but you can find out a lot about what types of questions will be on the test. We know—from published information such as the NYSTCE *Preparation Guide*s as well as from past tests—a lot about what question types will appear and what content will be tested. Familiarize yourself with the test objectives we will cover in chapters 4, 9, and 15 and get to know the question types you will face. Learn strategies for answering them now so you will save time on the day of the test. Some question types can be tricky and require a little getting used to. Better to do that now than to do it while the clock is ticking during the test. You're better off acquainting yourself with the rules of the game before the game begins.

STRATEGY 2: PRACTICE

You can't really know what the LAST, the ATS-W, and the Multi-Subject CST are like just by reading *about* them. If you really want to know what to expect, you should take a trial run. The best way to use the practice tests in this book is to take them under as close to testlike conditions as possible. Time yourself. Do a whole test in one sitting, with no more than one or two bathroom breaks. Don't just browse through the tests now and then, doing a question here and a question there. Don't even look at the questions until you're ready to take them seriously.

After you have taken a whole practice test, check your answers against the answer keys. You can use your results to determine where you might need extra help. Read all the answer explanations, even for the items you answered correctly. The explanations are detailed, offering all kinds of strategic advice and creative approaches to answering test questions.

After you've taken the practice tests in this book, if you have time, you might want to take the shorter sample tests in the NYSTCE *Liberal Arts and Sciences Test (LAST) Preparation Guide,* the NYSTCE *Assessment of Teaching Skills–Written (ATS-W) Preparation Guide,* and the NYSTCE *Multi-Subject CST Preparation Guide.* You may download these guides from www.nystce.nesinc.com.

STRATEGY 3: GET READY

Organize your life the last couple of days before the test to ensure that you are in top mental and physical condition while you're taking the test. You'll want to be properly rested, properly fed, properly dressed, and properly equipped.

Get a good night's sleep the night before the test. Don't stay up late studying—you can't learn that much more in a few hours, and you will most likely fatigue your body and your mind. You need your rest. Watch a movie, read a book or a magazine, and get to bed early.

On the morning of the test, eat the kind of nutritious breakfast you would eat before heading out for a hike. You have many hours of test taking ahead, and you want to be properly fueled up. Make sure not to experiment with food—eat something wholesome and simple that your body is used to eating. Don't drink coffee if you don't usually drink coffee; even if you are a regular coffee drinker, don't drink too much before the test. Not only will it put you on edge, it will also increase your need for time-consuming bathroom breaks.

Be prepared for any kind of climate. Dress in layers—even if it is sweltering outside, it might be very cold in the testing room, or the opposite. That way, you can peel off or put on whatever you need to feel comfortable.

Figure out in advance what you'll need to take with you to the test. Here's what you're *required* to bring:

- **Admission ticket.** If you register before the deadline, you will receive an admission ticket in the mail from NES at least a week before the test date.

> **KAPLAN TIP**
>
> The important thing to remember the day before a test is to relax and be well rested. Prepare, and put in plain sight, the admissions slip and your identification. Make snacks and lunch to take to the test. You may want to take a practice run to the test site in case you are unfamiliar with the location.

- **Government-issued photo ID.** Acceptable forms of identification include a driver's license, passport, or military ID.

- **One other piece of secondary ID.** Acceptable forms of secondary identification include a student ID, social security card, or employee ID card.

- **Several No. 2 pencils.** They should be sharpened, but not too sharp. It's easier and faster to fill in ovals when your pencils are slightly dull.

It is also recommended that you bring the following:

- **A simple twist-type pencil sharpener.** You do not need to waste time walking back and forth to a pencil sharpener if your point breaks.

- **A good eraser.** The tests are scored electronically. If you change an answer, you will need to erase the old answer completely before marking the new one. Also, you should erase any stray marks on the answer document and sweep away any eraser dust because the electronic scoring machine may misinterpret these.

- **A watch.** There may be a clock in the room, and the proctor is supposed to let you know when time is running out, but you'll be much more in control if you have your own timepiece to refer to.

Here are some optional items you might consider bringing:

- **Mints, hard candy, or gum.** You may need these for a quick energy boost if you get hungry or tired.

- **Earplugs.** If noises like the coughing of other examinees might be distracting to you, consider blocking out the noise with earplugs.

You are *not* allowed to bring calculators or calculator watches, watches that beep, photographic or recording devices, highlighters, dictionaries, slide rules, briefcases, backpacks, packages, cell phones, beepers, PDAs, notebooks, textbooks, scratch paper, or any written material inside the testing room. Also, you are *not* allowed to eat, drink, or smoke inside the testing room.

STRATEGY 4: PACE YOURSELF

You will have 4 hours to complete each test. It is a good idea to allot at least 1.5 hours to the written assignment. That means you will have about 2.5 hours to complete the multiple-choice section. This works out to be a little less than 2 minutes per question.

It is important that you move through the test at a steady pace, but do not rush (there are no extra points for finishing first). Try to work as rapidly as you can without being careless, using your watch to check the time occasionally.

Good pacing is a delicate balancing act. You want to proceed quickly enough to get to every question and to respond to the writing prompt, but not so quickly that you make careless mistakes. Use the practice tests in this book to measure your natural pace and then adjust to make the most of the time allotted on test day.

> **KAPLAN TIP**
>
> As you begin the multiple-choice portion of the test, find and mark the question at the halfway point. You will then expect to reach that question by the end of 1 hour 15 minutes. If you have not reached it by the halfway mark, you will need to work through the rest of the test at a faster pace.

STRATEGY 5: DO EASY QUESTIONS FIRST

Learn to recognize and deal first with the questions that are easier for you. That means temporarily skipping those that promise to be difficult and time consuming. You can always come back to them later, and if you run out of time, you're better off not getting to questions you might not have been able to answer correctly anyhow than not getting to questions that you would have had a shot at answering correctly.

The first time you look at a question, make a quick decision on how hard and time consuming it might be for you. Then decide whether to answer it immediately or skip it until later. Here's how:

- If the question looks comprehensible and of reasonable difficulty, do it right away.

- If the question looks tough and time consuming but ultimately doable, skip it, circle the question number in the test booklet, and come back to it later.

- If the question looks impossible, guess and move on, never to return.

> **KAPLAN TIP**
>
> Whenever you skip a question the first time through the test, put a big circle in your test booklet around the question number. You could even circle the whole question. When you go back later, such questions will be easy to locate.

STRATEGY 6: THINK FIRST

After you read the question, you would be wise to stop and think for a few seconds before you look at the answer choices. You might even want to reread the stem. If you jump right into the answer choices, you're more likely to fall for a trap. Try to anticipate the answer before you look at the answer choices. It's easier to spot the correct answer when you have some idea of what you're looking for.

STRATEGY 7: CONSIDER ALL OPTIONS

For most questions, you're ultimately better off if you read all the answer choices before deciding which one to choose. You might read choice (A) and be tempted to pick it, but you should check out the other choices first. You might find that choice (D) seems plausible, too. Then, when you go back and reconsider (A), you might find that it's not as good a choice as you first thought.

Watch out especially for words such as *not, least, except, likely, most likely, best,* and *first*. Always be sure you're answering the question that's being asked. On the ATS-W, the test maker often includes "tempting terminology"—phrases that point to ideas about teaching and learning that you recognize as good practices but don't apply to the question. Under the pressure of time, it's easy to fall for one of these red herrings, thinking that you know what's being asked. (We'll discuss ATS-W tempting terminology and other distractors in chapter 10.)

Critical reading is vital! Particularly in the case of the ATS-W, look for the words in the question stem that narrow and focus the specific purpose that must be addressed in the answer choice. Don't read too much into a question. The correct answer should not assume information that is not given in the question stem.

STRATEGY 8: WORK BY A PROCESS OF ELIMINATION

Sometimes the correct answer doesn't jump out at you the first time you look through the answer choices. In that case, go back and cross off the letters of the choices you know are wrong. Try your best to eliminate at least two answer choices. When you have done this but are struggling to choose between the last two answer choices, a helpful strategy is go back and reread the question stem again. Find the little "gem" of information you need—the key word or phrase that focuses the question and guides you to the correct answer choice. There *is* something in the wording of the question *and* in the wording of the correct answer choice that links them together. The little gem will also help you recognize that a distractor containing "tempting terminology" is *not* answering the actual question.

> **KAPLAN TIP**
>
> Feel free to underline or write whatever you want in your test booklet. Underline key phrases. Cross out the letters of answer choices as you eliminate them.

STRATEGY 9: ANSWER EVERY QUESTION

There is no penalty for wrong answers on the LAST, the ATS-W, and the CST. Some standardized tests, such as the SAT®, have a wrong-answer penalty, which makes advice about guessing complicated. But with these tests, there are no such complications.

You get full credit for a correct answer, even if it's just a lucky guess, and you lose nothing when you guess wrong. With nothing to lose and possibly full credit to gain, be sure to answer every single question. It's foolish to leave even one question unanswered.

STRATEGY 10: DON'T MISGRID

Your score for the multiple-choice portion of the test is based on the number of times you fill in the correct ovals on the answer sheet. You could know the correct answer to every question but still get a low score if you misgrid. So be careful! Don't disdain the process of filling in those little bubbles. Sure, it's pretty mindless, but under time pressure, it's easy to make mistakes.

Carefully and completely fill in the space corresponding to the answer you select for each question. Mark only one answer for each question. Be sure to mark each answer in the row with the same number as the question. If you skip a question, also skip the corresponding number on your answer sheet. If you change an answer, be sure to erase the old answer completely before marking the new one. Also, erase any stray marks on the answer document because the electronic scoring machine may misinterpret these.

STRESS MANAGEMENT

The countdown has begun. Your date with THE TEST is looming on the horizon. Anxiety is on the rise. Don't despair! It is possible to tame that anxiety and stress before and during the test. Lack of control is one of the prime causes of stress. Research shows that if you don't have a sense of control over what's happening in your life, you can easily end up feeling helpless and hopeless. So just having concrete things to do and to think about—taking control—will help reduce your stress. This chapter shows you how to take control during the days leading up to the NYSTCE and during the tests.

QUICK TIPS FOR THE DAYS JUST BEFORE THE EXAM

As the test gets closer, you may find your anxiety is on the rise. You shouldn't worry. After the preparation you've received from this book, you're in good shape for the exam. To calm any pretest jitters you may have though, let's go over a few strategies for the days before the test.

- The best test takers do less and less as the test approaches. Taper off your study schedule and take it easy on yourself.

- Positive self-talk can be extremely liberating and invigorating, especially as the test looms closer. Tell yourself things such as, "I choose to take this test," rather than "I have to"; "I will do well," rather than "I hope things go well"; "I can," rather than "I cannot." Be aware of negative, self-defeating thoughts and images and immediately counter any you become aware of.

- Get your act together sooner rather than later. Have everything (including choice of clothing) laid out days in advance. Most important, know where the test will be held, the easiest, quickest way to get there, and how to enter the building. Make dependable arrangements to get to the test center in plenty of time. If you plan to go by car, find out where to park. You will gain great peace of mind if you know that all the little details—gas in the car, directions, etc.—are firmly in your control before the day of the test.

- Forego any practice on the day before the test. It's in your best interest to marshal your physical and psychological resources for 24 hours or so. Keep the upcoming test out of your consciousness; go to a movie, take a pleasant hike, or just relax. Don't eat junk food or tons of sugar, and, of course, get plenty of rest the night before.

HANDLING STRESS DURING THE TEST

The biggest stress monster will be the day of the test itself. Fear not—here are methods of quelling your stress during the test.

- Keep moving forward instead of getting bogged down in a difficult question. You don't have to get everything right to achieve a fine score. So don't linger out of desperation on a question that is going nowhere, even after you've spent considerable time on it. The best test takers skip (temporarily) difficult material in search of the easier stuff. They mark the questions that require extra time and thought. This strategy buys time and builds confidence so you can handle the tough stuff later.

- Don't be thrown if other test takers seem to be working more busily and furiously than you are. Continue to spend your time patiently but doggedly thinking through your answers; it's going to lead to higher-quality test taking and better results. Don't mistake other people's sheer activity as a sign of progress and higher scores.

- *Keep breathing!* Weak test takers tend to share one major trait: they forget to breathe properly as the test proceeds. They start holding their breath without realizing it, or they breathe erratically or arhythmically. Improper breathing hurts confidence and accuracy. Just as important, it interferes with clear thinking.

- Some quick isometrics during the test—especially if concentration is wandering or energy is waning—can help. Try this: Put your palms together and press intensely for a few seconds. Concentrate on the tension you feel through your palms, wrists, forearms, and up into your biceps and shoulders. Then, quickly release the pressure. Feel the difference as you let go. Focus on the warm relaxation that floods through the muscles. Now you're ready to return to the task.

- When you receive the test, take several deep, slow breaths, exhaling slowly while mentally visualizing yourself performing successfully on it before you begin. Do not get upset if you feel nervous; most of the people taking the test with you will be experiencing some measure of anxiety. During the test, try to remain as calm as possible. Stop periodically and take several deep, slow breaths, exhaling slowly, to help you relax. This is your big day, the day you have been waiting and preparing for. Just do it!

With what you've learned here, you're armed and ready to do battle with the test. This book and your studies will give you the information you'll need to answer the questions. It's all firmly planted in your mind. You also know how to deal with any excess tension that might come along, both before the test and during the test. You've experienced everything you need to tame your test anxiety and stress. You're going to get a great score.

CHAPTER 3: THE WRITTEN ASSIGNMENT

The majority of test takers find the multiple-choice sections of these tests straightforward. It is the written assignments that can sometimes be more challenging. To give you a leg up, let's begin by addressing some frequently asked questions regarding the written assignment portion of the LAST, the ATS-W, and the Multi-Subject CST.

HOW LONG WILL I HAVE TO COMPLETE THE WRITTEN ASSIGNMENT?

You should allot 1.5 hours of the 4 hours allowed for each exam to the written assignment. You may find it helpful to start on the written assignment first so you can get a feel for the time it will take. Then you will be able to adjust your pacing on the multiple-choice section accordingly.

HOW IS THE WRITTEN ASSIGNMENT SCORED?

Two readers using a rating scale will evaluate your response to the written assignment. The test maker does not provide a scoring rubric for your review.

WHAT DO I NEED TO KNOW TO PASS THE LAST WRITTEN ASSIGNMENT?

The essay portion of the LAST assesses your ability to express and support your opinions in a 300- to 600-word, multiparagraph essay. The essay should show that you can organize and develop ideas, usually about a current issue. The assignment will present two sides of a general interest issue, ask you to evaluate each side of the issue, state the position you will argue, and defend that position with logical and relevant examples.

TACKLING THE LAST WRITTEN ASSIGNMENT

Your essay will be evaluated on your ability to express your opinions and then effectively support them; it will not be evaluated on the nature of the opinions you express. The NYSTCE graders will evaluate your response on the basis of the following criteria:

Focus and Unity	Your response should maintain a strong focus on the given topic and should avoid any unrelated information or irrelevant arguments. Each sentence of your essay should add to your argument.
Appropriateness	When crafting your essay, never lose sight of your purpose and audience. Keep the composition's level of language and tone appropriate and avoid clichés and slang.
Reason and Organization	Present your opinions clearly and directly, so there is no doubt as to what they are, and keep your supporting arguments consistent and easy to follow.
Support and Development	Develop strong support for your position using solid evidence and detailed examples. Be sure to show awareness of other positions.
Structure and Conventions	Your essay must conform to the conventions of edited American English. Be sure to leave time to proof your work to ensure it is free of subject-verb disagreements; run-on sentences; and distracting mechanical errors in spelling, punctuation, and capitalization. Be sure to use proper word choice.

WHAT DO I NEED TO KNOW TO PASS THE ATS-W WRITTEN ASSIGNMENT?

In this assignment, you must have strong essay-writing skills to communicate your knowledge. The evaluators will also be looking for proof that you can express understanding of teaching and learning. You must show that you have a grasp of the range of Objectives (0007–0015) found in Subarea II: Instruction and Assessment. See page 221 of this book for a complete list of these Objectives.

TACKLING THE ATS-W ASSIGNMENT

Your response on the ATS-W assignment will be evaluated on the basis of your understanding of the teacher's role in relation to learner characteristics, instructional design and delivery, and the teaching environment as these understandings pertain to the goal set forth in the writing prompt. The scorers will evaluate your response using a 4-point scale. A response that earns a score "4" will reflect a thorough command of the relevant knowledge and skills required to respond properly to the prompt; a response that earns a "1" will reflect little or no command of the relevant knowledge and skills to do so.

The scorers will look for the following in your written response:

Purpose	Does your response completely fulfill the charge of the prompt?
Application of Content	How well does your response apply the relevant knowledge and skills to fulfill the charge of the assignment?
Support	Did you support your response with appropriate examples and/or sound reasoning that reflects a strong understanding of the relevant knowledge and skills?

WHAT DO I NEED TO KNOW TO PASS THE MULTI-SUBJECT CST WRITTEN ASSIGNMENT?

For the Multi-Subject CST exam, you will be asked to write a 150- to 300-word response to a topic relevant to the skills outlined in Subarea I, objective 0001 (understand the foundations of reading development) and objective 0002 (understand skills and strategies involved in reading comprehension).

The scorers will evaluate your response using a 4-point scale. A response that earns a score "4" will reflect a thorough command of the relevant knowledge and skills required to properly respond to the prompt; a response that earns a "1" will reflect little or no command of the relevant knowledge and skills to do so.

The scorers will look for the following in your written response:

Purpose	Does your response completely fulfill the charge of the prompt?
Application of Content	How well does your response apply the relevant knowledge and skills to fulfill the charge of the assignment?
Support	Did you support your response with appropriate examples and/or sound reasoning that reflects a strong understanding of the relevant knowledge and skills?

USEFUL STRATEGIES FOR THE WRITTEN ASSIGNMENT

Now that we've identified what is difficult about this part of the tests, let's take a look at some strategies that will ease the pain of this task.

Create an Outline and Stick to It. If you organize your ideas in an outline, the essay will practically write itself. Two things to remember when you develop your outline are as follows:

- The prompt is your outline. The assignment will be divided into several sequential bulleted tasks. Go through these in order and be sure you actually do what each bulleted point tells you to do.

- Assume the test maker's mindset. Write in an objective fashion, using words similar to those found throughout the test objectives and the *NYSTCE Preparation Guide.* For the ATS-W, do not write about your classroom experiences; write about ideal teaching practices as reflected in the test objectives. (See chapters 4 , 9, and 15 for all the test objectives.) In other words, respond as if you work in the quintessential educational environment with smoothly functioning systems and access to unlimited resources. We all know that the research on teaching practice is sound in theory but may be unrealistic in some cases because of a number of factors. The written assignment will not be asking you to expound on these difficulties.

Manage Your Time. Again, we recommend that you spend 90 minutes on the written assignment. Practicing timed written responses as you prepare for the test will give you a feel for how long it takes to organize and write a multipart response. Understanding how to approach the assignment and how your time should be used is one way to ease anxiety and ensure completion of the test within the time allowed.

- Start with the written assignment. Just because the test begins with the multiple-choice questions does not mean you have to answer them first. You must pass the written assignment to pass the tests, and you must get a certain number of multiple-choice questions correct as well. There is no "guessing penalty" on the multiple-choice section—only correct answers are counted. So, if you do run out of time on a few multiple-choice questions, it is better to guess on them than to not complete the written assignment.

- Follow the steps of Kaplan's 5-Step Writing Process as outlined below. If you spend about 15 minutes on each step, your essay will be done (and done well) in no time.

KAPLAN'S 5-STEP WRITING PROCESS

1. Prewriting
2. Outlining
3. Drafting
4. Revising
5. Proofreading

Step 1: *Prewriting* is the planning stage during which you will brainstorm ideas.

Step 2: *Outlining* is the stage during which you will organize your response in the form of an outline.

Step 3: *Drafting* is the stage during which you will write your response in paragraph form, developing the outline with examples and facts.

Step 4: *Revising* is the stage during which you check your response, making sure that it follows the prompt and answers the question in full. This is the time to make changes in supporting information, sentence structure, or paragraph order.

Step 5: *Proofreading* is the polishing stage during which you will read your response for errors in fluency and conventions.

EXAMPLE

Here is a prompt like one you might see on the ATS-W:

Cross-cultural awareness is important to individual development and international accord. Understanding the historical, philosophical, social, and religious ideas that shape a culture broadens student appreciation of societal and individual differences. Imagine that the educational goal and objectives below have been established for all schools in your district.

GOAL: Students will develop cross-cultural understanding and communication skills

Learning objectives include the following:

- Students will gain awareness of the social and political differences between various cultures.

- Students will develop an understanding of the cultural forces that shape artistic and literary expression.

- Students will gain communication skills in languages other than English.

In an essay written for a group of New York State educators, frame your response by identifying a grade level/subject area for which you are prepared to teach. Then,

- explain the importance of helping students develop cross-cultural awareness and communication skills.

- describe two strategies you would use to achieve this educational goal.

- explain why the strategies you describe would be effective in achieving this educational goal.

KAPLAN TIP

The essay topic won't be hidden—it is stated in the very first sentence of the prompt.

Be sure to specify a grade level/subject area in your essay and frame your ideas so that an educator certified at your level (i.e., elementary or secondary) will be able to understand the basis for your response.

STEP 1: PREWRITING

Planning your response, or prewriting, involves three steps:

1. Identifying important information in the prompt

2. Brainstorming your ideas

3. Thinking through your response

Identifying Important Information

The prompt for the ATS-W written assignment may look intimidating, but the information presented in it can actually help you a lot!

The prompt serves three purposes. First, it presents the topic that you will have to discuss. Second, it states specific tasks—a breakdown of what should be included in your response. Third, it provides information that you can borrow as a starting point for your brainstorming.

> **KAPLAN TIP**
>
> Watch out for tasks that aren't bulleted.

Let's take a closer look.

Identify the Topic. Read the sample prompt. Identify the general topic that you are being asked to discuss: *The importance of helping students develop cross-cultural awareness and communication skills.*

Once you have identified the general educational goal about which you will be writing, you should determine exactly what is expected of you.

Determine Specific Tasks. Look at the prompt again. Identify the specific tasks that the prompt asks you to do.

- Explain the importance.
- Describe two strategies.
- Explain why the strategies will work.

The rest of the information in the prompt is there to give you a jump start on your response. The test maker has given you this information; draw from it to generate ideas.

Brainstorming Your Ideas

Once you have a clear understanding of the prompt and the useful information it provides, you'll probably experience a surge of ideas rushing into your head. To prevent these ideas from rushing right out again, you should write them down.

Brainstorming involves making a list or a web of everything that comes to your mind. Write freely. Don't create flowery sentences; just jot down the phrases that represent the essence of the ideas you want to include in your response. The purpose is to take down quickly all of the ideas that may be applicable to the topic and tasks at hand.

> **KAPLAN TIP**
>
> The prompt is going to ask you to describe two strategies for meeting the stated goal and to explain why each would be effective. If you are having difficulty thinking of strategies to write about, start working on the multiple-choice part of the test. The questions and answer choices may give you some good ideas!

Thinking Through Your Response

Now that you have all your ideas down on paper, it is time to do some thinking. Now is also the time to assume the test maker's mindset. Remember, this written assignment is assessing your understanding of the role of the teacher in relation to the following:

- Knowledge of the learner
- Instructional planning and assessment
- Instructional delivery
- The professional environment

In chapter 10 we will discuss the ideology on which the ATS-W is based. Below are some examples of ways to put theory into practice.

Sample Instructional Strategies	Sample Instructional Resources
• Discovery learning	• Overhead projector
• Cooperative learning	• Chalkboard/whiteboard/Smart Board
• Inquiry-based learning	• Computer lab
• Independent study	• Internet
• Hands-on activities	• DVD
• Peer tutoring	• Film projector
• Modeling	• Flip charts
• Role-playing	• Library
• Journals/Blogging	• Guest speakers
• Writing and reading workshops	• Field trips
• Research projects	• Tape recorder
	• Newspaper/magazines
	• Commercial textbooks

Sample Modifications	Sample Assessment Methods (Formal and Informal)
• Untimed testing	• Portfolios
• Guided practice	• Teacher-made tests
• Copies of teacher notes	• Projects
• Verbal testing	• Presentations
• Computer access	• Demonstrations
• Deadline extensions	• Rubrics
• Shortened assignments	• Teacher observations
• Seat location	• Self-checklists
• Books on tape	• Peer evaluation
• Tape-recorded teacher lectures	• Written reflection
• Peer tutoring	• Standardized achievement tests
• Afterschool assistance	

STEP 2: OUTLINING

Once you've generated some ideas, you'll need to organize them in an outline. The better your outline is organized, the easier it will be to write your response. Read through your ideas and determine what you will use in your essay and where each piece will go.

- Which ideas are strategies that you can describe?
- Which ideas are reasons you can give in your explanation of why a particular strategy would be effective?

If you have listed more than two strategies, choose the two that you can most fully describe and for which you can offer the best explanations of why they would be effective.

You'll want to use the prompt itself as the skeleton of your essay.

KAPLAN TIP

A well-organized outline will ensure a well-organized essay.

KAPLAN TIP

Remember, *describe* means to tell "what"—to list the characteristics of a strategy. *Explain* means to tell "why" and "how" the strategy would be effective in meeting the educational goal set forth in the prompt.

Let's review the ATS-W prompt. It asks you to do the following:

- Identify a level/subject. You can do this before you begin the essay or work it into the introduction. Just don't forget to include it.

- Explain the importance of the goal. This becomes paragraph 1, the introduction to your essay.

- Describe two strategies. Each strategy that you describe should be a paragraph in the body of your essay.

- Explain why each strategy would be effective. Your essay should include one paragraph that explains the effectiveness of the first strategy you described and another paragraph that explains the effectiveness of the second strategy you described.

Sample Outline

Consider the following outline for a response to the sample prompt.

Grade level/subject: Fifth-Grade Humanities

Paragraph I: It is important that students are taught cultural understanding and communication skills because:

 A. It allows students the opportunity to see their own heritage reflected in the classroom.

 B. It helps create an appreciation of the diversity in the classroom, community, and society at large.

 C. It enhances communication between English- and non–English-speaking students, preparing them for greater future opportunities in the arenas of work.

Paragraph II: One strategy I would use to achieve this goal is "Country of the Month."

 A. Surround students with pictures, stories, the language.

 B. Assign cooperative groups to research one of the five cultural components: geography, customs and rituals, food, artistic influence, language.

 C. Read stories and poems from the "Country of the Month."

Paragraph III: "Country of the Month" would be effective in achieving this goal because:

 A. It incorporates various instructional techniques so that students with different learning styles and abilities can benefit.

 B. It requires active involvement and encourages learning through discovery.

C. It provides meaningful interdisciplinary activities that help students make real-life connections to what they are learning in school.

Paragraph IV: Another strategy I would use to achieve this goal is to plan and implement an instructional unit on immigration.

A. Interview relatives and friends who immigrated to the U.S.

B. Field experience to Ellis Island and NY's tenement museum.

C. Student journals—students take on the role of a young person experiencing the immigration process.

Paragraph V: The immigration unit would be an effective strategy because:

A. It connects their knowledge from home to their learning in school.

B. It offers experiential learning through field trips.

C. It requires students to reflect on their learning through journals.

STEP 3: DRAFTING

Now that you have practiced outlining your ideas, it is time to write your response. The good news is that you have already done the hardest part. Once your ideas are organized, the essay should be as easy as one, two, three:

1. Introduction
2. Body
3. Conclusion

Before we practice writing each paragraph, let's take a look at the big picture. No matter what topic you are asked to write about, the skeleton of your ATS-W written response will be the same.

Consider this template.

ATS-W Written Assignment Response

Paragraph 1 (Introduction):

(Sentence 1) As a *(state the grade level and subject)* teacher, it is important that I *(restate the first sentence in the prompt)*.

(Sentences 2–5+) The educational goal *(rewrite the educational goal given in the prompt)* is important because *(EXPLAIN why the educational goal is important)*.

Paragraph 2:

(Sentence 1) One strategy that I would use to accomplish this goal is _____.

(Sentences 2–5+) *(DESCRIBE strategy #1: Tell just what this would look like in your classroom.)*

Paragraph 3:

(Sentence 1) This strategy would be effective in achieving the educational goal because . . . .

(Sentences 2–5+) *(EXPLAIN why and how strategy #1 would be effective in achieving the educational goal.)*

Paragraph 4:

(Sentence 1) Another strategy that I would use to accomplish this goal is _____.

(Sentences 2–5+) *(DESCRIBE strategy #2: Tell just what this would look like in your classroom.)*

Paragraph 5:

(Sentence 1) This strategy would be effective in achieving the educational goal because . . . .

(Sentences 2–5+) *(EXPLAIN why and how strategy #2 would be effective in achieving the educational goal.)*

Paragraph 6 (Conclusion):

(Sentence 1) Again, *(restate the goal given in the prompt)* is an important goal because *(summarize the reasons you gave in paragraph 1).*

(Sentence 2+) *(The first strategy you discussed)* and *(the second strategy you discussed)* are both excellent ways to achieve this goal in a *(restate grade level and subject)* classroom.

Simple, right? Let's take a closer look at each paragraph.

The Introduction

An effective first (introduction) paragraph for an ATS-W prompt

- states the grade level and content area with which you will deal;

- clearly describes the topic or thesis to be discussed; and

- briefly summarizes the points you will make and the order in which you will make them.

Sample Introductory Paragraph

As a fifth-grade humanities teacher, it is my responsibility to teach cross-cultural understanding and communication. This goal is important because it allows students the opportunity to see their own heritage reflected in the classroom while serving to create an appreciation of the diversity in the classroom, the community, and the world. Further, emphasizing cross-cultural communication builds bridges of understanding between English- and non-English-speaking students, preparing them for larger future opportunity in the arenas of work and travel.

> **KAPLAN TIP**
>
> Don't be afraid to "borrow" language from the prompt. In fact, use the exact wording of the prompt to formulate a topic sentence for each one of your paragraphs.

The Body

Stick to the outline and do exactly what each bulleted part of the prompt tells you to do. Weave in your understanding (in language that resembles the test maker's) of the following:

- Knowledge of the Learner

- Instructional Planning and Assessment

- Instructional Delivery

- The Professional Environment

Sample Body

One strategy I would use to achieve this goal is "Country of the Month." Each month I would designate a host country. Throughout the month, I would try to surround my students with the culture of that country by displaying visuals on the walls, inviting guests from that country, reading stories from or about the country, and introducing common phrases of that country's language. I would also divide students into cooperative-learning groups and have each group research one of the following cultural areas: geography, customs and values, food, art and literature, and language. Each group would prepare a presentation of their research based on a predetermined evaluation rubric.

This "Country of the Month" strategy is effective in achieving the educational goal for a number of reasons. First, it incorporates various instructional techniques so students with all different learning styles and abilities can benefit. It also requires active involvement and encourages learning through discovery. Finally, it provides meaningful, interdisciplinary activities that help students make real-life connections to what they're learning in school.

Another strategy I would use to achieve this goal is to develop an interdisciplinary unit on immigration. During this unit, I would have students interview relatives and friends who immigrated to the United States and then share what they learned with their classmates. I would also plan a field trip to Ellis Island and New York City's Tenement Museum. Further, throughout the unit, I would have students maintain journals in which they would write about immigration in the first person as though they were experiencing it.

The immigration unit would also be an effective strategy for a number of reasons. First, it connects students' knowledge from home to their learning in school. Second, it offers experiential learning through local museums. Finally, it requires students to extend and reflect on their learning in journals.

The Conclusion

Consider the concluding paragraph a "wrap-up" of your essay. Your last paragraph should simply bring your essay to a close. Consider the following conclusion for the sample response:

Sample Conclusion

Again, teaching students cross-cultural understanding and communication is important because it fosters an appreciation of differences and celebration of diversity that opens doors of opportunities for young people. "Country of the Month" and an interdisciplinary unit on immigration are both excellent ways to achieve this educational goal in a fifth-grade humanities classroom.

Note that the sample conclusion does not introduce any new ideas. Instead, it summarizes what has been discussed in the essay.

STEP 4: REVISING

Your draft should contain all or most of the ideas and information that you want to include, but the writing itself may need some fine-tuning. Revising your essay involves

1. checking the structure;
2. checking the content.

Checking the Structure

Checking the structure of your response means two things: (1) checking that you addressed all parts of the written assignment prompt and (2) checking that your response is clear, complete, and organized in a logical way.

Check Against the Prompt. When you revise your essay, make sure that you not only answered the question, but that you addressed *all parts* of the prompt. Read your draft. In which paragraphs did you address each task?

I explained the importance of the educational goal in paragraph(s) _____.

I described two strategies in paragraph(s) _____.

I explained the effectiveness of my two strategies in paragraph(s) _____.

I included my grade level and subject area in my response.

Check for Organization. Remember, you want to make your response easy for the scorer to read. Even though you are being scored primarily on content, your ideas should be organized so that the scorer can see clearly (and quickly) that you have completed your task.

Read through your response once again. Use the checklist below to verify that your essay is organized.

- ❑ My essay begins with an introductory sentence that (1) identifies the grade level and subject I teach and (2) restates the educational goal presented in the prompt.

- ❑ Each paragraph in the body of my essay begins with a topic sentence that clearly addresses one aspect of the prompt.

- ❑ My essay includes a short conclusion in which (1) I state that the educational goal is important and (2) I state that my two strategies are effective.

Checking the Content

The most important (and also the most challenging) task in the written assignment is the content. What this assignment is *really* testing is your understanding of practical applications of the ideology on which this test is based.

- Does your writing reflect your understanding of the role of the teacher in relation to learner characteristics, instructional design and delivery, and the professional environment?

- Based on your experience and your understanding of the ATS-W test objectives, have you included the best strategies, resources, and general teaching practices that could fit into this essay?

See pages 26–27 for the list of strategies, techniques, and resources that are test-maker-friendly.

Content Checklist

Use the following checklist to verify that your essay incorporates, as much as possible, words that reflect the test maker's mindset.

- ❑ I have explained, in at least one or two sentences, why the educational goal is important.

- ❑ I have considered the developmental characteristics and capabilities of my students in choosing the two strategies that I will use to achieve the given educational goal.

- ❑ The strategies I have chosen to write about take into consideration the various learning styles of students and incorporate a range of instructional and assessment techniques and resources.

- ❑ I have clearly described each strategy and explained why each would be effective in achieving the educational goal stated in the prompt.

- ❑ *All* of my information in my essay relates directly to the prompt.

Use both revision checklists when reviewing your essay and make any necessary changes and additions.

STEP 5: PROOFREADING

Once you have revised your response, you are ready to "polish" or proofread it. You are ready, in short, to finalize your response to the written assignment. Your goal is to clean up your prose by getting rid of errors in

- grammar,

- punctuation, and

- spelling.

Perhaps the most important point to bear in mind when writing your response is to KEEP IT SIMPLE. This applies to word choice and sentence structure. The more complicated (and wordy) your sentences, the more likely they will be plagued by errors. Don't worry that this will make your writing simplistic: simple is not simplistic! A clear, straightforward approach can be sophisticated.

Proofreading Checklist

Everybody has his or her own common mistakes. Some people confuse *its* and *it's*; others forget to capitalize the names of the months. Get to know what your common mistakes are and be on the lookout for them when you proofread!

Read through your response. Use the general checklist below to proofread your essay. Make note of your common errors and practice identifying them in your writing.

Grammar

❑ Complete Sentences: Does every sentence express a complete thought?

❑ Agreement: Make sure singular subjects have singular verbs. Make sure pronouns agree with the nouns they replace

Punctuation

❑ Check that apostrophes replace the correct letters in contractions.

❑ Check that each sentence ends with a correct end mark.

Spelling

❑ Watch out for misused homonyms such as *fair/fare*, *to/two/too*, and *there/they're/their*.

❑ Look for common misspellings and errors, including "ie" and "ei" as in *friend/receive*, and "cede" and "ceed" as in *recede/succeed*, etc.

THE LAST

CHAPTER 4: WHAT YOU NEED TO KNOW: THE LAST OBJECTIVES

The purpose of the LAST is to assess knowledge and skills of prospective teachers in New York State in five areas. The LAST is comprised of approximately 80 multiple-choice questions and a written assignment. The multiple-choice questions assess a student's general knowledge in the four subareas. The approximate number of questions in each subarea is broken down as follows:

Subarea	Content Area	No. of Questions
I. Scientific, Mathematical, and Technological Processes	Mathematics	12
	Science and Technology	12
II. Historical and Social Scientific Awareness	History/Social Science	20
III. Artistic Expression and the Humanities	Art	8
	Literature	8
	Humanities	4
IV. Communication and Research Skills	English/Communication and Research	16
V. Written Analysis and Expression		This is assessed through a written assignment (essay).

THE LAST OBJECTIVES AND ONLINE REVIEW GUIDE

The objectives you will find on the LAST are listed below, followed by focus statements that provide examples of the range, style, and level of content that may appear on the test. Because the LAST covers such a broad range of material, your previous coursework will give you the best leg up in many subjects and content areas. Use this background knowledge to help you understand the questions and to predict and select the best responses. Keep in mind that most of the information you need to answer a question will be within the question; your job is to determine the information relevant to answering the question correctly.

If you do want to do some extra background preparation before test day, the Internet is a great source of information. You can do a general search for sites on, say, "art history" or "civil rights." However, the amount of material online may be daunting, and perhaps you are not sure where to begin. To assist you, we have included with each of the following LAST Objectives a sample online review guide to help you study. The websites listed are a good place to start gathering information on general liberal arts and sciences knowledge. While we strongly suggest that you spend the majority of your pretest time practicing your critical reading, writing, and test-taking skills, you can also benefit from targeting content areas specified in the NYSTCE test objectives and reviewing the online resources that follow.

Check out Kaplan's website (www.kaptest.com) for additional resources to help you prepare for the LAST.

Subarea I: Scientific, Mathematical, and Technological Processes

0001 Use mathematical reasoning in problem-solving situations to arrive at logical conclusions and to analyze the problem-solving process. For example:

- Analyzing problem solutions for logical flaws
- Analyzing problems to determine missing information needed to solve them
- Analyzing a partial solution to a problem to determine an appropriate next step
- Analyzing the validity or logic of an argument or advertising claim that is based on statistics or probability

Topic	URL	Annotation
National Council of Teachers of Mathematics	www.nctm.org	NCTM, the largest nonprofit professional association of mathematics educators in the world, is dedicated to improving the teaching and learning of mathematics.
Mathematical reasoning	www.stolaf.edu/people/ steen/Papers/reason.html	This site presents 20 questions about mathematical reasoning.
Problem solving	www.hawaii.edu/ suremath/students.html	This site can be used to develop a coherent approach to problem solving across the curriculum. It features links to materials that form organized lessons in problem solving.
Problem-solving strategies	www. mathcounts.org	The MATHCOUNTS program provides problem-solving strategies such as looking for a pattern, drawing a diagram, making an organized list, and so on. The program also models possible approaches to teaching problem solving.

0002 Understand connections between mathematical representations and ideas; use mathematical terms and representations to organize, interpret, and communicate information. For example:

- Analyzing data and making inferences from two or more graphic sources (e.g., diagrams, graphs, equations)

- Restating a problem related to a concrete situation in mathematical terms

- Using mathematical modeling/multiple representations to present, interpret, communicate, and connect mathematical information and relationships

- Selecting an appropriate graph or table summarizing information presented in another form (e.g., a newspaper excerpt)

Topic	URL	Annotation
Mathematics information	http://mathforum.org	This site offers math resources by subject for students, teachers, parents, and citizens. The forum features Ask Dr. Math, discussion groups, problem of the week, Web units and lessons, and a math search engine.

0003 Apply knowledge of numerical, geometric, and algebraic relationships in problem-solving and mathematical contexts. For example:

- Representing and using numbers in a variety of equivalent forms (e.g., integer, fraction, decimal, percent)

- Applying operational algorithms to add, subtract, multiply, and divide fractions, decimals, and integers

- Using scales and ratios to interpret maps and models

- Using geometric concepts and formulas to solve problems (e.g., estimating the surface area of a floor to determine the approximate cost of floor covering)

- Solving problems using algebraic concepts and formulas (e.g., calculating wages based on sales commission)

- Applying appropriate algebraic equations to the solution of problems (e.g., determining the original price of a sale item given the rate of discount)

Topic	URL	Annotation
Basic algebra	www.math.com/ homeworkhelp/Algebra.html	At this excellent, comprehensive site dealing with many facets of mathematics, subjects are divided into logical content units with a practice quiz at the end of each.
Basic geometry	www.math.com/ homeworkhelp/Geometry.html	Excellent Web resource for all aspects of geometry.

0004 Understand major concepts, principles, and theories in science and technology and use that understanding to analyze phenomena in the natural world and to interpret information presented in illustrated or written form. For example:

- Using an appropriate illustration, graphic, or physical model to represent a scientific theory, concept, or relationship presented in an excerpt

- Relating a major scientific principle, concept, or theory to a natural phenomenon

- Using design processes and procedures to pose questions and select solutions to problems and situations

- Applying technological knowledge and skills to evaluate the degree to which products and systems meet human and environmental needs

- Analyzing excerpts describing recent scientific discoveries or technological advances in relation to underlying scientific principles, concepts, or themes

Topic	URL	Annotation
National Science Teachers Association	www.nsta.org	The National Science Teachers Association (NSTA) is the largest organization in the world committed to promoting excellence and innovation in science teaching and learning for all.
Scientific phenomena	www.newscientist.com	This site houses a collection of everyday science questions and answers drawn from the pages of *New Scientist*, the world's leading weekly science and technology magazine. This archive contains over 600 questions on scientific phenomena.

0005 Understand the historical development and cultural contexts of mathematics, science, and technology; the relationships and common themes that connect mathematics, science, and technology; and the impact of mathematics, science, and technology on human societies. For example:

- analyzing the historical, societal, or environmental effects of given developments in science and technology (e.g., computerization)

- recognizing how mathematical models can be used to understand scientific, social, or environmental phenomena

- evaluating how historical and societal factors have promoted or hindered developments in science and technology

- analyzing how developments in scientific knowledge may affect other areas of life (e.g., recognizing types of scientific data likely to affect government policy making regarding pollution control)

Topic	URL	Annotation
Computerization	www.december. com/ cmc/mag/1996/ aug/ kling.html	The article "Computerization at Work" by Rob Kling examines the extent to which computer-based systems have transformed information systems, ways of working, organization of work, work locations, etc.
Scientific data affecting policy	www.gcrmn.org	Strong actions taken as alarming new findings about coral reefs are released in a report, "Status of Coral Reefs of the World 2008."
Societal factors	www.nyu.edu/classes/ stephens/Winston%20 book%20page.htm	This review of the book *Media Technology and Society* by Brian Winston. outlines the influence of society on the adoption of new technology.

0006 Understand and apply skills, principles, and procedures associated with inquiry and problem solving in the sciences. For example:

- Applying scientific methods and principles (including nonquantitative methods such as case studies) to investigate a question or problem

- Formulating questions to guide research and experimentation toward explanations for phenomena and observations

- Inferring the scientific principles (e.g., reliance on experimental data, replication of results) or skills (e.g., observation, inductive reasoning, familiarity with statistics and probability) that contributed to a scientific development as described in an excerpt

- Demonstrating familiarity with electronic means for collecting, organizing, and analyzing information (e.g., databases, spreadsheets)

- Analyzing the components of a given experimental design (e.g., dependent and independent variables, experimental groups, control groups)

- demonstrating an understanding of the nature of scientific inquiry (including ethical dimensions) and the role of observation and experimentation in science

Topic	URL	Annotation
Case studies	http://library.buffalo. edu/libraries/projects/ cases/case.html	Although the case method has been used for years to teach law, business, and medicine, it is not common in science. The use of case studies holds great promise as a pedagogical technique for teaching science because it humanizes science and illustrates scientific methodology and values.
Nature of scientific inquiry	www.philosophy.umd. edu/Faculty/LDarden/ sciinq/	It's the nature of scientific inquiry that scientists publish hypotheses that may later be disproved by new evidence and replaced by a better rival. Eventually some hypotheses receive sufficient positive evidence. They become accepted as part of scientific knowledge, with the proviso that even the best theories may be revised in the light of new evidence.
Scientific method	http://teacher.nsrl. rochester. edu/ phy_labs/AppendixE/ AppendixE.html	The scientific method is a four-step process that is used to "construct an accurate representation of the world." This site also describes when the scientific method is applicable.
Spreadsheets and databases	www.ehow.com/ facts_5164254_ spreadsheets-vs-databases.html	If you have a pile of data to organize, you may be wondering whether to use a spreadsheet or a database. The ease of setting up a spreadsheet makes it a tempting choice. If you're looking at a lot of data, or if your security and sharing needs are complex, a database is the way to go.

SUBAREA II: HISTORICAL AND SOCIAL SCIENTIFIC AWARENESS

0007 Understand the interconnectedness of historical, geographic, cultural, economic, political, and social issues and factors. For example:

- Assessing the likely effects of human activities or trends (described in written or graphic form) on the local, regional, or global environment

- Assessing ways in which major transformations related to human work, thought, and belief (e.g., industrialization, the Scientific Revolution, the development and spread of Islam) have affected human society

- Inferring aspects of a society's social structure or group interactions based on information presented in an excerpt

- Analyzing ways in which social, cultural, geographic, and economic factors influence intergroup relations and the formation of values, beliefs, and attitudes

- Assessing the social or economic implications of political views presented in an excerpt

Topic	URL	Annotation
National Council for the Social Studies	www.ncss.org	Social studies educators teach students the content knowledge, intellectual skills, and civic values necessary for fulfilling the duties of citizenship in a participatory democracy. The mission of National Council for the Social Studies is to provide leadership, service, and support for all social studies educators.
Industrial Revolution	www.fordham. edu/halsall/mod/ modsbook14.html	The Industrial Revolution was a period (1700–1900) in which fundamental changes occurred in agriculture, textile and metal manufacturing, electricity, transportation, economic policies and the social structure in England.
Civil Rights Movement	http://directory.google. com/Top/Society/ History/By_Region/ North_America/United_ States/Civil_Rights_ Movement/	Google's directory of sites about the U.S. Civil Rights Movement.

Topic	URL	Annotation
Scientific Revolution	www.fordham. edu/halsall/mod/ modsbook09.html	Site offers a basic outline overview of the Scientific Revolution with links to important people and terms.

0008 Understand principles and assumptions underlying historical or contemporary arguments, interpretations, explanations, or developments.
For example:

- Inferring the political principles (e.g., popular sovereignty, separation of powers, due process of law) or assumptions (e.g., regarding the nature of power relationships) illustrated in given situations or arguments

- Recognizing assumptions (e.g., regarding the nature of power relationships) that inform the positions taken by political parties

- Analyzing assumptions on which given U.S. policies (e.g., national health insurance, foreign relations) are based

- Recognizing concepts and ideas underlying alternative interpretations of past events

- Inferring the economic principle (e.g., supply and demand, redistribution of wealth) upon which a given explanation is based

Topic	URL	Annotation
Economic systems	http://cowles.econ.yale. edu/P/cp/p03b/p0357. pdf	Here find a detailed discussion and comparison of the capitalist, socialist, and communist economic systems.
Supply and demand	http://ingrimayne. saintjoe.edu/econ/ DemandSupply/ OverviewSD.html	Interactive economics lecture discusses supply and demand.
Due process of law	www.lectlaw.com/files/ lws63.htm	The phrase "due process of law" originated in a 1355 restatement of the 1215 Magna Carta, which ordained that no person may be deprived of life, liberty, or property unless by a fundamentally rational law ("substantive due process") applied in a fundamentally fair proceeding ("procedural due process"). This site contains a mini outline and offers related information.

0009 Understand different perspectives and priorities underlying historical or contemporary arguments, interpretations, explanations, or developments. For example:

- Identifying the values (e.g., a commitment to democratic institutions) implicit in given political, economic, social, or religious points of view

- Recognizing the motives, beliefs, and interests that inform differing political, economic, social, or religious points of view (e.g., arguments related to equity, equality, and comparisons between groups or nations)

- Analyzing multiple perspectives within U.S. society regarding major historical and contemporary issues

- Recognizing the values or priorities implicit in given public policy positions

- Analyzing the perceptions or opinions of observers or participants from different cultures regarding a given world event or development

Topic	URL	Annotation
World religions	www.omsakthi.org/religions.html	Offers a comprehensive overview of the major world religions. More detailed resources are referenced.
World history	www.camelotintl. com/world	Site gives a timeline summary of the major world events, searchable by continent. Links provide further information on key names and locations.
U.S. history	www.historyplace.com/	Provides extensive information on America's history from its formation to the present day.
Public policy on technology	www.siggraph.org/pub-policy/ whitepaperGII. html	This white paper addresses the current state of the Global Information Structure (GII) and its interrelationship with computer graphics, as well as visualization and public policy issues related to computer graphics transmitted over or used on the GII.

0010 Understand and apply skills, principles, and procedures associated with inquiry, problem solving, and decision making in history and the social sciences. For example:

- Analyzing a description of research results to identify additional unanswered questions or to determine potential problems in research methodology

- Determining the relevance or sufficiency of given information for supporting or refuting a point of view

- Assessing the reliability of sources of information cited in historical or contemporary accounts or arguments and determining whether specific conclusions or generalizations are supported by verifiable evidence

- Evaluating the appropriateness of specific sources (e.g., atlas, periodical guide, economic database) to meet given information needs (e.g., the distribution of natural resources in a given region, the political philosophy of a presidential candidate)

- Distinguishing between unsupported and informed expressions of opinion

Topic	URL	Annotation
Research methodology	www.nrf.ac.za/yenza/	This site is "a guide to using the Internet for research and teaching in the Social Sciences and Humanities."
Evaluating sources of information	www.library.cornell.edu/okuref/research/skill26.htm	Here find an extensive guide to evaluating the reliability of books, articles, and web pages.

0011 Understand and interpret visual representations of historical and social scientific information. For example:

- translating written or graphic information from one form to another (e.g., selecting an appropriate graphic representation of information from an article on historical changes in global populations)

- relating information provided in graphic representations (e.g., regarding population or economic trends) to public policy decisions

- interpreting historical or social scientific information provided in one or more graphs, charts, tables, diagrams, or maps

- inferring significant information (e.g., geographic, economic, sociological) about a historical or contemporary society based on examination of a photograph, painting, drawing, or cartoon

Topic	URL	Annotation
Historical data	www.census.gov/ population/ www/censusdata/ hiscendata.html	Working with historical census data from the U.S. Census Bureau, this site uses graphs, charts, and tables to display raw data and information collected 1940–2000.
Political cartoons and cartoonists	http://roads.virginia. edu/~M1996/puck/part1. htm	Reviews the history of political cartooning from the beginning of the 19th century to the end of the century, when political cartoons emerged as one of the most popular and influential features of the daily press. Also documents some of their uses, from Thomas Nast's campaign of the 1870s to oust the Tweed Ring through portrayals of political leaders, issues, and world events during the first decades of the 20th century.

SUBAREA III: ARTISTIC EXPRESSION AND THE HUMANITIES

0012 Understand and analyze elements of form and content in works from the visual and performing arts from different periods and cultures. For example:

- Recognizing important elements in a given work of the visual or performing arts (e.g., focal point, symmetry, repetition of shapes, perspective, motif, rhythm)

- Determining how a sense of unity or balance is achieved in a given work from the visual or performing arts

- Characterizing the theme, mood, or tone of a given work from the visual or performing arts

- Determining how specific elements in a given work of the visual or performing arts (e.g., color, composition, scale, instrumentation, set design, choreography) affect audience perceptions of the content of the work

Topic	URL	Annotation
Perspective in art	http://mathforum.org/ sum95/math_and/ perspective/perspect. html	Site gives a simple explanation of perspective.
Symmetry	www.artlex.com	Symmetry or symmetrical balance is part of an image or object organized so that one side duplicates, or mirrors, the other (also known as "formal balance"). Also at ArtLex, find more than 3,100 terms along with thousands of images, pronunciation notes, great quotations, and links to other resources on the Web.
German Expressionism	www.ibiblio.org/wm/ paint/glo/expressionism/	Expressionism is an artistic movement that seeks to portray subjective emotions and responses. Expressionism manifested mostly in Germany.
Modern dance	www.pitt.edu/~gillis/ dance/disp.html	This site presents a historical overview of some of the most important figures in the early years of modern dance in the United States. Includes details about the dances they created, the music they worked with, and the cultural events that shaped their evolutions.

0013 Analyze and interpret works from the visual and performing arts representing different periods and cultures and understand the relationship of works of art to their social and historical contexts. For example:

- Identifying similarities and differences in forms and styles of art from different movements or periods of time

- Comparing and contrasting two or more works from the visual or performing arts in terms of mood, theme, or technique

- Demonstrating an understanding of art as a form of communication (e.g., conveying political or moral concepts, serving as a means of individual expression)

- Analyzing ways in which the content of a given work from the visual or performing arts reflects a specific cultural or historical context

Topic	URL	Annotation
History of jazz	www.documentaryfilms.net/Jazz/	The documentary *Jazz* by Ken Burns is a celebration of a unique American art form and of the people made it—Miles Davis, Louis Armstrong, John Coltrane, Duke Ellington, Charlie Parker, and Dizzy Gillespie. Burns traces jazz history from its beginnings in New Orleans to Dixieland to avant-garde, from the East Coast to the West Coast, and from predictable ensembles to totally free improvising.
Tragedy in theater	www.crystalinks.com/greektheater.html	Explains ancient Greek theater, including a substantial section on tragedy.
Political theater	www.nytimes.com/books/00/11/12/specials/miller-crucible90.html	*Reviews The Crucible*, Arthur Miller's most produced and continually relevant work of political theater. By focusing on the Salem witch hunts of the 17th century, the playwright placed the outrage of McCarthyism in historical perspective and created a drama that has remained meaningful to succeeding generations.

0014 Understand forms and themes used in literature from different periods and cultures. For example:

- Identifying characteristic features of various genres of fiction and nonfiction (e.g., novels, plays, essays, autobiographies)

- Distinguishing the dominant theme in a literary passage

- Recognizing common literary elements and techniques (e.g., imagery, metaphor, symbolism, allegory, foreshadowing, irony) and using those elements to interpret a literary passage

- Determining the meaning of figurative language used in a literary passage

Topic	URL	Annotation
National Council of Teachers of English	www.ncte.org	The National Council of Teachers of English is devoted to improving the teaching and learning of English and the language arts at all levels of education. Use the site map to find general categories of subject interest.
Moral message theme	http://tomsdomain.com/aesop/aesopmain.htm	Aesop's fables contain short narratives that seek to illustrate a hidden message, or moral. Generally, the fables use animals or objects as part of the narrative, yet the message is designed to apply to humans.
Poetry	www.writing.upenn.edu/~afilreis/88/poetic-terms.html	Explains 26 poetic terms from *assonance* to *tone*.

0015 Analyze and interpret literature from different periods and cultures and understand the relationship of works of literature to their social and historical contexts. For example:

- Analyzing how the parts of a literary passage contribute to the whole

- Comparing and contrasting the tone or mood of two or more literary passages

- Analyzing aspects of cultural or historical context implied in a literary passage

- Distinguishing characteristic features of different literary genres, periods, and traditions reflected in one or more literary passages

- Making inferences about character, setting, author's point of view, etc., based on the content of a literary passage

- Recognizing how a text conveys multiple levels of meaning

Topic	URL	Annotation
Langston Hughes	www.redhotjazz.com/ hughes.html	Hughes is particularly known for his insightful, colorful portrayals of black life in America from the 1920s through the 60s. His life and work were enormously important in shaping the artistic contributions of the Harlem Renaissance during the 1920s.
William Shakespeare	www.shakespeare-online. com/	Comprehensive site details the life and works of Western culture's arguably most influential poet/playwright.
Ayn Rand	www.aynrand.org	Russian writer and philosopher's most famous Objectivist works highlight the strength of the individual and comment on the pro-Communist world in which she grew up and the unstable political climate of the mid-20th century.

0016 Analyze and interpret examples of religious or philosophical ideas from various periods of time and understand their significance in shaping societies and cultures. For example:

- Distinguishing the religious and philosophical traditions associated with given cultures and world regions

- Recognizing assumptions and beliefs underlying ideas presented in religious or philosophical writing

- Analyzing societal implications of philosophical or religious ideas

- Comparing and contrasting key concepts presented in two excerpts reflecting different philosophical or religious traditions

Topic	URL	Annotation
Karl Marx	www.philosophypages.com/ ph/marx.htm	Marx made class struggle the central aspect of his theory on social evolution. "The history of all hitherto existing human society is the history of class struggles."
Mahatma Gandhi	www.mkgandhi.org/ articles/ index.htm	Gandhi maintained that there cannot be true and lasting peace unless there are equal opportunities for all. This is a comprehensive website on Gandhi's life, writings, and philosophy.
Martin Luther King Jr.	http://mlk-kpp01.stanford. edu	King was one of the most notable leaders of the American Civil Rights Movement, working for African-American equality through nonviolent social change. This website provides extensive resources on his life and work.

SUBAREA IV: COMMUNICATION AND RESEARCH SKILLS

0017 Derive information from a variety of sources (e.g., magazine articles, essays, websites). For example:

- Identifying the stated or implied main idea of a paragraph or passage

- Selecting an accurate summary or outline of a passage

- Organizing information presented on a website or other electronic means of communication

- Comprehending stated or implied relationships in an excerpt (e.g., cause and effect, sequence of events)

- Recognizing information that supports, illustrates, or elaborates the main idea of a passage

Topic	URL	Annotation
Reading comprehension	www.middleweb. com/Reading. html#anchor5515939	Links to practical articles on teaching reading.

0018 Analyze and interpret written materials from a variety of sources. For example:

- Recognizing a writer's purpose for writing (e.g., to persuade, to describe)
- Drawing conclusions or making generalizations based on information presented in an excerpt
- Interpreting figurative language in an excerpt
- Comparing and contrasting views or arguments presented in two or more excerpts

Topic	URL	Annotation
Figurative language	www.cod.edu/people/ faculty/fitchf/readlit/figspch. htm	Fairly comprehensive website reviews figurative techniques such as metaphors, imagery, and irony among others.

0019 Use critical reasoning skills to assess an author's treatment of content in written materials from a variety of sources. For example:

- Analyzing the logical structure of an argument in an excerpt and identifying possible instances of faulty reasoning
- Distinguishing between fact and opinion in written material
- Determining the relevance of specific facts, examples, or data to a writer's argument
- Interpreting the content, word choice, and phrasing of a passage to determine a writer's opinions, point of view, or position on an issue
- Evaluating the credibility, objectivity, or bias of an author's argument or sources

Topic	URL	Annotation
Author critique	www.goshen.edu/english/critique.html	Excellent site has essay review guidelines and techniques.

0020 Analyze and evaluate the effectiveness of expression in a written paragraph or passage according to the conventions of edited American English. For example:

- Revising text to correct problems relating to grammar (e.g., syntax, pronoun-antecedent agreement)

- Revising text to correct problems relating to sentence construction (e.g., those involving parallel structure, misplaced modifiers, run-on sentences)

- Revising text to improve unity and coherence (e.g., eliminating unnecessary sentences or paragraphs, adding a topic sentence or introductory paragraph, clarifying transitions between and relationships among ideas presented)

- Analyzing problems related to the organization of a given text (e.g., logical flow of ideas, grouping of related ideas, development of main points)

Topic	URL	Annotation
Writer's reference	www.bartleby.com/141/	Asserting that one must first know the rules to break them, *The Elements of Style* by strunk and white, a classic reference book, is a must-have for any student and conscientious writer. It gives in brief space the principal requirements of plain English style and concentrates on the rules of usage and principles of composition most commonly violated.

0021 Demonstrate the ability to locate, retrieve, organize, and interpret information from a variety of traditional and electronic sources. For example:

- Demonstrating familiarity with basic reference tools (e.g., encyclopedias, almanacs, bibliographies, databases, atlases, periodical guides)

- Recognizing the difference between primary and secondary sources

- Formulating research questions and hypotheses

- Applying procedures for retrieving information from traditional and technological sources (e.g., newspapers, CD-ROMs, the Internet)

- Interpreting data presented in visual, graphic, tabular, and quantitative forms (e.g., recognizing level of statistical significance)

- Organizing information into logical and coherent outlines

- Evaluating the reliability of different sources of information

Topic	URL	Annotation
Primary and secondary sources	www.mnwest.edu/larc/ library/research-help/ primarysecondary-sources/	Details the differences between primary and secondary sources.
Formulating a research question	www.theresearchassistant. com/tutorial/2.asp	This online tutorial discusses how a research goal is developed through the establishment of a research question.
Interpreting data	http://money.howstuffworks. com/personal-finance/ math-tutoring/tables-graphs/ reading-interpreting-data.htm	Find here a library of articles on reading and interpreting different types of data.
Organizing information into outlines	www.writeexpress.com/ writing-outline.html	This is an excellent article on writing an effective outline.
Evaluating reliability of information sources	www.library.cornell.edu/ olinuris/ref/research/evaluate. html	Comprehensive article evaluates the reliability of different sources of information.

SUBAREA V: WRITTEN ANALYSIS AND EXPRESSION

0022 Prepare an organized, developed composition in edited American English in response to instructions regarding content, purpose, and audience. For example:

- Taking a position on an issue of contemporary concern and defending that position with reasoned arguments and supporting examples

- Analyzing and responding to an opinion presented in an excerpt

- Comparing and contrasting conflicting viewpoints on a social, political, or educational topic, as presented in one or more excerpts

- Evaluating information and proposing a solution to a stated problem

- Synthesizing information presented in two or more excerpts

Topic	URL	Annotation
Edited American English	www.smu.edu/english/firstyearwriting/policies.asp#standards	Gives standards of evaluation for edited American English.
The Little, Brown Handbook	www.mantex.co.uk/reviews/fowler.htm	Reviews a reference guide to all aspects of academic writing that its authors say will answer almost any question you have about writing.

STUDYING FOR THE LAST

As you can see, the LAST is very much a gauge of a person's liberal arts and sciences knowledge at an introductory level. You often do not need to go beyond the information in the item to answer it correctly. The test will not contain complex mathematical equations and concepts or scientific processes, nor will it ask you to diagram sentences, have knowledge of languages other than English, be familiar with word origins, or require you to recall dates of historical events.

In the days and weeks prior to the test, it is helpful to do the following:

- Practice reading short passages—in newspapers, novels, and textbooks—to glean the important information.

- Look over graphs, charts, and maps learn how to read and interpret them.

- Recall basic grammar and English usage rules.

- Get a broad understanding of art, music and architecture and try to determine special qualities and meanings in work.
- Practice writing essays on general topics. Be sure to practice directly responding to a question, supporting your thesis with reasons and details. Be sure to respond in formal essay structure, including an introduction, body, and conclusion

In the preparation phase, it is of utmost importance to take a practice LAST under realistic conditions. This means finding a quiet room with no distractions and following the time guidelines. You will have 4 hours to complete the 80 multiple-choice questions and the 1 essay question. For the multiple-choice section, a key strategy is to focus on the information in the passage, graph, chart, picture, etc. and determine what will help you answer the question.

ATTACKING THE QUESTIONS

The multiple-choice questions may ask the following types of questions, as indicated by these keywords:

summarize

draw a conclusion based on information given

important theme

grammatical error

inference

interpreting data on a chart or map

implied meaning

main idea

mood or tone of voice of a passage

author's purpose

word substitution

comparisons

analyze

given a formula, calculate the answer

addition, subtraction, multiplication, and division symbols

The first step in answering a question is to *understand what the question is asking*. Look for key words or phrases that give you clues about what the author is asking. At this stage, another strategy is to *reword the question*. Putting the question into your own words helps you understand it better.

Once you read a question once, reread it to glean important information. Try to identify the *main idea*. In addition, note *details* that are relevant to the question (possibly by underlining them). *Predict* the answer to the question before you look at the choices. *Eliminate* incorrect answer choices right at the beginning. Remember—passages may seem complicated or unfamiliar, but the questions generally are not.

ELIMINATING WRONG ANSWERS

Incorrect answers on the LAST tend to fall into a few categories. Being able to recognize these will help you eliminate incorrect options.

> *Contradiction*: This states the view opposite from what is presented.
>
> *Distortion*: This changes the author's intent. It gives it a different meaning or interpretation than the author intended.
>
> *Extreme*: This is an all-or-none proposition. Rarely is something true all of the time or none of the time.
>
> *Wrong Scope*: The statement is generally accurate, but it is not the basic argument of the passage. It is usually a detail that supports the argument.

Try the following example.

1. Advocates of foreign language study have reacted with uncritical enthusiasm to recent surveys showing increased enrollment in college-level foreign language classes. Most of the classes in question, however, use conversational methods rather than the traditional exercises in grammar and rigorous analysis of literary texts. Unfortunately, by providing an easier way of meeting language requirements for the bachelor's degree, these classes will actually have the detrimental effect of decreasing the number of graduates who are capable of appreciating the subtleties of another culture's means of expression.

Which of the following is a major assumption of the argument above?

A. Abolishing the foreign language requirement for the bachelor's degree would make conversation language classes more attractive to students.

B. A conversation course typically attracts more students than does a literature course when a choice exists.

C. Conversational courses do not provide the linguistic insights that traditional grammar or literature courses do.

D. All college graduates should be required to have a reading knowledge of at least one foreign language.

Think about the main idea of this passage and put it into your own words:

The assumption behind the argument is that conversational classes do not provide as much insight into the language as classes that are more traditional.

The rest of the passage supports the main idea but is not helpful in answering the question.

Based on this information, the correct response for this question is (C).

Let's look at the incorrect responses:

Choice (A) is a *distortion* of the author's purpose. This statement is irrelevant to the passage. The paragraph says nothing about abolishing a foreign language requirement.

Choice (B) is an example of *wrong scope*. Whereas this statement may be true, it does not address the main idea of the passage.

As for (D), rarely is an *extreme* response the correct response (*all* college graduates . . .). Also, this response is not supported in the passage.

Predicting each answer before reading the given response and then eliminating incorrect responses will aid you greatly in successfully completing the LAST.

CHAPTER 5: **DIAGNOSTIC LAST**

Before taking this practice test, find a quiet room where you can work uninterrupted for 4 hours. Make sure you have a comfortable desk and several No. 2 pencils.

Use the answer sheet provided to record your answers.

Once you start this practice test, don't stop until you've finished. Remember, you can complete the sections of the test in any order you wish.

You will find an answer key and explanations following the test.

Good luck!

SAMPLE DIRECTIONS

This test booklet contains a multiple-choice section and a single written assignment section. You may complete the sections of the test in the order you choose.

Each question in the first section of this booklet is a multiple-choice question with four answer choices. Read each question CAREFULLY and choose the ONE best answer. Record your answer on the answer document in the space that corresponds to the question number. Completely fill in the space having the same letter as the answer you have chosen. *Use only a No. 2 lead pencil.*

Sample Question

1. What is the capital of New York?

    A. Buffalo

    B. New York City

    C. Albany

    D. Rochester

The correct answer to this question is (C). You would indicate that on the answer document as follows:

1.

You should answer all questions. Even if you are unsure of an answer, it is better to guess than not to answer a question at all. You may use the margins of the test booklet for scratch paper, but you will be scored only on the responses on your answer document.

The directions for the written assignment appear later in this test booklet.

FOR TEST SECURITY REASONS, YOU MAY NOT TAKE NOTES OR REMOVE ANY OF THE TEST MATERIALS FROM THE ROOM.

The words "End of Test" indicate that you have completed the test. You may go back and review your answers, but be sure you have answered all questions before raising your hand for dismissal. Your test materials must be returned to a test administrator when you finish the test.

If you have any questions, please ask them now before beginning the test.

STOP

DO NOT GO ON UNTIL YOU ARE TOLD TO DO SO.

LAST Answer Sheet

1.	Ⓐ Ⓑ Ⓒ Ⓓ	28. Ⓐ Ⓑ Ⓒ Ⓓ	55. Ⓐ Ⓑ Ⓒ Ⓓ
2.	Ⓐ Ⓑ Ⓒ Ⓓ	29. Ⓐ Ⓑ Ⓒ Ⓓ	56. Ⓐ Ⓑ Ⓒ Ⓓ
3.	Ⓐ Ⓑ Ⓒ Ⓓ	30. Ⓐ Ⓑ Ⓒ Ⓓ	57. Ⓐ Ⓑ Ⓒ Ⓓ
4.	Ⓐ Ⓑ Ⓒ Ⓓ	31. Ⓐ Ⓑ Ⓒ Ⓓ	58. Ⓐ Ⓑ Ⓒ Ⓓ
5.	Ⓐ Ⓑ Ⓒ Ⓓ	32. Ⓐ Ⓑ Ⓒ Ⓓ	59. Ⓐ Ⓑ Ⓒ Ⓓ
6.	Ⓐ Ⓑ Ⓒ Ⓓ	33. Ⓐ Ⓑ Ⓒ Ⓓ	60. Ⓐ Ⓑ Ⓒ Ⓓ
7.	Ⓐ Ⓑ Ⓒ Ⓓ	34. Ⓐ Ⓑ Ⓒ Ⓓ	61. Ⓐ Ⓑ Ⓒ Ⓓ
8.	Ⓐ Ⓑ Ⓒ Ⓓ	35. Ⓐ Ⓑ Ⓒ Ⓓ	62. Ⓐ Ⓑ Ⓒ Ⓓ
9.	Ⓐ Ⓑ Ⓒ Ⓓ	36. Ⓐ Ⓑ Ⓒ Ⓓ	63. Ⓐ Ⓑ Ⓒ Ⓓ
10.	Ⓐ Ⓑ Ⓒ Ⓓ	37. Ⓐ Ⓑ Ⓒ Ⓓ	64. Ⓐ Ⓑ Ⓒ Ⓓ
11.	Ⓐ Ⓑ Ⓒ Ⓓ	38. Ⓐ Ⓑ Ⓒ Ⓓ	65. Ⓐ Ⓑ Ⓒ Ⓓ
12.	Ⓐ Ⓑ Ⓒ Ⓓ	39. Ⓐ Ⓑ Ⓒ Ⓓ	66. Ⓐ Ⓑ Ⓒ Ⓓ
13.	Ⓐ Ⓑ Ⓒ Ⓓ	40. Ⓐ Ⓑ Ⓒ Ⓓ	67. Ⓐ Ⓑ Ⓒ Ⓓ
14.	Ⓐ Ⓑ Ⓒ Ⓓ	41. Ⓐ Ⓑ Ⓒ Ⓓ	68. Ⓐ Ⓑ Ⓒ Ⓓ
15.	Ⓐ Ⓑ Ⓒ Ⓓ	42. Ⓐ Ⓑ Ⓒ Ⓓ	69. Ⓐ Ⓑ Ⓒ Ⓓ
16.	Ⓐ Ⓑ Ⓒ Ⓓ	43. Ⓐ Ⓑ Ⓒ Ⓓ	70. Ⓐ Ⓑ Ⓒ Ⓓ
17.	Ⓐ Ⓑ Ⓒ Ⓓ	44. Ⓐ Ⓑ Ⓒ Ⓓ	71. Ⓐ Ⓑ Ⓒ Ⓓ
18.	Ⓐ Ⓑ Ⓒ Ⓓ	45. Ⓐ Ⓑ Ⓒ Ⓓ	72. Ⓐ Ⓑ Ⓒ Ⓓ
19.	Ⓐ Ⓑ Ⓒ Ⓓ	46. Ⓐ Ⓑ Ⓒ Ⓓ	73. Ⓐ Ⓑ Ⓒ Ⓓ
20.	Ⓐ Ⓑ Ⓒ Ⓓ	47. Ⓐ Ⓑ Ⓒ Ⓓ	74. Ⓐ Ⓑ Ⓒ Ⓓ
21.	Ⓐ Ⓑ Ⓒ Ⓓ	48. Ⓐ Ⓑ Ⓒ Ⓓ	75. Ⓐ Ⓑ Ⓒ Ⓓ
22.	Ⓐ Ⓑ Ⓒ Ⓓ	49. Ⓐ Ⓑ Ⓒ Ⓓ	76. Ⓐ Ⓑ Ⓒ Ⓓ
23.	Ⓐ Ⓑ Ⓒ Ⓓ	50. Ⓐ Ⓑ Ⓒ Ⓓ	77. Ⓐ Ⓑ Ⓒ Ⓓ
24.	Ⓐ Ⓑ Ⓒ Ⓓ	51. Ⓐ Ⓑ Ⓒ Ⓓ	78. Ⓐ Ⓑ Ⓒ Ⓓ
25.	Ⓐ Ⓑ Ⓒ Ⓓ	52. Ⓐ Ⓑ Ⓒ Ⓓ	79. Ⓐ Ⓑ Ⓒ Ⓓ
26.	Ⓐ Ⓑ Ⓒ Ⓓ	53. Ⓐ Ⓑ Ⓒ Ⓓ	80. Ⓐ Ⓑ Ⓒ Ⓓ
27.	Ⓐ Ⓑ Ⓒ Ⓓ	54. Ⓐ Ⓑ Ⓒ Ⓓ	

Use the passage below to answer the question that follows.

Because a healthy economy benefits almost everyone and a stagnant one hurts most people, policies aimed at improving the economy are debated. Presidents become dependent on economic experts and their theories to keep the economy moving forward.

1. Which of the following statements best describes an example of an economic theory?

    A. Monetary policy is an attempt to use the amount of money and bank deposits and the price of money (interest rate) to affect the economy.

    B. Fiscal policy is an attempt to use taxes and expenditures to affect the economy.

    C. Monetarism means that the government should have a steady, predictable increase in the money supply about equal to the growth of the economy.

    D. Federal Reserve Board determines interest rates to be charged by regional banks.

Read the passage below, excerpted from *Foundations of American Education* (Allyn and Bacon, © 1999); then, answer the question that follows.

"According to the Goals 2000 education act passed by Congress in 1994, schools must provide all students the opportunity to learn the skills outlined in national standards for mathematics, science, English, the arts, foreign languages, history, geography, civics, and economics. The provision of remediation for the underserved is no longer the focus. The expectation is that all students can learn. Because Goals 2000 also expects U.S. students to achieve better on international tests than students in any other part of the world, one may wonder whether opportunity to learn actually means the ability to perform well on some tests. More optimistically, national standards could help prevent students from being tracked into courses and programs that limit their access to higher-level knowledge. They could even encourage critical thinking and the ability to view the world and academic subjects from multiple perspectives."

2. Which of the following conclusions is best supported by information presented in the passage?

    A. Students in the United States are higher achievers than students in many other countries.

    B. Equality of education for all students should be a higher priority.

    C. The national standards in Goals 2000 are difficult to achieve.

    D. Academic tracking is prevalent in the U.S. educational system.

Read the sonnet below, written by Shakespeare when he was growing old; then, answer the question that follows.

That time of year thou mayst in me behold
When yellow leaves, or none, or few, do hang
Upon these boughs which shake against the cold,
Bare ruined choirs, where late the sweet bird sang.
In me thou seest the twilight of such day
As after sunset fadeth in the west,
Which by and by black night doth take away,
Death's second self, that seals up all in rest.
In me thou seest the glowing of such fire,
That on the ashes of his youth doth lie,
As the deathbed whereon it must expire,
Consumed by that it was nourished by.
This thou perceiv'st, which makes thy love more strong,
To love that well which thou must leave ere long.

3. The poet expresses the central idea that

    A. He dislikes autumn when the leaves fall from the trees and the air becomes cold and bitter.

    B. Friendship and love are everlasting and make the pain of old age increasingly more bearable.

    C. Friendship is more valued when both people realize that their time together will be brief.

    D. Old age and death are terrifying prospects.

Read the passage below, which contains a grammatical error; then, answer the question that follows.

(1) The proper role of schools, then, is to do the educating not done or not done easy elsewhere in the culture. (2) In creating schools, one might well begin by seeking to discover what educating the culture already is doing well or conceivably could do well. (3) In rethinking what existing schools should be doing now and in the future, one should seek to find out what they currently are doing that the rest of the culture is doing or could do better. (4) To define or appraise the role of schools apart from the total ecology within which they function is myopic.

4.   Which part of the passage should be rewritten?

    A.   Part 1: to correct an error in an adverb.

    B.   Part 2: to correct an error in prepositional phrasing

    C.   Part 3: to correct an error in subject-verb agreement

    D   Part 4: to correct an error in tense

5.   You are traveling 140 miles on the New York State Thruway and are able to maintain a constant 60 mph rate of speed. The formula for distance is $d = rt$ (distance = rate × time). About how long will it take you to reach your destination?

    A.   2 hours, 40 minutes

    B.   2 hours, 20 minutes

    C.   1 hour, 25 minutes

    D.   1 hour, 50 minutes

6.   Kelley Collins is saving the money from her summer job to go to college. She earns $6.75 per hour and works 35 hours per week. She saves half of this gross income and deposits it into a savings account earning 5.5%. If she works for 9 weeks, how much money total will she have in her account (principle plus interest)?

    A. $1,121.60

    B. $5,330.65

    C. $53.30

    D. $2,126.25

7. Billy finished the 600-meter run in P.E. class in 2 minutes, 29.7 seconds. Gretchen finished 2.6 seconds slower. What was Gretchen's time?

   A. 2:27.1

   B. 2:55.7

   C. 2:32.3

   D. 2:25.7

8. Which of the following describes the geographical setting in which early civilization was most likely to emerge?

   A. an open, grassy plain with plenty of room and food for livestock

   B. rolling hills that provided vantage points from which to scout for enemy invasions

   C. a temperate river delta that flooded regularly, resulting in fertile soil for crops

   D. dense jungle with edible plants and game enough for hunting and gathering

Use the passage below to answer the question that follows.

Automobiles were very expensive in the early 20th century because each one was made individually by hand. The hood, wheels, and seats varied slightly with each vehicle made. However, with the invention of _____, more people were able to afford an automobile because they were cheaper to produce.

9. What phrase best fits in the blank?

   A. the steam engine

   B. standard parts

   C. gasoline

   D. the workers' union

10. Emotional language is language that appeals to a reader's emotions, rather than logic or solid arguments. Which of these is an example of the use of emotional language?

    A. If you do not use a child safety seat for your infant, he will die in a car accident.

    B. The frequency of violent acts in schools increased in 2000.

    C. A greater percentage of Caucasians than African Americans have type B blood.

    D. The Constitution of the United States was ratified in 1789.

In questions 11 and 12, choose the letter of the underlined phrase that contains a grammatical error. Select choice D if there is no error in the sentence.

11. Neither <u>the magician</u> <u>or his assistant</u> knew <u>how to get out</u> of the box. <u>No error</u>
               A.   B.   C.   D.

12. <u>Lindsay and Yao</u> <u>went</u> to the supermarket <u>to buy</u> a loaf of bread. <u>No error</u>
         A.   B.   C.   D.

13. Three cucumbers can be purchased for $1.50. Maria has N dollars. How many cucumbers can she buy?

    A. $3 \times \left(\dfrac{N}{\$1.50} \right)$

    B. $3 \times N \times \$1.50$

    C. $\left(\dfrac{\$1.50 \times 3}{N} \right)$

    D. $\left(\dfrac{N \times \$1.50}{3} \right)$

14. Vertebrates are members of the animal kingdom that have backbones. Which of these is NOT a vertebrate?

    A. human

    B. trout

    C. alligator

    D. earthworm

15. Theodore Roosevelt is remembered as being a progressive president who was opposed to business monopolies. With which of these statements would Theodore Roosevelt probably agree?

    A. Big businesses always look out for the best interests of the consumer.

    B. Private businesses should be abolished, and the government should take control of the means of production.

    C. Small, locally owned businesses that have a great deal of competition tend to operate in the best interests of the consumer.

    D. The profits obtained from a business monopoly are rewards that businesspeople deserve for exploiting the capitalist system to their own advantage.

16. Lauren finished a 1,500-meter race in 4 minutes, 59 seconds. Jenny was 2.4 seconds slower. What was Jenny's time?

    A. 4 minutes, 56.6 seconds

    B. 4 minutes, 56.4 seconds

    C. 5 minutes, 23 seconds

    D. 5 minutes, 1.4 seconds

17. Alliteration is the repetition of a consonantal sound at the beginning of several words. Which of these sentences exhibits alliteration?

    A. Annie ate apples all day.

    B. Birte brought Billy a ball.

    C. Cesar did his homework.

    D. Your eyes are like pools of water.

18. The world population doubled between about 650 and 1650. It doubled again between 1650 and 1850. It doubled again between 1850 and 1930. The world population once again doubled between 1930 and 1975. What can be inferred from this data?

    A. The population is currently growing at a faster rate than it was 1,000 years ago.

    B. The population is probably decreasing now.

    C. In 1850, there were 400 million more people on Earth than there were in 650.

    D. About 7 billion people currently live on Earth.

19. Which of the following modern disciplines was NOT influenced by the civilization of ancient Greece?

    A. philosophy

    B. anthropology

    C. theater

    D. mathematics

20. Which of the following best expresses one reason that slavery became entrenched in the southern colonies prior to the Revolutionary War but never took hold in the northern colonies?

    A. The southern colonies were settled primarily by Spain, which had no moral qualms about slavery; but the English, who abhorred slavery, settled in the north.

    B. The southern colonies were settled primarily as penal colonies, with an anything-goes attitude, but the northern colonies were more strictly governed by England.

    C. Geographically speaking, the southern colonies were closer to the route the slave traders took from Africa, so southern slavery was more economically feasible.

    D. The geography of the northern colonies was less conducive to highly labor-intensive cash crop agriculture than was the geography of southern colonies.

21. Which of the following most accurately describes the central goal of the women's suffrage movement in the United States?

    A. to abolish the practice of slavery

    B. to ensure equitable salaries for women

    C. to obtain the right for women to vote

    D. to prohibit the use of alcohol

Use the passage below to answer the question that follows.

The sun sank rapidly; the silvery light had faded from the bare boughs and the watery twilight was settling in when Wilson at last walked down the hill, descending into cooler and cooler depths of grayish shadow. His nostril, long unused to it, was quick to detect the smell of wood smoke in the air, blended with the odor of moist spring earth and the saltiness that came up the river with the tide.

—from *Alexander's Bridge* by Willa Cather

22. The passage above contains characteristic elements of which of the following literary genres?

    A. fable

    B. autobiography

    C. folktale

    D. realistic fiction

Use the chart below to answer the four questions that follow.

Table 1. The Length of Each Planet's Year

Planet	Period of Revolution
Mercury	88 days
Venus	225 days
Earth	365 days
Mars	687 days
Jupiter	12 years
Saturn	30 years
Uranus	84 years
Neptune	165 years
Pluto	248 years

Source: *Earth Science* by Danielson and Denecke, 1989.

23. About how many times longer than Venus's period of revolution is Mars's period of revolution?

    A. $\frac{1}{3}$

    B. 2

    C. 3

    D. 462

24. Which planet takes the longest amount of time to revolve around the sun?

    A. Mercury

    B. Earth

    C. Mars

    D. Pluto

25. Which planet does NOT have a period of revolution longer than that of Earth?

    A. Venus

    B. Mars

    C. Saturn

    D. Pluto

26. Which of the following conclusions can be inferred from this table?

    A. Venus is closer to the sun than Neptune is.

    B. Uranus is closer to the sun than Saturn is.

    C. Pluto is approximately 80 miles farther from the sun than Neptune is.

    D. Saturn is larger than Jupiter.

In questions 27 and 28, fill in the blank with the word choice that best fits logically and structurally.

27. Juanita is a(n) _____ person. She always tends to see the negative side of a situation.

   A. optimist

   B. optimistic

   C. pessimist

   D. pessimistic

28. LaTisha is the one _____ ate the last piece of cake.

   A. who

   B. whom

   C. which

   D. did

**Vincent van Gogh, *Starry Night*, oil on canvas;
The Museum of Modern Art, New York**

29. Vincent van Gogh painted *Starry Night* while in an asylum in Saint Remy. It was painted from memory and not outdoors, as was his preference. What emotion best characterizes van Gogh's state of mind while painting this picture?

    A. euphoric

    B. sad

    C. tumultuous

    D. afraid of the dark

Use the graph below to answer the two questions that follow.

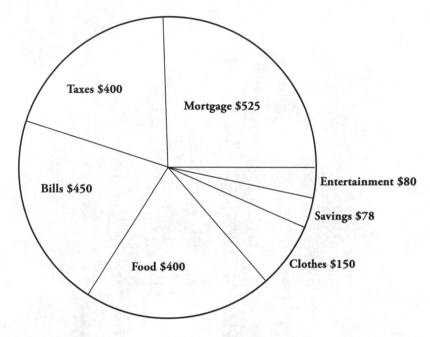

30. The monthly household expenses total $2,083.33. Approximately what percent of this total is spent on the mortgage?

    A. 20%

    B. 40%

    C. 15%

    D. 25%

31. This family wants to save for a television that costs $625. If they used all their savings and entertainment allowance, how many months would it take to earn enough for the television?

    A. 6 months

    B. 12 months

    C. 4 months

    D. 2 months

32. All of the following exterior features serve to accentuate the height of the building pictured above EXCEPT

    A. the horizontal lines that separate the stories.

    B. the vertical alignment of the windows.

    C. the flat wall surfaces with no setbacks.

    D. the steeply pitched roofs.

33. To what power of 10 would you multiply 5.83 to get 58,300,000?

    A. 10^5

    B. 10^7

    C. 10^6

    D. 10^8

34. Which of the following describes the example above?

    A. It is a good example of the single-point perspective system.

    B. The clothing reveals the artist's preoccupation with human anatomy.

    C. The figures are arranged symmetrically and exhibit little interaction.

    D. The rocks establish a shallow, stagelike space that frames the action.

$(11:27.03 + 11:06.2 + 11:12.5 + 10:55.9) \div 4 = $ _____

35. Which of the following statements could result in the number sentence above?

    A. Lauren wanted to find the median time of her 3,000-meter runs.

    B. Lauren wanted to find the mean of her 3,000-meter runs.

    C. Lauren wanted to find the product of her 3,000-meter runs.

    D. Lauren wanted to find the sum of the quotient of her 3,000-meter runs.

Use the map below to answer the two questions that follow.

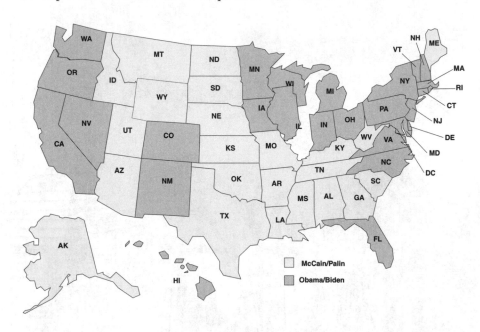

Presidential Election of 2008

36. The shading on this map shows a visual representation of

    A. the number of electoral votes each candidate won.

    B. which states have more Republicans than Democrats.

    C. the states in which each candidate won the popular vote.

    D. Obama winning the election 35–15.

37. What conclusion might you reasonably draw from this map?

    A. McCain is from Tennessee.

    B. The Northeast is a Republican area.

    C. If not for Texas, McCain would have won the election.

    D. The Southern states are heavily Republican.

Use the passage below to answer the three questions that follow.

1.
Nevertheless, I ran it. There were only two of us brave girls out there, and neither of us had ever run this before. In fact, the first time I actually jumped (well, climbed) over a steeple was about five minutes before the race. So, equally unprepared, we walked toward the starting line, fearing the worst but hoping it would be fun. After all, how often do distance runners get to _____ over hurdles?

2.
Today I ran the steeplechase for the first time. Two thousand meters, 30 degrees, high winds, and 25 steeples were sure to make for an interesting experience, to say the least. Thoughtfully, the hosts of the meet emptied the water jump for us. Being cold and wet would have made things even more miserable. But it was a mixed blessing, for the cushioning that the water usually provided was absent. I would have to jump off a steeple into an empty pit, instead.

3.
The gun went off, and we went out slowly. The first two laps were run side by side. We were both equally tentative about taking the lead, and neither of us wanted to push the pace since we had no idea how tired we would eventually get and did not want to waste our energy on the early, easier laps. I began to let the other runner take the lead by a few steps. I made excuses to myself: "you're doing it on purpose; you're letting her block the wind for you; she's got a steeplechase on her school's track and you don't."

38. What is the correct order of the paragraphs above?

    A. 1, 2, 3

    B. 2, 3, 1

    C. 3, 1, 2

    D. 2, 1, 3

39. What word best fits into the blank?

    A. run

    B. steeple

    C. jump

    D. climb

40. Which primary form of rhetoric does the author use in this passage?

    A. reflection

    B. exposition

    C. narration

    D. argumentation

Use the passage below to answer the question that follows.

Much phosphorous is found in rock and sedimentary deposits. It is released by weathering, leaching, and mining. It can also transfer to other places by traveling through fresh water and being transported by the death and decay of plants, grazers, and parasites. Most of it, however, is deposited in the sea in shallow sediments or in ocean depths. Phosphorous is brought back to the land through fish harvests and by the collection of fish deposited by sea birds.

41. Which of the following questions can be answered from the passage above?

    A. How is phosphorous released from sedimentary rock?

    B. What is leaching?

    C. Can phosphorous exist in a combined form with other elements?

    D. How is the phosphorous cycle completed?

Use the passage below to answer the two questions that follow.

"Give me liberty or give me death." This was the cry of the founding fathers, men who felt oppressed and used because they were being governed without having any input as to who would govern them. Today it seems that we may have forgotten the noble ideas for which the founders fought, as voter turnout has fallen in recent decades. In 1860, 80 percent of eligible voters voted. By 1996—a low point—that figure was down to 49 percent. The 2008 elections showed a bit of a rebound with a 63 percent turnout, but that number is still significantly lower than in 1860. However, this perceived low turnout may not be as low as it seems. It is well known that the political machines of the late nineteenth century "stuffed" ballot boxes by having some people vote multiple times and simply adding ballots to boxes if necessary. Because there are no accurate records of actual voter turnout, it is difficult to see if the numbers we have today are really that much lower than they were in the 1800s.

Even so, it is generally agreed that voter turnout has gone down markedly. Most frighteningly, our nation's youth are abstaining from the voting booth in record numbers. In 2008, only about one half of those eligible to vote between the ages of 18 and 24 actually cast ballots.

42. Which of the following statements can be inferred from the passage?

    A. The number of voters has decreased by 17%.

    B. People cared more about the country in 1860.

    C. People between 18 and 24 don't care about politics.

    D. It is difficult to tell the actual number of people who voted in 1860.

43. Which of the following words is the most appropriate substitution for "stuffed" in sentence 8?

    A. added votes to

    B. charged additional money for

    C. determined the winner of

    D. voted for

Use the passage below to answer the three questions that follow.

Many countries seek to control alcohol-related problems among teenagers by setting a minimum legal drinking age. The effectiveness of such legislation, however, varies from country to country. Research shows that in North America, such legislation does little to deter teenagers from drinking (although it may lower the level of consumption). The fact that such measures are not taken very seriously in North America—either by the populace or enforcement agencies—reflects a legal tradition that has frequently seen laws passed simply to express moral concern. In European countries, on the other hand, symbolic legislation is rarely enacted. However, when it is, it is both more strictly enforced and more strictly observed because cultural traditions encourage an attitude of absolute respect for the law.

44. The main purpose of this passage is to

   A. draw attention to the seriousness of the problems caused by illegal alcohol consumption by teenagers.

   B. explain a major point of difference between the legislative process in Europe and in North America.

   C. support the view that teenage drinking is primarily a moral problem rather than a problem of law enforcement.

   D. discuss some of the factors influencing the effectiveness of alcohol-control legislation in different countries.

45. According to the passage, the effectiveness of legislation setting a minimum drinking age is likely to be determined primarily by

   A. whether the population perceives its primary purpose to be the complete elimination of underage drinking or simply the lowering of consumption levels.

   B. the extent to which it expresses a society's moral disapproval of alcohol consumption and alcohol-related problems.

   C. the frequency with which symbolic legislation is enacted in the country in which the law is passed.

   D. how the provisions of the law are interpreted by the agencies responsible for enforcing it in each country.

46. On the basis of the information provided in the passage, it can be inferred that the effectiveness of alcohol-control legislation in deterring teenagers from drinking would probably be greater in Europe than in North America because

   A. North American teenagers tend to be more immoral than their European counterparts.

   B. It is to be expected that European teenagers would follow the tradition in European countries of absolute respect for the law.

   C. European teenagers would be morally opposed to consumption of alcoholic beverages.

   D. It is to be expected that North American teenagers would follow the tradition in North America of absolute respect for the law.

Use the passage below to answer the three questions that follow.

Some positive aspects of additives are the obvious benefits they provide, such as the improved taste, coloration, texture, and consistency they can add to food. They can also help stop moisture absorption and lumping, prevent mold from forming on a food, keep foam from forming during manufacture, stop materials from separating from each other, keep foods from becoming soft, maintain an acceptable moisture level, and cause bread and cakes to rise. They can also help increase the nutritional level of foods, stop bacteria from growing, help dispense food from aerosol cans, trap small amounts of substances that would spoil food, and make your central nervous system work faster. However, there are also some negative aspects to additives. Many can produce harmful side effects. Some common side effects include headaches, nausea, runny nose, loss of appetite, fever, hives, liver damage, ulcers, and rashes. Even more serious side effects can occur in people with a history of migraines and asthma. For people who are allergic to a certain additive, ingesting it can even result in death.

47. The tone of this passage is best described as

    A. angry.

    B. objective.

    C. nervous.

    D. sarcastic.

48. The author's primary purpose for writing this passage is to

    A. persuade.

    B. debate.

    C. inform.

    D. entertain.

49. What main point is the author making in this passage?

    A. The positive effects of food additives outweigh the negative effects.

    B. Food additives are only used when food becomes moldy.

    C. Food additives are the best way to attain hives.

    D. There are both positive and negative aspects to food additives.

Use the passage below to answer the six questions that follow.

There were many factors that set the stage for World War I. Military buildup, nationalistic feelings, and rival alliances all played a part in causing the war that would affect the entire world.

Military buildup had been occurring in all the European countries since the 1890s,
5   when the arms race began. Countries such as Great Britain, Russia, Germany, and Austria-Hungary had all doubled the amount of money spent on weapons from 1890 to 1914, which was when the war began. In addition, nearly all the Great Powers had large standing armies. Highly detailed plans were developed for mobilization or the ability to organize and move troops in case of a war. The large and strong standing
10   armies and the supposedly sure-fire plans of the generals created strong nationalistic feelings in the citizens of these countries.

Nationalism, a deep devotion to one's own nation, had the power to bring the people of a nation together. It also had the power to create a rivalry among competing nations. It helped create competition between all of Europe's Great Powers to see
15   which nation could overpower the others. They competed to overpower the others in many aspects, including materials and markets; industry, finance, and shipping; and territory; many of the countries were prepared to use any means necessary to achieve their goals. Nationalistic feelings also led to demands for independence in Serbia, Bulgaria, and Romania. After Serbia's demand for independence, Austria-Hungary
20   claimed that Serbs allowed secret societies to be formed against the monarch of Austria-Hungary and thought that the Serbs had too much free press and needless agitation. They then demanded a formal assurance that there would be no opposition to the monarch and that Serbia had to allow Austria-Hungary representatives into Serbia to stop any movement against the monarch.

25   The international rivalries led to a complex alliance system, which also played a part in causing the war. However, they were originally intended to keep peace throughout Europe. Otto von Bismarck of Germany thought that France was the biggest threat to maintaining peace in Europe and tried to isolate it by taking away its allies and forming the Triple Alliance along with Austria-Hungary and Italy. He also signed
30   a treaty with Russia. Later, however, Kaiser Wilhelm II became ruler of Germany and forced Bismarck to resign. He then let his treaty with Russia lapse, and Russia responded by forming an alliance with France. Then Kaiser decided to challenge Great Britain, who then decided to form the Triple Entente with France and Russia. The two rival alliances were a source of great bitterness among all the nations involved because
35   of broken promises and changing loyalties. This played a large part in causing the war.

Germany eventually landed all the responsibility for the war, but the causes were also as Count Brockdorff-Rantzau stated: policies of retaliation, expansion, the disregard for the right of the people to be able to determine their own destiny, the mobilization of Russia, and the murder of the Archduke. Another opinion was that every European

40   country was in some way responsible
because each had leaders that did things to lead to war or had leaders who failed to do things to prevent the war.

Although everyone involved seemed to have a different opinion, most people now agree on what caused World War I: military buildup, nationalistic feelings, and a

45   complex alliance system were the major factors.

50. All of the following statements can be infrrred from the passage EXCEPT

A. An arms race began and caused nations to build up their militaries.

B. Whereas nationalism had the power to bring a nation together, it could also start conflicts.

C. Broken promises were a source of bitterness, which led to rivalry between the two alliances.

D. Germany took responsibility for the war because it had the most money and could pay for it.

51. Which of the following words is the most appropriate replacement for "agitation" in line 22?

A. restlessness

B. war

C. censorship

D. creativity

52. Which of the following is the correct chronology in which Russia formed an alliances?

A. France—Great Britain—United States

B. Germany—France—Great Britain

C. Germany—Serbia—Great Britain

D. Serbia—United States—Germany

53. What can be inferred about Kaiser Wilhelm from lines 30–35 of the passage?

    A. He made many efforts to prevent war from breaking out.

    B. He was a coward and always backed down from a challenge.

    C. He was loyal to all the countries that he had an alliance with.

    D. He was not trustworthy or reliable.

54. Based on the passage, which of the following words best describes why Germany had to take responsibility for World War I?

    A. mobilization

    B. wealth

    C. instigation

    D. prevention

55. What main point is the author making in this passage?

    A. There were several causes of World War I.

    B. Many countries are still bitter because of World War I.

    C. The alliances formed before and during World War I are still strong today.

    D. The policy of mobilization is the best strategy for winning a war.

Use the passage below to answer the question that follows.

In literature, the antagonist is in opposition to the hero. An example is Cinderella's wicked stepmother. She is as evil as Cinderella is good. This opposition drives the narrative forward.

56. Which of the following would be an example of a protagonist/antagonist relationship?

    A. Hansel and Gretel

    B. Little Red Riding Hood and the Wolf

    C. Snow White and the Seven Dwarfs

    D. Dorothy Gale and the Lion

57. It is thought that people go into teaching for a variety of reasons: interpersonal, service, material benefits, or time compatibility. Jane wants to be a teacher because she is diabetic and is attracted by the excellent health benefits. This is an example of which of the following?

    A. interpersonal

    B. service

    C. material benefits

    D. time compatibility

58. A ladder has 12 rungs. Each rung is 9 inches apart, with the bottom rung being 9 inches off the ground. How high off the ground is the top rung?

    A. 9 feet

    B. 7 feet

    C. 99 inches

    D. 12 feet

Use the passage below to answer the question that follows.

The Supreme Court of the United States first assembled in February 1790. Originally, there was a Chief Justice and five Associate Justices. Since 1869, the number of justices has been nine. Members of the Supreme Court are appointed by the president, subject to approval of the Senate. The justices are to be independent and protected from partisan pressures. For this reason, they serve what has generally meant life terms.

59. Based on the information in this passage, which of the following statements is NOT true?

    A. Congress can help determine the makeup of the Supreme Court justices.

    B. Once a justice is appointed, he or she may remain until he dies.

    C. The number of justices has increased since the beginning.

    D. Justices are under a lot of pressure to vote the will of the president.

Use the passage below to answer the three questions that follow.

The stars were shining, and the leaves rustled in the woods ever so mournful; and I heard an owl, away off, who-whooing about somebody that was dead, and a whippowill and a dog crying about somebody that was going to die; and the wind was trying to whisper something to me, and I couldn't make out what it was, and so it made the cold shivers run over me.

—from *The Adventures of Huckleberry Finn*, by Mark Twain

60. The style of writing employed in this passage can best be described as

    A. standard English.

    B. formal English.

    C. jargon.

    D. dialect.

61. The author's use of language in this passage helps to demonstrate the speaker's

    A. lack of intelligence.

    B. lack of education.

    C. good-heartedness.

    D. confusion.

62. The author uses imagery in this section to illustrate Huck's

    A. fear and loneliness.

    B. awareness of his environment.

    C. loss of his father.

    D. moral dilemma.

63. What subject matter is most likely to be found in a parable?

    A. the origins of the Earth and human beings

    B. a moral tale involving animals as characters

    C. the history of a culture

    D. the importance of love

Use the map below to answer the two questions that follow.

2005–2006—Per Pupil Expenditure in American Public Schools

Digest of Education Statistics, U.S. Department of Education, 2008

64. Approximately how much more money is spent on District of Columbia students than on students in Mississippi?

   A. About three times as much

   B. About two-thirds more

   C. About twice as much

   D. About one-third more

65. Which regional comparison about per pupil expenditure can be made?

   A. On average, more money is spent on children in the Northeast.

   B. On average, more money is spent on children in the South.

   C. On average, more money is spent on children in the Southwest.

   D. No comparisons can be made.

Use the passage below to answer the two questions that follow.

The HIV virus is not deadly, but because it weakens and finally consumes the immune system, it makes the victims particularly vulnerable to infection. It destroys an integral part of the immune system, the helper T-cells. When HIV, which stands for *human immunodeficiency virus*, enters your body, it weakens your immune system and makes you susceptible to over 20 deadly diseases and infections called AIDS. There is no cure for HIV, but an extraordinary number of researchers are working on treatments and vaccines. However, new drug therapies, such as protease inhibitors, often prolong and improve the lives of people living with HIV and AIDS.

66. What is the main point of this passage?

    A. Although HIV is potentially very harmful, many treatments are being developed to improve the quality of the lives of those living with the virus.

    B. Helper T-cells are the most important part of the immune system.

    C. The people infected with the HIV virus have a very high quality of life.

    D. HIV stands for *human immunodefiency virus*.

67. Based on the passage, which of these questions CANNOT be answered?

    A. Does HIV make the bodies of its victims particularly susceptible to infection?

    B. Is it possible to improve the qualities of the lives of those living with the HIV virus?

    C. What does HIV stand for?

    D. What does AIDS stand for?

68. Herbert Hoover served as the 31st president from 1929 to 1933. Franklin Delano Roosevelt served as the 32nd president from 1933 to 1945. Harry Truman served as the 33rd president from 1945 to 1953. Dwight D. Eisenhower served as the 34th from 1953 to 1961. John F. Kennedy served as the 35th president from 1961 to 1963. Which president broke the two-term precedent that had been set by George Washington?

    A. Herbert Hoover

    B. Franklin Delano Roosevelt

    C. Dwight D. Eisenhower

    D. John F. Kennedy

69. Historical fiction and nonfiction are two related genres of literature. What is one way in which these genres are similar?

    A. They both are customarily written in the second-person voice.

    B. They both deal with characters that actually existed.

    C. They always re-create conversations word for word based on documents such as audiotapes and written letters.

    D. They both attempt to capture the cultural traditions of the time period in which they are set.

Use the information below to answer the question that follows.

Each of these groups contain an incomplete list of U.S. presidents who correctly fit a particular description:

U.S. Presidents: John Adams, Abraham Lincoln, Ulysses S. Grant, Herbert Hoover, Franklin D. Roosevelt, Lyndon B. Johnson, Ronald Reagan, George H. W. Bush, George W. Bush

Republicans: Abraham Lincoln, Ulysses S. Grant, Herbert Hoover, Ronald Reagan, George H. W. Bush, George W. Bush

People Who Were President in the Twentieth Century: Herbert Hoover, Franklin D. Roosevelt, Lyndon Johnson, Ronald Reagan, George H. W. Bush

Presidents Whose Last Name is "Bush": George H. W. Bush, George W. Bush

70. Which group contains only Republican presidents who served in the twentieth century?

    A. Lincoln, Grant, Hoover, Reagan, G. H. W. Bush, G. W. Bush

    B. Hoover, Reagan, G. H. W. Bush, G. W. Bush

    C. Hoover, F. D. Roosevelt, L. B. Johnson, Reagan, G. H. W. Bush

    D. Hoover, Reagan, G. H. W. Bush

71. Which of the following describes the facade pictured above?

    A. Only the vertical ground is rusticated.

    B. Vertical pilasters counterbalance the narrow horizontal moldings that separate the stories.

    C. The design is composed principally of rectangles and round arches.

    D. The three stories diminish progressively in height from the lower story to the upper story.

Use the passage below to answer the question that follows.

From 1840 to 1845, New England mill owners sponsored the publication of the *Lowell Offering*, a collection of writings by female millhands. Perhaps predictably, its pages largely offered idealized vignettes of "millgirls" working selflessly to support their orphaned siblings or widowed mothers. Recent demographic research has provided a more complex view, one with positive and negative sides.

The industrialization of textile production after 1815 brought sweeping changes in the economy of the New England family farm. The hand-spun textiles, with which many families had supplemented their incomes, could not compete with cheaper factory-spun cloth, but the factories created a new role for the farm daughter as a paid hand. The family she left behind would profit from a share of her wages, while she gained access to money—whether to save or to spend on the consumer goods created by the new industrial society. Thus, mill work was often a deliberate step toward personal advancement from a limited, but not destitute, farm background. For most of the native-born millgirls of the 1820s and 1830s, factory work brought a move away from their families into a new social structure, the company-owned boarding house. Strictly controlled by mill management, which at first required millgirls without local families to reside in company housing, these all-female establishments fostered strong friendships as well as strivings for the type of cultural expression reflected in the *Offering*. The company boardinghouse reinforced an existing homogeneity of age and working together 24 hours a day. Ironically, this may well have played an important role in forging the solidarity reflected in the early strikes of millgirls.

72. This passage best illustrates which of the following cultural changes brought about by the emergence of the Industrial Revolution?

   A. The Industrial Revolution brought about factory labor that stifled human ambition and endeavor.

   B. The Industrial Revolution rescued humanity from a life of backbreaking toil on the farm.

   C. The Industrial Revolution created new social settings and new ways of relating to the world.

   D. The Industrial Revolution made small-scale farming techniques obsolete.

73. In an attempt to walk across a frozen lake, a skier tries to determine the best method for getting across the ice without cracking it. She takes into account pressure and force. Which of the following methods would most likely help the skier get across the lake without cracking the ice? (Hint: Pressure = Force/Area)

   A. tiptoeing

   B. walking upright

   C. standing on one foot

   D. crawling

74. The atomic theory could be used to analyze which of the following?

    A. properties of hydrogen

    B. the proliferation of bacteria

    C. the AIDS epidemic

    D. the motion of an object

75. By 2050, the world's population will reach 9 billion people. Which of the following environmental effects will likely accompany population growth?

    I.   increased supply of groundwater

    II. consumption of natural resources

    III. destruction of habitats

    IV. decreased pollution

    A. I and II only

    B. II and III only

    C. I and III only

    D. II and IV only

76. Forty-nine hours of overtime must be split among three workers. The second worker will be assigned twice as many hours as the first. The third worker will be assigned seven less than twice as many hours as the second. What equation matches this scenario?

    A. $x + 2x + (2x - 7) = 49$

    B. $x + 2x + 2 + (2x - 7) = 49$

    C. $x + 2x + 2 - (2x - 7) = 49$

    D. $x + 2x + (4x - 7) = 49$

77. If two brown-eyed parents have a blue-eyed child, the probability that their next child will have blue eyes is

    A. zero.

    B. 1 in 2.

    C. 1 in 3.

    D. 1 in 4.

78. Which of the following groups of Middle Eastern tribes is credited with bringing the concept of monotheism to the world?

    A. Hebrews

    B. Egyptians

    C. Kush

    D. Persians

79. The tenets listed below are most accurately attributed to which of the following religious belief systems?

    I. belief in reincarnation (rebirth after death)

    II. practice of a caste system with four social groups, membership in which is determined by birth

    III. drive to attain enlightenment, which brings freedom from rebirth

    IV. belief in the concept of karma, that one's fate is earned by one's past deeds

    A. Buddhism

    B. Islam

    C. Confucianism

    D. Hinduism

**Mary Cassatt, *Mother and Child*;
National Gallery of Art, Washington, D.C.**

80. Mary Cassatt, an American who lived and worked in France, was an impressionist painter. She was influenced by Japanese woodcuts and began to emphasize line rather than form or mass. She specialized in informal, natural gestures and positions. Which of the following elements of the painting characterizes this style?

　A. the sunflower

　B. the child sitting on her mother's lap

　C. the child's reflection in the mirror

　D. the mother's long gown

SAMPLE DIRECTIONS FOR THE WRITTEN ASSIGNMENT

This section of the test consists of a written assignment. You are asked to prepare a written response of approximately 300–600 words on the assigned topic. The assignment can be found on the next page. You should use your time to plan, write, review, and edit what you have written for the assignment.

Read the assignment carefully before you begin to write. Think about how you will organize what you plan to write. You may use any blank space provided on the following pages to make notes, write an outline, or otherwise prepare your response. However, your score will be based solely on the response you write in the written response booklet.

Your response to the written assignment will be evaluated on the basis of the following criteria.

- **FOCUS AND UNITY:** Comprehend and focus on a unified, controlling topic.

- **APPROPRIATENESS:** Select and use a strategy of expression that is appropriate for the intended audience and purpose.

- **REASON AND ORGANIZATION:** Present a reasoned, organized argument or exposition.

- **SUPPORT AND DEVELOPMENT:** Use support and evidence to develop and bolster one's own ideas and account for the views of others.

- **STRUCTURE AND CONVENTIONS:** Express oneself clearly and without distractions caused by inattention to sentence and paragraph structure, choice and use of words, and mechanics (i.e., spelling, punctuation, capitalization).

Your response will be evaluated based on your demonstrated ability to express and support opinions, not on the nature or content of the opinions expressed. The final version of the response should conform to the conventions of edited American English. This should be your original work, written in your own words, and not copied or paraphrased from some other work.

Be sure to write about the assigned topic and use multiple paragraphs. Please write legibly. You may not use any reference materials during the test. Remember to review what you have written and make any changes you think will improve your response.

Written Assignment—Diagnostic LAST

With more violent acts occurring in our schools, there is a call for more obvious security measures in schools, such as metal detectors, security guards in the hallway, banning backpacks, and requiring students to wear uniforms.

Do you believe these or other security measures are a good or bad idea?

Write an essay to support your position.

Answers and explanations for the Diagnostic LAST content review are in the next chapter.

CHAPTER 6: DIAGNOSTIC LAST REVIEW

As you can see, the questions on the LAST require very little previous knowledge—they are really reading comprehension problems in disguise. The key to answering the multiple-choice questions lies in understanding the question and carefully reading all the information provided, because you will generally not need to go beyond what the test makers give you.

In chapter 4, we outlined the process you should use to attack the LAST questions. First, you must understand the question—be certain what it is asking. Next, you should reread the question or passage to identify key words and the main idea. Finally, you need to predict your answer and select the one that most closely matches your prediction.

We have already provided you with one of the best ways to prepare for the LAST— Kaplan's Top 10 Test-Taking Strategies. Be sure to review chapter 2 and apply our proven methods to the test questions.

USING THIS DIAGNOSTIC

On the following pages you will find detailed answer explanations for each question on the Diagnostic LAST you've just completed, as well the LAST Objective that corresponds to each of those questions. As you assess your results on this practice test, note those areas in which you feel you need additional review. Be sure to use the online review links provided with each Objective in chapter 4 as well the ample resources around you. Your school is a great place to start! For example, if art is not your strong suit, get your hands on a syllabus for an introductory art course to get a cursory review of what art students learn, or check out the textbook that accompanies the introductory art course. You can also head to the library's art section, or browse through an encyclopedia or a basic review book of liberal arts and sciences such as *Kaplan's GED*. Even just talking to a friend who's an art major—or simply one who's taken a course in art—can give you a brief rundown of the basics.

Check out Kaplan's website (**kaptest.com**) for additional resources to help you prepare for the LAST.

ANSWER KEY FOR THE DIAGNOSTIC LAST

Below are the answers for the Diagnostic LAST found in chapter 5.

1.	C	21.	C	41.	A	61.	D
2.	B	22.	D	42.	D	62.	A
3.	C	23.	C	43.	A	63.	B
4.	A	24.	D	44.	D	64.	C
5.	B	25.	A	45.	D	65.	A
6.	A	26.	A	46.	B	66.	A
7.	C	27.	D	47.	B	67.	D
8.	C	28.	A	48.	C	68.	B
9.	B	29.	C	49.	D	69.	D
10.	A	30.	D	50.	D	70.	D
11.	B	31.	C	51.	A	71.	C
12.	D	32.	A	52.	B	72.	C
13.	A	33.	B	53.	D	73.	D
14.	D	34.	D	54.	C	74.	A
15.	C	35.	B	55.	A	75.	B
16.	D	36.	C	56.	B	76.	D
17.	B	37.	D	57.	C	77.	D
18.	A	38.	D	58.	A	78.	A
19.	B	39.	C	59.	D	79.	D
20.	D	40.	A	60.	D	80.	B

ANSWERS AND EXPLANATIONS

1. C

The primary focus of this question is Objective 0008:

Understand principles and assumptions underlying historical or contemporary arguments, interpretations, explanations, or developments.

Choice (C) is an example of an economic theory. Monetarists believe that inflation occurs when there is too much money to buy too few goods. The government then cuts back on the amount of money in circulation. A recession can ensue, with slowing economic growth and an increase in unemployment. Choices (A) and (B) are incorrect because neither is an example of an economic theory; rather, they are both economic policies. Similarly, (D) is not an example of an economic theory but describes one of the activities of the Federal Reserve Board.

2. B

The primary focus of this question is Objective 0007:

Understand the interrelatedness of historical, geographic, cultural, economic, political, and social issues and factors.

In the first sentence, it states "schools must provide all students the opportunity to learn . . . ." The rest of the passage expands on how and why this should happen. Choice (A) is not supported in the excerpt. It states that a goal (expectation) is that students from the United States will achieve better on tests than students of other countries, but this is only in the context of whether learning is equated with doing well on certain tests. Choice (C) is not justified by the passage: the passage does not discuss the difficulty level of the standards. Choice (D) is not justified, either. The excerpt states that tracking exists but does not mention its prevalence.

3. C

The primary focus of this question is Objective 0014:

Understand forms and themes used in literature from different periods and cultures.

As with most sonnets, the central theme is found at the end: "This thou perceiv'st, which makes thy love more strong,/To love that well which thou must leave ere long." The answer choice that best expresses this sentiment is (C). Choice (A) fails to take into account that autumn is a metaphor in the poem, symbolizing Shakespeare's advancing age. As for (B), nothing is said about love's being everlasting. Neither is the pain of old age mentioned. Choice (D) is incorrect because the poet simply describes his state; he does not express fear of it.

4. A

The primary focus of this question is Objective 0020:

Analyze and evaluate the effectiveness of expression in a written paragraph or passage according to the conventions of edited American English.

The word *easy* should be "easily." *Easy* is an adjective that can modify only nouns. In this sentence, the adverb "easily" modifies the verb "done." Choice (B) contains no grammatical error. The prepositional phrase "in creating schools" is correctly placed and phrased. In part 3, (C), the sentence has correct subject-verb agreement. *They* and *are* are both plural; *culture* and *is* are both singular. Part 4, (D), is also grammatically correct. The verb *is* is in agreement with the rest of the passage.

5. B

The primary focus of this question is Objective 0003:

Apply knowledge of numerical, geometric, and algebraic relationships in problem-solving and mathematical contexts.

Using the formula $d = rt$ (distance = rate × time), you have the following equation:

$$140 = 60t$$

To solve for t, the equation changes to $\frac{140}{60} = t$.

$2\left(\frac{20}{60}\right) = 2\frac{1}{3} = 2$ hours, 20 minutes.

6. A

The primary focus of this question is Objective 0003:

Apply knowledge of numerical, geometric, and algebraic relationships in problem-solving and mathematical contexts.

Her weekly gross income is $236.25 ($6.75 × 35 hours).

Over the course of nine weeks, she earns $2,126.25 (236.25 × 9 weeks).

Half of this total is $1,063.13 ($2,126.25 ÷ 2).

If this money earns 5.5%, it adds $58.47 cents to the total, making her income $1,121.60.

7. C

The primary focus of this question is Objective 0003:

Apply knowledge of numerical, geometric, and algebraic relationships in problem-solving and mathematical contexts.

By adding 2.6 seconds to Billy's time of 2:29.7, Gretchen's time is 2:32.3.

8. C

The primary focus of this question is Objective 0007:

Understand the interrelatedness of historical, geographic, cultural, economic, political, and social issues and factors.

The earliest civilizations were in the so-called Fertile Crescent in the Middle East, along the Tigris and Euphrates rivers. These rivers provided ideal conditions for agriculture to emerge, and regular crops provided enough respite from the grind of daily hunting and gathering that people could devote time and attention to the pursuits of civilization—art, religion, learning—that require leisure time. The locations described in the other answers are all viable habitats for humans, but agriculture is considered a prerequisite for the development of civilization.

9. B

The primary focus of this question is Objective 0020:

Analyze and evaluate the effectiveness of expression in a written paragraph or passage according to the conventions of edited American English.

The word *however* shows that this sentence is going in a different direction than the previous sentence. The previous sentence mentions varying parts. Thus, "standard parts" follows the "however." The issues cited in (A), (C), and (D) (engine type, fuel, and labor) are not mentioned in the passage as reasons that earlier cars were more expensive.

10. A

The primary focus of this question is Objective 0019:

Use critical-reasoning skills to assess an author's treatment of content in written materials from a variety of sources.

The statement in (A) is not supported by factual evidence. It seeks only to appeal to readers' love of their children. Responses (B), (C), and (D) are all verifiable facts. Their truth value can be indisputably determined.

11. B

The primary focus of this question is Objective 0020:

Analyze and evaluate the effectiveness of expression in a written paragraph or passage according to the conventions of edited American English.

Because it is preceded by *neither*, the statement should read "*nor* his assistant." *Neither/nor* are compatible conjunctions. In (A), "the magician" is the correct use of an article, and (C)'s "how to get out" is the correct use of a verb.

12. D

The primary focus of this question is Objective 0020:

Analyze and evaluate the effectiveness of expression in a written paragraph or passage according to the conventions of edited American English.

All elements of the sentence are grammatically correct. "Lindsay and Yao" (A) are the correct (compound) subject nouns, "went" (B) is the correct past tense verb, and "to buy" (C) is the correct use of the verb.

13. A

The primary focus of this question is Objective 0002:

Understand connections between mathematical representations and ideas and use mathematical terms and representations to organize, interpret and communicate information.

If 3 cucumbers are $1.50, then they are $0.50 each. $\frac{N}{50}$ can also be expressed as $3 \times \left(\frac{N}{\$150} \right)$.

14. D

The primary focus of this question is Objective 0004:

Understand major concepts, principles, and theories in science and technology and use that understanding to analyze phenomena in the natural world and to interpret information presented in illustrated or written form.

An earthworm does not have a backbone. All of the other answer choices have backbones.

15. C

The primary focus of this question is Objective 0008:

Understand principles and assumptions underlying historical or contemporary arguments, interpretations, explanations, or developments.

A business monopoly is a company having exclusive control over a particular market, with little or no competition for the product. For example, Bill Gates was accused by some of having a monopoly over the software business (i.e., by having Windows installed in all computers). Some believe this can lead to higher prices. Therefore, Theodore Roosevelt was opposed to business monopolies, he was in favor of many smaller companies competing with each other. He felt that would be in the best interests of the consumer because the product would need to be of high quality and the price lower (or the consumer would buy from a competitor).

16. D

The primary focus of this question is Objective 0003:

Apply knowledge of numerical, geometric, and algebraic relationships in problem-solving and mathematical contexts.

Adding 2.4 seconds to 4:59 gives you 5:01.4. Therefore, Jenny's time is 5 minutes, 1.4 seconds.

17. B

The primary focus of this question is Objective 0014:

Understand forms and themes used in literature from different periods and cultures.

The repeating consonant is *b*—**B**irte **b**rought **B**illy a **b**all. In *Annie ate apples all day* (A), it is a vowel, *a*, that is repeating at the beginning of each word rather than a consonant. Neither (C) nor (D) includes repeating sounds.

18. A

The primary focus of this question is Objective 0002:

Understand connections between mathematical representations and ideas and use mathematical terms and representations to organize, interpret, and communicate information.

Because the population continues to double, the starting rate for the number is larger than it was 1,000 years ago. Even if the proportion of the rate of increase remains constant, the actual number is greater. For example, if you double 1, you get 2. If you double 2, you get 4. If you double 4, you get 8. Even though your proportion (doubling) is the same, your number gets exponentially larger. There is no evidence to support the statement in (B), and (C) and (D) cannot be inferred because no actual numbers for population are given.

19. B

The primary focus of this question is Objective 0009:

Understand different perspectives and priorities underlying historical or contemporary arguments, interpretations, explanations, or developments.

Anthropology—the study of peoples—was not founded as a discipline until the twentieth century. Today's philosophy (Aristotle, Socrates, Plato), theater (Sophocles, Aristophanes, tragedy as a form), and mathematics (particularly geometry) were all greatly influenced by the ancient Greeks, as were art, architecture, medicine, and many other disciplines. The Greeks were also our predecessors in practicing an early form of democracy.

20. D

The primary focus of this question is Objective 0007:

Understand the interrelatedness of historical, geographic, cultural, economic, political, and social issues and factors.

Those who settled in the New England and mid-Atlantic colonies did not see slavery as a righteous institution. Those who settled the southern colonies tended to be more interested in furthering their economic status than in religious freedom. Also, the southern climate was more conducive to the large plantations that made slavery economically feasible. Choice (C) is only partially correct, in that the south is closer to Africa. Statements in (A) and (B) are incorrect.

21. C

The primary focus of this question is Objective 0009:

Understand different perspectives and priorities underlying historical or contemporary arguments, interpretations, explanations, or developments.

By definition, the suffrage movement was about obtaining the right to vote for women, choice (C). The Abolitionist movement sought to abolish slavery, (A). Choice (B) is a tempting trap, but equal pay for equal work was the focus of supporters of the Equal Rights Amendment, or ERA, in the late twentieth century. The Temperance movement sought to prohibit the use of alcohol, (D).

22. D

The primary focus of this question is Objective 0015:

Analyze and interpret literature from different periods and cultures and understand the relationship of works of literature to their social and historical contexts.

This passage appears to be telling a story about a character named Wilson. The story is told in the third person and appears to use the standard devices of realistic fiction, (D). A fable, choice (A), is a fictitious story, usually involving animals, that attempts to illustrate a universal truth or moral. An autobiography, choice (B), is a self-written life story. Consequently, autobiographies are always in the first person, and (B) can be eliminated. A folktale, choice (C), is a characteristically anonymous, timeless, and placeless tale that is normally communicated orally.

23. C

The primary focus of this question is Objective 0003:

Apply knowledge of numerical, geometric, and algebraic relationships in problem-solving and mathematical contexts.

If you divide Mars's period of revolution by Venus's period of revolution ($687 \div 225$), you come out with 3.05. Therefore, the closest interpretation is 3 times longer.

24. D

The primary focus of this question is Objective 0021:

Demonstrate the ability to locate, retrieve, organize, and interpret information from a variety of traditional and electronic sources.

Pluto takes the longest to revolve around the sun—248 years. The largest number (Mars's) is 687 days, a much shorter time period. The farther from the sun that the planet is, the longer it takes to revolve around the sun.

25. A

The primary focus of this question is Objective 0021:

Demonstrate the ability to locate, retrieve, organize, and interpret information from a variety of traditional and electronic sources.

Venus is the correct response because it takes only 225 days to revolve around the sun, whereas it takes Earth 365 days, or one year, to do so. So Venus's revolution takes 140 days less than Earth's. You may have been able to answer immediately if you noted that Venus is closer to the sun and would therefore require less revolution time. As for the other choices: Mars takes 322 more days than Earth to revolve around the sun (B); it takes Saturn 29 more years than Earth to revolve around the sun (C); and Pluto takes 247 more years than Earth to revolve around the sun (D).

26. A

The primary focus of this question is Objective 0002:

Understand connections between mathematical representations and ideas and use mathematical terms and representations to organize, interpret, and communicate information.

The closer the planet is to the sun, the less time it takes to revolve around the sun. As for choice (C): Nothing can be inferred about the actual mileage from the sun or size of the planet from the information given.

27. D

The primary focus of this question is Objective 0020:

Analyze and evaluate the effectiveness of expression in a written paragraph or passage according to the conventions of edited American English.

An *optimist* (noun) is someone who looks at the bright side of things. A *pessimist* (noun) looks at the negative side of a situation. In this sentence, the adjective form of the word is needed to fill in the blank (and describe "person"). *Pessimistic* is the correct word because it describes a person who looks at the negative side of a situation.

28. A

The primary focus of this question is Objective 0020:

Analyze and evaluate the effectiveness of expression in a written paragraph or passage according to the conventions of edited American English.

Who is a pronoun referring to a person (LaTisha) in the subjective position (referring to the subject of a sentence). *Whom* (B) is the objective case (referring to the object of a sentence). *Which* (C) refers to a collection of people or things. *Did* (D) is a verb and is the past tense of *do*—to perform an action. It is inappropriate in this sentence.

29. C

The primary focus of this question is Objective 0012:

Understand and analyze elements of form and content in works from the visual and performing arts from different periods and cultures.

The stars in the night sky are raging. This is said to reflect van Gogh's tortured (tumultuous) mind at the time. *Euphoric* (A) means to be in a state of well-being or happiness. Also, whereas van Gogh may have been sad at the time (B), the whirling stars would not support this response. The phrase in choice (D), "afraid of the dark," simply has no bearing on the picture.

30. D

The primary focus of this question is Objective 0002:

Understand connections between mathematical representations and ideas and use mathematical terms and representations to organize, interpret, and communicate information.

The mortgage is \$525. If you apply the percent formula $\left(\dfrac{\text{part}}{\text{whole}} = \text{percent} \right)$, you will see that $\dfrac{\$525}{\$2{,}083.33} = 0.252$, or 25%, choice (D). Alternatively, you can work backwards from the answer choices, eliminating wrong answers as you go. Twenty-five percent of \$2,083.33 is \$521. Therefore, approximately 25% of the total monthly income is \$525.

31. C

The primary focus of this question is Objective 0002:

Understand connections between mathematical representations and ideas and use mathematical terms and representations to organize, interpret, and communicate information.

By adding the monthly entertainment and savings together ($80 + $78), you get $158. Then $625 ÷ $158 = 3.96 months. In other words, it would take about four months to save enough for the television.

32. A

The primary focus of this question is Objective 0012:

Understand and analyze elements of form and content in works from the visual and performing arts from different periods and cultures.

Horizontal lines generally serve to emphasize width; vertical lines emphasize height. Each of these items serves to accentuate the building's height: vertical alignment of the windows (B), vertical walls without setbacks (C), and roofs that are more vertical than horizontal (D).

33. B

The primary focus of this question is Objective 0003:

Apply knowledge of numerical, geometric, and algebraic relationships in problem-solving and mathematical contexts.

This answer can be derived by counting the number of places (7) the decimal has to be moved from the original number (5.83) to the new number (58,300,000). The zeros are added as additional placeholders.

34. D

The primary focus of this question is Objective 0012:

Understand and analyze elements of form and content in works from the visual and performing arts from different periods and cultures.

The rocks do indeed create a wall behind the figures, restricting the depth of the action. Let's take a look at the other choices. Cross off (A): the picture is not a good example of single-point perspective—there's not much depth to the picture, and the lines in the building on the right stay parallel, even when receding. Choice (B) is incorrect, as the clothing mostly hangs like massive cylinders, not revealing much of the figures' anatomies. (C) is out; the figures are not arranged symmetrically, and they do seem to be interacting.

35. B

The primary focus of this question is Objective 0001: *Use mathematical reasoning in problem-solving situations to arrive at logical conclusions and to analyze the problem-solving process.*

The *mean* is the average of several numbers. To calculate the mean, you add all the numbers and divide by the number of numbers. In this case, there are four times, so you add all the times together and divide by 4. In (A), *median* is the middle time (50% are above; 50% are below). With four numbers, the two middle numbers are the median. *Product* (C) is the answer you get when you multiply numbers together, *sum* (D) is addition, and *quotient* is division.

36. C

The primary focus of this question is Objective 0011:

Understand and interpret visual representations of historical and social scientific information.

The lightly shaded areas show the states where McCain won the popular vote; the darkly shaded states are those states that Obama won. From the map shown, we cannot infer anything about the number of electoral votes (A), the number of Democrats and Republicans (B), or the fact that Obama won the election (D). Remember, you must use and apply only the information given to you by the test makers.

37. D

The primary focus of this question is Objective 0011:

Understand and interpret visual representations of historical and social scientific information.

Because the majority of Midwestern states voted Republican, it can be assumed that it is a Republican area of the country. Although McCain won the electoral votes in Tennessee, there is no information about where the candidates were from (A). Choice (B) is incorrect, because most Northeast states were won by Obama. (C) is wrong: McCain did win Texas.

38. D

The primary focus of this question is Objective 0020:

Analyze and evaluate the effectiveness of expression in a written paragraph or passage according to the conventions of edited American English.

Paragraph 2 comes first in the chronology. It is an introductory explanation of the event that is about to take place. Next comes paragraph 1, the time leading up to the actual race. In sentences 3 and 4 of paragraph 1, the author talks of walking toward the starting line. The third paragraph concludes with the gun going off, which is the signal for the start of the race. The only logical order of the three paragraphs is 2, 1, 3.

39. C

The primary focus of this question is Objective 0018:

Analyze and interpret written materials from a variety of sources.

The steeplechase is an event in which the runner runs on the track and jumps over five steeples, similar to hurdles, through each lap. Sentence 2 makes this clear when the author states that she jumped over a steeple just before the start of the race. This would lead one to assume it is similar to a hurdle.

40. A

The primary focus of this question is Objective 0019:

Use critical reasoning skills to assess an author's treatment of content in written materials from a variety of sources.

This is an example of a *reflection*: the author is reflecting on her feelings about the upcoming event and how she felt when she started.

41. A

The primary focus of this question is Objective 0004:

Understand major concepts, principles, and theories in science and technology and use that understanding to analyze phenomena in the natural world and to interpret information presented in illustrated or written form.

The first sentence states where phosphorous is found, and the second sentence begins the explanation of how phosphorous is released. It can be inferred, then, that phosphorous is released from sedimentary rock. Let's look at the other responses.

Eliminate (B)—there is no explanation of leaching. Eliminate (C) as well, because nothing is stated in the passage about combining phosphorous with other elements. Finally, there is no explanation in the passage about the phosphorous cycle (D).

42. D

The primary focus of this question is Objective 0010:

Understand and apply skills, principles, and procedures associated with inquiry, problem solving, and decision making in history and the social sciences.

There is nothing in the passage to indicate the exact number of voters in 1860 or at any other time in our history. Whereas the percentage of eligible voters has declined by 17 percent, we do not know the actual *number* of voters (A). Because there were more people eligible to vote in 1996 and 2008 than in 1860, the actual number of voters may well be higher. Choices (B) and (C) are also incorrect: based on this passage, nothing can be inferred about people's feelings for the country or about people's interest in politics at any age.

43. A

The primary focus of this question is Objective 0018:

Analyze and interpret written materials from a variety of sources.

In this context, *stuffed* means adding votes—putting extra votes for a candidate into the ballot box.

44. D

The primary focus of this question is Objective 0017:

Derive information from a variety of sources (e.g., magazine articles, essays, websites).

The author's topic is introduced early in the passage—the varying effectiveness of legislation aimed at curbing underage drinking. The central thesis is that the effectiveness of such legislation varies from country to country. The rest of the passage goes on to consider reasons this is so. Thus, (D) best expresses the overall purpose of the passage. Whereas the passage implies that teenage drinking is a serious problem, the point made in (A) remains an unstated assumption underlying the issues discussed in the passage. Choice (B) confuses the effectiveness of legislation in different countries with differences in legislative process. Choice (C) is inaccurate in that the passage does not focus on the problem of teenage drinking as such.

45. D

The primary focus of this question is Objective 0018:

Analyze and interpret written materials from a variety of sources.

The passage mentions a number of factors that might determine the effectiveness of legislation aimed at curbing underage drinking, but in essence, they all pertain to how well such legislation is observed and enforced. The implication of the last sentence is that in Europe, all legislation is more effective because there is a cultural tradition of absolute respect for the law. By implication, it is the absence of such a tradition that renders North American legislation less effective. As for the other choices: you can eliminate (A) because the ultimate aim of the law is perceived to be a lesser determinant than that given in (D). In (B), the extent to which the law reflects a particular moral stance is a lesser determinant than that given in (D). Likewise, the respect accorded symbolic legislation (C) is a lesser determinant than that given in (D).

46. B

The primary focus of this question is Objective 0007:

Understand the interrelatedness of historical, geographic, cultural, economic, political, and social issues and factors.

The effectiveness of alcohol-control legislation in deterring teenagers from drinking would probably be greater in Europe than in North America because it is to be expected that European teenagers would follow the cultural tradition of absolute respect for the law that prevails in European countries. Choices (A) and (C) distort the information presented in the passage. The passage does not support the inferences stated in these responses. Choice (D) is incorrect because its statement contradicts the information in the passage.

47. B

The primary focus of this question is Objective 0019:

Use critical reasoning skills to assess an author's treatment of content in written materials from a variety of sources.

Objective means being free from personal opinions. In writing, it is stating information free of one's own opinions or biases. The author achieves this tone by clearly stating a number of facts in a balanced manner. The word choice and tone do not convey anger (A), nervousness (C), or sarcasm (D).

48. C

The primary focus of this question is Objective 0018:

Analyze and interpret written materials from a variety of sources.

This passage is stating information about the benefits of additives in food. It is meant to *inform* the consumer. Although some readers may be persuaded (A) to avoid additives, persuasian is not the primary purpose of the passage. The passage could inspire a debate (B), but its neutral tone makes it primarily informative. And, although the passage may entertain (D) some readers, those readers would be the exception and entertainment is not the author's primary purpose.

49. D

The primary focus of this question is Objective 0017:

Derive information from a variety of sources (e.g., magazine articles, essays, websites).

The passage begins by stating several benefits of additives, and about two-thirds into the passage it also lists several negative aspects of additives. It does not state that one or the other is more important, making (D) the correct choice.

50. D

The primary focus of this question is Objective 0007:

Understand the interrelatedness of historical, geographic, cultural, economic, political, and social issues and factors.

Some people believed that Germany should take the responsibility for starting the war because of its broken promises and changing loyalties when it created an alliance. You can eliminate (A) because this is stated in lines 4–5. Choice (B) can be inferred from the passage because of the statement that nationalism had the power to create rivalries between competing countries. These rivalries can lead to conflicts. As for (C), alliances were forged and later changed; a treaty with Russia was signed and then broken. These broken trusts played a large part in causing the war.

51. A

The primary focus of this question is Objective 0018:

Analyze and interpret written materials from a variety of sources.

Agitation means a commotion or strong emotional disturbance. In this context, *agitation* means strong feelings toward nationalization and demand for independence. This causes *restlessness*. Agitation does not necessarily lead to *war* (B)—it cannot be assumed that the feelings were warlike. *Censorship* (C) means suppressing something objectionable, and *creativity* (D) is characterized by original thought. Neither word fits in this context.

52. B

The primary focus of this question is Objective 0021:

Demonstrate the ability to locate, retrieve, organize, and interpret information from a variety of traditional and electronic sources.

Start at lines 29–30. Here, it states that Otto von Bismarck of Germany signed a treaty with Russia (1). After that treaty lapsed, Russia formed an alliance with France (2). Finally those two joined with Great Britain (3) to form the Triple Entente.

53. D

The primary focus of this question is Objective 0008:

Understand principles and assumptions underlying historical or contemporary arguments, interpretations, explanations, or developments.

Kaiser Wilhelm forced the previous leader to resign and then broke a treaty with Russia and formed an Alliance with France. Next he challenged Great Britain. This caused all three to form an alliance against Germany. It led people to believe his word was not to be trusted. You cannot infer (A) from the passage: many people believe Wilhelm played a large role in starting the war. Nor is there any indication he backed down from any challenge (B). Finally, he was not loyal to his allies (C). He broke a treaty with Russia and broke the alliance with France.

54. C

The primary focus of this question is Objective 0008:

Understand principles and assumptions underlying historical or contemporary arguments, interpretations, explanations, or developments.

Instigation means to incite or to goad. According to the passage, it is believed by some that German leaders were responsible for starting the war. You can eliminate (A), (B), and (D). *Mobilization* (A) means to assemble troops to prepare for war. Many European countries, not just Germany, were mobilizing troops and building up arms. There is no mention in the passage about *wealth* (B) being a factor in starting the war, and Germany made no effort to *prevent* the war (D).

55. A

The primary focus of this question is Objective 0017:

Derive information from a variety of sources (e.g., magazine articles, essays, websites).

The first paragraph answers this question by stating three main factors that caused World War I. The other three responses cannot be inferred based on the information in the passage.

56. B

The primary focus of this question is Objective 0014:

Understand forms and themes used in literature from different periods and cultures.

The protagonist is the leading character, usually a champion of good, whereas the antagonist opposes the leading character, usually for bad purposes. Little Red Riding Hood is doing a good deed by bringing a basket to her grandmother. The Big Bad Wolf is trying to defeat Red Riding Hood. In (A), recall that Hansel and Gretel were brother and sister; both were the protagonists. The antagonist in that story was the witch in the house of candy. Choice (C)'s Snow White was the protagonist with the dwarves as her friends and allies. The antagonist was the wicked queen, who was her stepmother. Finally, Dorothy (D) was the protagonist, and the lion helped her resolve her dilemma. The Wicked Witch of the West was the antagonist in that story.

57. C

The primary focus of this question is Objective 0009:

Understand different perspectives and priorities underlying historical or contemporary arguments, interpretations, explanations, or developments.

Material benefits are anything tangible that you receive. For most jobs, these include a paycheck and health benefits. Jane was attracted to teaching because of the health benefits offered. Let's take a look at the other choices. *Interpersonal* (A) means "between people." This is not related to health benefits. In (B), people go into teaching because of the *service* aspect—hoping to help other people. Vacations and summer are also reasons some people state for going into teaching. The time involved is *compatible* (D) with their children's schedules.

58. A

The primary focus of this question is Objective 0003:

Apply knowledge of numerical, geometric, and algebraic relationships in problem-solving and mathematical contexts.

The response is calculated by multiplying 12 rungs by 9 inches to arrive at 108 inches. Because there are 12 inches in 1 foot, you divide 108 inches by 12 inches to get 9 feet.

59. D

The primary focus of this question is Objective 0008:

Understand principles and assumptions underlying historical or contemporary arguments, interpretations, explanations, or developments.

As stated, Supreme Court justices are to be independent and protected from pressures. Even though they are appointed by the president, he or she cannot threaten to fire them if they do not vote his will because they serve life terms. Choice (A) is true: because the Senate has to approve the Supreme Court candidates, it can have a say in determining the court. Similarly, (B) is correct in that justices may serve until they retire or die in office. Choice (C) is true as well: there were originally six justices, now there are nine.

60. D

The primary focus of this question is Objective 0014:

Understand forms and themes used in literature from different periods and cultures.

Scan the question stems before digging into the passage to find out what, exactly, you will need to know. For questions 60 and 61, you need only have a general sense of the language being used, which in this case is a regional dialect, (D). Choice (A) is incorrect; there is nothing standard about Huck's use of English. Choice (B) is certainly incorrect, as Huck's speech is far from formal. Choice (C) may be confusing if you are unsure of the meaning of the word *jargon*, terminology specific to an occupation or hobby.

61. D

The primary focus of this question is Objective 0015:

Analyze and interpret literature from different periods and cultures and understand the relationship of works of literature to their social and historical contexts.

You might be tempted by (A), but nothing in the passage indicates that Huck is stupid. He is, however, uneducated and superstitious, so (B) is correct. Choice (C) may be tempting to test takers thinking about the overall message of the novel. Huck is, indeed, good-hearted. But there is nothing in this particular passage to indicate this and certainly not his way of speaking. Choice (D) is incorrect; Huck is lonely and scared in the passage but not confused. Some test takers may think of his superstitions as confusion. However, Huck's way of speaking does not illustrate this.

62. A

The primary focus of this question is Objective 0014:

Understand forms and themes used in literature from different periods and cultures.

The imagery in this selection helps to illustrate Huck's isolation and fear, so (A) is correct. The fact that Huck hears and sees these things certainly indicates that he is aware of his environment, choice (B), but this argument is circular; Huck's apparent awareness does not illustrate his awareness. What he sees and hears illustrates something beyond merely hearing and seeing; it shows a state of mind. Choice (C) is tempting to those who remember the rest of the novel. Huck does lose his father in the novel, but that has nothing to do with this excerpt. Choice (D) is also tempting. Huck does face a moral dilemma in the novel—but again, not in this particular selection.

63. B

The primary focus of this question is Objective 0014:

Understand forms and themes used in literature from different periods and cultures.

Parables, fables, and allegories are all storytelling forms that present a moral tale, often one involving animals as characters. Therefore, choice (B) is the best answer. The origins of the Earth and human beings, choice (A), are usually explored in the mythology of an ancient culture. The history of a culture, choice (C), does not imply a moral lesson, as with a parable, fable, or allegory. The importance of love, choice (D), may be one lesson learned from a particular parable, but it is not the subject matter most likely to be found in a parable.

64. C

The primary focus of this question is Objective 0011:

Understand and interpret visual representations of historical and social scientific information.

You can calculate this response by dividing the number spent per pupil in the District of Columbia by the number spent per pupil in Mississippi: $15,626 ÷ $7,800 = 2.003. Rounded, this is 2, or twice as much. Three times as much as spent on students in Mississippi would be $23,400 (A); two-thirds as much as was spent on students in Mississippi would be $13,000 (B); one-third more than was spent on students in Mississippi would be about $10,397 (D).

65. A

The primary focus of this question is Objective 0021:

Demonstrate the ability to locate, retrieve, organize, and interpret information from a variety of traditional and electronic sources.

Based on this data, the Northeast region spends between $11,615 (New Hampshire) and $16,587 (New Jersey) per pupil. This exceeds the other regions. The South region spends between $7,742 (Tennessee) and $9,854 (Florida), whereas the Southwest region spends between $7,749 (Arizona) and $9,514 (Nevada). Response (D) is incorrect: clearly, the data does allow us to make comparisons by region.

66. A

The primary focus of this question is Objective 0017:

Derive information from a variety of sources (e.g., magazine articles, essays, websites).

Choice (A) is the best response for this question. It's basically a summary of the last two sentences of the passage. Reviewing the other choices, you'll see that whereas the passage states that the helper T-cells are an integral part of the immune system, it says nothing about their being the most important, (B). You can eliminate (C): the quality of life of those with HIV is improving over what it has been in the past, but the passage doesn't state the level of their quality of life. As for (D), although this statement is correct, it is an informational fact, clarifying the meaning of the acronym. It is not a major part of the passage.

67. D

The primary focus of this question is Objective 0018:

Analyze and interpret written materials from a variety of sources.

AIDS stands for Acquired Immune Deficiency Syndrome, but this is not stated in the passage. Therefore, (D) is the correct answer. The first sentence states the answer to the question posed in (A), and the last sentence states that new drug therapies are improving the quality of life for those with HIV and AIDS, so (B) is out. Choice (C) is wrong as well: HIV stands for human immunodeficiency virus, and this is stated in lines 3–4.

68. B

The primary focus of this question is Objective 0001:

Use mathematical reasoning in problem-solving situations to arrive at logical conclusions and to analyze the problem-solving process.

Presidential terms are four years long. Thus, any president who served more than eight years, as Roosevelt did, served for more than two terms, breaking the two-term tradition. Roosevelt served three terms, or 12 years.

69. D

The primary focus of this question is Objective 0014:

Understand forms and themes used in literature from different periods and cultures.

Historical fiction and nonfiction both attempt to capture the cultural traditions of the time period in which they take place. The difference is that nonfiction attempts to re-create a true story, whereas historical fiction makes up a story based on realistic time and place. Let's take a look at the other answer choices. Both historical fiction and nonfiction may be written in any voice (but they are usually written in the first or third person), so we can cross out (A). Choice (B) is wrong as well: historical fiction may deal with fictional characters created to make a realistic story. Finally, in both types of literature, conversations are usually roughly re-created to match the tone of the time period—especially in ancient times, conversations were not generally recorded. Choice (C) is therefore inaccurate.

70. D

The primary focus of this question is Objective 0010:

Understand and apply skills, principles, and procedures associated with inquiry, problem solving, and decision making in history and the social sciences.

Each of the presidents listed in answer choice (D) can be categorized as Republicans who served in the 20th century. Responses (A), (B), and (C) can be eliminated. Lincoln, Grant, and G. W. Bush did not serve in the 20th century (Bush's term began in 2001), therefore eliminating (A) and (B); F. D. Roosevelt and L. B. Johnson were not Republicans, eliminating (C).

71. C

The primary focus of this question is Objective 0012:

Understand and analyze elements of form and content in works from the visual and performing arts from different periods and cultures.

The door, windows, bricks, and even overall shape of the facade are all made of rectangles and semicircles. Cross off (A), because all three stories are rusticated, meaning they are made of rough-surfaced masonry brick with pronounced joints. (B) is out because there are no pilasters, which are like columns flattened against a wall. Finally, the three stories are much the same height, so (D) is incorrect.

72. C

The primary focus of this question is Objective 0007:

Understand the interrelatedness of historical, geographic, cultural, economic, political, and social issues and factors.

The passage describes the many ways the social and economic circumstances of the mill employees changed as they made the transition from farm to factory. Choice (A) contradicts the passage because the mill work was often "a deliberate step toward personal advancement." (B) is not supported by the passage, and (D) is incorrect because the passage does not speak of farming techniques.

73. D

The primary focus of this question is Objective 0006:

Understand and apply skills, principles, and procedures associated with inquiry and problem solving in the sciences.

Because $P = \dfrac{\text{Force}}{\text{Area}}$, the more surface area the skier covers, the lower the pressure exerted on the ice, thereby reducing the possibility of cracking the ice. Standing on one foot, (C), creates the most pressure on the ice because this method provides the least amount of surface area. Tiptoeing, (A), and walking upright, (B), create more surface area than standing on one foot, but crawling, (D), provides the maximum amount of surface area of all the choices. Therefore, (D) is correct.

74. A

The primary focus of this question is Objective 0004:

Understand major concepts, principles, and theories in science and technology and use that understanding to analyze phenomena in the natural world and to interpret information presented in illustrated or written form.

The atomic theory would be used to analyze the properties of hydrogen because it deals with the atomic level of matter. Choice (B) is a phenomenon that bacteriologists or microbiologists might study; it would not be studied in relation to the atomic theory. Choice (C) is an example of an epidemiological study, while (D) is a concept studied in physics that might be analyzed by Newton's laws.

75. B

The primary focus of this question is Objective 0005:

Understand the historical development and cultural contexts of mathematics, science, and technology; the relationships and common themes that connect mathematics, science, and technology; and the impact of mathematics, science, and technology on human societies.

As the world's population grows, crowding will likely generate more pollution, destroy natural habitats, and strain the water supply and other natural resources. Scientists believe that the size of the human population directly affects environmental problems, including global warming, ozone depletion, and rain forest destruction. Statement I, which regards an increased supply of groundwater, is not related to population growth. This automatically makes (A) and (C) incorrect. Since pollution will increase, not decrease as suggested in statement IV, (D) can also be eliminated.

76. D

The primary focus of this question is Objective 0002:

Understand connections between mathematical representations and ideas and use mathematical terms and representations to organize, interpret, and communicate information.

Translating words into algebraic equations is the skill required here. A total of 49 hours is divided among 3 workers. Let x be the first worker; $2x$ is the second worker with twice as many hours as the first; $4x - 7$ is the third worker, who has seven less than twice the second.

77. D

The primary focus of this question is Objective 0006:

Understand and apply skills, principles, and procedures associated with inquiry and problem solving in the sciences.

If two brown-eyed parents have a blue-eyed child, the probability that their next child will have blue eyes is 1 in 4. The blue-eyed gene (b) is recessive to the brown-eyed gene (B), so if both parents have brown eyes and one of the children has blue eyes, both parents carry the recessive blue-eyed gene (Bb). Thus, the chances of any more of their children being blue-eyed (bb) is 1 in 4.

78. A

The primary focus of this question is Objective 0016:

Analyze and interpret examples of religious or philosophical ideas from various periods of time and understand their significance in shaping societies and cultures.

Today's Jews worship the one God their Hebrew ancestors worshipped 3,000 years ago. At that time, their neighbors and other groups still practiced polytheism, the worship of more than one god. Christians and Muslims derived their monotheistic concepts from the Jewish, or Hebrew, philosophy of one God. The other groups mentioned all worshipped multiple gods when the Hebrews developed monotheism.

79. D

The primary focus of this question is Objective 0016:

Analyze and interpret examples of religious or philosophical ideas from various periods of time and understand their significance in shaping societies and cultures.

While both Hinduism (D) and Buddhism (A) share a belief in karma and the possibility of enlightenment (which brings relief from the burden of reincarnation, Statement I), Buddhists do not practice the caste system (Statement II). Confucianism (C) is a philosophical system practiced in China that emphasizes respect for others, especially authority. Islam (B) does not share any tenets listed in the question with Hinduism.

80. B

The primary focus of this question is Objective 0013:

Analyze and interpret works from the visual and performing arts representing different periods and cultures and understand the relationship of works of art to their social and historical contexts.

A child sitting on a mother's lap is a very intimate, domestic, natural gesture, making (B) the correct choice. Let's look at the other choices. A mother holding a sunflower (A) is not a truly natural gesture. Whereas a child's reflection in the mirror may be natural (C), it is not a common, intimate gesture. The long gown (D) is not generally thought of as an intimate, natural gesture.

SCORING YOUR WRITTEN ASSIGNMENT

The official LAST scorers will evaluate your written assignment using the following performance characteristics as a guide.

Focus and Unity	Did you comprehend the writing topic and focus your writing on that controlling topic?
Appropriateness	Did you select and use a strategy of expression appropriate for the intended audience and purpose?
Reason and Organization	Does your response present a reasoned, organized argument or exposition?
Support and Development	Did you use support and evidence to develop and bolster your own ideas and account for the views of others?
Structure and Conventions	Did you express yourself clearly in the response, without distractions caused by inattention to sentence and paragraph structure, choice and use of words, and mechanics (i.e., spelling, punctuation, and capitalization)?

LAST WRITTEN ASSIGNMENT SCORING SCALE

The written assignment is scored according to the following scale:

Score Point	Score Point Description
4	**The "4" response gives evidence of strong skills of written expression.**

- The writer clearly addresses the stated task, states or strongly implies a purpose for writing and a controlling topic, and maintains a steady focus on that topic.
- The chosen expressive approach is consistent with the writer's purpose and audience.
- Opinions are presented clearly, and arguments and/or expositions are well organized and ably reasoned.
- The writer offers relevant evidence and details to develop and support the position taken, showing awareness of other potential or actual positions.
- The response is free of distracting flaws in sentence structure (e.g., subject-verb disagreements, run-on sentences) and paragraph structure (e.g., lack of paragraph breaks to coincide with thought transitions), shows proficient use and choice of words, and avoids disruptive mechanical errors (e.g., inappropriate capitalization, misspellings of common words).

3   **The "3" response gives evidence of satisfactory skills of written expression.**

- The writer addresses the stated task, states or at least implies a purpose for writing and a controlling topic, and generally maintains a focus on that topic, with few digressions or extraneous points.
- The chosen expressive approach is generally consistent with the writer's purpose and audience.
- Opinions are presented clearly, and arguments and/or expositions give evidence of organization and reason, although some minor flaws in these areas may be present.
- The writer offers evidence and details to develop and support the position taken and generally acknowledges other potential or actual positions.
- The response contains very few distracting flaws in sentence structure and/or paragraph structure, shows generally competent use and choice of words, and avoids most disruptive mechanical errors.

2   **The "2" response gives evidence of limited skill in written expression.**

- The writer attempts to address the stated task but does so incompletely, and the purpose for writing and the topic may be unclear. The focus on the topic may not be consistently maintained, and several digressions may be present.
- The chosen expressive approach may be partially inconsistent with the writer's purpose and audience.
- Opinions may not be presented clearly, and arguments and/or expositions may give little evidence of organization and reason.
- Little or no evidence or detail may be provided to develop and support positions, and the existence of other potential or actual positions may not be recognized.
- The response may contain distracting flaws in sentence structure and/or paragraph structure, inappropriate use and choice of words, and disruptive mechanical errors.

1   **The "1" response gives evidence of a lack of skill in written expression.**

- The writer may attempt to address the stated task but does so incompletely, and the purpose for writing and the topic are generally unclear.
- There is little or no sense of intended audience.
- Opinions may not be presented clearly or may simply be asserted without support, elaboration, or detail.
- If arguments and/or expositions are present, they give little or no evidence of organization or reason. The existence of other potential or actual positions is generally not recognized.
- The response usually contains distracting flaws in sentence structure and/or paragraph structure, inappropriate use and choice of words, and disruptive mechanical errors that interfere with understanding.

LAST Diagnostic Written Assignment

Sample Response

> Prompt: With more violent acts occurring in our schools, there is a call for more obvious security measures in schools, such as metal detectors, security guards in the hallway, banning backpacks, and requiring students to wear uniforms.
>
> Do you believe these or other security measures are a good or bad idea?
>
> Write an essay to support your position.

What follows is an example of a strong response to the written assignment on the diagnostic test.

I believe that some security measures in a school are important. If the idea of the security is actually to keep children safe while at school, it is a very good thing. If the idea has no safety value but infringes on the rights of the students, I would not be in favor of the measures. Let me explain my position with examples.

Security guards in the school, and even a local police precinct located in a school, can be a very positive thing for all involved. In this way, students and police generally get to know each other on a more personal basis and can begin to trust and respect each other. If a policeperson knew the students on a personal, informal basis, it might help him or her not to jump to conclusions based on a student's appearance or perceived behavior. It also might afford the students the opportunity to talk to the police when they thought trouble might be coming.

Because it is easy to hide a weapon in a backpack, another safeguard that might be helpful is not allowing students to carry backpacks to class. The backpacks can be kept in the lockers, and only books carried to class. Schools might need to adjust the time allowed for changing between classes so students have the time to go to their lockers to exchange their books. This would be a minor modification and could mean a big difference in the safety of all the students.

An example that I believe is not a good safety measure would be requiring students to wear uniforms. Granted, in some schools, certain dress may have the appearance of gang clothing, but I think this is a limited argument. Dress, as long as it does not contain obscene material and sufficiently covers the student, is a matter of personal style. I do not believe it is the school's job to try to make everyone alike. Schools attempt to create individuals who can think critically and take a stand on an issue.

By making everyone look alike, they tend to send the message that everyone should think alike. I do not believe that this is the job of school.

In summary, I believe that there are measures that can be taken to improve safety in schools. They should be well thought out, and not unduly infringe on the rights of students in the school. In other words, the measures taken should have the sole purpose of improving safety of everyone in the school.

CHAPTER 7: **PRACTICE LAST**

Before taking this practice test, find a quiet room where you can work uninterrupted for 4 hours. Make sure you have a comfortable desk and several No. 2 pencils.

Use the answer sheet provided to record your answers.

Once you start this practice test, don't stop until you've finished. Remember, you can complete the sections of the test in any order you wish.

You will find an answer key and explanations following the test.

Good luck!

SAMPLE DIRECTIONS

This test booklet contains a multiple-choice section and a single written assignment section. You may complete the sections of the test in the order you choose.

Each question in the first section of this booklet is a multiple-choice question with four answer choices. Read each question CAREFULLY and choose the ONE best answer. Record your answer on the answer document in the space that corresponds to the question number. Completely fill in the space having the same letter as the answer you have chosen. *Use only a No. 2 lead pencil.*

Sample Question

1. What is the capital of New York?

       A.   Buffalo

       B.   New York City

       C.   Albany

       D.   Rochester

The correct answer to this question is (C). You would indicate that on the answer document as follows:

1.   (A)   (B)   ●   (D)

You should answer all questions. Even if you are unsure of an answer, it is better to guess than not to answer a question at all. You may use the margins of the test booklet for scratch paper, but you will be scored only on the responses on your answer document.

The directions for the written assignment appear later in this test booklet.

FOR TEST SECURITY REASONS, YOU MAY NOT TAKE NOTES OR REMOVE ANY OF THE TEST MATERIALS FROM THE ROOM.

The words "End of Test" indicate that you have completed the test. You may go back and review your answers, but be sure you have answered all questions before raising your hand for dismissal. Your test materials must be returned to a test administrator when you finish the test.

If you have any questions, please ask them now before beginning the test.

STOP

DO NOT GO ON UNTIL YOU ARE TOLD TO DO SO.

LAST Answer Sheet

1.	Ⓐ Ⓑ Ⓒ Ⓓ	28. Ⓐ Ⓑ Ⓒ Ⓓ	55. Ⓐ Ⓑ Ⓒ Ⓓ
2.	Ⓐ Ⓑ Ⓒ Ⓓ	29. Ⓐ Ⓑ Ⓒ Ⓓ	56. Ⓐ Ⓑ Ⓒ Ⓓ
3.	Ⓐ Ⓑ Ⓒ Ⓓ	30. Ⓐ Ⓑ Ⓒ Ⓓ	57. Ⓐ Ⓑ Ⓒ Ⓓ
4.	Ⓐ Ⓑ Ⓒ Ⓓ	31. Ⓐ Ⓑ Ⓒ Ⓓ	58. Ⓐ Ⓑ Ⓒ Ⓓ
5.	Ⓐ Ⓑ Ⓒ Ⓓ	32. Ⓐ Ⓑ Ⓒ Ⓓ	59. Ⓐ Ⓑ Ⓒ Ⓓ
6.	Ⓐ Ⓑ Ⓒ Ⓓ	33. Ⓐ Ⓑ Ⓒ Ⓓ	60. Ⓐ Ⓑ Ⓒ Ⓓ
7.	Ⓐ Ⓑ Ⓒ Ⓓ	34. Ⓐ Ⓑ Ⓒ Ⓓ	61. Ⓐ Ⓑ Ⓒ Ⓓ
8.	Ⓐ Ⓑ Ⓒ Ⓓ	35. Ⓐ Ⓑ Ⓒ Ⓓ	62. Ⓐ Ⓑ Ⓒ Ⓓ
9.	Ⓐ Ⓑ Ⓒ Ⓓ	36. Ⓐ Ⓑ Ⓒ Ⓓ	63. Ⓐ Ⓑ Ⓒ Ⓓ
10.	Ⓐ Ⓑ Ⓒ Ⓓ	37. Ⓐ Ⓑ Ⓒ Ⓓ	64. Ⓐ Ⓑ Ⓒ Ⓓ
11.	Ⓐ Ⓑ Ⓒ Ⓓ	38. Ⓐ Ⓑ Ⓒ Ⓓ	65. Ⓐ Ⓑ Ⓒ Ⓓ
12.	Ⓐ Ⓑ Ⓒ Ⓓ	39. Ⓐ Ⓑ Ⓒ Ⓓ	66. Ⓐ Ⓑ Ⓒ Ⓓ
13.	Ⓐ Ⓑ Ⓒ Ⓓ	40. Ⓐ Ⓑ Ⓒ Ⓓ	67. Ⓐ Ⓑ Ⓒ Ⓓ
14.	Ⓐ Ⓑ Ⓒ Ⓓ	41. Ⓐ Ⓑ Ⓒ Ⓓ	68. Ⓐ Ⓑ Ⓒ Ⓓ
15.	Ⓐ Ⓑ Ⓒ Ⓓ	42. Ⓐ Ⓑ Ⓒ Ⓓ	69. Ⓐ Ⓑ Ⓒ Ⓓ
16.	Ⓐ Ⓑ Ⓒ Ⓓ	43. Ⓐ Ⓑ Ⓒ Ⓓ	70. Ⓐ Ⓑ Ⓒ Ⓓ
17.	Ⓐ Ⓑ Ⓒ Ⓓ	44. Ⓐ Ⓑ Ⓒ Ⓓ	71. Ⓐ Ⓑ Ⓒ Ⓓ
18.	Ⓐ Ⓑ Ⓒ Ⓓ	45. Ⓐ Ⓑ Ⓒ Ⓓ	72. Ⓐ Ⓑ Ⓒ Ⓓ
19.	Ⓐ Ⓑ Ⓒ Ⓓ	46. Ⓐ Ⓑ Ⓒ Ⓓ	73. Ⓐ Ⓑ Ⓒ Ⓓ
20.	Ⓐ Ⓑ Ⓒ Ⓓ	47. Ⓐ Ⓑ Ⓒ Ⓓ	74. Ⓐ Ⓑ Ⓒ Ⓓ
21.	Ⓐ Ⓑ Ⓒ Ⓓ	48. Ⓐ Ⓑ Ⓒ Ⓓ	75. Ⓐ Ⓑ Ⓒ Ⓓ
22.	Ⓐ Ⓑ Ⓒ Ⓓ	49. Ⓐ Ⓑ Ⓒ Ⓓ	76. Ⓐ Ⓑ Ⓒ Ⓓ
23.	Ⓐ Ⓑ Ⓒ Ⓓ	50. Ⓐ Ⓑ Ⓒ Ⓓ	77. Ⓐ Ⓑ Ⓒ Ⓓ
24.	Ⓐ Ⓑ Ⓒ Ⓓ	51. Ⓐ Ⓑ Ⓒ Ⓓ	78. Ⓐ Ⓑ Ⓒ Ⓓ
25.	Ⓐ Ⓑ Ⓒ Ⓓ	52. Ⓐ Ⓑ Ⓒ Ⓓ	79. Ⓐ Ⓑ Ⓒ Ⓓ
26.	Ⓐ Ⓑ Ⓒ Ⓓ	53. Ⓐ Ⓑ Ⓒ Ⓓ	80. Ⓐ Ⓑ Ⓒ Ⓓ
27.	Ⓐ Ⓑ Ⓒ Ⓓ	54. Ⓐ Ⓑ Ⓒ Ⓓ	

"Let a woman modestly yield to others: let her respect others; let her put others first, herself last. Should she do something good, let her not mention it; should she do something bad, let her not deny it."

1. What idea does this quotation, by a Chinese author in 1901, communicate about the role of women in China in the years preceding the communist revolution?

    A. They often held powerful positions.

    B. Men and women had equal rights in most areas of society.

    C. Women were regarded as inferior.

    D. Women were praised for their good deeds.

2. In China, most citizens are engaged in agricultural activities. Thus, China is a(n) _____ society.

    A. market

    B. feudal

    C. technologically advanced

    D. agrarian

Use the passage below to answer the question that follows.

Regeneration is the ability to replace body parts. For example, when a flatworm is cut in half, the head end will grow a new tail, and the tail end will grow a new head. Starfish also have the ability to regenerate lost parts. There are usually limitations on the size or portion of an organism that can be regenerated. In humans and other vertebrates, small wounds heal by regeneration of new tissues to replace damaged tissues. Regeneration occurs by mitosis.

3. Sponges can regenerate. How can this fact be of commercial value?

   A. The consumer will never have to buy a new sponge because the one that they buy, which is dead, can be cut into pieces and used infinitely to create new sponges.

   B. Sponges, which can regenerate, have twice the cleaning power of nonregenerating organisms.

   C. Regeneration in sponges has no commercial value.

   D. The manufacturer can cut off part of a living sponge, dry it, and sell it as a cleaning instrument. The remaining live sponge can regenerate and be used as a source for more sponges. This decreases the manufacturer's need to kill sponges and buy new ones to sell.

Read the selection below from a poem written by Emily Dickinson; then, answer the two questions that follow.

1   I can wade Grief—
       Whole Pools of it—
       I'm used to that—
       But the least push of Joy
5   Breaks up my feet—
       And I tip—drunken—
       Let no Pebble smile—
       'Twas the New Liquor—
       That was all!

4. In line 8 of the poem, to what do the words "New Liquor" refer?

   A. happiness

   B. alcoholic drink

   C. the water in the pool

   D. emotion

5. The author uses metaphor to suggest that

   A. People find the speaker's drunken behavior amusing.

   B. The speaker's life contains nothing but grief.

   C. The speaker is unused to pleasant emotions.

   D. Happiness makes the speaker drunk.

KAPLAN

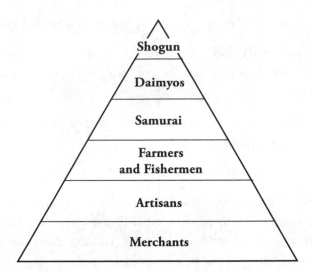

6. Based on the pyramid above, merchants occupy the lowest position in this social pyramid of feudal Japan because they

    A. made up the largest percentage of Japan's population at that time.

    B. were regarded as having little status in the society.

    C. had the greatest impact on society and culture.

    D. did not subscribe to the major religion of the day, Shinto.

7. The formula for distance is $d = rt$ (distance = rate × time). You are traveling 60 miles of back roads from Buffalo to Rochester. If you average 35 mph for the trip, about how long will it take you to reach your destination?

    A. 1 hour, 40 minutes

    B. 1 hour

    C. 35 minutes

    D. 1 hour, 35 minutes

The famous satirist Finley Peter Dunne created the "Mr. Dooley" character, who was a keen and often caustic commentator on and observer of the American scene, at the turn of the century. Use the "Mr. Dooley" piece written by Dunne in 1898 to answer the question that follows.

"I know wht I'd do if I was Mack," said Mr. Hennessy, "I'd hist a flag over the Ph'lippeens, an' I'd take in the whole lot iv thim."

"An' yet," said Mr. Dooley, "'tis not more thin two months since ye learned whether they were islands or canned goods? If yer son Packy was to ask ye where th' Ph'lippeens is, cud ye give him anny good idea whether they was in Rooshia or jus' west iv the' tracks?

"Mebbe I cuddn't," said Mr. Hennessy, haughtily, "but I'm f'r taking thim in, annyhow."

8. Which of the following points was most probably the author's intent of this humorous interchange?

   A. The U.S. invasion of the Philippines was an act of unacceptable aggression.

   B. Some citizens of the United States felt that intervention in the Philippines was unavoidable.

   C. Certain American citizens have supported U.S. expansionism as an end in itself.

   D. Most Americans are gravely deficient in knowledge of foreign geography and politics.

Use the passage below to answer the question that follows.

Among the protozoa, respiration is accomplished by the diffusion of dissolved oxygen and carbon dioxide through the cell membrane. Oxygen dissolved in the surrounding water diffuses into the organism and is carried throughout the cell by cyclosis and diffusion. Carbon dioxide, which is produced within the cell, diffuses out through the cell membrane into the surrounding medium.

9. What is the respiratory surface of the protozoa?

    A. the cell membrane

    B. the surrounding medium

    C. the cell's cytoplasm

    D. carbon dioxide and oxygen

Use the passage below to answer the question that follows.

I watched the little bike teeter, then straighten, and begin to take off across the playground. Money came hard these days, and it meant a lot to be able to buy that bike. He took off like Icarus, seeming to fly along the path. "I can ride!" he shouted. "Daddy, Daddy, look at me fly!" He never saw the rock. I heard the thud and saw the small body hurled upward toward the sun. And I knew that my pride was the pride of Daedalus and that wings are a dangerous gift to the very young.

10. The images in the passage above were most probably drawn from

    A. The Old Testament.

    B. The Odyssey.

    C. Greek mythology.

    D. Arthurian legend.

Read the excerpt below from "America the Beautiful"; then, answer the question that follows.

America, America, God mend thy every flaw
Confirm thy soul in self-control
Thy liberty in law.

11. The lines printed above are unusual in that

    A. they do not rhyme.

    B. patriotic songs usually do not allude to a nation's faults.

    C. they set law as a necessary condition of liberty.

    D. patriotic songs usually do not contain references to God.

12. Billy and Peter, two friends, are saving their allowance to buy a Game Boy™. The games cost $29.99 plus 7% sales tax. If Billy earns an allowance of $5.00 per week, and Peter earns $7.00 per week, how much sooner will Peter be able to buy the game than Billy?

    A. 5 weeks

    B. 1 week

    C. 2 weeks

    D. 7 weeks

In questions 13 and 14, choose the letter of the underlined phrase that contains a grammatical error. Select choice (D) if there is no error in the sentence.

13. Neither Beth <u>or her friend</u>, Liz, <u>had enough money</u> <u>to buy</u> the concert tickets. <u>No error</u>
          A.   B.   C.   D.

14. There <u>has never been</u> a better time <u>to begin</u> <u>a exercise program</u>. <u>No error</u>
           A.   B.   C.   D.

15. Many problems faced in the world today resemble similar situations that took place in the 17th century. Which modern-day social problem was NOT a concern before 1700?

    A. world trade

    B. destruction of the rain forest

    C. racism

    D. religious conflict

Use the passage below to answer the question that follows.

(1) Early in this century, the patient viewed the physician as more of a comforter than a healer. (2) The doctor was present to predict the progress of a disease and to help the patient cope with a struggle or an imminent defeat; the doctor was not expected to work miracles. (3) This situation, however, changed with the coming of such drugs as penicillin and other antibiotics. (4) Penicillin was discovered in 1928 by Sir Alexander Fleming. (5) These effective drugs, as well as other technological developments of contemporary medicine, have put the medical professional under pressure to defeat every disease, correct every physical defect, and maximize the patient's quality of life. (6) Ultimately, patients today expect results rather than sympathy from their physicians.

16. Sentence 4 can be characterized as

    A. a relevant elaboration on sentence 3.

    B. a relevant but parenthetical detail.

    C. an irrelevant detail.

    D. redundant.

Use the passage below to answer the question that follows.

The "Great Awakening" was a revival of religious zeal in America in the late 18th century. It was brought about by clerical intellectualism and lay liberalism. Before the Great Awakening, priests and ministers delivered long, unemotional sermons. Key characteristics of the Great Awakening included a rise in the popularity of younger religious leaders, the "splintering" of Protestantism, and a widespread feeling of colonial unity. During and after the Great Awakening, many people became enthusiastic about religion and were eager to demonstrate this emotion.

17. Which of the following was NOT a direct effect of the Great Awakening?

    A. suspicion and harassment of members of nontraditional churches

    B. growth in church membership

    C. opposition to many established churches

    D. religious diversity increased

Use the information below to answer the question that follows.

Several important political figures in the early 19th century had very divergent views about tariffs, internal improvements by the federal government, and a proposed Bank of the United States.

> John Q. Adams: Supported high tariffs, many internal improvements, and a Bank of the United States.
>
> Andrew Jackson: Supported low tariffs, few internal improvements, and no Bank of the United States.
>
> Henry Clay: Supported high tariffs, many internal improvements, and a Bank of the United States.
>
> Daniel Webster: Supported high tariffs, many internal improvements, and a Bank of the United States.
>
> John C. Calhoun: Supported low tariffs, many internal improvements, and no Bank of the United States.

There were two major parties in the United States at this time, the Democrats and the Whigs. The Democrats favored local rule, limited government, free trade, and equal economic opportunity for white males. They opposed monopolies, a national bank, high tariffs, and high land prices. The Whig Party generally favored Henry Clay's American System (a national bank, federal funding of internal improvements, and a protective tariff); they opposed immorality, vice, and crime, some of which they blamed on immigrants.

18. Based on the information given, to which party did the historical figures belong?

　　A. Democratic: Adams, Clay, Webster; Whig: Jackson; Neither: Calhoun

　　B. Democratic: Jackson, Calhoun; Whig: Adams, Clay, Webster

　　C. Democratic: Adams, Webster; Whig: Jackson, Clay, Calhoun

　　D. Democratic: Jackson; Whig: Adams, Clay, Webster; Neither: Calhoun

19. Identify the underlined section containing the error in the following sentence. If there is no error in the sentence, select choice (D).

"Actually, <u>we never</u> married," said <u>Gwen</u>, the <u>5-foot-11</u> songstress. <u>No error</u>
         A.   B.   C.   D.

Use the information below to answer the question that follows.

An isosceles triangle is a triangle that has two equal (congruent) sides called the legs. The angles opposite the legs are called base angles, and the side that they include is the base. The angle opposite the base is called the vertex angle. The three angles of any triangle add up to 180 degrees.

20. If the degree measure of the vertex angle of an isosceles triangle is 80, what is the degree measure of each base angle?

    A.   8

    B. 180

    C. 100

    D. 50

21. A zookeeper has only ostriches and sheep in his zoo. If the animals in his zoo have a total of 60 heads and 140 legs, how many ostriches and how many sheep are in his zoo?

    A. 0 ostriches, 60 sheep

    B. 40 ostriches, 20 sheep

    C. 36 ostriches, 24 sheep

    D. 50 ostriches, 10 sheep

22. The exclusionary rule is where evidence cannot be used in the court of law if it has been obtained improperly. A politician who advocates the discontinuance of the exclusionary rule in court cases most probably would be content to be viewed in which of the following ways?

    A. law-and-order candidate

    B. defender of the status quo

    C. liberal

    D. sympathetic toward criminals

Read the song lyrics below, written by Jose Marti; then, answer the two questions that follow.

Guantanamera*

Guantanamera
The peasant Guantanamera
Guantanamera
The peasant Guantanamera

I am a sincere man
From where the palms grow
I am a sincere man
From where the palms grow
And before I die I want
To cast my verses from my soul

Guantanamera
The peasant Guantanamera
Guantanamera
The peasant Guantanamera

My verse is of a clear green
And of a burning jasmine
My verse is of a clear green
And of a burning jasmine

My verse is from a dear heaven
That we will seek as refuge
Guantanamera
The peasant Guantanamera
Guantanamera
The peasant Guantanamera

With the poor people of the land
I want to cast my luck
With the poor people of the land
I want to cast my luck
The stream of the mountain
Pleases me more than the sea

Guantanamcra
The peasant Guantanamera
Guantanamera.
The peasant Guantanamera...

*A *guantanamera* is a woman from Guantanamo, Cuba.

23. The tone of this song is

    A. exuberant.

    B. hateful.

    C. aggressive.

    D. introspective.

24. How does the author view his verses?

    A. as important lessons that must be preserved so others can learn from them

    B. as useless lines that he must cast from him before he dies

    C. as only applicable to peasants and other members of the lower class

    D. as dangerous things that should be burned with jasmine as an offering

Read the passage below, written by a young student; then, answer the question that follows.

Soon the old woman returns again to Tarquinius, but six books were carried with her but of the same price, because it had been asked for before, it was demanded. Again she has been dismissed by the king.

25. Which of the following corrections is best stylistically and best preserves the meaning of the original?

    A. Soon the old woman again returned to Tarquinius, carrying six books of the same price. They had been demanded several times before. However, just as in the past, she was dismissed by him.

    B. Soon the old woman returned again to Tarquinius, the king, but six books that were being carried by the hands of her had been demanded again. And again, she was dismissed by Tarquinius.

    C. Again and again the old woman returned to Tarquinius. "Here are the books for which you asked," she said each time.

       "I don't want any books! Have them burned! Leave immediately!" he cried. The executioners descended upon the wretched woman.

    D. Keep the passage as it is.

Use the passage below to answer the question that follows.

Masks served two very important purposes on the Roman stage. First, they allowed the actors to play many different characters in a single play. Second, the peculiar formation of the mask with its wide-open mouth amplified the actor's voice, which would otherwise be hard to hear in a large open-air theater. Occasionally, modern authors like Eugene O'Neill have employed the mask to indicate a dual personality of a character.

26. Which of the following does the passage NOT mention as a use for masks in theater?

    A. to demonstrate two opposing personalities in a character

    B. to fortify the strength of the actor's voice

    C. to induce prescribed reactions in audience members

    D. to allow a play to be staged with fewer actors

The following is a translation of a Roman sepulchral inscription.

To the deified spirits of Epaphroditus, driver for the Red stable; he won 178 times, and after being manumitted to the Purples he won 8 times. Beia Felicula made this monument for her deserving husband.

—Gilbert Lawall

27. What attitude did Beia Felicula most likely have toward her husband?

    A. pride and reverence

    B. disdain and jealousy

    C. arrogance and egotism

    D. hate and sharpness

Use the passage below to answer the question that follows.

Writing in verse form can in no way qualify as poetry unless it awakens the senses on the nonverbal level or elevates the emotions. Obviously, not every verse can be deemed a poem. The criterion for classifying verse as poetry is thus its effect on the reader (or, better, the listener). Every British schoolchild knows the old verse about Dr. Fell, but it is certainly not a poem.

28. The author's conclusion that the verse about Dr. Fell is not a poem apparently rests on the author's belief that

   A. The verse has proven popular only with schoolchildren.

   B. The verse cannot truthfully be said to elevate the emotions or the senses.

   C. The assessment of a poem can only be undertaken when one understands the relationship between poem and reader.

   D. The only important quality of a poem is that it be emotionally moving.

Use the passage below to answer the two questions that follow.

The University's decision to keep the library open around the clock was a key element in the rejuvenation of the Collegeside neighborhood, where the marked increase in late-night street traffic led to the expansion of existing businesses and the opening of several new ones. But the new schedule's positive effect on the local economy was not a factor in the University's decision. Similarly, the University Computer Center's gradual shift, during the 1960s and '70s, away from punched cards and printed output was not intended to throw the local paper recycling project out of business.

29. Which of the following can be inferred from the passage?

   A. The University policy makers would have preferred that Collegeside remain undeveloped.

   B. The Collegeside economy would never have expanded if the University had not extended its hours.

   C. The extended library hours brought more potential customers into the Collegeside neighborhood.

   D. The use of punched cards and printed output at the Computer Center became impractical when the new library schedule vastly increased computer usage.

30. Which of the following is most probably the point the author would go on to make next?

    A. The shift from punched cards and printed output represented a major revolution in the data-processing industry.

    B. The failure of the local paper-recycling project was an unintentional consequence of the Computer Center's new policy.

    C. The reasons for the University's extending library hours were similar to those behind the Computer Center's change in output formats.

    D. Major shifts in policy on the part of a university are likely to be misinterpreted by the surrounding nonacademic community.

31. A department store regularly sells twill jean shorts for $34. The company offers a choice of colors among apple green, hot pink, stone, mid-blue, and white. During the end-of-season sale, the twill jean shorts are offered for 32% off the regular price. To the nearest dollar, for how much do the shorts sell during the sale?

    A. $34

    B. $11

    C. $45

    D. $23

32. In 2001, the Fujimori family bought a young apple tree. In 2001, 2002, 2003, and 2004, it yielded no apples. In 2005, the tree yielded 20 apples. In 2006, it yielded 34 apples. In 2007, it yielded 59 apples. In 2008, it yielded 97 apples. In 2009, it yielded 145 apples. In 2010, it yielded 202 apples. What is the most reasonable prediction for number of apples yielded by the tree in 2011?

    A. 145 apples

    B. 202 apples

    C. 210 apples

    D. 275 apples

Use the information below to answer the question that follows.

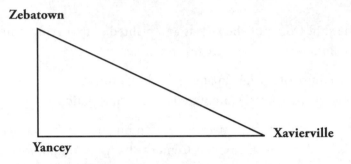

The Pythagorean theorem states that $a^2 + b^2 = c^2$, with a and b representing the legs of a triangle that form a right (90 degree) angle and c representing the hypotenuse (diagonal).

33. Zebatown and Yancey are 30 miles apart. Yancey and Xavierville are 40 miles apart. What is the shortest possible distance between Zebatown and Xavierville?

    A. 10 miles

    B. 40 miles

    C. 50 miles

    D. 70 miles

This is an excerpt from the Bradford Bulls football team's record books.

Bulls' 100-Yard Rushing Performances

Name	Date	Number of Rushing Attempts	Total Yards Rushed
Antoine	12/23/00	17	147
Truman	11/30/97	18	104
Darren	11/3/96	22	122
Kent	11/22/92	20	161
Lance	10/29/89	21	121
Otis	12/16/73	34	200

34. Which player had the highest number of average yards per rushing attempt?

  A. Antoine

  B. Darren

  C. Kent

  D Otis

35. It used to be said that "the sun never sets on the British Empire." The most accurate interpretation of this saying is:

  A. The British military never sleeps.

  B. The Greenwich Meridian is central to the world's timekeeping system.

  C. British rule will never end.

  D. Britain rules lands all around the globe.

36. Emotional language is language that appeals to a reader's emotions, rather than logic or solid arguments. Which of these sentences is an example of the use of emotional language?

  A. Francis Scott Key wrote the national anthem.

  B. Billy's birthday is September 1.

  C. If you don't pick up the crumbs, you will have ugly bugs all over your room.

  D. The transcripts you requested will take two weeks to be sent.

Use the passage below to answer the question that follows.

The fierce competitiveness shown by many parents seeking to enroll their children in exclusive preschool programs is ironic in light of the avowed purpose of such programs, which typically emphasize individually paced growth and the development of social skills through compromise and cooperation.

37. Which of the following best accounts for the author's characterization of the parents' competitiveness as ironic?

    A. the fact that the parents are behaving like children

    B. the incongruity between the parents' actions and the values they wish instilled in their children

    C. the inconsistency of programs that emphasize sociability while restricting enrollment

    D. the contrast between the individual orientation of the preschool programs and the conformism of the parents

38. A hardware store sells a 10.1 oz. tube of caulk with silicone for $0.89. Marty has $10.59. How many tubes of caulk can he buy? (Disregard any tax.)

    A.   11

    B.   12

    C. 11.9

    D.   1

Use the information below to answer the question that follows.

Henry, Phil, Shawn, and Ruben play football for the Appleville Astronauts.

Name	First Season	Height	Weight	Birthdate	Birthplace
Henry	1991	6'0"	200	12/29/67	Missouri
Phil	1991	6'5"	273	5/20/68	North Dakota
Shawn	1996	6'4"	290	3/28/70	California
Ruben	1995	6'3"	304	2/13/72	New Jersey

39. Which player has the least amount of experience as an Astronaut?

    A. Henry

    B. Phil

    C. Shawn

    D. Ruben

40. It took Jenna 35 minutes to do her English homework. Math is more difficult, and it took her 56 more minutes to complete that homework. How long did it take Jenna to do her math homework?

    A. 1 hour, 31 minutes

    B. 21 minutes

    C. 56 minutes

    D. 1 hour, 56 minutes

41. Which of the following empires splintered from the Egyptian empire and established a vigorous trade in precious metals while retaining many characteristics of Egyptian civilization?

    A. Phoenician

    B. Mayan

    C. Babylonian

    D. Kush

$(23 + 27 + 42 + 19 + 33) ÷ (5) = $ _____

42. Which of the following statements could result in the number sentence above?

    A. Lindsay wanted to find the sum of her playing time.

    B. Lindsay wanted to find the median of her playing time.

    C. Lindsay wanted to find the quotient of her playing time.

    D. Lindsay wanted to find the mean of her playing time.

43. Appliance stores tend to raise prices of fans and air conditioners as the hottest months of the year approach. This is consistent with which of the following economic principles?

    A. deflation

    B. supply and demand

    C. deficit spending

    D. diminishing returns

44. Tragedy is a form of drama that can be traced as far back as Greek theater. The hallmarks of a tragedy are all but which of the following?

    A. The hero's pain appears to the audience to be just and fair.

    B. The hero's pain is to some extent redemptive.

    C. The play's denouement is catastrophic.

    D. The play's denouement is inevitable.

45. Which of the following is a stately court dance in triple time that originated as a rustic French dance and was introduced to the court in the seventeenth century?

    A. waltz

    B. minuet

    C. scherzo

    D. paso doble

Use the statement below to answer the two questions that follow.

The League of Women Voters is a *nonpartisan* organization that promotes political responsibility, including active participation in government. It was organized the same year that the 19th Amendment was ratified.

46. Based on this statement, what conclusion can best be drawn?

    A. Women vote as a bloc on issues the League determines important.

    B. The League of Women Voters has little political clout.

    C. The 19th Amendment gave women the right to vote.

    D. The League does not trust men to make the best decisions regarding their future.

47. What is the best meaning for the word *nonpartisan*?

    A. nonpolitical

    B. pro-women

    C. pro-political

    D. taking no sides on an issue

48. Which of the following is NOT a central aspect of the Reformation?

    A. Martin Luther's 95 theses

    B. Henry VIII's divorce

    C. The Catholic church's practice of indulgences

    D. The works of Shakespeare, Michelangelo, and Da Vinci

49. Some moots are noots. All zoots are either moots or doots. No doots are moots. All doots are noots. All woots are moots. No _____ are woots.

    Which word best fits the blank?

    A. doots

    B. noots

    C. zoots

    D. moots

Use the information below to answer the question that follows.

Four students were contestants in a figure-skating competition. The following chart shows the scores they received from each judge.

Contestant	Judge #1	Judge #2	Judge #3	Judge #4	Judge #5
Ling	4	5	6	2	5
Collette	8	7	9	10	7
Salchicha	1	9	2	2	1
Larga	9	9	9	9	9

50. The competition winner was determined by the contestant with the highest average score. Who won the competition?

    A. Ling

    B. Collette

    C. Salchicha

    D. Larga

51. Kimberly ran 40 miles in week 1, 42 miles in week 2, 39 miles in week 3, 37 miles in week 4, and 42 miles in week 5. What is the average (mean) number of miles she ran per week?

    A. 37

    B. 39.5

    C. 40

    D. 42

52. Which of the following pairs of colonies BEST represents truly tolerant havens for religious freedom, rather than being devoted to the practice of only one brand of religion?

    A. Rhode Island and Pennsylvania

    B. Massachusetts and New York

    C. Connecticut and New Hampshire

    D. Maryland and Virginia

53. The concept of Manifest Destiny, which was popular in the nineteenth century, is best exemplified by which of the following U.S. actions?

    A. the Louisiana Purchase

    B. the impeachment of President Andrew Johnson

    C. the Civil War

    D. the Mexican-American War

54. Which of the following words acquired new definitions due to technological advances and developments in the twentieth century?

    I. Mouse

    II. Surfing

    III. Cookie

    IV. Desktop

    A. I and III only

    B. II and IV only

    C. I, II, and III only

    D. I, II, III, and IV

Use the information below to answer the question that follows.

There is a tiny village deep in the rain forest inhabited by only three kinds of people. Anties always tell the truth, Burks always lie, and Crabapplies sometimes lie and sometimes tell the truth. You approach a group of villagers.

VILLAGER 1: "I am not a Burk."
VILLAGER 2: "Yes, he is! Villager 1 is a Burk!"
VILLAGER 3: "Villager 2 is right. Villager 1 is a Burk."
VILLAGER 1: "I am an Antie. Villager 2 is a Burk."
VILLAGER 2: "Villagers 1 and 3 are both Burks."
VILLAGER 3: "Of course I'm a Burk."
VILLAGER 1: "Villager 3 is a Crabapplie."
VILLAGER 3: "That's correct. I'm a Crabapplie."
VILLAGER 2: "No way! Villager 3's an Antie!"

55. Which of these choices is correct?

    A. VILLAGER 1 = Antie; VILLAGER 2 = Burk; VILLAGER 3 = Crabapplie

    B. VILLAGER 1 = Burk; VILLAGER 2 = Antie; VILLAGER 3 = Crabapplie

    C. VILLAGER 1 = Antie; VILLAGER 2 = Crabapplie; VILLAGER 3 = Burk

    D. VILLAGER 1 = Burk; VILLAGER 2 = Crabapplie; VILLAGER 3 = Antie

Read the excerpt below from Carl Sandburg's poem "Chicago" and answer the two questions that follow.

Chicago

Hog Butcher for the World,
Tool Maker, Stacker of Wheat,
Player with Railroads and the Nation's Freight Handler;
Stormy, husky, brawling,
City of the Big Shoulders.

56. In this poem, Sandburg suggests that the source of Chicago's raw energy and optimism is

    A. its vigorous laboring class.

    B. a muscular, male pair of shoulders.

    C. the nation's railroad system, which connects it with other urban centers.

    D. the production of meat.

57. What literary device is Sandburg using when addressing the city of Chicago as an individual?

    A. allusion

    B. simile

    C. alliteration

    D. personification

Use the quote below to answer the question that follows.

"I'm a professional, so I don't vacation. I have surgery."—Joan Rivers, to *People* magazine, on why she doesn't have any "crummy vacation" stories.

58. What is the tone of this quotation?

    A. humorous

    B. serious

    C. businesslike

    D. naive

Use the advertisement below to answer the question that follows.

A Mann for All Seasons
Thomas Mann's Handyman Service

Need a Handyman? Call Thomas Mann's Handyman Service at 555-KL5H. We have experts in all manner of household labor, from snow shoveling to lawn mowing. Low hourly rates!

---

59. The headline of the advertisement uses a literary device. Which literary device is used?

    A. pun

    B. personification

    C. allusion

    D. alliteration

Use the below passage to answer the three questions that follow.

A mammal is an animal that raises its young on milk. Mammals are vertebrates (i.e., they have a backbone), and most are covered with hair or fur. Most mammals give birth to live young. Those that do not are called monotremes and are highly unusual among mammals. Most mammal babies are completely helpless when they are born, initially relying on their mothers for food. This close link between mother and offspring produces strong family ties, with young mammals learning to copy their mothers' behavior. Mammals also have a recognizable intelligence not seen in lower animals. Some of the most familiar animals are cats, dogs, gorillas, whales, and humans.

60. Which of the following choices was NOT mentioned in the passage as a characteristic of MOST mammals?

    A. offspring supported by their mothers' milk during early life

    B. covered with hair or fur

    C. live birth

    D. ability to fly and/or swim

The chart below describes the characteristics of several animals.

Species (Common Name)	Fur/Hair?	Backbone?	Gives Birth to Live Young?
Gorilla	Yes	Yes	Yes
Trout	No	Yes	No
Whale	Yes	Yes	Yes
Platypus	Yes	Yes	No
Squirrel	Yes	Yes	Yes
Jellyfish	No	No	No
Sponge	No	No	No
Blue Jay	No	Yes	No

61. According to the passage and the chart, which of the following is NOT a mammal?

    A. gorilla

    B. whale

    C. squirrel

    D. blue jay

62. Which of the following is a monotreme?

    A. squirrel

    B. platypus

    C. trout

    D. jellyfish

Pierre Auguste Renoir, *Lucie Berard (Child in White)*, 1883, Art Institute of Chicago

63. Based on this picture by Renoir, impressionism can best be characterized by which of the following?

    A. realism

    B. murkiness

    C. landscape paintings

    D. abstraction

64. From the following list of words used in a poem, determine the tone the poet establishes: *long, silent, blind, blackness, stumble, fall, silent, dry, run, runs, turn, nobody, dark, doorless, turning, forever, nobody, waits, follows, pursue, stumbles, rises, nobody.*

    A. anxious

    B. ordinary

    C. passive

    D. angry

65. The first 10 amendments to the Constitution of the United States are often referred to as the Bill of Rights. This is because

   A. they are focused on individual rights.

   B. they set forth the laws of the country.

   C. they list the rights and responsibilities of citizenship.

   D. they are more right than is the rest of the Constitution.

Use the information below to answer the four questions that follow.

Mountain	Location	State	Above Sea Level	Interesting Detail
Mount McKinley	Denali National Park and Preserve	South, Central Alaska	20,320 ft.	highest peak in North America
Pikes Peak	Colorado Springs	Colorado	14,110 ft.	inspired writing of "America the Beautiful"
Mount Marcy	Adirondack Mountains	Northeast New York	5,344 ft.	composed mainly of metamorphic and igneous rock
Cadillac Mountain	Desert Island	Maine	1,530 ft.	first place in U.S. to see sunrise

66. About how much higher is Mount Marcy than Cadillac Mountain?

   A. more than three times as high

   B. twice as high

   C. about 3,800 meters higher

   D. five times as high

67. Which mountain is the furthest north?

   A. Mount McKinley

   B. Pikes Peak

   C. Mount Marcy

   D. Cadillac Mountain

68. Which piece of information tells you about the easternmost mountain?

    A. "Northeast New York"

    B. "Highest peak in North America"

    C. "First place in U.S. to see sunrise"

    D. "Pikes Peak"

69. Which of the following conclusions can be inferred from this table?

    A. Pikes Peak has the most beautiful view.

    B. Mount McKinley is the southernmost of all the mountains listed.

    C. All Maine mountains are smaller than New York mountains.

    D. The Adirondack Mountains were formed from a volcano.

Use the following passage to answer the question that follows.

A second-grade science class is studying different types of soil. They have designed an experiment with settling jars to see which kind of soil has the most layers. Each team of students examines three different types of soil: sand, clay, and loam. They look at each sample through a magnifying glass and thoroughly examine it. Students then make a prediction as to which type of soil will have the most layers when it settles in a jar of water.

They notice that sand particles are slightly larger and more varied than the dusty clay particles. They also notice loam has the most sizes and types of particles, including some decaying vegetation and redwood bark.

Next, each team labels three different jars "sand," "clay," and "loam" and then places three tablespoons of each type of soil into the appropriately labeled jars. They add two-thirds of a cup of water to each jar, put the lids on, and shake each jar.

70. According to the students' observations, which type of soil is most likely to have the most layers when the soil settles?

    A. sand

    B. clay

    C. loam

    D. They will all have just one layer.

71. The Proclamation of 1763 was an unpopular edict that led to further unrest in the British colonies. Which of the following best represents the content of this proclamation?

    A. Colonists were forbidden to move west of the Appalachian Mountains.

    B. Colonists were required to pay for the housing of British troops.

    C. Colonists were required to pay taxes on many imported goods.

    D. Colonists were required to sign oaths of loyalty to the English king.

72. Which line in the table below best matches the name of an event in the Revolutionary War to an accurate description of the event's effect?

Line	Event	Effect
1	Battle of Concord	Caused massive defection of British troops.
2	Battle of Saratoga	Persuaded France to ally with the revolutionaries.
3	Crossing the Delaware	Captured badly needed food supplies for starving revolutionary army.
4	Battle of Yorktown	Decimated revolutionary troops and prolonged the war.

    A. Line 1

    B. Line 2

    C. Line 3

    D. Line 4

73. Which of the following sums up the reasons the Articles of Confederation proved inadequate governing documents for the newly formed United States?

    A. They concentrated too much power in the hands of too few.

    B. They did not adequately protect the interests of minorities.

    C. They gave the federal government too few powers.

    D. They did not give women the right to vote.

74. Which type of dance is developed through the traditions of a culture and passed down from generation to generation?

    A. ballroom dance

    B. folk dance

    C. modern dance

    D. ballet

75. In literature, an *oxymoron* is a linkage of two terms that are normally thought to be opposites. Which of the following sentences contains an oxymoron?

    A. The melancholy boy watched his mother leave.

    B. The burning ice left an imprint on my hand.

    C. The sly fox figured out how to enter the henhouse and scare the chickens.

    D. The thin little girl stood patiently in line for lunch.

The Louvre, Paris, France.   (photo: Del Franz)

76. This addition to the Louvre in Paris by I. M. Pei is an example of what type of architecture?

    A. neoclassical

    B. prairie

    C. art deco

    D. eclectic modernism

Use the passage below to answer the two questions that follow.

Andy Warhol was one of the first artists to understand the importance of mass media. He painted subjects that are easily identifiable in the culture of the day, ranging from Campbell's soup cans to the faces of celebrities. He isolated his subjects on the canvas and made them larger than life.

77. What might Andy Warhol's style of art be called?

    A. gothic

    B. cubism

    C. pop art

    D. impressionism

78. What else might have been a subject of an Andy Warhol painting?

    A. dollar bill

    B. the White House

    C. a landscape

    D. flowers

79. When doing research on the life of an important figure, you would probably give more credence to a biography than you would to an autobiography, due to the memoirist's

    A. verbosity.

    B. creativity.

    C. subjectivity.

    D experiences.

80. All of the following are true of map projections EXCEPT that

    A. map projections are flat.

    B. map projections are the most accurate representations of the surface of the Earth.

    C. map projections create distortions.

    D. map projections use grid lines of longitude and latitude.

SAMPLE DIRECTIONS FOR THE WRITTEN ASSIGNMENT

This section of the test consists of a written assignment. You are asked to prepare a written response of approximately 300–600 words on the assigned topic. The assignment can be found on the next page. You should use your time to plan, write, review, and edit what you have written for the assignment.

Read the assignment carefully before you begin to write. Think about how you will organize what you plan to write. You may use any blank space provided on the following pages to make notes, write an outline, or otherwise prepare your response. However, your score will be based solely on the response you write in the written response booklet.

Your response to the written assignment will be evaluated on the basis of the following criteria:

- Taking a position on an issue of contemporary concern and defending that position with reasoned arguments and supporting examples.

- Analyzing and responding to an opinion presented in an excerpt.

- Comparing and contrasting conflicting viewpoints on a social, political, or educational topic, as presented in one or more excerpts.

- Evaluating information and proposing a solution to a stated problem.

- Synthesizing information presented in two or more excerpts.

Your response will be evaluated based on your demonstrated ability to express and support opinions, not on the nature or content of the opinions expressed. The final version of the response should conform to the conventions of edited American English. This should be your original work, written in your own words, and not copied or paraphrased from some other work.

Be sure to write about the assigned topic and use multiple paragraphs. Please write legibly. You may not use any reference materials during the test. Remember to review what you have written and make any changes you think will improve your response.

Written Assignment—Practice LAST

There has been much research and evidence presented that schools are not providing an equal education for boys and girls. Among other things, it has been shown that teachers call on boys more often, allow boys to call out answers while requiring girls to raise their hands, allow boys more time to respond to questions, and give boys more feedback.

You do not need to agree or disagree with the above statements, but present examples of both sides of the issue (equal versus unequal treatment of girls and boys) and state examples of things teachers can do to alter this situation.

CHAPTER 8: **PRACTICE LAST ANSWERS AND EXPLANATIONS**

Answer Key

1. C	17. A	33. C	49. A	65. A
2. D	18. D	34. A	50. D	66. A
3. D	19. D	35. D	51. C	67. A
4. A	20. D	36. C	52. A	68. C
5 C	21. D	37. B	53. D	69. D
6. B	22. A	38. A	54. D	70. C
7. A	23. D	39. C	55. A	71. A
8. C	24. A	40. A	56. A	72. B
9. A	25. A	41. D	57. D	73. C
10. C	26. C	42. D	58. A	74. B
11. B	27. A	43. B	59. A	75. B
12. C	28. B	44. A	60. D	76. D
13. A	29. C	45. B	61. D	77. C
14. C	30. B	46. C	62. B	78. A
15. B	31. D	47. D	63. A	79. C
16. C	32. D	48. D	64. A	80. B

ANSWERS AND EXPLANATIONS

1. C

The primary focus of this question is Objective 0007:

Understand the interrelatedness of historical, geographic, cultural, economic, political, and social issues and factors.

The main idea communicated in the quotation can be found in the first sentence: "let her put others first, herself last." In other words, (C) women were regarded as inferior. Choice (A) states the opposite view of the quote, and (D)'s response is not supported in any way by the quotation. As for (B), the quotation did not mention in any area that men and women were considered equal; in fact, it states women are to put themselves last.

2. D

The primary focus of this question is Objective 0007:

Understand the interrelatedness of historical, geographic, cultural, economic, political, and social issues and factors.

Agrarian means "agricultural." In predicting the correct response, one should look at the similarities in the words. *Agricultural* and *agrarian* have the same root, *agri*. A market society (A) is based on an economic system. Feudal societies (B) were more common in the Middle Ages when a lord of a manor had serfs do the work. A technologically advanced society (C) uses many types of technologies. This is not supported by the statement.

3. D

The primary focus of this question is Objective 0006:

Understand and apply skills, principles, and procedures associated with inquiry and problem solving in the sciences.

The statement in (D) says everything; the fact that a sponge regenerates decreases the manufacturer's need to kill sponges and buy new ones. Choice (A) is incorrect because regeneration occurs only in live animals. Eliminate (B); there is no information given regarding the cleaning power of sponges. Finally, the statement in (C) is not supported by the passage.

4. A

The primary focus of this question is Objective 0014:

Understand forms and themes used in literature from different periods and cultures.

The speaker says that the least push of joy causes her to tip, meaning that it unsettles her. She then compares her state to drunkenness. She continues this analogy with the reference to the "new liquor." The words are a metaphor for the joy—or, one might say, happiness—that unnerves her and produces a tipsy quality. Choice (B) fails to recognize that the words "new liquor" are metaphoric. The speaker is not referring to actual drunkenness. As for (C), the only reference to a pool is in the second line, describing the speaker's capacity for grief—not the joy that is like "new liquor." "Emotion" (D) is too vague because it can denote either grief or joy.

5. C

The primary focus of this question is Objective 0014:

Understand forms and themes used in literature from different periods and cultures.

Grief, even a lot of it, does not trouble the speaker because she is used to it, but the smallest bit of joy—a pleasant emotion—is unsettling. Obviously, she is unused to experiencing pleasant emotions. Choices (A) and (D) fail to detect the metaphoric quality of the allusion to drunkenness. (B) considers only the first three lines of the poem without recognizing that the thrust of the work is the speaker's reaction to joy, not grief.

6. B

The primary focus of this question is Objective 0011:

Understand and interpret visual representations of historical and social scientific information.

The key phrase in this question is "bottom of this social pyramid." Therefore, one can deduce that the question is asking about *social status* (B). Whereas merchants may have made up the largest part of the population (A), this was not what the question is asking. Choices (C) and (D) are irrelevant as well—there is nothing in the pyramid or question relating to societal impact or religion.

7. A

The primary focus of this question is Objective 0003:

Apply knowledge of numerical, geometric, and algebraic relationships in problem-solving and mathematical contexts.

The formula given is $d = rt$. In this problem, the distance is given as 60 miles; the rate is 35 mph. The question is asking for the time (t). Therefore, the equation can be set up as $60 = 35t$, or $\frac{60}{35} = t$. So $t = 1.714$. Leave the 1 off right now (remember it equals 1 hour) and focus on the decimal.

$$\frac{714}{100} = \frac{t}{60}$$

$714 \times 60 = 100t$

$42{,}840 = 100t$

$42.84 = t$

$43 = t$ (to the nearest minute)

Now remember to add back in the first hour.

So, 1 hour and 43 minutes is the approximate time it would take to drive from Buffalo to Rochester. The closest response from the choices given is 1 hour, 40 minutes (A).

8. C

The primary focus of this question is Objective 0019:

Use critical reasoning skills to assess an author's treatment of content in written materials from a variety of sources.

In 1898, the Spanish-American War was ending. The discussion in the passage is about whether the United States should annex the Philippines as opposed to giving them back to Spain or letting them fend for themselves. For his part, Mr. Hennessy advocates "taking in" the Philippines, even though he isn't sure where they are and, only just recently, found out *what* they are. Supporting U.S. takeover of territory with such a limited understanding of the situation strongly suggests that Hennessy is in favor of expansionism for its own sake, which is the point made in choice (C). None of the remaining choices are supported by the passage. (A) conveys a harsh sentiment not supported by the piece's airy tone. We can rule out (B) because neither Hennessy nor Dooley brings up whether the intervention is inevitable, just whether it is desirable. As for (D), Hennessy certainly demonstrates gaps in his knowledge of geography and world politics, but we cannot be sure that the author considers these deficiencies to be grave or that he believes most Americans share them.

9. A

The primary focus of this question is Objective 0006:

Understand and apply skills, principles, and procedures associated with inquiry and problem solving in the sciences.

The first sentence is key here—it states that protozoa dissolve oxygen and carbon dioxide through the cell membrane (A). This is the first (or surface) level of the respiratory system. The surrounding medium (B) is the next level for respiration, and carbon dioxide and oxygen (D) are gases. Choice (C) is irrelevant because cytoplasm is not mentioned in the passage.

10. C

The primary focus of this question is Objective 0015:

Analyze and interpret literature from different periods and cultures and understand the relationship of works of literature to their social and historical contexts.

The key references in this passage are to the mythological characters of Icarus and Daedalus. Daedalus made wings for his son Icarus. The boy flew too close to the sun, the wax that held together the wings melted, and he plunged to his death. There is no reference to Icarus and Daedalus in the Old Testament, so you can eliminate (A). *The Odyssey* concerns the travels of Ulysses, or Odysseus. There is no reference to Icarus and Daedalus in the story, so (B) can also be eliminated. Regarding (D), there is no reference to Icarus and Daedalus in the Arthurian legend, which concerns King Arthur and the Knights of the Round Table.

11. B

The primary focus of this question is Objective 0015:

Analyze and interpret literature from different periods and cultures and understand the relationship of works of literature to their social and historical contexts.

What makes these lines distinctive is the request: "God mend thy every flaw." Most patriotic songs mention only good things about a country; this line suggests that the country may have faults. Thus, (B) is the best answer. Choice (A) is incorrect because the first and third lines rhyme. Choice (C) distorts the meaning of the lines. The lines ask God to confirm, or reinforce, America's liberty through law. They do not set law as a necessary condition of liberty. It is not unusual for patriotic songs to contain references to God; for example, "God Bless America" and "The Battle Hymn of the Republic" contain references to God. (D) is incorrect.

12. C

The primary focus of this question is Objective 0003:

Apply knowledge of numerical, geometric, and algebraic relationships in problem-solving and mathematical contexts.

The total cost of the Game Boy is 29.99×1.07 (sales tax) = $32.09. Billy would have enough money to buy the Game Boy in 7 weeks: $\frac{32.09}{5} = 6.418$ weeks. (Because he gets his allowance once a week, it would be the seventh week that gives him the correct amount.) Peter would have enough money in 5 weeks: $\frac{32.09}{7} = 4.584$ weeks. (Again, this needs to be rounded to the next week.) Then $7 - 5 = 2$ weeks. Peter would have the Game Boy two weeks earlier than Billy.

13. A

The primary focus of this question is Objective 0020:

Analyze and evaluate the effectiveness of expression in a written paragraph or passage according to the conventions of edited American English.

The companion conjunction with *neither* is *nor*. (The conjunction *either* would be correct with *or*.) The verb-adjective-noun phrase "had enough money" in (B) is correct, as is the infinitive "to buy" in (C).

14. C

The primary focus of this question is Objective 0020:

Analyze and evaluate the effectiveness of expression in a written paragraph or passage according to the conventions of edited American English.

The article *a* precedes a noun or adjective that starts with a consonant. *An* must be used before a word that starts with a vowel (*exercise*). The proper tense ("has never been") is used in (A), and the infinitive "to begin" (B) is correct as well.

15. B

The primary focus of this question is Objective 0007:

Understand the interrelatedness of historical, geographic, cultural, economic, political, and social issues and factors.

Only natives lived in the rain forest before the 1700s, and by all accounts, they took care of their environment. Shipping of goods to other continents has occurred for hundreds of years; Christopher Columbus is sometimes viewed as an early world trader. This eliminates (A). Cross off (B), too, as there are accounts of racism for hundreds of years, especially with slave trade—the settlers in this country imported slaves from the Caribbean in the 1600s. Finally, religious wars have been documented since very early in the history of man. Many wars and conflicts around the world were based on religious disagreements. (D) is incorrect.

16. C

The primary focus of this question is Objective 0020:

Analyze and evaluate the effectiveness of expression in a written paragraph or passage according to the conventions of edited American English.

Sentence 4 supplies a detail about penicillin that does not contribute to the logical thread of the paragraph, thus making it an irrelevant detail. Since the detail is irrelevant, eliminate (A) and (B), which both contain the word *relevant*. Choice (D), *redundant*, means the needless repetition of a concept; redundancy is not exemplified by sentence 4, making (D) incorrect.

17. A

The primary focus of this question is Objective 0018:

Analyze and interpret written materials from a variety of sources.

Only (A) is irrelevant to the passage: no mention is made about how others felt about nontraditional churches and their members. It can be assumed that, with a *rise* in the popularity of younger religious leaders, there would be growth in the church, so (B) can be considered a direct effect of the Great Awakening. The "splintering" of the church probably led to opposition (C) and more religious diversity (D).

KAPLAN

18. D

The primary focus of this question is Objective 0017:

Derive information from a variety of sources (e.g., magazine articles, essays, websites).

Given the positions of the specific leaders and the description of Democrats and Whigs, (D) is the logical choice. Based on their beliefs, these leaders belonged to the following parties: John Q. Adams, Whig; Andrew Jackson, Democrat; Henry Clay, Whig; Daniel Webster, Whig. As for John C. Calhoun, he supported aspects of both parties but neither entirely.

19. D

The primary focus of this question is Objective 0020:

Analyze and evaluate the effectiveness of expression in a written paragraph or passage according to the conventions of edited American English.

This sentence is correct as written.

20. D

The primary focus of this question is Objective 0003:

Apply knowledge of numerical, geometric, and algebraic relationships in problem-solving and mathematical contexts.

It may help to draw the triangle described. Next, subtract the vertex angle (80) from the sum of the angles (180) to find out what the other two angles need to add up to (100). Because the information states that the two legs are equal, we know that we can divide 100 in half and that each of the remaining two angles must be 50 degrees.

21. D

The primary focus of this question is Objective 0001:

Use mathematical reasoning in problem-solving situations to arrive at logical conclusions and to analyze the problem-solving process.

Ostriches and sheep each have one head only. This means, if there are 60 heads, there must 60 animals total. Ostriches have two legs; sheep have four legs. The best way to tackle this question is to work backwards from the answer choices provided. In (A), if there are 60 sheep and no ostriches, there would be 240 legs (60 × 4). In (B), 40 ostriches would add up to 80 legs (40 × 2), plus the 80 legs of the 20 sheep

(20 × 4), for a total of 160 legs. In (C), there are 72 legs for the ostriches (36 × 2) and 96 legs for the 24 sheep (24 × 4). That's 168 legs. In (D), the 50 ostriches would have 100 legs, and the 10 sheep would have 40 legs for a total of 140 legs, making (D) the correct answer.

22. A

The primary focus of this question is Objective 0009:

Understand different perspectives and priorities underlying historical or contemporary arguments, interpretations, explanations, or developments.

Although generally considered a valid means of ensuring that police activities stay within constitutional limits, applying the exclusionary rule does limit the state's ability to prosecute criminals in certain cases. This has given the exclusionary rule a pro-criminal gloss, and a politician who advocates discontinuance of the rule would most likely hold conservative views and want to be as a law-and-order candidate. Let's look at the remaining choices. Because the exclusionary rule is the status quo, this role would be in conflict with the view that the rule should be discontinued, so (B) is out. We can eliminate (C) on the basis that a politician who holds conservative views would probably not want to be viewed as a liberal. (D) is incorrect because a politician who advocates discontinuance of the rule would most likely be unsympathetic toward criminals.

23. D

The primary focus of this question is Objective 0012:

Understand and analyze elements of form and content in works from the visual and performing arts from different periods and cultures.

The lyricist is writing a poem about himself and his surroundings. *Introspection* (D) means to look into oneself. *Exuberant* (A) means to be very happy and excited, but the tone of these lyrics is almost the opposite. The author might be a little sad, but there is no indication he is *hateful* (B). Nor is the tone *aggressive* (C).

24. A

The primary focus of this question is Objective 0013:

Analyze and interpret works from the visual and performing arts representing different periods and cultures and understand the relationship of works of art to their social and historical contexts.

In the second stanza, the author says, "And before I die I want / To cast my verses from my soul." This indicates the author wants others to know and understand his verses, not have them die with him. As for the remaining choices: when he states he is a sincere man and is so earnest in stating his verses, it is doubtful he sees them as useless lines, so choice (B) is out. Neither (C) nor (D) is indicated in the lyrics.

25. A

The primary focus of this question is Objective 0020:

Analyze and evaluate the effectiveness of expression in a written paragraph or passage according to the conventions of edited American English.

The paragraph in (A) corrects what appears to be a translation into proper English. The first sentence of the original piece is actually three run-on sentences. Choice (B) does not correct this problem; in fact, it muddles it further. Choice (C) makes up extraneous information—the king wanted the books burned and the woman executed.

26. C

The primary focus of this question is Objective 0018:

Analyze and interpret written materials from a variety of sources.

To induce "prescribed reactions" would be to plan the reaction of the audience. This is not indicated in the passage. The second sentence of the passage states that masks allow an actor to play more than one role, so we can eliminate (A). Choice (B) is also mentioned as a use for the masks—that the wide-open mouth of the masks *amplifies* the actors' voices, or makes them louder and stronger. Choice (D) can be justified because if actors could play multiple roles, fewer people would be needed to stage the plays.

27. A

The primary focus of this question is Objective 0015:

Analyze and interpret literature from different periods and cultures and understand the relationship of works of literature to their social and historical contexts.

The last sentence of the inscription states her feelings—she made a "monument for her deserving husband." She is proud of him. Choices (B), (C), and (D) are all negative responses, and the inscription is clearly a positive one.

28. B

The primary focus of this question is Objective 0018:

Analyze and interpret written materials from a variety of sources.

In the author's view, a piece of verse qualifies as a poem only if it affects the reader or listener in such a way as to awaken the senses on a nonverbal level or elevate the emotions. A verse, such as the Dr. Fell verse, that fails to produce these effects is "certainly not a poem." As for the other choices: popularity with schoolchildren is not mentioned by the author as a reason to disqualify a piece of verse as a poem, so (A) is out. Choice (C) states a principle with which the author likely agrees, but asserting the importance of the poem-reader relationship does not in itself provide a criterion by which verses can be judged as poems. Finally, (D) does not address the question, which is about the author's belief about what qualifies a verse as a poem, not what the author believes about poetry in general.

29. C

The primary focus of this question is Objective 0018:

Analyze and interpret written materials from a variety of sources.

The author claims that the new extended library hours resulted in more late-night street traffic, which in turn led to the expansion of existing businesses and the opening of several new ones in the Collegeside neighborhood. That extra traffic must have consisted of potential customers for the new and expanded businesses. Whereas the positive effects of the changed schedule on the Collegeside economy were not a factor in the University's decision, this doesn't imply that the University harbored objections to the development of the neighborhood (A). Also, you cannot assume that the local economy would not have expanded in response to other influences (B). Finally, there is nothing in the passage that logically suggests a cause-and-effect relationship between the new library schedule and the shift away from punched cards and printouts (D).

30. B

The primary focus of this question is Objective 0019:

Use critical reasoning skills to assess an author's treatment of content in written materials from a variety of sources.

This question requires that you extrapolate a probable continuation on the basis of information provided in the passage. Choice (B) is strongly indicated by the structure and tone of the passage. The author has explained that, whereas the University did not intend to rejuvenate the local community through its library decision, that benefit was nonetheless an outcome of the University's decision. *Similarly* (author's structural clue), the University Computer Center's decision was not intended to cause the failure of the local recycling project. To make this latter situation parallel to the previous one, the author would have to assert that the demise of the recycling project was nonetheless a consequence of the Computer Center's decision. Choice (A), though plausible, is too far removed from the topic of the passage, which concerns the effects of the University's decisions on the local community. Eliminate (C): There is nothing in the passage that logically suggests a causal link between the University's decision about the library hours and the Computer Center's decision to change output formats. Choice (D) is too broad; the author is concerned quite specifically with the role of the University in Collegeside and with explaining the effects of two particular decisions.

31. D

The primary focus of this question is Objective 0003:

Apply knowledge of numerical, geometric, and algebraic relationships in problem-solving and mathematical contexts.

You first need to determine the amount of the discount: $34.00 × 0.32 (or 32%) is $10.88; $10.88 is the amount the pants will be reduced. Therefore; $34.00 − $10.88 = $23.12. Rounded to the nearest dollar, the correct response is $23.

32. D

The primary focus of this question is Objective 0001:

Use mathematical reasoning in problem-solving situations to arrive at logical conclusions and to analyze the problem-solving process.

Because the apple tree is yielding more apples each year, we can automatically eliminate responses (A) and (B). Now we must decide if (C) or (D) is the most reasonable prediction. Choice (C), 210 apples, would mean there was a very slight increase in the yield. Based on the previous years' output, one would expect the yield to increase significantly more. Therefore, this response is not the most likely. Choice (D), 275 apples, would be the best prediction.

33. C

The primary focus of this question is Objective 0003:

Apply knowledge of numerical, geometric, and algebraic relationships in problem-solving and mathematical contexts.

With the information provided, we see that:

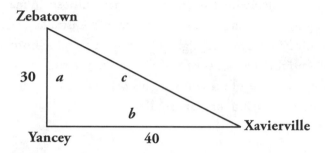

Now, plug the numbers into the Pythagorean theorem to get $30^2 + 40^2 = c^2$, or $900 + 1,600 = c^2$; c^2 therefore equals 2,500, the square root of which is 50.

34. A

The primary focus of this question is Objective 0002:

Understand connections between mathematical representations and ideas and use mathematical terms and representations to organize, interpret, and communicate information.

To figure out the average rushing yards per attempt, we need to divide the "total yards rushed" by the "number of rushing attempts." In the case of Antoine (A), he had 17 attempts for 147 yards; $\frac{147}{17} = 8.65$ yards per carry.

Truman (B) had 18 attempts for 104 yards; $\frac{104}{18} = 5.78$ yards per carry.

Darren (C) had 22 attempts for 122 yards; $\frac{122}{22} = 5.55$ yards per carry.

Kent (D) had 20 attempts for 161 yards; $\frac{161}{20} = 8.05$ yards per carry. Based on these calculations, Antoine averages the most yards per carry of all the players listed in the answer choices.

35. D

The primary focus of this question is Objective 0008:

Understand principles and assumptions underlying historical or contemporary arguments, interpretations, explanations, or developments.

From the beginning of the Age of Exploration until the mid-20th century, Great Britain established and maintained an empire that had outposts in many areas of the world. If it was nighttime in England, it was daytime in Australia. If Canada was dark, Rhodesia (now Zimbabwe) was light. One way to examine history is to look at the succession of empires in various parts of the world. The rise, expansion, and fall of empires gives a good sense of the course of history and provides lessons that can productively be applied to contemporary studies.

36. C

The primary focus of this question is Objective 0019:

Use critical reasoning skills to assess an author's treatment of content in written materials from a variety of sources.

The sentence in (C) is someone's opinion that tries to appeal to the audience's dislike for bugs rather than use solid evidence (except maybe experience). The statements in responses (A), (B), and (D) are rooted in fact.

37. B

The primary focus of this question is Objective 0017:

Derive information from a variety of sources (e.g., magazine articles, essays, websites)

The use of the word *ironic* suggests that some obvious incongruity is discernible in a given set of circumstances. In the context of the passage, the parents' competitiveness in the enrollment process clashes with their expectations regarding its ultimate outcome—the acquisition of social skills based on compromise and cooperation (qualities that stand in stark contrast to competitiveness). The passage does not tell you how the author expects either adults or children to behave; you cannot assume that the author believes the parents are behaving like children. Cross out (A). Choice (C) does not address the question, which is about the parents, not about preschool programs. Finally, (D) is incorrect because the author gives no indication in the passage that the parents' competitiveness is a kind of conformism; you would have to make an unwarranted assumption to equate the two.

38. A

The primary focus of this question is Objective 0003:

Apply knowledge of numerical, geometric, and algebraic relationships in problem-solving and mathematical contexts.

We can calculate $\frac{\$10.59}{0.89} = 11.9$. Because you cannot buy 0.9 of a tube of caulk, you must round down to the nearest number, 11.

39. C

The primary focus of this question is Objective 0002:

Understand connections between mathematical representations and ideas and use mathematical terms and representations to organize, interpret, and communicate information.

The key to answering this question is the "First Season" column. Shawn began playing for the Astronauts in 1996. This is the most recent year listed. Shawn has been playing for the fewest years and is thus the least experienced. Henry (A) and Phil (B) began playing in 1991, and Ruben (D) began in 1995. These are all earlier years than 1996, and we can therefore conclude that Henry, Phil, and Ruben all have more experience than Shawn.

40. A

The primary focus of this question is Objective 0001:

Use mathematical reasoning in problem-solving situations to arrive at logical conclusions and to analyze the problem-solving process.

To find out how long it took Jenna to complete her math homework, we can set up this equation: 35 minutes + 56 minutes = 91 minutes. Looking at the answer choices, it's clear we need to convert 91 minutes into hours and minutes. There are 60 minutes in an hour: 91 – 60 = 31. Therefore, it took Jenna 1 hour and 31 minutes to complete her math homework.

41. D

The primary focus of this question is Objective 0007:

Understand the interrelatedness of historical, geographic, cultural, economic, political, and social issues and factors.

Originally dominated for centuries—both politically and culturally—by the Egyptians, the people of Kush (also known as Nubia), in what is now Sudan, became a powerful force in about 750 BCE. They were located on trade routes in northern Africa and benefited from rich gold and emerald mines in their land. The land also yielded iron ore and the timber required to fuel the processing of ore into usable iron, so they also had a thriving iron industry. The Babylonian civilization (C) preceded the Kush and could not be considered a splinter kingdom of Egypt, nor could the Phoenician (A) or the Mayan (B) civilizations.

42. D

The primary focus of this question is Objective 0002:

Understand connections between mathematical representations and ideas and use mathematical terms and representations to organize, interpret, and communicate information.

The key to answering this question is knowing the definitions of the math terms *sum*, *median*, *quotient*, and *mean*. *Mean*, in a mathematical sense, means "average." To find the mean, one would add together all of the pieces of data and then divide by the number of pieces of data. This process is seen in the equation. *Sum* (A) means the answer to an addition problem. Because there is division in this equation, it is not merely a "sum" problem. *Median* (B) means finding the middle number in a group of numbers listed in order. There are no mathematical operations involved; one simply lists the numbers in either ascending or descending order and then finds the middle number in the list. Finally, *quotient* (D) means the answer to a division problem. Because there is addition in this equation, it is not merely a "quotient" problem.

43. B

The primary focus of this question is Objective 0008:

Understand principles and assumptions underlying historical or contemporary arguments, interpretations, explanations, or developments.

The fact that prices of fans and air conditioners go up during the hottest months of the year is consistent with the principle of supply and demand. When demand is greatest or supply is lowest, prices tend to go up.

44. A

The primary focus of this question is Objective 0012:

Understand and analyze elements of form and content in works from the visual and performing arts from different periods and cultures.

In a classic tragedy, the play's denouement is inevitable (D) and catastrophic (C). The hero's suffering is disproportionate to his guilt; the hero's anguish appears to the audience as unjust and unfair (the opposite of (A), making it the correct choice). The hero's pain appears to be beyond human endurance, and the hero's pain is to some extent redemptive (B).

45. B

The primary focus of this question is Objective 0012:

Understand and analyze elements of form and content in works from the visual and performing arts from different periods and cultures.

The minuet—a dance so called because of its small, dainty steps—was popular in 17th-century European royal courts. The minuet was adapted as a musical form by such composers as Lully, Mozart, and Haydn. The waltz was introduced to the royal courts in the 18th century, so (A) is incorrect. The scherzo (C) developed from the minuet and shares its three-four time signature, but it is a musical device found in symphonies, string quartets, sonatas, and similar works—not a dance. The paso doble (D) is a Spanish style of dance that was developed in France.

46. C

The primary focus of this question is Objective 0008:

Understand principles and assumptions underlying historical or contemporary arguments, interpretations, explanations, or developments.

The connection between the League of Women Voters and the 19th Amendment is implied in the statement. Because it says that the League "promotes political responsibility," one can infer that it has something to do with voting. Because it was organized in the same year that the 19th Amendment was ratified, the most likely conclusion is (C). We can rule out the remaining choices. Because the League is nonpartisan, it does not deem issues important; thus, women do not vote as a bloc on these issues (A). The statement implies neither that the League is powerful nor that it is weak. There is nothing in the statement that supports the assumption that the League has little political clout, so (B) is out. The statement does not imply that the League does not trust men (D); it simply says that the League wants women to have active participation in government.

47. D

The primary focus of this question is Objective 0010:

Understand and apply skills, principles, and procedures associated with inquiry, problem solving, and decision making in history and the social sciences.

Nonpartisan is rooted in the word *party* and the prefix *non- Non-* means "no" or "without." A "party," in the political sense, is a faction or group that takes sides on one or more issues. Thus, a "nonpartisan" group does not take sides on issues. (D) is the best choice. Because the statement says that the League "promotes political responsibility," it is a political group; that is, it is involved in politics. Thus, it is not "nonpolitical" (A). *Nonpartisan* does not mean "pro-women" (B) or "pro-politics" (C). *Nonpartisan* means "not tied to either political party."

48. D

The primary focus of this question is Objective 0016:

Analyze and interpret examples of religious or philosophical ideas from various periods of time and understand their significance in shaping societies and cultures.

The works of Shakespeare, Michelangelo, and Da Vinci are associated with the Renaissance, not the Reformation, so (D) is correct. Luther's 95 Theses, (A), were what he nailed to the church door in Wittenburg to signal the beginning of the Reformation and Lutheranism. Henry VIII's divorce, (B), was a key component of the Reformation and led to his founding of the Church of England. The Catholic Church's practice of selling indulgences (C), or pardons from sins, was one of the main aspects of its corruption that led to the Reformation.

49. A

The primary focus of this question is Objective 0001:

Use mathematical reasoning in problem-solving situations to arrive at logical conclusions and to analyze the problem-solving process.

Start with sentence 3, "No doots are moots." This says that doots and moots are two separate entities. Nothing that is a doot is also a moot. Now focus on sentence 5, "All woots are moots." This says that every woot is a moot; that is, woots are a subset of moots. Because no doots are moots, then it follows that no doots are woots, because all woots are moots.

Let's look at the other choices.

Choice (B): Start with sentence 1, "Some moots are noots." This means that in some cases, a moot equals a noot. Because "all woots are moots" (sentence 5), then one cannot be sure whether or not there is an overlap of woots and noots in the moot set. Thus, we cannot say definitively that no noots are woots.

Choice (C): Start with sentence 2, "All zoots are either moots or doots." You cannot be sure if a particular zoot is a moot or a doot. If it is a doot, then it is true that it is not a woot. But if it is a moot, then it *is* a woot. So we cannot say definitively whether or not a zoot is a woot.

Choice (D): Start with sentence 5, "All woots are moots." Because all woots are moots, woots are a subset of moots. Thus, some moots are woots.

50. D

The primary focus of this question is Objective 0002:

Understand connections between mathematical representations and ideas and use mathematical terms and representations to organize, interpret, and communicate information.

To find the average of a set of numbers, you need to add them up and divide by the number of numbers. Thus, Ling's average score is 4.4 $\left(\frac{22}{5}\right)$; Collette's average score is 8.4 $\left(\frac{42}{5}\right)$; Salchicha's average score is 3 $\left(\frac{15}{5}\right)$; and Larga's average score is 9 $\left(\frac{45}{5}\right)$.

The winner is the person with the highest average score: Larga (D) with 9.

51. C

The primary focus of this question is Objective 0003:

Apply knowledge of numerical, geometric, and algebraic relationships in problem-solving and mathematical contexts.

Again, the average is all the pieces of data added together divided by the number of pieces of data.

So we can set up this equation:

$$\frac{40 + 42 + 39 + 37 + 42}{5}$$

$$\frac{200}{5} = 40$$

52. A

The primary focus of this question is Objective 0009:

Understand different perspectives and priorities underlying historical or contemporary arguments, interpretations, explanations, or developments.

Roger Williams was expelled from Massachusetts for disagreeing with its religious leaders. He made his way to Rhode Island and established that colony as the first to recognize the separation of church and state. William Penn, a Quaker, established Pennsylvania as a haven of tolerance for the religious beliefs of even non-Quakers and enshrined those principles in the colony's constitution. None of the other answer choices is correct. The states mentioned in (B), (C), and (D) were not established as havens for religious freedom seekers.

53. D

The primary focus of this question is Objective 0009:

Understand different perspectives and priorities underlying historical or contemporary arguments, interpretations, explanations, or developments.

A newspaper editor coined the phrase *Manifest Destiny* in 1845. Those two words described the American people's vision of themselves as destined to spread their political philosophy throughout the hemisphere. In particular, they saw the United States as stretching from "sea to shining sea." The Louisiana Purchase in 1803 (A) greatly expanded U.S. territory, but prior to the coining of the term. Choices (B) and (C) do not relate to Manifest Destiny. However, the Mexican-American War was a thinly disguised land grab that helped fulfill that destiny.

54. D

The primary focus of this question is Objective 0005:

Understand the historical development and cultural contexts of mathematics, science, and technology; the relationships and common themes that connect mathematics, science, and technology; and the impact of mathematics, science, and technology on human societies.

Each of the listed terms acquired a new meaning in the 20th century. A mouse (I) is a device used to navigate computer screens. Surfing (II) refers to browsing through Internet sites, as in "surfing the Web." A cookie (III) is an electronic trail recording websites visited. The desktop (IV) refers to the files and programs accessible from a computer's initial screen.

55. A

The primary focus of this question is Objective 0001:

Use mathematical reasoning in problem-solving situations to arrive at logical conclusions and to analyze the problem-solving process.

The best way to approach this question is to assume each choice is correct and work backward. We'll assume (A) is correct. Because Villager 1 is an Antie, he is telling the truth when he says in statement 1, "I am not a Burk." He is also telling the truth when he says, in statement 4, "I am an Antie. Villager 2 is a Burk." Thus, we now know that Villager 2 is a Burk. This is consistent with (A). Because (A) is the only choice that has Villager 1 as an Antie and Villager 2 as a Burk, then we know that it is correct.

Let's now assume (B) is correct. In this case, Villager 1, who is a Burk, would be lying when he says in statement 7 that Villager 3 is a Crabapplie. But in (B), Villager 3 *is* a Crabapplie. Thus, (B) cannot be correct. If we assume (C) is correct, then Villager 3 would be lying when, in statement 6, he says that he is a Burk. However, because he *is* a Burk, then that is not a lie. If Burks always lie, then (C) is not correct. Finally, if we assume (D) is correct, Villager 3, who is an Antie, would be telling the truth when he says, in statement 6, that he is a Burk. However, this is a lie, because he is an Antie, and because Anties never lie, (D) cannot be correct.

56. A

The primary focus of this question is Objective 0014:

Understand forms and themes used in literature from different periods and cultures.

The excerpt opens Sandburg's poem "Chicago," which is a lively portrait of a flourishing urban center. The poem begins with (and maintains) a lot of energy, its initial images being of a butcher, tool maker, harvester, and freight handler—the laboring class (A). "Player with Railroads" and "Stormy, husky, brawling," suggest giants full of energy and optimism. Choice (B) is wrong because Sandburg is not being literal with the image of "Big Shoulders"; rather, they serve as a metaphor for Chicago's strength and its national status as freight capital. Railroads (C) and meat production (D) are just two of the several types of hard labor Sandburg cites.

57. D

The primary focus of this question is Objective 0014:

Understand forms and themes used in literature from different periods and cultures.

Recall that *personification* attributes human qualities to nonhuman animals or objects. Even in this brief excerpt, Sandburg personifies Chicago by calling it Butcher, Maker, Stacker, Player, and Handler and by using human characteristics such as "husky," "brawling," and "big shoulders." Choice (A) is incorrect because *allusion* is an indirect device and Sandburg's images are very direct. A *simile* (B) is a figure of speech that expresses a resemblance between things of different kinds using *like* or *as*—words not found in the excerpt. *Alliteration* (C) is the repetition of the same sound and has nothing to do with addressing Chicago as an individual.

58. A

The primary focus of this question is Objective 0018:

Analyze and interpret written materials from a variety of sources.

"I don't vacation. I have surgery," is a tongue-in-cheek comment on celebrities—that they are always supposed to look perfect. Rivers is referencing plastic surgery and is sarcastically mocking Hollywood's fixation on physical appearance. *Humorous* (A) is the best answer. Rivers is not being *serious* (B) or *businesslike* (C). She does not mean that she has never taken a vacation and that every single time she has time off she has plastic surgery; she is using hyperbole, irony, satire, and sarcasm. Rivers is not *naive* (D) in making this comment. In fact, she sounds rather jaded when it comes to show business.

59. A

The primary focus of this question is Objective 0014:

Understand forms and themes used in literature from different periods and cultures.

A *pun* (A) is a play on words. A pun uses words in a nontraditional sense to gain a desired effect on the audience. In a literal sense, the headline would read "A Man for All Seasons," but the author of the advertisement decided to use that common phrase to integrate the name of the business, Mann's, into the headline in order to make it more memorable. Let's look at the other literary devices listed as answer choices. *Personification* (B) is giving human qualities to a nonhuman object or idea. There is no evidence of that in the headline. *Allusion* (C) is referencing another work of literature or a historical event in a work of literature. There is no evidence of that in the headline, either. *Alliteration* (D) is the repetition of the initial consonant in several consecutive words. There is no alliteration in the headline.

60. D

The primary focus of this question is Objective 0006:

Understand and apply skills, principles, and procedures associated with inquiry and problem solving in the sciences.

"Ability to fly and/or swim" is not mentioned anywhere in the passage as a characteristic of most mammals. In fact, many mammals can neither fly nor swim. You can eliminate (A), (B), and (C), as the passage states that most mammals initially rely on their mothers for food, are covered with fur, and give birth to live young.

61. D

The primary focus of this question is Objective 0021:

Demonstrate the ability to locate, retrieve, organize, and interpret information from a variety of traditional and electronic sources.

According to the passage and chart, a blue jay does not have fur or hair, and it does not give birth to live young. Therefore, it is not a mammal because all mammals have fur/hair and all except monotremes give birth to live young. Gorillas (A), whales (B), and squirrels (C) are all mammals because they all exhibit mammalian characteristics: they have fur/hair and a backbone, and they give birth to live young.

62. B

The primary focus of this question is Objective 0021:

Demonstrate the ability to locate, retrieve, organize, and interpret information from a variety of traditional and electronic sources.

The passage states that a *monotreme* is a mammal that does not give birth to live young. According to the chart, a platypus (B) does not give birth to live young. Neither does a trout (C), but a trout is not a mammal.

63. A

The primary focus of this question is Objective 0013:

Analyze and interpret works from the visual and performing arts representing different periods and cultures and understand the relationship of works of art to their social and historical contexts.

This is a realistic painting of the little girl. We can therefore infer that impressionism, as represented by Renoir and his work in this question, is marked by *realism* (A). Looking at the picture and the answer choices, we can easily eliminate (B), (C), and (D). If the picture was characterized by *murkiness*, the girl's features would not be clear. *Landscape paintings* are characterized by outdoor scenery, none of which is found in the example. *Abstract* paintings would distort the features of the subject of the painting; this is not the case in *Child in White*.

64. A

The primary focus of this question is Objective 0014:

Understand forms and themes used in literature from different periods and cultures.

These words are from the poem "The Street" by Octavio Paz. When you read a poem or other text, underline words that evoke feelings, images, and associations. These are the words that will point you toward the author's meaning and intentions, which are often conveyed as much by tone as by literal word meanings. On the LAST, you are more likely to see an entire poem than a list of words like this, so it will be up to you to compile your own list as you read the text.

65. A

The primary focus of this question is Objective 0008:

Understand principles and assumptions underlying historical or contemporary arguments, interpretations, explanations, or developments.

The first 10 amendments were drafted by James Madison in response to Anti-Federalist complaints that the Constitution did not protect individuals and states from abuses of the federal government. The Federalists had written a Constitution that created a strong federal government, reacting to the weak Articles of Confederation that had failed to guide the country. The Anti-Federalists became alarmed that individual rights were in danger and demanded provisions that would protect important individual rights, such as the right to free speech and free assembly, and the protection against unreasonable search and seizure.

66. A

The primary focus of this question is Objective 0002:

Understand connections between mathematical representations and ideas and use mathematical terms and representations to organize, interpret, and communicate information.

Mount Marcy is 5,344 feet high, whereas Cadillac Mountain is 1,530 feet. If we set up the equation $\frac{5,344}{1,530}$, we get 3.5 as the answer. Now look for the answer choice that comes closest: (A), it is more than three times as high. If you weren't sure how to go about answering the question, you could have worked backward from the answer choices and eliminated wrong numbers as necessary. For (B) to be correct, Mount Marcy would have to be twice as high as Cadillac Mountain, about 3,000 feet. The chart tells us differently. For (C) to be correct, Mount Marcy would have to be 11,400 feet, which the chart contradicts (3,800 meters is equivalent to 11,400 feet). For (D) to be the correct answer, Mount Marcy would need to measure 7,650 feet (five times 1,530)—much too high.

67. A

The primary focus of this question is Objective 0004:

Understand major concepts, principles, and theories in science and technology and use that understanding to analyze phenomena in the natural world and to interpret information presented in illustrated or written form.

Alaska is the northernmost state in the United States, so Mount McKinley is the correct answer.

68. C

The primary focus of this question is Objective 0004:

Understand major concepts, principles, and theories in science and technology and use that understanding to analyze phenomena in the natural world and to interpret information presented in illustrated or written form.

Because the sun rises in the east, it can be assumed that the first place to see the sunrise would be the easternmost mountain. Choice (A) is wrong because there are places further east than northeast New York. In (B), the highest peak won't see the sunrise first if it is not furthest east. Mount McKinley sees the sun several hours later than Cadillac Mountain in Maine. (D) gives no information about Pikes Peak's location and is therefore irrelevant to answering the question.

69. D

The primary focus of this question is Objective 0021:

Demonstrate the ability to locate, retrieve, organize, and interpret information from a variety of traditional and electronic sources.

The details included with Mount Marcy—that it is part of the Adirondack Mountains and that it is made of metamorphic and igneous rock, which are volcanic matter—lead us to conclude that, (D), the Adirondacks were formed from a volcano. Eliminate (A) because this is an opinion and not necessarily true. Choice (B) is out, because even if Mount McKinley is in southern Alaska, it is still in the northernmost U.S. state to begin with. Cross out (C), too: no information is given on the lowest mountains.

70. C

The primary focus of this question is Objective 0006:

Understand and apply skills, principles, and procedures associated with inquiry and problem solving in the sciences.

The students noticed that loam has the most varied types and sizes of particles, which indicates that, when placed in a jar of water, it will most likely produce the most layers. Sand, (A), has the next largest size and variety of particles, but the loam should produce more layers in water because it will also contain the floating particles from the decaying vegetation and bark, eliminating choice (A). The fact that the decaying vegetation and bark floats ensures that the loam at least will have more than one layer, eliminating choice (D). Clay, (B), has fine, uniform, particles, which will create fewer layers than the loam.

71. A

The primary focus of this question is Objective 0007:

Understand the interrelatedness of historical, geographic, cultural, economic, political, and social issues and factors.

After the end of the French and Indian War, England wanted to avoid angering the Native Americans in the newly acquired Ohio Valley and to keep the colonists where they could be controlled more easily. The Proclamation of 1763 forbade them to move west, thereby angering the colonists. This proclamation was the first in a string of edicts that inflamed rebellion, including those described in (B) and (C). Choice (D) does not describe an actual edict.

72. B

The primary focus of this question is Objective 0008:

Understand principles and assumptions underlying historical or contemporary arguments, interpretations, explanations, or developments.

The Battle of Saratoga was a decisive victory for the revolutionaries and was all the impetus the French needed to join cause with the rebels against the British. This alliance proved to be a major turning point in the war. The Battle of Concord (A), usually linked with Lexington, was the first skirmish in the war. The crossing of the Delaware (C) led to much-needed victory but was not carried out to obtain food. The Battle of Yorktown (D) was a huge victory against the British, one that hastened the end of the war, not prolonged the war as stated in the answer choice.

73. C

The primary focus of this question is Objective 0007:

Understand the interrelatedness of historical, geographic, cultural, economic, political, and social issues and factors.

Among the powers not granted to the federal government in the Articles of Confederation were the ability to raise money from the states (hence, no money to spend), the ability to regulate interstate trade, and the ability to conduct national foreign policy. Although thought by some to be true, none of the other issues stated in the answer choices—the concentration of power in the hands of few (A), the inadequate protection of minority groups' interests (B), and the exclusion of women from voting (D)—was crucial to the debate over the governing documents.

74. B

The primary focus of this question is Objective 0013:

Analyze and interpret works from the visual and performing arts representing different periods and cultures and understand the relationship of works of art to their social and historical contexts.

Folk dance is also called ethnic dance, traditional dance, or country dance and derives from the traditions, music, and costumes of a specific culture. For example, a dance included in all Russian folk dance repertoires is the "troika" (meaning three-horse team), where dancers in teams of three imitate the prancing of horses pulling a sled or a carriage. Ballroom dance (A), a form of dance involving specific patterns performed by a pair of dancers, was developed in the European courts of the 17th century. Modern dance (C) was developed in 20th-century America as an offshoot of ballet (D), which originated in 17th- and 18th-century France.

75. B

The primary focus of this question is Objective 0014:

Understand forms and themes used in literature from different periods and cultures.

We usually think of *ice* as very cold and *burning* as being as being very hot, but in this sentence, the ice is so cold it feels as though it is burning. This is an example of an oxymoron.

76. D

The primary focus of this question is Objective 0012:

Understand and analyze elements of form and content in works from the visual and performing arts from different periods and cultures.

The addition contrasts highly with the original Louvre building. With its pyramid shape and diamond-shaped glass blocks, the addition, as pictured, is an example of *eclectic modernism* (D). If you aren't sure what eclectic modernism is, try working backward from the answer choices and eliminating those you are sure are incorrect. *Neoclassical* (A) is, as the stem words indicate, an adaptation of the classical style of architecture. This picture has no elements of classical architecture; it is definitely modern looking. *Prairie* (B) architecture would have characteristics of the Midwest, not clean, modern lines. *Art deco* (C) architecture is characterized by bold outlines and geometric and zigzag designs. It was popular in the 1920s and '30s.

77. C

The primary focus of this question is Objective 0013:

Analyze and interpret works from the visual and performing arts representing different periods and cultures and understand the relationship of works of art to their social and historical contexts.

Pop is short for *popular*. According to the information provided, Warhol used the media and easily identifiable subjects—as such, *pop art* is an apt description. *Gothic* (A) is an architectural style characterized by narrow spires and heavier buttresses. *Impressionism* (D) uses paints to mute the work; famous impressionists include Monet and Manet. As for (B), *cubism* is characterized by distorted and abstract depictions of the world—objects are not likely to be easily identifiable. Examples of cubist artists include Picasso and Braque.

78. A

The primary focus of this question is Objective 0018:

Analyze and interpret written materials from a variety of sources

Once again, you need only to consider the information provided. The passage says that Warhol understood "mass media," "painted subjects easily identifiable with [the] culture," and made his subjects "larger than life." The dollar bill is important to all Americans and is a highly recognizable object. It can certainly be made to seem larger than life. Whereas the White House (B) is easily identifiable, it isn't an object of mass consumption and cannot be painted larger than life. A landscape (C) cannot be painted larger than life, either, and besides, landscapes aren't generally thought of as popular culture. Finally, flowers (D) can be painted larger than life, but no specific flower is easily identifiable with American popular culture.

79. C

The primary focus of this question is Objective 0010:

Understand and apply skills, principles, and procedures associated with inquiry, problem solving, and decision making in history and the social sciences.

Where is an autobiography most likely to differ from a third-person account of a life? In the subjectivity of the author, choice (C). A third-person life history is usually more reliable as an objective account of events. Choice (A), wordiness, is a problem that could affect biographers as well as autobiographers. Choice (B), creativity, is not necessarily a liability. You may read too much into this answer choice and think of it as "lying." Remember to read only what is given. Choice (D) is an asset for research, not a liability, and is expected more of a biographer than an autobiographer.

80. B

The primary focus of this question is Objective 0010:

Understand and apply skills, principles, and procedures associated with inquiry, problem solving, and decision making in history and the social sciences.

Remember on EXCEPT questions that you are looking for the one answer choice that does NOT apply. In this question about map projections, choice (B) is the exception. Map projections are NOT the most accurate representations of the surface of the Earth. A globe or some other three-dimensional object would be more accurate. Note that map projections are flat; they create distortions due to their attempt to represent three dimensions in a two-dimensional map, and they frequently use grid lines of longitude and latitude.

SCORING YOUR WRITTEN ASSIGNMENT

The official LAST scorers will evaluate your written assignment using the following performance characteristics as guide.

Focus and Unity	Did you comprehend the writing topic and focus your writing on that controlling topic?
Appropriateness	Did you select and use a strategy of expression appropriate for the intended audience and purpose?
Reason and Organization	Does your response present a reasoned, organized argument or exposition?
Support and Development	Did you use support and evidence to develop and bolster your own ideas and account for the views of others?
Structure and Conventions	Did you express yourself clearly in the response, without distractions caused by inattention to sentence and paragraph structure, choice and use of words, and mechanics (i.e., spelling, punctuation, and capitalization)?

LAST Written Assignment Scoring Scale

The written assignment is scored according to the following scale:

Score Point	Score Point Description

4   **The "4" response gives evidence of strong skills of written expression.**

- The writer clearly addresses the stated task states or strongly implies a purpose for writing and a controlling topic, and maintains a steady focus on that topic.

- The chosen expressive approach is consistent with the writer's purpose and audience.

- Opinions are presented clearly, and arguments and/or expositions are well organized and ably reasoned.

- The writer offers relevant evidence and details to develop and support the position taken, showing awareness of other potential or actual positions.

- The response is free of distracting flaws in sentence structure (e.g., subject-verb disagreements, run-on sentences) and paragraph structure (e.g., lack of paragraph breaks to coincide with thought transitions), shows proficient use and choice of words, and avoids disruptive mechanical errors (e.g., inappropriate capitalization, misspellings of common words).

3   **The "3" response gives evidence of satisfactory skills of written expression.**

- The writer addresses the stated task, states or at least implies a purpose for writing and a controlling topic, and generally maintains a focus on that topic, with few digressions or extraneous points.

- The chosen expressive approach is generally consistent with the writer's purpose and audience.

- Opinions are presented clearly, and arguments and/or expositions give evidence of organization and reason, although some minor flaws in these areas may be present.

- The writer offers evidence and details to develop and support the position taken and generally acknowledges other potential or actual positions.

Score Point	Score Point Description
	• The response contains very few distracting flaws in sentence structure and/or paragraph structure, shows generally competent use and choice of words, and avoids most disruptive mechanical errors.
2	**The "2" response gives evidence of limited skill in written expression.**
	• The writer attempts to address the stated task but does so incompletely, and the purpose for writing and the topic may be unclear. The focus on the topic may not be consistently maintained, and several digressions may be present.
	• The chosen expressive approach may be partially inconsistent with the writer's purpose and audience.
	• Opinions may not be presented clearly, and arguments and/or expositions may give little evidence of organization and reason.
	• Little or no evidence or detail may be provided to develop and support positions, and the existence of other potential or actual positions may not be recognized.
	• The response may contain distracting flaws in sentence structure and/or paragraph structure, inappropriate use and choice of words, and disruptive mechanical errors.
1	**The "1" response gives evidence of a lack of skill in written expression.**
	• The writer may attempt to address the stated task but does so incompletely, and the purpose for writing and the topic are generally unclear.
	• There is little or no sense of intended audience.
	• Opinions may not be presented clearly or may simply be asserted without support, elaboration, or detail.
	• If arguments and/or expositions are present, they give little or no evidence of organization or reason. The existence of other potential or actual positions is generally not recognized.
	• The response usually contains distracting flaws in sentence structure and/or paragraph structure, inappropriate use and choice of words, and disruptive mechanical errors that interfere with understanding.

Practice LAST Written Assignment Sample Response

> Prompt: There has been much research and evidence presented that schools are not providing an equal education for boys and girls. Among other things, it has been shown that teachers call on boys more often, allow boys to call out answers while requiring girls to raise their hands, allow boys more time to respond to questions, and give boys more feedback.
>
> You do not need to agree or disagree with the above statements, but present examples of both sides of the issue (equal versus unequal treatment of girls and boys) and state examples of things teachers can do to alter this situation.

What follows is an example of a strong response to the written assignment on the practice test.

In my 16 years as a student in the public schools, I have witnessed education favoring boys at certain times and girls at other times. This has been true from elementary school through college. I will give an example at each level: elementary school, high school, and college.

In elementary school, we were divided into reading groups. The high group was always mostly girls. Once you were put into a group (high, medium, or low), you were almost never moved, so it was difficult for boys to achieve the high group. Boys were often more active in elementary school, so they would get into trouble for being loud or getting out of their seats.

In high school, it seemed that the education had pretty much evened out. I went to a school where girls were encouraged to take math and science courses, though there were more boys in chemistry, physics, and precalculus. When we did group work, the girls talked a lot but didn't usually get into trouble. The teacher probably thought they were talking about the project. Boys got into trouble for talking, because they usually yelled across the room. Sometimes the girls didn't get to participate as much in class because boys called out answers, and the teachers accepted them. If a girl tried to just call out an answer, she was usually told to hush and raise her hand.

In college, I am majoring in elementary education, and there are very few men in the program. It is hard to say if this is unequal. Were they discouraged from going into elementary education because the little kids are for women and the high school content areas are for men? It is hard for me to say if this is true, but it seems a likely idea. Elementary schools need more male teachers so the reading groups even out and the boisterous boys don't lose their playfulness. It might even help some girls find their inner playfulness.

In summary, based on my experiences, I believe there have been unequal opportunities for boys and girls in school. My hope, though, is that in the end it all evens out, and everyone has gained equal knowledge.

THE ATS–W

CHAPTER 9: WHAT YOU NEED TO KNOW: THE ATS-W OBJECTIVES

The ATS-W is designed to measure proficiency in four subareas: Knowledge of the Learner, Instructional Planning and Assessment, Instructional Delivery, and the Professional Environment. Each subarea is defined by a set of objectives. These objectives provide specific information about the pedagogical knowledge and skills that teachers need to teach effectively the approved curriculum in New York State public schools. Focus statements providing examples of the range, type, and level of content that may appear on the test further define each objective.

THE ATS-W OBJECTIVES AND ONLINE REVIEW GUIDE

Test items on the ATS-W are designed to measure specific test objectives. The number of objectives within a given subarea generally determines the number of items that will address the content of that subarea on the test. Thus, the subareas with more objectives will receive more emphasis on the test and in the scoring process than those with fewer objectives. A listing of the ATS-W subareas, objectives, and focus statements follows. In addition, included with each Objective is an online review to guide you to current information from experts in each field that will be assessed on the test. Be sure to take a look at these helpful Web resources to target the specified ATS-W content areas. You may also want to check out Kaplan's website (kaptest. com/education/) for additions or updates to our Internet resource guide (click on the NYSTCE tab to access test-specific resources and study guides).

SUBAREA I—STUDENT DEVELOPMENT AND LEARNING

0001 Understand human development, including developmental processes and variations, and use this understanding to promote student development and learning. For example:

Elementary only:

- Demonstrating knowledge of the major concepts, principles, and theories of human development (physical, cognitive, linguistic, social, emotional, and moral) as related to children from birth to Grade 6

- Identifying sequences (milestones) and variations of physical, cognitive, linguistic, social, emotional, and moral development in children from birth to Grade 6

- Recognizing the range of individual developmental differences in children within any given age group from birth to Grade 6 and the implications of this developmental variation for instructional decision making

- Identifying ways in which a child's development in one domain (physical, cognitive, linguistic, social, emotional, moral) may affect learning and development in other domains

- Applying knowledge of developmental characteristics of learners from birth to Grade 6 to evaluate alternative instructional goals and plans

- Selecting appropriate instructional strategies, approaches, and delivery systems to promote development in given learners from birth to Grade 6

Secondary only:

- Demonstrating knowledge of the major concepts, principles, and theories of human development (physical, cognitive, linguistic, social, emotional, and moral) as related to young adolescents and adolescents (i.e., as related to students in Grades 5 to 12)

- Identifying sequences (milestones) and variations of physical, cognitive, linguistic, social, emotional, and moral development of young adolescents and adolescents

- Recognizing the range of individual developmental differences in students within any given age group in Grades 5 to 12 and the implications of this developmental variation for instructional decision making

- Identifying ways in which a young adolescent's or adolescent's development in one domain (physical, cognitive, linguistic, social, emotional, moral) may affect learning and development in other domains

- Applying knowledge of developmental characteristics of young adolescents and adolescents to evaluate alternative instructional goals and plans

- Selecting appropriate instructional strategies, approaches, and delivery systems to promote young adolescents' and adolescents' development and learning

Topic	URL	Annotation
Cognitive development	www.edpsycinteractive.org/topics/cogsys/piaget.html	Describes the theory, processes, and stages of cognitive development. Areas of focus include attention, memory, conceptual knowledge and its formation, learning, reasoning, decision making, problem solving, executive functioning, principles and mechanisms of development, intelligence, action, and motor control.
Developmental characteristics	http://childdevelopmentinfo.com/development/devsequence.shtml	Provides a comprehensive list of the developmental characteristics and stages displayed by many children.
General development	www.childdevelopmentinfo.com/development/	Provides information on physical, mental, and emotional growth and development in children and teenagers. Also provides resources on how to help children and adolescents reach their full potential as they grow and develop.
Affective development	www.nichd.nih.gov/about/org/crmc/cdb/index.cfm	Provides studies of personality, temperament, emotion, and motivation (particularly achievement, school-related, pro- and antisocial) and the relationship among these domains.
Instructional strategies	www.sabine.k12.la.us/vrschool/instructstrat.htm	Provides a comprehensive listing and explanation of instructional strategies.

0002 Understand learning processes and use this understanding to promote student development and learning. For example:

- Analyzing ways in which development and learning processes interact

- Analyzing processes by which students construct meaning and develop skills and applying strategies to facilitate learning in given situations (e.g., by building connections between new information and prior knowledge; by relating learning to world issues and community concerns; by engaging students in purposeful practice and application of knowledge and skills; by using tools, materials, and resources)

- Demonstrating knowledge of different types of learning strategies (e.g., rehearsal, elaboration, organization, metacognition) and how learners use each type of strategy

- Analyzing factors that affect students' learning (e.g., learning styles, contextually supported learning versus decontextualized learning) and adapting instructional practices to promote learning in given situations

- Recognizing how various teacher roles (e.g., direct instructor, facilitator) and student roles (e.g., self-directed learner, group participant, passive observer) may affect learning processes and outcomes

- Recognizing effective strategies for promoting independent thinking and learning (e.g., by helping students develop critical-thinking, decision-making, and problem-solving skills; by enabling students to pursue topics of personal interest) and for promoting students' sense of ownership and responsibility in relation to their own learning

Topic	URL	Annotation
Constructivist learning	www.ncrel.org/sdrs/areas/ issues/content/cntareas/ science/sc5model.htm	The key notion in constructivist theory is that people learn best by actively constructing their own understanding.
Prior knowledge	www.ncrel.org/sdrs/areas/ issues/students/learning/ lr100.htm	When teachers link new information to the student's prior knowledge, they activate the student's interest and curiosity and infuse instruction with a sense of purpose.

Topic	URL	Annotation
Student role in learning	http://oregonstate.edu/instruct/pte/theory/studrole.htm	Students who are engaged in their own learning often assume roles of the explorer, the cognitive apprentice, teacher, producers of knowledge, and self-directed managers of their own learning.
Teacher as facilitator	www.infed.org/thinkers/et-rogers.htm	The role of the teacher is to act as a facilitator, guide, and co-learner. As a facilitator, the teacher creates an environment in which students do authentic tasks and collaborate. This site contains information on Carl Rogers, the father of this theory.
Multiple intelligences	www.thomasarmstrong.com/multiple_intelligences.htm	Dr. Howard Gardner, of the Harvard Graduate School of Education, has developed a theory of multiple intelligences that suggests that people have different "intelligences," or areas of strength. Through a working knowledge of students' learning styles and "intelligences," teachers are better able to tailor lessons and activities to bring out an individual student's potential.
Bloom's taxonomy	http://faculty.washington.edu/~krumme/guides/bloom.html	In 1956, Benjamin Bloom headed a group of educational psychologists who developed a classification of levels of intellectual behavior important in learning.

0003 Understand how factors in the home, school, and community may affect students' development and readiness to learn and use this understanding to create a classroom environment within which all students can develop and learn. For example:

- Recognizing the impact of sociocultural factors (e.g., culture, heritage, language, socioeconomic profile) in the home, school, and community on students' development and learning

- Analyzing ways in which students' personal health, safety, nutrition, and past or present exposure to abusive or dangerous environments may affect their development and learning in various domains (e.g., physical, cognitive, linguistic, social, emotional, moral) and their readiness to learn

- Recognizing the significance of family life and the home environment for student development and learning (e.g., nature of the expectations of parents, guardians, and caregivers; degree of their involvement in the student's education)

- Analyzing how schoolwide structures (e.g., tracking) and classroom factors (e.g., homogeneous versus heterogeneous grouping, student-teacher interactions) may affect students' self-concept and learning

- Identifying effective strategies for creating a classroom environment that promotes student development and learning by taking advantage of positive factors (e.g., culture, heritage, language) in the home, school, and community and minimizing the effects of negative factors (e.g., minimal family support)

- Analyzing ways in which peer interactions (e.g., acceptance versus isolation, bullying) may promote or hinder a student's development and success in school and determining effective strategies for dealing with peer-related issues in given classroom situations

- Demonstrating knowledge of health, sexuality, and peer-related issues for students (e.g., self-image, physical appearance and fitness, peer-group conformity) and the interrelated nature of these issues and recognizing how specific behaviors related to health, sexuality, and peer issues (e.g., eating disorders, drug and alcohol use, gang involvement) can affect development and learning

Topic	URL	Annotation
Sociocultural issues	www.ncrel.org/sdrs/areas/ issues/students/earlycld/ ea700.htm	Comprehensive website provides resources on promoting children's readiness to learn.
Preventing and managing challenging classroom situations	www.worcester.edu/ Currents/Archives/ Volume_1_Number_2/ CurrentsV1N2WingertP4.pdf	This is a basic toolkit of strategies and resources to support and to improve the overall teaching and learning environment.
Peer pressure	www.cedu.niu.edu/ ~shumow/itt/doc/ PeerPressure.pdf	"Teacher's Guide to Peer Pressure"

0004 Understand language and literacy development and use this knowledge in all content areas to develop the listening, speaking, reading, and writing skills of students, including students for whom English is not their primary language. For example:

- Identifying factors that influence language acquisition and analyzing ways students' language skills affect their overall development and learning

- Identifying expected stages and patterns of second-language acquisition, including analyzing factors that affect second-language acquisition

- Identifying approaches that are effective in promoting English language learners' development of English language proficiency, including adapting teaching strategies and consulting and collaborating with teachers in the ESL program

- Recognizing the role of oral language development, including vocabulary development, and the role of the alphabetic principle, including phonemic awareness and other phonological skills, in the development of English literacy and identifying expected stages and patterns in English literacy development

- Identifying factors that influence students' literacy development and demonstrating knowledge of research-validated instructional strategies for addressing the literacy needs of students at all stages of literacy development, including applying strategies for facilitating students' comprehension of texts before, during, and after reading, and using modeling and explicit instruction to teach students how to use comprehension strategies effectively

- Recognizing similarities and differences between the English literacy development of native English speakers and English language learners, including how literacy development in the primary language influences literacy development in English, and applying strategies for helping English language learners transfer literacy skills in the primary language to English

- Using knowledge of literacy development to select instructional strategies that help students use literacy skills as tools for learning; that teach students how to use, access, and evaluate information from various resources; and that support students' development of content-area reading skills

Topic	URL	Annotation
ESL teacher resources	http://owl.english.purdue.edu/owl/resource/586/1/	Lists theoretical and practical professional resources. The list includes links to organizations and journals of interest to language teachers and language policy developers, as well as to a selection of online teaching and reference materials. Each of these links is a portal to an extensive collection of further resources for the professional ESL community.
Second language acquisition	www.everythingesl.net/inservices/language_stages.php	Informative article discusses the stages of second language acquisition.
English as a second language (ESL)	http://everythingesl.net	Great website for K–12 ESL/EFL educators features staff development ideas, content-based lesson plans, downloadable activities, tips on classroom resources, interactive discussion boards, and more.

0005 Understand diverse student populations and use knowledge of diversity within the school and the community to address the needs of all learners, to create a sense of community among students, and to promote students' appreciation of and respect for individuals and groups. For example:

- Recognizing appropriate strategies for teachers to use to enhance their own understanding of students (e.g., learning about students' family situations, cultural backgrounds, individual needs) and to promote a sense of community among diverse groups in the classroom

- Applying strategies for working effectively with students from all cultures, students of both genders, students from various socioeconomic circumstances, students from homes where English is not the primary language, and students whose home situations involve various family arrangements and lifestyles

- Applying strategies for promoting students' understanding and appreciation of diversity and for using diversity that exists within the classroom and the community to enhance all students' learning

- Analyzing how classroom environments that respect diversity promote positive student experiences

Topic	URL	Annotation
Teaching diversity	http://teacher.scholastic.com/professional/teachdive/manylanguages.htm	Provides suggestions and strategies for teaching children about racial, cultural, and linguistic diversity and how to live and work together respectfully.
Diversity in the classroom	www.indiana.edu/~icy/diversity.html	Gives teaching tips on inclusion and diversity.
Gifted children	www.ri.net/gifted_talented/character.html	Lists characteristics and behaviors of gifted children.
Diverse classroom environments	http://cte.tamu.edu/documents/tt.teach_cultural_diverse_class.pdf	Discusses the learning styles of international students.

0006 Understand the characteristics and needs of students with disabilities, developmental delays, and exceptional abilities (including gifted and talented students) and use this knowledge to help students reach their highest levels of achievement and independence. For example:

- Demonstrating awareness of types of disabilities, developmental delays, and exceptional abilities and of the implications for learning associated with these differences

- Applying criteria and procedures for evaluating, selecting, creating, and modifying materials and equipment to address individual special needs and recognizing the importance of consulting with specialists to identify appropriate materials and equipment, including assistive technology, when working with students with disabilities, developmental delays, or exceptional abilities

- Identifying teacher responsibilities and requirements associated with referring students who may have special needs and with developing and implementing Individualized Education Plans (IEPs) and recognizing appropriate ways to integrate goals from IEPs into instructional activities and daily routines

- Demonstrating knowledge of basic service delivery models (e.g., inclusion models) for students with special needs and identifying strategies and resources (e.g., special education staff) that help support instruction in inclusive settings

- Demonstrating knowledge of strategies to ensure that students with special needs and exceptional abilities are an integral part of the class and participate to the greatest extent possible in all classroom activities

Topic	URL	Annotation
Types of disabilities	www.irsc.org	Directory includes different types of physical and mental disabilities.
Characteristics of learning disabilities	www.kidsource.com/NICHCY/ learning_disabilities.html	General resource website features basic facts and information about learning disabilities.

Topic	URL	Annotation
Resources on disabilities	http://ericec.org	Find here FAQs, information, and resources from the ERIC Clearinghouse on Disabilities and Gifted Education.
Developmental delays	www.keepkidshealthy. com/welcome/conditions/ developmentaldelays.html	Developmental milestones are determined by the average age at which children attain each skill. About 3% of children will not meet them on time but will eventually develop normally over time, although a little later than expected. Early identification and screening of children with developmental disabilities leads to effective therapy of conditions for which treatment is available.
Exceptional children	www.cec.sped.org/index.html	The Council for Exceptional Children (CEC) is the largest international professional organization dedicated to improving educational outcomes for individuals with exceptionalities, students with disabilities, and/or the gifted.
Evaluating, selecting, and modifying materials and equipment	www.cast.org/ncac/	CAST has established a National Center on Accessing the General Curriculum to provide a vision of how new curricula, teaching practices, and policies can be woven together to create practical approaches for improved access to the general curriculum by students with disabilities.

Topic	URL	Annotation
Assistive technology	www.abledata.com	Documents how educators can effectively use assistive technology, a range of "supplementary aids and services," to educate students with disabilities with their nondisabled peers.
Individualized Education Plans (IEPs)	http://kidshealth.org/parent/ positive/learning/iep.html	Students with disabilities are the most likely to need an Individualized Education Plan. A diverse team of professionals creates the plan, which can later be revised and edited as needed.
Individualized Family Service Plans (IFSPs)	www.health.state.ny.us/nysdoh/ child/english/step4.htm	Children in New York State are eligible for the Early Intervention Program if they are under three years old *and* have a disability *or* developmental delay. An IFSP is a written plan for early intervention services.
Classroom strategies for children with special needs	www.educationworld. com/a_curr/curr139.shtml	This is a compilation of online resources is devoted to the education of children with special needs.
Inclusion classrooms	www.associatedcontent.com/ article/66531/inclusion_in_the_ classroom_the_teaching.html	Provides a breakdown of the five methods used in a full-inclusion classroom.

SUBAREA II—INSTRUCTION AND ASSESSMENT

0007 Understand how to structure and manage a classroom to create a safe, healthy, and secure learning environment. For example:

- Analyzing relationships between classroom management strategies (e.g., in relation to discipline, student decision making, establishing and maintaining standards of behavior) and student learning, attitudes, and behaviors

- Recognizing issues related to the creation of a classroom climate (e.g., with regard to shared values and goals, shared experiences, patterns of communication)

- Demonstrating knowledge of basic socialization strategies, including how to support social interaction and facilitate conflict resolution among learners, and applying strategies for instructing students on the principles of honesty, personal responsibility, respect for others, observance of laws and rules, courtesy, dignity, and other traits that will enhance the quality of their experiences in, and contributions to, the class and the greater community

- Organizing a daily schedule that takes into consideration and capitalizes on the developmental characteristics of learners

- Evaluating, selecting, and using various methods for managing transitions (e.g., between lessons, when students enter and leave the classroom) and handling routine classroom tasks and unanticipated situations

- Analyzing the effects of the physical environment, including different spatial arrangements, on student learning and behavior

Topic	URL	Annotation
Discipline	www.ascd.org	Eleven techniques can be used in the classroom to help achieve effective group management and control.
Behaviors	www.disciplinehelp.com	Index of student behaviors includes a description of each behavior, its effects, and common mistakes that may perpetuate the problem.

Topic	URL	Annotation
Classroom transitions	www.cpin.us/docs/classroomtransitions.doc	Describes how to manage student transitions successfully.
Classroom spatial arrangement	www.designshare.com/Research/BrainBasedLearn98.htm	Schools that incorporate specific design principles in their learning environments have the flexibility to accommodate a wide array of learning styles.

0008 Understand curriculum development and apply knowledge of factors and processes in curricular decision making. For example:

- Applying procedures used in classroom curricular decision making (e.g., evaluating the current curriculum, defining scope and sequence)

- Evaluating curriculum materials and resources for their effectiveness in addressing the developmental and learning needs of given students

- Applying strategies for modifying curriculum based on learner characteristics

- Applying strategies for integrating curricula (e.g., incorporating interdisciplinary themes)

Topic	URL	Annotation
NYS curriculum resources	www.emsc.nysed.gov/ciai/pub.html	Website contains New York State learning standards and resource guides with core curriculums.
Scope and sequence	http://schools.nyc.gov/Teachers/QuickLinks/scopesequence.htm	Resource page details the length of time spent on each classroom unit.
Interdisciplinary themes	www.thirteen.org/edonline/concept2class/interdisciplinary/index.html	This is an online workshop on interdisciplinary learning in the classroom

0009 Understand the interrelationship between assessment and instruction and how to use formal and informal assessment to learn about students, plan instruction, monitor student understanding in the context of instruction, and make effective instructional modifications. For example:

- Demonstrating understanding that assessment and instruction must be closely integrated

- Demonstrating familiarity with basic assessment approaches, including the instructional advantages and limitations of various assessment instruments and techniques (e.g., portfolio, teacher-designed classroom test, performance assessment, peer assessment, student self-assessment, teacher observation, criterion-referenced test, norm-referenced test)

- Using knowledge of the different purposes (e.g., screening, diagnosing, comparing, monitoring) of various assessments and knowledge of assessment concepts (e.g., validity, reliability, bias) to select the most appropriate assessment instrument or technique for a given situation

- Using rubrics and interpreting and using information derived from a given assessment

- Recognizing strategies for planning, adjusting, or modifying lessons and activities based on assessment results

Topic	URL	Annotation
Portfolios	www.ed.gov/pubs/OR/ ConsumerGuides/classuse.html	Portfolios enable children to participate in assessing their own work, help teachers keep track of an individual child's progress, and provide a basis for evaluating the quality of children's overall performance.
Performance assessment	www.eduplace.com/rdg/res/ litass/auth.html	Performance assessment, also known as alternative or authentic assessment, is a form of testing that requires students to perform a task rather than select an answer from a ready-made list.

Topic	URL	Annotation
Informal and formal assessment techniques	http://teacher.scholastic.com/ professional/assessment/ studentprogress.htm	Interview with assessment expert, Grant Wiggins, discusses important questions about measuring student progress.
Achievement tests	http://epaa.asu.edu/epaa/ v8n46.html	Analyzes the merits of using achievement tests to judge school quality.
Standardized tests	www.kidsource.com/kidsource/ content2/talking.assessment. k12.4.html	Answers questions about the how, what, and why of standardized tests.
Appropriate assessment instruments	www.nclrc.org/essentials/ assessing/alternative.htm	The challenge for educators is to determine what forms of alternative assessment are most useful for what purposes and how to evaluate the quality of the measures.

0010 Understand instructional planning and apply knowledge of planning processes to design effective instruction that promotes the learning of all students. For example:

- Recognizing key factors to consider in planning instruction (e.g., New York State Learning Standards for students, instructional goals and strategies, the nature of the content and/or skills to be taught, students' characteristics and prior experiences, students' current knowledge and skills as determined by assessment results, available time and other resources)

- Analyzing and applying given information about specific planning factors (see above statement) to define lesson and unit objectives, select appropriate instructional approach(es) to use in a given lesson (e.g., discovery learning, explicit instruction), determine the appropriate sequence of instruction/learning for given content or learners within a lesson and unit, and develop specific lesson and unit plans

- Identifying the background knowledge and prerequisite skills required by a given lesson and applying strategies for determining students' readiness for learning (e.g., through teacher observation, student self-assessment, pretesting)

and for ensuring students' success in learning (e.g., by planning sufficient time to preteach key concepts or vocabulary, by planning differentiated instruction)

- Using assessment information before, during, and after instruction to modify plans and to adapt instruction for individual learners

- Analyzing a given lesson or unit plan in terms of organization, completeness, feasibility, etc.

- Applying strategies for collaborating with others to plan and implement instruction

Topic	URL	Annotation
Developing lesson plans	www.adprima.com/lesson.htm	Provides information on the importance of lesson plans and how to build them effectively.

0011 Understand various instructional approaches and use this knowledge to facilitate student learning. For example:

- Analyzing the uses, benefits, or limitations of a specific instructional approach (e.g., direct instruction, cooperative learning, interdisciplinary instruction, exploration, discovery learning, independent study, lectures, hands-on activities, peer tutoring, technology-based approach, various discussion methods such as guided discussion, various questioning methods) in relation to given purposes and learners

- Recognizing appropriate strategies for varying the role of the teacher (e.g., working with students as instructor, facilitator, observer; working with other adults in the classroom) in relation to the situation and the instructional approach used

- Applying procedures for promoting positive and productive small-group interactions (e.g., establishing rules for working with other students in cooperative learning situations)

- Comparing instructional approaches in terms of teacher and student responsibilities, expected student outcomes, usefulness for achieving instructional purposes, etc.

0012 Understand principles and procedures for organizing and implementing lessons and use this knowledge to promote student learning and achievement. For example:

- Evaluating strengths and weaknesses of various strategies for organizing and implementing a given lesson (e.g., in relation to introducing and closing a lesson, using inductive and deductive instruction, building on students' prior knowledge and experiences)

- Recognizing the importance of organizing instruction to include multiple strategies for teaching the same content so as to provide the kind and amount of instruction/practice needed by each student in the class

- Evaluating various instructional resources (e.g., textbooks and other print resources, primary documents or artifacts, guest speakers, films and other audiovisual materials, computers and other technological resources) in relation to given content, learners (including those with special needs), and goals

- Demonstrating understanding of the developmental characteristics of students (e.g., with regard to attention and focus, writing or reading for extended periods of time) when organizing and implementing lessons

- Applying strategies for adjusting lessons in response to student performance and student feedback (e.g., responding to student comments regarding relevant personal experiences, changing the pace of a lesson as appropriate)

Topic	URL	Annotation
Cooperative learning	www.co-operation.org	Cooperative learning encourages small groups of mixed-ability students to work together to reach a common goal. Students must work together as an interdependent team to construct knowledge.

Topic	URL	Annotation
Direct instruction	www.jefflindsay.com/EducData.shtml	A theory of instruction claims that learning can be greatly accelerated in any endeavor if instructional presentations are clear and rule out likely misinterpretations while facilitating generalizations. The instructional programs and lessons developed are carefully scripted and tightly sequenced.
Instructional methods	www.adprima.com/teachmeth.htm	This site compares various methods to help teachers select an instructional method that best fits one's particular teaching style and the lesson situation.
Inquiry-based teaching	www.thirteen.org/edonline/concept2class/inquiry/	This workshop covers inquiry-based teaching and learning.
Critical thinking skills	www.edpsycinteractive.org/topics/cogsys/critthnk.html	Critical thinking skills figure prominently among the goals for education. This article presents a useful model of critical thinking.
Peer tutoring	www.ericdigests.org/1994/peer.htm	Research on peer tutoring indicates that the intervention is relatively effective in improving both tutees' and tutors' academic and social development.
Technology-based instruction	http://learnweb.harvard.edu/ent/home/index.cfm	Education with New Technologies (ENT) is a networked community designed to help educators teach for understanding through the effective use of computers, the Internet, and other interactive tools. This website offers access to thoughtful colleagues, detailed examples of technology-enhanced education, and a valuable collection of online resources.

0013 Understand the relationship between student motivation and achievement and how motivational principles and practices can be used to promote and sustain student cooperation in learning. For example:

- Distinguishing between motivational strategies that use intrinsic and extrinsic rewards and identifying the likely benefits and limitations of each approach

- Analyzing the effects of using various intrinsic and extrinsic motivational strategies in given situations

- Recognizing factors (e.g., expectations, methods of providing specific feedback) and situations that tend to promote or diminish student motivation

- Recognizing the relationship between direct engagement in learning and students' interest in lessons/activities

- Applying procedures for enhancing student interest and helping students find their own motivation (e.g., relating concepts presented in the classroom to students' everyday experiences; encouraging students to ask questions, initiate activities, and pursue problems that are meaningful to them; highlighting connections between academic learning and the workplace)

- Recognizing the importance of utilizing play to benefit young children's learning (elementary only)

- Recognizing the importance of encouragement in sustaining students' interest and cooperation in learning

- Recognizing the importance of utilizing peers (e.g., as peer mentors, in group activities) to benefit students' learning and to sustain their interest and cooperation

Topic	URL	Annotation
Enhancing student motivation	www.engines4ed.org/ hyperbook/nodes/NODE-62-pg. html	Student motivation is crucial to learning. Although the focus of much of a student's motivation is beyond a teacher's control, there is much that teachers can do to influence the motivation of students
Active engagement in learning	www.ncrel.org/sdrs/ areas/issues/content/cntareas/ math/ma2lindi.htm	Indicators of engaged learning have been excerpted and summarized from "Designing Learning and Technology for Educational Reform."
Motivation factors, intrinsic/extrinsic strategies	www.kidsource.com/kidsource/ content2/Student_Motivatation. html	Awareness of students' attitudes and beliefs about learning and what facilitates learning can assist educators in reducing student apathy.

0014 Understand communication practices that are effective in promoting student learning and creating a climate of trust and support in the classroom and how to use a variety of communication modes to support instruction. For example:

- Analyzing how cultural, gender, and age differences affect communication in the classroom (e.g., eye contact, use of colloquialisms, interpretation of body language) and recognizing effective methods for enhancing communication with all students, including being a thoughtful and responsive listener

- Applying strategies to promote effective classroom interactions that support learning, including teacher-student and student-student interactions

- Analyzing teacher-student interactions with regard to communication issues (e.g., those related to communicating expectations, providing feedback, building student self-esteem, modeling appropriate communication techniques for specific situations)

- Recognizing purposes for questioning (e.g., encouraging risk taking and problem solving, maintaining student engagement, facilitating factual recall, assessing student understanding) and selecting appropriate questioning techniques

KAPLAN

- Applying strategies for adjusting communication to enhance student understanding (e.g., by providing examples, simplifying a complex problem, using verbal and nonverbal modes of communication, using audiovisual and technological tools of communication)

- Demonstrating knowledge of the limits of verbal understanding of students at various ages and with different linguistic backgrounds and strategies for ensuring that these limitations do not become barriers to learning (e.g., by linking to known language; by saying things in more than one way; by supporting verbalization with gestures, physical demonstrations, dramatizations, and/or media and manipulatives)

Topic	URL	Annotation
Gender differences in communication	www.umm.maine.edu/ resources/beharchive/ bexstudents/MarkTripp/ mt320.html	Examines research literature related to how the genders are perceived to express themselves differently in the form of communications.
Classroom interactions	http://classobservation. com/docs/research_papers/ CLASS_PolicyBrief_single.pdf	Describesh how to create effective teacher/student interactions.
Questioning techniques	www.grrec.ky.gov/ MathAlliance/Questioning% 20Techniques%20For%20 the%20Classroom.pdf	Gives a brief run-down of questioning techniques.
Nonverbal communication in the classroom	http://honolulu.hawaii. edu/intranet/committees/ FacDevCom/guidebk/ teachtip/commun-1.htm	Discusses six ways to improve your nonverbal communications.

0015 Understand uses of technology, including instructional and assistive technology, in teaching and learning and apply this knowledge to use technology effectively and to teach students how to use technology to enhance their learning. For example:

- Demonstrating knowledge of educational uses of various technology tools, such as calculators, software applications, input devices (e.g., keyboard, mouse, scanner, modem, CD-ROM), and the Internet

- Recognizing purposes and uses of common types of assistive technology (e.g., amplification devices, communication boards)

- Recognizing issues related to the appropriate use of technology (e.g., privacy issues, security issues, copyright laws and issues, ethical issues regarding the acquisition and use of information from technology resources) and identifying procedures that ensure the legal and ethical use of technology resources

- Identifying and addressing equity issues related to the use of technology in the classroom (e.g., equal access to technology for all students)

- Identifying effective instructional uses of current technology in relation to communication (e.g., audio and visual recording and display devices)

- Applying strategies for helping students acquire, analyze, and evaluate electronic information (e.g., locating specific information on the Internet and verifying its accuracy and validity)

- Evaluating students' technologically produced products using established criteria related to content, delivery, and the objective(s) of the assignment

Topic	URL	Annotation
Technology in education	www.newhorizons.org/ strategies/technology/ front_tech.htm	Find here a number of informative articles on technology in education.
Assistive technology	http://atto.buffalo.edu/ registered/ATBasics/Foundation/ intro/index.php	Online learning module provides an overview of assistive technology.

SUBAREA III—THE PROFESSIONAL ENVIRONMENT

0016 Understand the history, philosophy, and role of education in New York State and the broader society. For example:

- Analyzing relationships between education and society (e.g., schools reflecting and affecting social values, historical dimensions of the school-society relationship, the role of education in a democratic society, the role of education in promoting equity in society)

- Demonstrating knowledge of the historical foundations of education in the United States and of past and current philosophical issues in education (e.g., teacher-directed versus child-centered instruction)

- Applying procedures for working collaboratively and cooperatively with various members of the New York State educational system to accomplish a variety of educational goals

- Analyzing differences between school-based and centralized models of decision making

- Applying knowledge of the roles and responsibilities of different components of the education system in New York (e.g., local school boards, Board of Regents, district superintendents, school principals, Boards of Cooperative Educational Services [BOCES], higher education, unions, professional organizations, parent organizations)

Topic	URL	Annotation
Board of Regents	www.regents.nysed.gov/about/	Introduces the Board of Regents and their responsibilities as supervisors of all educational activities within the state.
Urban school superintendents	www.cgcs.org/Pubs/Urban_Indicator_08-09.pdf	"Urban School Superintendents: Characteristics, Tenure, and Salary; Sixth Survey and Report"

Topic	URL	Annotation
District superintendents	www.emsc.nysed.gov/irts/ chapter655/2003/home.html	Gives information about public school districts based on geographical, political, and employment characteristics of counties.
Superintendents of schools	www.superintendentofschools. com	This resource for superintendents in New York State outlines the challenges that face superintendents and the common mistakes made by superintendents.
Board of Cooperative Educational Services (BOCES)	www.nassauboces.org	BOCES offers services to students and adults in local school districts that would be too costly or ineffective to provide individually.
Higher Education: Bank Street College	www.bankstreet.edu	Since its beginning in 1916, Bank Street College of Education has been a leader in education, a pioneer in improving the quality of classroom education, and an advocate for children and families.
City University of New York (CUNY)	www.cuny.edu	The City University of New York (CUNY) is the largest urban university in the United States. Some 200,000 students are enrolled for degrees on 20 campuses in all five boroughs of New York City. Another 150,000 students take adult and continuing education courses.

Topic	URL	Annotation
New York University (NYU)	http://steinhardt.nyu.edu	NYU's School of Education is a professional school with a wide range of both undergraduate and graduate programs. It is a center for research and community service, committed to activities aimed at improving the urban environment. The school also serves as a source of continuing education for working professionals who seek career advancement and enrichment.
State University of New York (SUNY)	www.suny.edu	SUNY is a unified public university in New York State. A statewide system of 64 campuses enrolling more than 400,000 students, SUNY's 13 University Colleges offer programs of academic study through the master's degree in a wide range of liberal arts and professional disciplines and have deep roots in teacher education.
Teachers College, Columbia University	www.teacherscollege.edu	Teachers College was founded in 1887 to provide a new kind of schooling for the teachers of the poor children of New York. The College continues its mission through collaborative research with urban and suburban school systems to strengthen teaching in areas such as reading, writing, science, mathematics, and the arts. It also prepares leaders to develop and administer programs in schools, hospitals, and community agencies and advances the use of technology for the classroom.

Topic	URL	Annotation
Unions: American Federation of Teachers (AFT)	www.aft.org	The AFT is known for its democratic ideals and its cutting-edge work on behalf of its more than 1 million members nationwide.
National Education Association (NEA)	www.nea.org	The NEA claims more than 2.5 million members who work at every level of education, from preschool to university graduate programs. The NEA has affiliates in every state as well as in over 13,000 local communities across the United States.
New York State United Teachers (NYSUT)	www.nysut.org	NYSUT serves nearly 450,000 people who work in, or are retired from, New York's schools, colleges, and healthcare facilities.
United Federation of Teachers (UFT)	www.uft.org	With more than 140,000 members, the UFT is the sole bargaining agent for most of the nonsupervisory educators who work in the New York City public schools, representing approximately 74,000 teachers, 17,000 paraprofessionals, other employees, and retired members.
Association of Supervision and Curriculum Development (ASCD)	www.ascd.org	ASCD is an international, nonprofit, nonpartisan association of professional educators whose jobs cross all grade levels and subject areas. Members share a commitment to excellence in education.

Topic	URL	Annotation
Education Commission of the States (ECS)	www.ecs.org	ECS is a national, nonprofit organization that helps governors, legislators, state education officials, and others identify, develop, and implement policies to improve student learning at all levels.
International Reading Association (IRA)	www.reading.org	The IRA promotes high levels of literacy for all by improving the quality of reading instruction through studying the reading process and teaching techniques; serving as a clearinghouse for the dissemination of reading research through conferences, journals, and other publications; and actively encouraging the lifetime reading habit.
National Council of Social Studies (NCSS)	www.ncss.org	Founded in 1921, the NCSS is the largest association in the country devoted solely to strengthening and advocating social studies education.
National Council of Teachers of English (NCTE)	www.ncte.org	The NCTE is devoted to improving the teaching and learning of English and the language arts at all levels of education. Since 1911, NCTE has provided a forum for the profession, an array of opportunities for teachers to continue their professional growth, and a framework to deal with issues that affect the teaching of English.

Topic	URL	Annotation
National Science Teachers Association (NSTA)	www.nsta.org	NSTA is the largest organization in the world committed to promoting excellence and innovation in science teaching and learning for all. NSTA's membership of more than 53,000 includes science teachers, science supervisors, administrators, scientists, business and industry representatives, and others involved in science education.
National Council of Teachers of Mathematics (NCTM)	www.nctm.org	With about 110,000 members, NCTM is the largest nonprofit professional association of mathematics educators in the world dedicated to improving the teaching and learning of mathematics. NCTM offers vision, leadership, and avenues of communication for mathematics educators at the elementary, middle, high school, and college and university levels.
Society for Information Technology and Teacher Education (SITE)	www.aace.org/site/	SITE is an international association of individual teacher educators and affiliated organizations who are interested in the creation and dissemination of knowledge about the use of information technology in teacher education and faculty/staff development.

Topic	URL	Annotation
The Knowledge Loom	http://knowledgeloom.org	The Knowledge Loom is an active online teaching and learning community where educators can review current research; view stories about real teachers, schools, and districts; learn new strategies; participate in online events and discussions; and discover other supporting organizations and resources.

0017 Understand how to reflect productively on one's own teaching practice and how to update one's professional knowledge, skills, and effectiveness. For example:

- Assessing one's own teaching strengths and weaknesses

- Using different types of resources and opportunities (e.g., journals, inservice programs, continuing education, higher education, professional organizations, other educators) to enhance one's teaching effectiveness

- Applying strategies for working effectively with members of the immediate school community (e.g., colleagues, mentor, supervisor, special needs professionals, principal, building staff) to increase one's knowledge or skills in a given situation

- Analyzing ways of evaluating and responding to feedback (e.g., from supervisors, students, parents, colleagues)

Topic	URL	Annotation
Teacher reflection	www.sedl.org/pubs/1001/	When teachers place student learning at the center of their practice, they will develop a more meaningful practice. Teacher reflection plays a critical part in the process.

Topic	URL	Annotation
Professional development	www.ncrel.org/sdrs/areas/ issues/envrnmnt/go/94-4over. htm	This overview explores changes in our assumptions about effective professional development, new visions of teaching and learning, and the implications of these new approaches for schools.
National Staff Development Council (NSDC)	www.nsdc.org	NSDC, founded in 1969, is the largest nonprofit professional association committed to ensuring success for all students through staff development and school improvement.

0018 Understand the importance of and apply strategies for promoting productive relationships and interactions among the school, home, and community to enhance student learning. For example:

- Identifying strategies for initiating and maintaining effective communication between the teacher and parents or other caregivers and recognizing factors that may facilitate or impede communication in given situations (including parent-teacher conferences)

- Identifying a variety of strategies for working with parents, caregivers, and others to help students from diverse backgrounds reinforce in-school learning outside the school environment

- Applying strategies for using community resources to enrich learning experiences

- Recognizing various ways in which school personnel, local citizens, and community institutions (e.g., businesses, cultural institutions, colleges and universities, social agencies) can work together to promote a sense of neighborhood and community

Topic	URL	Annotation
Parent involvement	http://educationnorthwest.org/webfm_send/112	Report addresses the fact that although the No Child Left Behind Act of 2001 spells out parent involvement requirements for schools in need of improvement, the majority (54%) of the 84% of Northwest Region school improvement plans reviewed failed to include such provisions.
National Parent Teacher Association (PTA)	www.pta.org	The National PTA is the oldest and largest volunteer association in the United States, having worked to promote the education, health, and safety of children and families for over 100 years.

0019 Understand reciprocal rights and responsibilities in situations involving interactions between teachers and students, parents/guardians, community members, colleagues, school administrators, and other school personnel.
For example:

- Applying knowledge of laws related to students' rights in various situations (e.g., in relation to due process, discrimination, harassment, confidentiality, discipline, privacy)

- Applying knowledge of a teacher's rights and responsibilities in various situations (e.g., in relation to students with disabilities, potential abuse, safety issues)

- Applying knowledge of parents' rights and responsibilities in various situations (e.g., in relation to student records, school attendance)

- Analyzing the appropriateness of a teacher's response to a parent, a community member, another educator, or a student in various situations (e.g., when dealing with differences of opinion in regard to current or emerging policy)

Topic	URL	Annotation
Student rights/ responsibilities	http://schools.nyc. gov/RulesPolicies/ StudentBillofRights/default.htm	Bill of Rights and Responsibilities for Learning focuses on improving student conduct and academic achievement.
Discipline	www.aft.org/pdfs/teachers/ tips_discipline99.pdf	Offers tips for student discipline, including steps teachers can take to help establish, maintain, or restore order.
Teachers' rights	http://nysut.org/newmember	This comprehensive document from NYSUT stresses how school employees can behave in ways to avoid certain situations and actions and to protect themselves physically, medically, legally, and professionally.
Students with disabilities	www.weac.org/Issues_Advocacy/ Resource_Pages_On_Issues_ one/Special_Education/special_ education_inclusion.aspx	Inclusion remains a controversial concept in education because it relates to educational and social values, as well as to our sense of individual worth.
School policy	www.ed.gov/pubs/OR/ ResearchRpts/whos.html	Report discusses teachers' views on control over school policy and classroom practices.
Parents' rights	http://archive.aft.org/parents/	The American Federation of Teachers' parent page covers topics ranging from academic standards to communicating with school staff, as well as class size, school discipline, and homework.

SUBAREA IV—INSTRUCTION AND ASSESSMENT: CONSTRUCTED RESPONSE ITEM

The content to be addressed by the constructed-response assignment is described in Subarea II, Objectives 07–15.

As you can see, the ATS-W test objectives are broad statements of skills, knowledge, and understanding that you need in order to be an effective classroom teacher in New York State. You should read them carefully to familiarize yourself with the specific knowledge you will need to demonstrate on the test. You should reflect on them so that you understand their meanings and can apply the terms and concepts used in them to actual teaching situations. This book is designed to help you learn to do that.

CHAPTER 10: **STUDYING FOR THE ATS-W**

The best way to prepare for the ATS-W exam is to familiarize yourself with the content outlined and reviewed in the test objectives in chapter 9. The key to performing well on this exam is to step into the test makers' shoes by analyzing the test objectives, adopting the "ATS-W Mindset," and learning the types of questions and answer choices you'll face.

ANALYZING THE ATS-W OBJECTIVES

When you looked at the 19 ATS-W Test Objectives in the previous chapter and their bulleted focus statements, it probably become clear that the test maker favors certain notions about teaching and learning. We have listed some of these "in" ideas here, as well as on our online review guide chapter 9, to point you to current information from experts in each field that will be assessed on the test.

GETTING INTO THE ATS-W MINDSET

A very distinct ideology—a rationale about teaching and learning—undergirds the entire ATS-W. This is what we call the ATS-W Mindset. One way to think of the mindset is to think of putting on a specialized pair of rose-colored glasses. The lenses enable you to interpret the multiple-choice questions and the answer choices as the test maker means them to be interpreted. To do this, you may have to take off your own glasses of practical experience. Assuming the ideology of the test maker is more important than trying to reason according to pragmatism. One good rule of thumb is "Don't think first of what you *would* do in the real world—think of what you *should* do in the *test maker's* ideal world."

The ATS-W is firmly based on a constructivist theory of pedagogy. What does this mean? Tenets of constructivism as represented on the ATS-W include the following:

- Students come to class with a mental framework (or cognitive schema) of previous experiences and understandings. As they encounter new experiences or information, they relate it to what they already know, finding a place to "hang it" on the existing framework of previous knowledge or revising the framework according to the new information. In this way, they make sense of—or construct meaning from—new information.

- Students actively build their own learning while interacting with the environment. Therefore, the role of student is that of worker, not of passive recipient of information.

- Student work must be purposeful, authentic work done for a meaningful audience. Students must have a sense of ownership and responsibility toward their work.

- Students are self-motivated, self-regulated learners.

- The role of the teacher is to arrange, organize, manage, and orchestrate the available time, materials, physical space, special resources, and student tasks, activities, and assignments to promote students' active (mental) engagement in learning.

- The teacher provides rich problem-solving situations that invite students to question, explore, and find connections among ideas. The teacher's responsibility is to accommodate each student's learning needs by creating a classroom environment that offers instructional support, help in maintaining focus, and consistent feedback to students on the progress of their work.

Assume a constructivist mindset as you make decisions about answer choices on the multiple-choice portion of the test and as you respond to the written assignment. Doing so will greatly improve your ability to answer correctly on the ATS-W.

ATTACKING THE QUESTIONS

There are two basic types of question formats used on the ATS-W:

1. Single-response questions
2. Multiple-response questions

In single-response questions, you are given a question stem followed by four answer choices—A, B, C, or D—from which you must select the correct answer choice. Multiple-response questions have a question stem followed by a set of Roman numerals. You are given answer choices—A, B, C, or D—that offer combinations of the Roman numeral responses from which to make your selection.

Some question stems on the ATS-W are priority-setting questions. Priority-setting questions ask you to select the item among the responses that, for example,

> *best illustrates, best describes,* etc.
>
> *is likely, most likely,* etc.
>
> *is the primary purpose, primary reason,* etc.
>
> *is the first step, initial step,* etc.

DISTRACTOR TRAITS

Regardless of the format used, the test maker has created one best answer choice for each multiple-choice question on the ATS-W. This does not mean that all the other answer choices are clearly "wrong." You won't see "one truth and three lies." It may be that all four of the answer choices are on the right track; however, some recognizable characteristics of incorrect answer choices can be eliminated if you can detect them.

Usually each incorrect answer choice can be eliminated on the basis of one or some combination of the following traits.

Tempting terminology. The answer choice contains phrases that point to ideas about teaching and learning that are indeed consistent with a constructivist philosophy and, thus, highly favored by the test maker—which makes you think this could be the correct answer choice. You almost feel guilty not choosing an answer choice with tempting terminology in it! Some examples of tempting terminology are as follows:

> *cooperative-learning groups*
>
> *critical thinking*
>
> *inclusion*
>
> *student choice*
>
> *teacher as facilitator*

Decoy objective ideas. The answer choice contains key concepts from an objective other than the objective that is the *primary* focus of the question.

Practitioner's perspective. The answer choice represents something you probably *would* do out of practicality in the real world, but is not the best thing you *should* do if you assume the ideal world of the test maker's mindset.

Improper teacher role. The answer choice places the responsibility of the teacher on other parties, such as students, parents, special needs personnel, supervisor, etc.

Philosophical clash. The answer choice falls outside the test maker's mindset; in other words, it is not consistent with a constructivist approach.

Truism. The answer choice expresses a self-evident truth that is too broad or too vague to address the actual question stem.

EXAMPLES

Let's try a single-response example that may appear on an Elementary ATS-W exam.

1. During the first week of school, Mr. Hadley has his class of 19 first graders participate in a whole-class activity in which the success of the activity depends upon the cooperation and participation of the entire group working as a team. Mr. Hadley's primary purpose for the activity is

    A. to foster a view of learning as a purposeful pursuit

    B. to encourage students to assume responsibility for their own learning

    C. to encourage student-initiated activities

    D. to promote student ownership in a safe and productive learning environment

The best strategy to use when answering a single-response question is to read the question stem carefully. Think about what aspect of the classroom situation is under discussion in the question and which ATS-W objective is its primary focus. Then read each answer choice, trying to eliminate any that are clearly incorrect or implausible based on the information provided in the question stem, your knowledge about the relevant objective, and principles and concepts that relate to the pedagogy of the situation.

This is a priority-setting question—you must select the *primary* purpose of the activity. When you read the question stem, two aspects that should catch your attention is that Mr. Hadley's whole-group activity is conducted during the *first week* of school and that the success of the activity depends on the class *working as a team*. Teachers typically plan activities during the first week of school that will help their classrooms become places where learning can occur—where students are responsible, cooperative, purposeful, and mutually supportive. They should recognize issues related to the creation of a productive classroom climate (e.g., with regard to shared values, shared experiences, or patterns of communication). These ideas are related to *classroom management* (Objective 0007), which is clearly the primary focus of this question.

Eliminate (A) and (B) because they deal with *learning processes* (Objective 0002) and (C) because it deals with *motivational principles* (Objective 0013)—all of which undoubtedly will receive Mr. Hadley's attention *after* he has established a suitable climate for learning. These distractors are examples of both tempting terminology and decoy objective ideas. (Tempting terminology often comes from the key ideas of nonrelated objectives.) Fostering a view of learning as a purposeful pursuit, encouraging students to assume responsibility for their own learning, and encouraging student-initiated activities are sound constructivist-based practices, *but* these ideas are not directly pertinent to what is actually being asked in this question.

Mr. Hadley encourages the students to work as a team during the class activity. Clearly, during this *first week* of school, he wants to promote student ownership in a safe and productive learning environment. Choice (D) is the correct response.

Now let's try a multiple-response example.

1. Ms. Harrison is concerned because in her eighth-grade social studies class, she has several students who seem especially unmotivated. These students rarely participate in class discussions and regularly fail to turn in completed homework assignments. Ms. Harrison can increase motivation to learn in her classroom by

    I. selecting content that is relevant to the students' lives

    II. encouraging students to assist in planning instructional activities

    III. using "I" messages when dealing with student misbehavior

    IV. using simulations and role-play

    A. I and II only

    B. I, II, and IV only

    C. II, III, and IV only

    D. I, II, III, and IV

Using a two-step process is the best approach when answering a multiple-response question. As a first step, you should identify Roman numeral responses you are sure are correct and eliminate any Roman numeral responses that are clearly incorrect or implausible. Read the stimulus and question stem carefully. Then read each Roman numeral choice and put a check next to any you feel are correct while crossing out the numeral of any response that you are sure should be eliminated. Next, cross out the letter of an answer choice if it does not include a Roman numeral you feel is correct or if it includes a Roman numeral you have eliminated.

Now give it a try. The question stem tells us that the question is about *motivation*, so its primary focus is Objective 0013:

> *Understand the relationship between student motivation and achievement and how motivational principles and practices can be used to promote and sustain student cooperation in learning.*

Read the four Roman numeral responses and try to identify one with which you totally agree or one with which you totally disagree, whichever seems easier. Eliminate Roman numeral III because it deals with *classroom management* (Objective 0007), not motivation. This is an example of tempting terminology—it *is* correct that teachers should use "I" messages as opposed to "you" messages when dealing with student misbehavior, *but* this question is concerned with how to motivate students, not how to deal with misbehavior. Eliminate answer choices (C) and (D) because they both include III. Choices (A) and (B) both include I and II. Thus, you need only decide whether Roman IV is an appropriate strategy for increasing motivation. Simulations and role-play can increase motivation by making the learning more relevant to students' lives. Teachers should apply procedures for enhancing student interest and helping students find their own motivation (e.g., relating concepts presented in the classroom to students' everyday experiences, allowing students to have choices in their learning, or encouraging student-initiated activities) and recognize factors and situations that tend to promote or diminish student motivation. They can increase motivation to learn in their classrooms by selecting content that is relevant to the students' lives (I), encouraging students to assist in planning instruction (II), and using simulations and role-playing (IV). Choice (B) is the correct response.

You will have additional opportunities to practice the strategies you have learned thus far when you take the practice tests. Consciously think about the strategies as you work through the tests to increase your confidence in using them.

GIVE YOURSELF AN ADDITIONAL EDGE

Besides using Kaplan's Top 10 Strategies outlined in chapter 2, getting in the "mindset," and reviewing the suggested education-related materials presented in this chapter, you can give yourself an additional edge on the ATS-W by applying careful knowledge and understanding of the test objectives. What do we mean by this?

When you read an ATS-W question, you should immediately try to identify which ATS-W objective is the *primary* focus of the question. Do this by looking for aspects of the question stem that relate to key ideas as expressed in the focus statements of the objectives. Once you are confident you have identified the relevant objective, you can eliminate answer choices that do not apply to that objective—particularly answer choices that contain key ideas from other objectives, which may be distractors. The edge that you will have when you take the ATS-W is that these questions will be *easier* for you because you can readily eliminate distractors based on your knowledge of the key ideas in the objectives. After eliminating as many distractors as you can in this manner, select the answer choice that is most consistent with educational theory of effective practice related to the relevant objective.

A Word of Caution. In general, the strategy of identifying the objective when you read the question will be very helpful to you in achieving success on the ATS-W. Nevertheless, you may not always be able to figure out which objective applies to the question when you first read the question; further, occasionally the question may use language or wording that will cause you to misidentify the objective. You need to be prepared to shift gears and take a different approach if this occurs.

Another caution is that the objectives are not independent of each other—many times they overlap. For example, when teachers are *planning* (Objective 0010), they must consider *instructional approaches* (Objective 0011). Therefore, it may occur, for example, that two objectives apply to a single question. In this case, even if you decide that one of them *best* applies, you are likely to need ideas from both objectives to answer such a question. The main point is, *don't get bogged down because you're trying to figure out the objective*—just go on and use a different strategy.

Remember, you are the master of your test-taking experience. Do the questions in the order you want and the way you want. Use your time for one purpose—to maximize your score. Don't get bogged down or agonize. Remember, you don't get points for suffering, but you do earn points for moving on to the next question and getting it right.

Don't let the ATS-W intimidate you. Fear and self-doubt will cause you to perform below your true ability level and will result in scores that do not reflect your knowledge and skills. Think of the test not as an obstacle to be overcome but as an opportunity to show what you know and can do. Learn and use the 10 fundamental Kaplan strategies and the test taker's edge, and you'll be well on your way to achieving your goal of becoming a teacher in New York State.

We can't stress enough the power of practice. To help you, we've prepared two practice tests that mirror the types of questions you will encounter on the actual ATS-W. Keep in mind that the content of both versions of the ATS-W—Elementary and Secondary—is very similar. The major differences occur in the subareas of Knowledge of the Learner (questions derived from Objective 001 about developmental characteristics of specific age groups) and Instructional Planning and Assessment (specifically, questions about developmentally appropriate practice). So, regardless of which version of the ATS-W you plan to take, it would be worth your while to complete the two practice tests in this book.

You will want to familiarize yourself with the key terminology used by the NYSTCE test makers. Turn to the appendix at the back of this book for a comprehensive glossary of important ATS-W terms.

CHAPTER 11: PRACTICE ATS-W—ELEMENTARY

Before taking this practice test, find a quiet room where you can work uninterrupted for 4 hours. Make sure you have a comfortable desk and several No. 2 pencils.

Use the answer sheet provided to record your answers.

Once you start this practice test, don't stop until you've finished. Remember, you can complete the sections of the test in any order you wish.

You will find an answer key and explanations following the test.

Good luck!

SAMPLE DIRECTIONS

This test booklet contains a multiple-choice section and a single written assignment section. You may complete the sections of the test in the order you choose.

Each question in the first section of this booklet is a multiple-choice question with four answer choices. Read each question CAREFULLY and choose the ONE best answer. Record your answer on the answer document in the space that corresponds to the question number. Completely fill in the space having the same letter as the answer you have chosen. *Use only a No. 2 lead pencil.*

Sample Question
1. What is the capital of New York?

    A.   Buffalo

    B.   New York City

    C.   Albany

    D.   Rochester

The correct answer to this question is (C). You would indicate that on the answer document as follows:

1.

You should answer all questions. Even if you are unsure of an answer, it is better to guess than not to answer a question at all. You may use the margins of the test booklet for scratch paper, but you will be scored only on the responses on your answer document.

The directions for the written assignment appear later in this test booklet.

FOR TEST SECURITY REASONS, YOU MAY NOT TAKE NOTES OR REMOVE ANY OF THE TEST MATERIALS FROM THE ROOM.

The words "End of Test" indicate that you have completed the test. You may go back and review your answers, but be sure you have answered all questions before raising your hand for dismissal. Your test materials must be returned to a test administrator when you finish the test.

If you have any questions, please ask them now before beginning the test.

DO NOT GO ON UNTIL YOU ARE TOLD TO DO SO.

ATS-W ANSWER SHEET

1. (A) (B) (C) (D)	28. (A) (B) (C) (D)	55. (A) (B) (C) (D)
2. (A) (B) (C) (D)	29. (A) (B) (C) (D)	56. (A) (B) (C) (D)
3. (A) (B) (C) (D)	30. (A) (B) (C) (D)	57. (A) (B) (C) (D)
4. (A) (B) (C) (D)	31. (A) (B) (C) (D)	58. (A) (B) (C) (D)
5. (A) (B) (C) (D)	32. (A) (B) (C) (D)	59. (A) (B) (C) (D)
6. (A) (B) (C) (D)	33. (A) (B) (C) (D)	60. (A) (B) (C) (D)
7. (A) (B) (C) (D)	34. (A) (B) (C) (D)	61. (A) (B) (C) (D)
8. (A) (B) (C) (D)	35. (A) (B) (C) (D)	62. (A) (B) (C) (D)
9. (A) (B) (C) (D)	36. (A) (B) (C) (D)	63. (A) (B) (C) (D)
10. (A) (B) (C) (D)	37. (A) (B) (C) (D)	64. (A) (B) (C) (D)
11. (A) (B) (C) (D)	38. (A) (B) (C) (D)	65. (A) (B) (C) (D)
12. (A) (B) (C) (D)	39. (A) (B) (C) (D)	66. (A) (B) (C) (D)
13. (A) (B) (C) (D)	40. (A) (B) (C) (D)	67. (A) (B) (C) (D)
14. (A) (B) (C) (D)	41. (A) (B) (C) (D)	68. (A) (B) (C) (D)
15. (A) (B) (C) (D)	42. (A) (B) (C) (D)	69. (A) (B) (C) (D)
16. (A) (B) (C) (D)	43. (A) (B) (C) (D)	70. (A) (B) (C) (D)
17. (A) (B) (C) (D)	44. (A) (B) (C) (D)	71. (A) (B) (C) (D)
18. (A) (B) (C) (D)	45. (A) (B) (C) (D)	72. (A) (B) (C) (D)
19. (A) (B) (C) (D)	46. (A) (B) (C) (D)	73. (A) (B) (C) (D)
20. (A) (B) (C) (D)	47. (A) (B) (C) (D)	74. (A) (B) (C) (D)
21. (A) (B) (C) (D)	48. (A) (B) (C) (D)	75. (A) (B) (C) (D)
22. (A) (B) (C) (D)	49. (A) (B) (C) (D)	76. (A) (B) (C) (D)
23. (A) (B) (C) (D)	50. (A) (B) (C) (D)	77. (A) (B) (C) (D)
24. (A) (B) (C) (D)	51. (A) (B) (C) (D)	78. (A) (B) (C) (D)
25. (A) (B) (C) (D)	52. (A) (B) (C) (D)	79. (A) (B) (C) (D)
26. (A) (B) (C) (D)	53. (A) (B) (C) (D)	80. (A) (B) (C) (D)
27. (A) (B) (C) (D)	54. (A) (B) (C) (D)	

Learners in Carla Raptor's fourth-grade class are performing inquiry investigations to produce a final unit project reflecting what they've learned about geometric shapes and angles in the world around them. In her class of 25 students, Ms. Raptor has 5 students whom she considers "at risk." These five students have socioeconomic challenges that place them at a disadvantage in achieving academic success, and for this project, they are hesitant to begin work for fear of yet another failing grade.

1. Which two of the following practices would be best for Ms. Raptor to implement to engage these students in completing the geometry project?

   I. Offer students a limited number of meaningful choices about which subtopics to pursue and about how they may compile and present their findings.

   II. Award incentives like stickers to each student as she or he reaches a goal on a teacher-created timeline of how the project should be progressing at periodic intervals.

   III. Pair each at-risk student with a high-achieving student to complete the project.

   IV. Develop a rubric at the beginning of the project that defines clear goals and expectations for both effort and actual products, and be sure that all students understand how their effort and their products are being evaluated.

   A. I and III only

   B. I and IV only

   C. II and III only

   D. II and IV only

Use the information below to answer the two questions that follow.

In evaluating her own performance in the classroom, sixth-grade English language arts teacher LaRhonda Callahan begins to suspect that she has not always been successful in conveying feedback to students about their progress.

2. In order to improve this important aspect of her teaching, Ms. Callahan most probably should concentrate on

   A. meeting periodically with each student and assessing his or her achievement in general and inclusive terms

   B. writing positive and encouraging comments of some length on weekly assignments, no matter how incomplete or unsuccessful the student's effort

   C. analyzing each student's progress in front of the rest of the class, pointing out problems but carefully moderating the negative aspects

   D. giving immediate and specific feedback, whether in writing or in one-to-one consultation, and assessing whether or not such feedback seems to be helpful

3. Ms. Callahan's decision to evaluate her own classroom performance best illustrates which of the following principles?

   A. Teachers should analyze teacher-student interactions with regard to providing feedback.

   B. Teachers should reflect on their own practice to enhance effectiveness.

   C. Teachers should analyze ways of evaluating and responding to student feedback.

   D. Teachers should apply strategies for initiating and maintaining effective communication.

4. A group of 30 eighth graders participate in a demonstration against the canceling of the appearance of a popular radio personality at the school. The demonstration occurs in the hallways during class hours and consists of participants loudly shouting and banging on lockers to attract the attention of the students in class. The school principal stops the demonstration. The principal's action is

    A. an infringement of the students' right to free speech as described under the First Amendment.

    B. within the duties of the principal because the protest was not supervised by a teacher.

    C. within the duties of the principal because the demonstration disrupted students' class time.

    D. in accord with the principal's duties because the principal felt the radio personality was not an appropriate role model for the students.

5. A fire partially destroys a school facility. During the projected six-week rebuilding period, two fourth-grade classes will be merged, meeting in a classroom designed for one. Which of the following responses to students' complaints by Mr. Fritz, the teacher, will best facilitate class adjustment to the situation?

    A. "There's nothing I can do about it—the fire wasn't my fault. It wasn't anybody's fault. I don't like it any more than you do."

    B. "Oh, it's not such a big deal. If the whole school had burned down, we couldn't hold classes at all."

    C. "It's not going to go on like this forever. In fact, I'll bet the repairs will be done in only four weeks, and we'll be back to normal that soon."

    D. "It's only temporary. Maybe it will be good for us all to work together for a little while. It might even be fun. Let's give it a try."

6. Maggie Piazza, a kindergarten teacher, constructs a model of the friendship and interaction patterns of the children in her class. Ms. Piazza's primary purpose for doing this is to

    A. compare and contrast the socioeconomic backgrounds of her students.

    B. supplement and clarify information gained from observation about her students' peer relationships.

    C. discover how she can most efficiently redirect existing patterns in classroom friendships.

    D. record individual instructional needs of each student.

Use the information below to answer the two questions that follow.

Boupha Libdeh, an English language arts teacher, has a class of students from diverse ethnic and racial backgrounds. Mr. Libdeh wants to address the needs of all learners and to create a classroom climate in which both the diversity and the similarities of groups and individuals are appreciated.

7. Which of the following activities would most effectively familiarize the students with each other's backgrounds while promoting self-pride and self-respect?

    A. Read and discuss with the class stories that illustrate the achievements and cultural uniqueness of the varied groups.

    B. Prepare a handout that briefly describes each represented group.

    C. Have students go to the library and research information about their respective backgrounds.

    D. Ask the students to name their respective backgrounds.

8. Mr. Libdeh is concerned about assessment of spoken English skills by the ESL students in his culturally mixed classroom. These students who are English language learners rarely volunteer comments during classroom discussions. It is most important that Mr. Libdeh be aware that

   A. Most students who are learning English as a second language are handicapped by an overly strict upbringing.

   B. Students who are more willing to speak in class usually are more proficient language users than are students who are reluctant to speak.

   C. Cultural factors as well as language ability affect the extent to which ESL students speak out in class.

   D. ESL learners should not be assessed on their spoken English skills because it may cause them undue stress.

9. In 1985, the New York State Board of Regents adopted Rule 19.5, which prohibits the use of corporal punishment in New York public schools. However, the State does allow the use of "reasonable physical force" to prevent injury to people or damage to property. The Supreme Court determined that, as long as students' right to due process is honored, states have the right to adopt measures that allow the use of physical force on students because

   A. The federal government has no right to interfere in how students are disciplined in school.

   B. Common law recognizes the right of teachers to use reasonable but not excessive force when it is necessary to discipline a student.

   C. Students are minors under the law, so schools are obliged to act in the place of parents.

   D. A student who is not disciplined may well become a chronic discipline problem.

Use the information below to answer the two questions that follow.

Ariel Estrada, a sixth-grade social studies teacher, is teaching a unit on citizenship. To reinforce the concept of citizenship, Ms. Estrada has her students salute the flag by reciting the Pledge of Allegiance at the beginning of class every day.

10. One afternoon she receives a call from Mitzi Feuer's mother informing her that Mitzi will no longer be participating in the Pledge activity. This parent is

   A. within her rights, based on a Supreme Court decision stating that no student can be compelled to salute the flag

   B. within her rights, because her daughter is protected under the due process clause of the Fourteenth Amendment

   C. not within her rights, because the school may require all students to salute the flag

   D. not within her rights, because her daughter would be advocating a specific belief on school grounds

11. Throughout the unit, Ms. Estrada uses a variety of assessment strategies to determine her students' understanding of the unit. At the end of the unit, Ms. Estrada gives a comprehensive teacher-made test as a summative assessment. In assessing her class with the comprehensive teacher-made test, which of the following is information to be gained by Ms. Estrada?

   I. the success of her instructional materials and teaching methods

   II. the relationship of the class median to nationwide norms

   III. the progress of the class in the attainment of unit objectives

   IV. the specific weaknesses of individual students with regard to the unit

   A. I and II only

   B. II and III only

   C. III and IV only

   D. I, III, and IV only

12. Jacob Wechsler, a fourth-grade teacher, is concerned that the books he selects for his students to read in language arts be free from bias, promote constructive social thinking, and not be offensive to anyone in his multiethnic class. What is the best way to determine this?

    A. reading the material himself, forming his own determination

    B. a money-back guarantee from the publisher that such is the case

    C. a statement from the school librarian that such is the case

    D. approval of the books by the New York State Regents

13. When deciding upon the fitness of a teacher providing instructional services to serve as a New York State public school teacher, a district

    A. must use as the sole basis for its decision the teacher's conduct and competence in the classroom.

    B. may include the teacher's personal behavior outside the classroom as part of its evaluation.

    C. is required to investigate all of the teacher's activities and supplementary employment in the community.

    D. must rule to grant the teacher tenure if a majority of the criteria specified on the district's professional performance review plan are met.

Use the information below to answer the two questions that follow.

Claudia Cavuto has started a new job as a seventh-grade teacher in a school that is known to have students involved in gang-related activities. As a new teacher, Ms. Cavuto is concerned that she may have students who are such discipline problems that she will not be able to handle them in class.

14. Which of the following behaviors, if exhibited by a student, would warrant removal from Ms. Cavuto's class?

    A. negative attitude expressed toward the subject matter

    B. inability to concentrate as evidenced by slack posture and drooping eyelids

    C. indication of strong, suppressed personal hostility toward the teacher or other students

    D. disruption of the class that detracts from the learning process of other students

KAPLAN

15. Although not required by law to do so, the school where Ms. Cavuto teaches notifies parents within 24 hours of all impending internal suspensions. Which two of the following are probable purposes of this policy?

   I. to promote a partnership between the school and parents in matters of student discipline

   II. to make sure parents are informed of their child's behavior so that they can be held accountable

   III. to make sure the child is disciplined at home for his or her misbehavior

   IV. to ensure that the child spends the internal suspension working productively

   A. I and II

   B. I and IV

   C. II and III

   D. III and IV

Use the information below to answer the four questions that follow.

Mike O'Grady is a first-year second-grade teacher. He has a positive outlook and holds high expectations for his students.

16. In monitoring his students' progress, Mr. O'Grady should be most concerned when a student

   A. learns more slowly than his or her peers do.

   B. responds more readily to visual than to verbal presentation of material.

   C. cannot be convinced that the subject under discussion is relevant to his or her personal life.

   D. cannot apply the concepts he or she has supposedly learned.

17. Mr. O'Grady wants his students to engage in activities that will promote their development of higher-order thinking skills. Which of the following tasks is most likely to achieve this purpose?

    A. filling in missing components of a pattern

    B. naming the characters of a favorite story

    C. writing a thank-you letter

    D. writing a recipe for "silly putty"

18. Participation of his students in class is a high priority for Mr. O'Grady. Of the following physical aspects of a classroom, which is most important in determining student class participation?

    A. size of the room

    B. spatial arrangement of the room

    C. number of windows

    D. location of the room in the building

19. Dividing his class up into groups of three or four, Mr. O'Grady provides each group with an empty milk carton. He challenges the groups to come up with as many new and different ways to use such a milk carton as possible. Which of the following is Mr. O'Grady encouraging his students to engage in with this activity?

    I. brainstorming

    II. affective learning

    III. divergent thinking

    IV. cooperative learning

    A. I, II, and III only

    B. II and IV only

    C. I, III, and IV only

    D. I, II, III, and IV

20. Hanna Selig is a veteran middle school teacher of 20 years. Throughout her teaching career, she has observed that middle school girls and boys behave differently both socially and academically. This is caused by

    A. biological factors.

    B. cultural influences.

    C. home backgrounds.

    D. biological and cultural factors in combination.

21. In which of the following has the proper allocation of responsibility for the IEP of a student who is learning disabled and whose placement is in the regular education classroom been observed?

    A. The principal defines educational objectives, whereas the classroom and resource teachers choose instructional strategies.

    B. The classroom teacher defines objectives, and the resource teacher chooses strategies.

    C. The resource teacher defines objectives and chooses strategics.

    D. The parents of the child define objectives, and the classroom and resource teachers choose instructional strategies.

22. Loren Rudovsky, an eighth-grade social studies teacher, assigns her class to read and discuss a controversial novel containing scenes depicting the real-life bombing of Dresden by the United States during World War II. The parent of a student calls Ms. Rudovsky and irately objects to the assignment, saying that the book is unpatriotic and that Ms. Rudovsky should be fired for making her students read it. The most professional reaction on Ms.Rudovsky's part would be to

    A. arrange a conference with the parent, giving that student an alternative assignment if the parent's objections are not assuaged afterward.

    B. argue that the novel is a recognized classic and that it is not unpatriotic to discuss some of the nation's questionable actions of the past.

    C. acquiesce to the objection and withdraw the assignment for any student who agree that the book's point of view is unpatriotic.

    D. turn the matter over to the school board for a decision.

23. Federal laws and regulations must be complied with in a New York State school district

    A. because the U.S. Congress has a constitutional mandate to regulate education across the nation.

    B. only in cases involving the civil rights of a student or faculty member in contention with the school administration.

    C. whenever federal monies are received by the district.

    D. at no time and in no situation because the power to regulate education is constitutionally the province of the individual states.

24. Dr. Rhodes, the principal at Magglio Johnson's school, asks Mr. Johnson to give her copies of his monthly lesson plans two months in advance because she is required by the superintendent to do so. Mr. Johnson thinks this is too far in advance. His best course of action is to

    A. comply with the request, but write very cursory lesson plans.

    B. comply with the request, but explain that the lesson plans may change and offer to provide Dr. Rhodes copies of such changes.

    C. find out what the other teachers are doing about this and do what they do.

    D. refuse politely, explaining his position.

Use the information below to answer the four questions that follow.

Ichiro Sato is a middle school English language arts teacher. Mr. Sato's class includes students with a wide range of abilities and from diverse cultural backgrounds, including several students who were in bilingual education programs in elementary school.

25. Mr. Sato should be aware that bilingual education is meant to foster

    I. increased proficiency in the native language.

    II. maintenance of nonlanguage academic skills while the student is learning English.

    III. fostering of pride in the student's native background.

    IV. replacement over time of the native language.

    A. I and III only

    B. I, II, and III only

    C. II and IV only

    D. II, III, and IV only

26. To increase social harmony among his students, Mr. Sato should

    A. avoid discussing racial or ethnic relations with the class.

    B. have the students engage in competitive activities.

    C. use cooperative groups that are racially and ethnically balanced.

    D. assign English language learners to a separate group for group activities.

27. Mr. Sato holds high expectations for all his students, regardless of their differences and diverse abilities. This attitude best illustrates that teachers should understand

   A. how developmental variations among learners affect instructional decision making in given situations.

   B. how classroom factors may affect students' self-concepts and learning.

   C. how classroom environments that respect diversity foster positive student experiences.

   D. how to apply strategies to ensure that children with special needs participate to the greatest extent possible in all classroom activities.

28. Mr. Sato probably is aware that with middle school students, teacher's expectations tend to have the least effect on

   A. student performance.

   B. student grades.

   C. student peer relations.

   D. student discipline.

29. Abbe is a new student in Jena Ruiz's fourth-grade class. He has trouble sitting still, and his in-class writing assignments are poorly done, although his homework is somewhat better. Abbe gets along well with other children and is well liked among his classmates. After checking Abbe's school academic records, Ms. Ruiz decides to meet with the counselor to discuss her concerns about Abbe. This decision is an example of a teacher

   A. recognizing that a student's writing ability is impacted by factors outside of the classroom.

   B. understanding that she is a member of a learning community and should work with other members of the community to enhance her own effectiveness.

   C. identifying issues related to the creation of a smoothly functioning classroom community.

   D. exploring various ways school personnel can work together to promote a sense of community in the school.

Use the information below to answer the three questions that follow.

Hava Akhtar, a new third-grade teacher, wants to foster critical thinking and enhance problem-solving skills in her students.

30. When teaching a lesson on light, which of the following would Ms. Akhtar likely do?

   A. In cooperative groups, have the students complete a worksheet on the different properties of light.

   B. Demonstrate to the students how light of different colors combines and have them take notes.

   C. In small groups, have the students read aloud about light from their science books.

   D. In cooperative groups, have the students experiment with light.

31. Which of the following would be likely to enhance the critical thinking skills of Ms. Akhtar's students?

   I. establishing a teacher-centered, textbook-focused learning environment

   II. encouraging students to discuss their conclusions with each other

   III. having students memorize and recite metacognitive strategies to each other

   IV. requiring students to justify the reasoning behind their conclusions

   A. I, II, and III only

   B. II and III only

   C. II and IV only

   D. III and IV only

32. Ms. Akhtar prefers using groups for science activities because this approach keeps her students actively engaged in learning. Her class has a wide range of achievement levels. Which of the following grouping practices would be most appropriate for Ms. Akhtar to use?

    A. Group according to academic ability level.

    B. Group slow learners together, but use mixed-ability groups with the rest of the class.

    C. Use mixed-ability groups for the whole class.

    D. Use whole-class activities, rather than small-group activities.

33. For two years while in graduate school, Julia Ramon was the church basketball league coach for Alex, a student who is now in Ms. Ramon's fifth-grade class. Alex, delighted to see Ms. Ramon, calls her by her first name as he always did when she coached him. How should Ms. Ramon handle the situation?

    A. Ignore this behavior as unimportant.

    B. Tell Alex in front of the class that this behavior is inappropriate.

    C. Explain to Alex, privately and as soon as possible after class, that the classroom context requires more formal address.

    D. Rather than reprove Alex, allow all the students to call her by her first name.

34. Cheragh Fatemah's second-grade class has been highly unruly the past few days. Ms. Fatemah decides to hold a class meeting to discuss the problem. Holding the class meeting illustrates Ms. Fatemah's understanding that

    A. she should work effectively with members of the school community to promote appropriate behavior.

    B. she should promote student ownership in a smoothly functioning learning community.

    C. she must impart expectations and ideas to create a climate of trust.

    D. she must help students become self-initiated learners.

Use the information below to answer the two questions that follow.

Sergei Nestor teaches health education in an inner-city middle school. Mr. Nestor wants to educate his seventh- and eighth-grade students about the dangers of risky behaviors, such as riding in a car with someone who has been drinking alcohol.

35. Mr. Nestor is most likely to achieve this goal if his instructional planning takes into account that, in general, young people of this age

    A. feel invincible and believe that bad things happen to other people, not to them

    B. have high regard for adult authorities as a source of ideas and values

    C. are incapable of reasoning hypothetically about a situation contrary to fact

    D. usually respond positively to severe warnings about risky behaviors

36. Mr. Nestor observes that Ellen, a homeless student who is doing poorly in his class, exhibits low self-esteem. Which of the following would be most effective for Mr. Nestor to use to enhance Ellen's self-esteem?

    A. Provide a caring environment in which Ellen is urged to try harder.

    B. Allow Ellen to be more involved in making decisions about her assignments.

    C. Routinely present Ellen with challenging activities at which she is able to achieve success through her own efforts.

    D. Plan activities in which the whole class discusses the importance of feeling good about oneself.

37. Cynara Spagnola, a seventh-grade mathematics teacher, is teaching a unit on measurement. How should Ms. Spagnola prepare her students for a lesson on the metric system?

    A. The day before the lesson, give the students a list of the metric prefixes and tell them to memorize them before they come to class the next day.

    B. The day before the lesson, have the students write down and discuss in small groups all the things they already know about the metric system.

    C. The day of the lesson, begin by having the students preview a worksheet that they will have to complete at the end of class.

    D. The day of the lesson, begin by showing students a step-by-step procedure for how to convert from one unit to another.

38. Frederic was suspended from school for vandalism. His friends wear armbands to school bearing the statement "Frederic is innocent." A group of teachers find the armbands and the students' attitude intimidating. The best course of action for these teachers would be to

    A. ask the principal to establish a dress code that would prohibit armbands.

    B. ask the principal to reconsider the suspension.

    C. do nothing as long as the students do not disrupt the learning environment.

    D. call a meeting with these students and allow them to voice their protests.

39. Which of the following outcomes is the most compelling reason for an eighth-grade English language arts teacher to reteach a literature unit introducing the stories and characters of Shakespeare's *Romeo and Juliet*?

    A. Fewer than half of the students are inspired by the unit to read another Shakespearean tragedy.

    B. Fewer than half of the students exhibit confidence when reading lines of verse from the play.

    C. Fewer than half of the students can explain why Juliet commits suicide.

    D. Most of the students admit to enjoying the film version more than reading the play.

40. Zhang Jingjoy, a social studies teacher, wishes to evaluate the performance of his class. Which of the following information would be most useful for this purpose?

   I. the distribution of grades in the other social studies classes

  II. scores his students achieved on the state social studies assessment

 III. pre- and postgain scores on a unit mastery test

 IV. his cumulative class anecdotal records

  A. I and III only

  B. II only

  C. I and II only

  D. II, III, and IV only

Use the information below to answer the two questions that follow.

In her seventh-grade English language arts classroom, Jenelle Kirby is working with her students on improving their writing skills. In providing feedback on their writing to her students, Ms. Kirby wants to promote student learning and foster a climate of trust and support in the classroom.

41. Which of the following is the most appropriate way to grade and comment on writing assignments?

  A. Point out all errors and assign an overall grade.

  B. Give an overall grade and write a short paragraph pointing out all errors the student made.

  C. Give one grade for content and another for mechanics.

  D. Point out strengths and one to three problem areas for the student to work on in the next writing assignment.

42. To increase her students' intrinsic motivation to engage in writing, Ms. Kirby should

   A. praise their writing regardless of its quality.

   B. give tangible rewards to students who voluntarily write more papers than other students do.

   C. permit students to choose from a list of interesting topics, that they want to write about.

   D. have students write on topics that she personally finds interesting.

Use the information below to answer the two questions that follow.

Sasha Montoya, an eighth-grade Spanish teacher, is the team leader of an interdisciplinary team at the middle school where she teaches. Ms. Montoya's team includes an English language arts teacher, a mathematics teacher, a science teacher, a social studies teacher, and a physical education teacher. Together this same group of teachers instructs 102 students. They share a common planning period so that they can meet regularly to plan the curriculum and discuss the progress and needs of their students.

43. Establishing interdisciplinary teams as a method of curriculum organization has which of the following advantages over more traditional organizational patterns?

   I. It offers greater opportunities for teachers on the team to contribute to one another's professional growth.

   II. Students are more likely to see the interrelationships between different subject areas.

   III. Students are more likely to have opportunities for realistic problem solving.

   IV. The particular talents of a teacher may be called upon more fully due to opportunities for integrated lessons.

   A. I and II only

   B. I, II, and III only

   C. II and IV only

   D. I, II, III, and IV

44. To enrich her teaching of language skills, Ms. Montoya asks the physical education teacher to visit her class and teach the students some basic dance movements linked with the words of a Spanish song. The method will probably be most beneficial for those students who best learn

 A. visually.

 B. tactilely.

 C. aurally.

 D. kinesthetically.

45. In early spring Lilia Truela is concerned because her third graders have difficulty remembering important concepts the class worked on at the beginning of the school year. Which of the following are effective techniques to improve memory?

 I. mnemonics

 II. chunking

 III. rote learning

 IV. rehearsal

 A. I and II only

 B. I, II, and IV only

 C. II and III only

 D. II, III, and IV only

46. A teacher who wishes to stimulate divergent thinking would use which of the following questions?

 A. What is the product of 24 and 35?

 B. What countries were involved in World War I?

 C. How many ways can a person travel from New York to Los Angeles?

 D. When was Abraham Lincoln born?

47. Bobby Honea, a first-year teacher, has just finished teaching a science unit on mammals to his class of first graders. Mr. Honea's evaluation of the unit indicates that the students did not adequately meet his objectives for the unit. Mr. Honea should

    A. teach the unit over again, this time urging the students to try harder.

    B. give additional outside work to those students who did poorly and move on to the next unit.

    C. give all the students additional work to do at home and move on to the next unit.

    D. reteach the material in which the students did poorly, using different strategies.

Use the information below to answer the three questions that follow.

Jessica Cooper has recently been employed as a kindergarten teacher in a school district that has made a strong commitment to the inclusion of students with disabilities into the total school program.

48. In planning for instruction, which of the following instructional methods will Ms. Cooper find to be most in accord with the district's commitment?

    A. ability grouping

    B. independent learning projects

    C. cooperative learning

    D. computer-assisted instruction

49. Ms. Cooper will have several children with disabilities in her classroom. In preparing for the inclusion of a child with a disability into a general education classroom, it is appropriate for a teacher to

   I. set aside an area of the classroom where the child will be confined so as not to be treated in an unacceptable way by the other children.

   II. consult with the child's parents regarding the child's IEP.

   III. explain to the other children the nature of the child's disability.

   IV. modify instructional techniques and materials to provide for the unique needs of the child.

   A. I, II, and IV only

   B. I, III, and IV only

   C. II and III only

   D. II, III, and IV only

50. Which of the following is most important for Ms. Cooper to consider when planning a field trip for her class?

   A. the accessibility for children with disabilities

   B. the distractibility of some of the children with special needs

   C. the difficulty of monitoring student behavior on field trips

   D. the need to determine alternative, but meaningful, activities for the children with special needs

51. Christine, a student in Roger Fuesdon's seventh-grade class, comes to Mr. Fuesdon very upset. She claims that everyone picks on her and that she has no friends in the class. Given the developmental characteristics of children at this age, Mr. Fuesdon should

    A. arrange a time to talk with Christine about the problem.

    B. tell Christine that she is well liked and is imagining her problem.

    C. speak with the other children and insist that they change their behavior toward Christine.

    D. ask the counselor to contact Christine's parents about obtaining professional help for her.

Use the information below to answer the four questions that follow.

In her social studies class, DeShala Washington uses a computer simulation activity to help her students learn about geography. She assigns the students to teams who must decide among themselves the most effective strategies for accomplishing tasks posed in the simulation.

52. In making her decision to use a computer simulation activity, Ms. Washington likely used her ability to

    A. apply procedures for promoting positive and productive small-group interactions.

    B. analyze the advantages and disadvantages of having students acquire information through a variety of modes and formats.

    C. recognize issues related to the creation of a productive classroom climate.

    D. apply strategies for using community resources to enrich learning experiences.

53. Ms. Washington probably selected the simulation activity because it will

    A. require less time than expository teaching methods.

    B. enhance students' community awareness.

    C. enhance the students' role-playing skills.

    D. encourage students to seek out knowledge actively.

54. While Ms. Washington's students are working in their teams, it is important that she actively monitor the groups at all times to

    A. prevent errors and illogical thinking on the part of students.

    B. direct student strategies for accomplishing tasks.

    C. assign students to tell others what to do if the team takes too much time.

    D. assess and guide individual and team collaborative skills.

55. As part of her ongoing effort to encourage her students to use higher-order thinking skills, which of the following should Ms. Washington do at the end of the simulation activity to promote evaluation-level thinking?

    A. Give a comprehensive multiple-choice exam on geography terms.

    B. Hold a class discussion on the merits of the computer simulation activity.

    C. Have students write a paragraph explaining how they participated in the computer simulation activity.

    D. Have students make a chart listing the major ideas they learned from the simulation activity.

Use the information below to answer the three questions that follow.

Mary Crowfoot believes that students learn mathematics better if it is taught through problem solving. She regularly poses complex problems to her class of fifth graders and asks them to work in pairs to come up with solutions. Before discussing their solutions with the whole class, pairs in the class explain their solutions to another pair, and they critique each other's solutions.

56. Ms. Crowfoot's instructional strategy is an especially good one because of its

    A. emphasis on fostering students' ownership and responsibility in relation to their own learning.

    B. emphasis on using concrete objects as problem-solving tools.

    C. responsiveness to a variety of learning styles.

    D. responsiveness to individual students' personal interests and needs.

57. Ms. Crowfoot's likely purpose for allowing the student pairs to critique each other's solutions is that

    A. individual students will have the opportunity to assess critically their own strengths and weaknesses in regard to their problem-solving ability.

    B. students will have the opportunity to clarify their own thinking and, at the same time, help and encourage each other.

    C. the brighter students can correct the other students' mistakes before the whole class sees the solutions.

    D. students who are poor problem solvers will have an opportunity to compare their skills to more capable students and, as a result, be inspired to try harder.

58. One day in class, Aki complains that she doesn't like math and, besides, girls don't need to know it. Others in the class nod their heads in agreement. Which of the following would be the best way for Ms. Crowfoot to dispel stereotypical impressions about women and mathematics?

    A. Explain to the class that mathematics is important for girls and boys alike.

    B. Have the students research and write reports on famous women mathematicians.

    C. Plan a week in which the class learns about how mathematics is used in various careers.

    D. Arrange for men and women in the community to visit the class throughout the year to talk about how they use math in their work and everyday lives.

Use the information below to answer the two questions that follow.

A school invites parents, grandparents, and other community members to serve as volunteers several hours a week in teachers' classrooms. The volunteers assist the teachers in various ways, including by tutoring individual students.

59. Besides helping the students academically, the most probable benefit of this arrangement will be that it will

    A. create community awareness of teachers' problems.

    B. allow students the opportunity to discuss their problems with a sympathetic outsider.

    C. foster positive ties between the school and the community.

    D. improve student behavior in the classroom.

60. Carmen Drew, a teacher at the school, is planning a field trip. She asks the volunteers in her classroom to accompany her and her students on the field trip. What is most important for Ms. Drew to do to prepare the volunteers for the field trip?

    A. Make sure they know the names of the students they will be supervising.

    B. Make sure they know what to do if a student misbehaves.

    C. Meet with them beforehand and teach them the objectives for the field trip.

    D. Ask them to read a brochure about the field trip destination beforehand.

Use the information below to answer the two questions that follow.

When Kathryn Chertoff uses cooperative-learning groups in her third-grade class, she assigns specific roles to each group member: leader, recorder, checker, spokesperson, and so on. She also establishes rules for working with other students in groups such as listening actively, giving clear explanations, avoiding rudeness, and including other people.

61. When assigning group roles, Ms. Chertoff should make sure that

    A. the more capable students get the more demanding roles.

    B. the groups operate with the same group leader over time to ensure continuity.

    C. leadership responsibility is given in some measure to all group members over time.

    D. the students with more innate leadership ability are assigned as group leaders.

62. With regard to the rules she has established, which of the following is a key consideration Ms. Chertoff should take into account when planning for cooperative-learning activities?

    A. She will need to spend time in class teaching students the desired behaviors.

    B. Posting the rules prominently is usually sufficient to ensure learners' compliance.

    C. Children's natural desire to work in isolation will operate against their acting appropriately toward one another in groups.

    D. She will need to require the students to memorize the rules before cooperative-learning activities are implemented.

63. A local school board decides to reduce athletic expenditures by eliminating the girls' softball team. Because girls are forbidden to play on the boys' softball team, this would effectively eliminate softball for girls in the district. A group of girls decides to organize a protest and seeks the advice of a teacher. Because the school district receives federal funding, the teacher can best help the girls by suggesting that they

   A. organize a girls' boycott of all school athletic activities.

   B. try to accept the board's viewpoint and become involved in other activities.

   C. write a letter to the school board citing pertinent provisions of Title IX.

   D. play softball with a local team organized through the Boys and Girls Club.

64. Cameron is a new student in Lonnie Dizier's sixth-grade class. Cameron has trouble sitting still in class and often disrupts other students when she needs to be working independently on assignments. Mr. Dizier wonders if Cameron may have a learning disability. Which of the following are probable indications of a learning disability?

   I. difficulty in understanding social cues

   II. impulsive behavior coupled with marked hyperactivity

   III. poor reading comprehension coupled with word recognition errors when reading

   IV. inability to apply what is learned in one setting to another

   A. I, II, and III only

   B. I, III, and IV only

   C. II, III, and IV only

   D. I, II, III, and IV

65. To find out about any unusual fears or phobias a middle school student might have, a teacher would get the most accurate information from which of the following?

   A. parent interview

   B. colleagues who have previously taught the student

   C. peers who seem particularly observant and insightful

   D. a structured interview with the student

66. Danny Lozek, a middle school health education teacher, is teaching a unit on human sexuality to his eighth graders because he believes such instruction is an effective means of meeting certain components, related to family life, of the New York State standards for health education. A parents' group learns about the unit and objects to it, demanding that the principal prevent Mr. Lozek from teaching the unit. To handle the situation in the most professional manner, Mr. Lozek should

   A. do nothing, because it is the principal's role to convince the parents that the unit should be taught.

   B. suggest to the principal that a meeting with the parents be set up for them to express their viewpoints and for Mr. Lozek to explain the unit objectives and content and how these relate to the health education standards.

   C. take a poll of his students' attitudes about the unit and release the results to the parents to convince them of the need for such a unit.

   D. rely on the good sense of all concerned to resolve the matter in a constructive fashion.

67. In his seventh-grade science class, Jason Blum is teaching a lesson on atoms and molecules. Akina, who has been doing very well in the class, asks a question about DNA, to which Mr. Blum does not know the answer. How should he handle Akina's question?

    A. Say that he is sorry but that he does not know the answer.

    B. Admit that he does not know the answer and suggest ways that he and Akina can find the answer and inform the class.

    C. Suggest that Akina confine her attention to the course material she should know to pass the class.

    D. Admit that he does not know the answer and suggest that Akina research it on the Internet and inform the class.

68. To'nuel, a third grader, is assigned a research project and decides to write a report on panda bears. He asks his teacher, Ms. Yuan, to help him get started. Ms. Yuan suggests that To'nuel begin by creating the web shown below, listing everything To'nuel currently knows and wants to know about pandas.

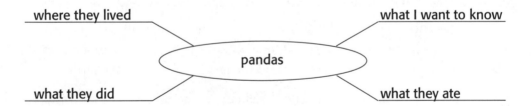

Creating such a web is likely to help To'nuel to

    I. organize his information about the topic.

    II. connect new information to previous knowledge.

    III. develop skill in using descriptive language.

    IV. make predictions about the topic.

    A. I and II only

    B. I and IV only

    C. II and III only

    D. III and IV only

69. Liang Freeman has arranged a parent-teacher conference with Mr. and Mrs. Ahmadi, the parents of Chera, a student in Ms. Freeman's class who is having academic difficulties. Ms. Freeman has observed that when Chera is working on assignments, she concentrates more on speed than on accuracy. When Ms. Freeman meets with Chera's parents, which of the following is appropriate for Ms. Freeman to do?

    A. To avoid wasting valuable time, begin immediately by telling them about Chera's hasty work habits.

    B. To reassure them that Chera does not have a learning disability, tell them that she thinks Chera is an underachiever.

    C. To lessen their anxiety about Chera, assure them that other students in the class are doing poorly as well.

    D. To end on a positive note, share some information about Chera's accomplishments at the close of the conference.

Use the information below to answer the two questions that follow.

70. A school district experiences a large increase in the number of Asian students, most of whom are English language learners who speak Chinese as their primary language. Ling, one of the Chinese students, has been placed in Azizeh Nejad's seventh-grade science class. Which of the following is an appropriate way for Mr. Nejad to address Ling's academic needs?

    A. Encourage Ling to speak her primary language at home only.

    B. Have a conference with Ling's parents to convince them that she would be better served in an ESL classroom for science instruction.

    C. Use drawings, demonstrations, concrete objects, and other visuals to explain concepts.

    D. Give Ling remedial assignments in science until her English improves.

71. During question-and-answer activities, Mr. Nejad should

    A. address questions to Ling that require only yes or no responses.

    B. question Nejad only in those areas of science in which she has demonstrated competence.

    C. address questions to Ling using body language and gestures to enhance meaning.

    D. call on Ling only when she volunteers to avoid embarrassing her.

72. As a new teacher, Calli Harper is nervous about student-teacher interactions with regard to communication issues. She is especially concerned about making sure that feedback to students is helpful in attaining learning objectives. To this end, Ms. Harper should give feedback that is

    I. immediate.

    II. specific.

    III. withheld during initial learning.

    IV. given about both correct and incorrect performances.

    A. I only

    B. II and III only

    C. I, II, and III only

    D. I, II, and IV only

73. Rob Naughton invites a scientist from a local university to give a presentation on global warming in the Americas to his middle school science students. Before the scientist's visit, Mr. Naughton plans to engage the students in a discussion in which they explore how North and South America differ with respect to man-made pollutants in the atmosphere. This discussion is most likely to facilitate student learning during the scientist's presentation by

   A. giving the students an indication of how they will be assessed on what the scientist presents.

   B. encouraging students to make predictions they can test during the presentation.

   C. enhancing the students' understanding of the society in which they live.

   D. outlining for the students what they should expect to learn from the presentation.

74. Cotina Martin, a fourth-grade teacher, is teaching a unit on the solar system. She begins a lesson about the planets by mentioning a popular science fiction television program about aliens and asks the students if anyone knows why these characters are called "aliens." Ms. Martin is attempting to motivate her students by

   A. relating the material in the lesson to the students' cultural experiences.

   B. convincing them of the importance of the material in the lesson.

   C. providing a tangible incentive for learning the material in the lesson.

   D. highlighting connections between the material in the lesson and the workplace.

75. Barbara Twomey, a first-year kindergarten teacher, wants to enhance her teaching effectiveness. Which of the following methods would most help Ms. Twomey in improving her own practice?

   A. Attend workshops on effective teaching at professional conferences.

   B. Study recent professional literature on effective teaching.

   C. Keep a reflective journal in which she deliberates on the quality of her teaching and is responsive to what she determines.

   D. Regularly observe a colleague who is known to be an effective teacher.

76. When designing curriculum for the middle school, educators should be aware that in general, middle school children

   A. are interested in investigating realistic problems and situations.

   B. have difficulty mentally reversing observable physical actions.

   C. have an emerging ability to reason logically about familiar phenomena.

   D. have already made clear-cut decisions about careers and ideology.

Use the information below to answer the two questions that follow.

When learners in Grinny Qiyue's second-grade class are problem solving in mathematics, Ms. Qiyue has them write out explanations for their solutions in their math journals. Even when students fail to solve a problem, she expects them to show the ideas and the work that they have considered.

77. Having students write out their reasoning for problems is most likely intended to

   A. highlight the relevance of problem solving to other subjects.

   B. motivate them to record the results of activities accurately.

   C. help them construct their own understanding of concepts.

   D. relate the ideas in the problem to their real-life concerns.

78. Writing in their math journals is likely to benefit students by

   A. enhancing their ability to access and use information effectively.

   B. helping them reflect on what they are learning.

   C. providing feedback that can be used to determine grades.

   D. fostering their ability to apply knowledge in varied contexts.

79. In ruling that it is unconstitutional to teach creationism as the sole explanation for the beginning of life, the Supreme Court based its reasoning upon

   A. scientific evidence accumulated by Darwin and his adherents.

   B. the majority opinion of biologists who teach and engage in research at present.

   C. the sound pedagogical principle that diversity of viewpoint should be exploited whenever possible.

   D. the constitutional prohibition against favoring one religion over another.

80. Tarishe Clooney teaches technology education in a school with a diverse student population. Ms. Clooney requires her students to participate in a group Internet "scavenger hunt" as an introductory activity to a unit on learning to use the Web. Carlos is a special education student in Ms. Clooney's class who is visually impaired. Carlos has "low vision," which means he can read print although he needs optical aids, such as magnifying lenses or other means, to enlarge the size of the print. Ms. Clooney is concerned that Carlos's low vision impairment is likely to make it difficult for him to participate fully in the introductory Internet activity. Which of the following should Ms. Clooney do to best fulfill her legal and ethical responsibilities toward Carlos?

   A. Provide him with an alternative assignment that he can do independently and successfully.

   B. Volunteer to stay after school with him to help him do the activity on his own.

   C. Make sure he has access to adaptive equipment that will allow him to participate fully in the group activity.

   D. Assign a partner to work with Carlos who will be his "eyes" during the activity.

KAPLAN

SAMPLE DIRECTIONS FOR THE WRITTEN ASSIGNMENT

This section of the test consists of a written assignment. You are asked to prepare a written response of approximately 300–600 words on the assigned topic. The assignment can be found on the next page. You should use your time to plan, write, review, and edit what you have written for the assignment.

Read the assignment carefully before you begin to write. Think about how you will organize what you plan to write. You may use any blank space provided on the following pages to make notes, write an outline, or otherwise prepare your response. However, your score will be based solely on the response you write in the written response booklet.

Your response will be evaluated on the basis of the following criteria:

- **PURPOSE:** Fulfill the charge of the assignment.
- **APPLICATION OF CONTENT:** Accurately and effectively apply the relevant knowledge and skills.
- **SUPPORT:** Support the response with appropriate examples and/or sound reasoning reflecting an understanding of the relevant knowledge and skills.

The ATS written assignment is intended to assess teaching knowledge and skills, not writing ability. However, candidates' responses must be communicated clearly enough to permit valid judgment of these factors by scorers. Candidates should present a thoughtful, reasonable response to the assignment supported by detail, argument, and evidence. The final version of the response should conform to the conventions of edited American English. This should be your original work, written in your own words, and not copied or paraphrased from some other work.

Be sure to write about the assigned topic and use multiple paragraphs. Please write legibly. You may not use any reference materials during the test. Remember to review what you have written and make any changes you think will improve your response.

Practice Written Assignment—Elementary ATS-W

Students come not only in different shapes and sizes, but with different backgrounds and different learning styles as well. It is important for teachers to recognize this diversity and create a classroom environment that fosters the learning of all children in the class.

Imagine the following statement was established as part of a mission statement at your school:

> Every student will be taught in a well-managed classroom environment that fosters and supports his or her active engagement in learning.

In an essay written for a group of New York State educators, frame your response by identifying a grade level/subject area for which you are prepared to teach. Then:

- explain the importance of providing valuable learning opportunities to all students in your classroom;
- describe two strategies you would use to achieve this goal; and
- explain why the strategies you describe would be effective in achieving this educational goal.

Be sure to specify a grade level/subject area in your essay, and frame your ideas so that an educator certified at your level (i.e., elementary or secondary) will be able to understand the basis for your response.

CHAPTER 12: PRACTICE ATS-W— ELEMENTARY ANSWERS AND EXPLANATIONS

Answer Key

1. B	21. B	41. D	61. C
2. D	22. A	42. C	62. A
3. B	23. C	43. D	63. C
4. C	24. B	44. D	64. B
5. D	25. B	45. B	65. A
6. B	26. C	46. C	66. B
7. A	27. B	47. D	67. B
8. C	28. C	48. C	68. A
9. B	29. B	49. D	69. D
10. A	30. D	50. A	70. C
11. D	31. C	51. A	71. C
12. A	32. C	52. B	72. D
13. B	33. C	53. D	73. B
14. D	34. B	54. D	74. A
15. A	35. A	55. B	75. C
16. D	36. C	56. A	76. A
17. A	37. B	57. B	77. C
18. B	38. C	58. D	78. B
19. C	39. C	59. C	79. D
20. D	40. D	60. B	80. C

ANSWERS AND EXPLANATIONS

1. B

The primary focus of this question is Objective 0013:

Understand the relationship between student motivation and achievement and how motivational principles and practices can be used to promote and sustain student cooperation in learning.

This is a multiple-response question. Read the statements and try to identify one with which you strongly agree or one with which you strongly disagree, whichever seems easier. Eliminate Statement II because an inquiry-based project seldom proceeds in a step-by-step progression, which renders a system of extrinsic rewards for steps completed problematic. Further, the goal of an inquiry-based project is purposeful, meaningful learning rather than externally motivated activity. Eliminate (C) and (D) because they contain Statement II. Choices (A) and (B) both contain Statement I, which therefore must be correct. Thus, you need decide only whether Statement III or Statement IV should be included in the answer choice. Statement III is a tempting choice because although in many instances students gain from working together— such as in mixed-ability cooperative-learning groups—in this case, such pairings could result in a further sense of inadequacy on the part of the at-risk students. Eliminate (A). Statement I is correct because giving students options about the project will allow the at-risk students to feel more in control of their participation in the project. Statement IV represents a sound approach because students understand the expectations for the project from the beginning and, more importantly, they know that they will receive credit for effort as well as for their end result, a stipulation likely to reduce the at-risk students' fear of failure. Choice (B) is the correct response.

2. D

The primary focus of this question is Objective 0014:

Understand communication practices that are effective in promoting student learning and creating a climate of trust and support in the classroom and how to use a variety of communication modes to support instruction.

Eliminate (A) because, whereas this approach isn't a bad idea all by itself, having feedback wait until specified times is. Feedback should be delivered as quickly as possible while the work is being discussed and is still fresh in the student's mind. Eliminate (B) because an important aspect of teacher feedback is to help students clearly identify areas that need strengthening and ways to work on those areas. Offering only positive feedback does not serve this purpose. Eliminate (C) because feedback tends to be less successful when it's delivered in public. Student embarrassment and suspicion about the teacher's motivation are two very real problems that could prevent public feedback from doing any good at all. Ms. Callahan somehow realizes that her feedback just isn't getting across. It's likely that part of her problem is that she isn't conveying feedback in a way that's clear to the students and in a way that they're comfortable with. Choice (D) takes care of both of these problems and, thus, is the correct response.

3. B

The primary focus of this question is Objective 0017:

Understand how to reflect productively on one's own teaching practice and how to update one's professional knowledge, skills, and effectiveness.

Notice that the question is asking what Ms. Callahan's *decision* to evaluate her own classroom performance *best* illustrates. Ms. Callahan's decision shows her desire to reflect on her own practice, which relates to *professional development* (Objective 0017). Eliminate (A) and (D) because these principles are focused on what Ms. Callahan does *after* her decision to evaluate her classroom performance. Further, these principles are related to *communication* (Objective 0012). Eliminate (C) because this principle is not focused on Ms. Callahan's decision. Further, the question does not support it— the students are not providing feedback. Ms. Callahan's decision to evaluate her own classroom performance best illustrates that she should reflect on her own practice to enhance her effectiveness in the classroom. Choice (B) is the correct response.

4. C

The primary focus of this question is Objective 0019:

Understand reciprocal rights and responsibilities in situations involving interactions between teachers and students, parents/guardians, community members, colleagues, school administrators, and other school personnel.

Eliminate (A) because the students are entitled to free speech in the school, but only as long as they don't deprive other students of the education to which they are entitled. Because the students are disrupting the education of the other students in the school, (A) is incorrect. Eliminate (B) because it is an out-of-focus response. It brings up a completely irrelevant issue. Whether or not a teacher is supervising the demonstration, the demonstration is disruptive and has to be stopped. Choice (D) supports the principal's decision for the wrong reason. The principal is not entitled to stop such a demonstration simply because the principal disagrees with the students' position. The students are entitled to free speech. The principal cannot interfere with that right unless the students are interfering with the other students' right to an education. Once students become so disruptive that they disturb the learning environment for others, that activity has to stop. Even though the demonstrators are entitled to express their opinions because they are entitled to free speech, just as everyone else is, they are not entitled to disrupt the classes of the other students, and that's why the principal has the right to stop the demonstration. Choice (C) is the correct response.

5. D

The primary focus of this question is Objective 0003:

Understand how factors in the home, school, and community may affect students' development and readiness to learn and use this understanding to create a classroom environment within which all students can develop and learn.

This is a priority-setting question. You're presented with a situation that requires you to decide which of the four responses offered would best facilitate class adjustment to the problem caused by the fire. Eliminate (A) because the teacher takes a defensive attitude instead of guiding the students. He is not teaching the students anything about how to handle an inconvenient and stressful situation gracefully. Eliminate (B) because it does not take the complaints of the students very seriously. It ignores the fact that there is a real inconvenience involved in sharing the classroom. Eliminate (C) because the teacher is encouraging unrealistic expectations in the students. It's not likely that the repairs will take only four weeks. The best response is (D). The first thing the teacher does is acknowledge that the situation is inconvenient. He's being honest with the students. The second thing he does is offer some positive aspects of the situation for the students to consider. He encourages them to look past the inconvenience and try out the new arrangement. By being honest with his students, but still encouraging them to think and behave well in the situation, the teacher is showing his students a way to handle a stressful situation with as much maturity as they can. Choice (D) is the correct response.

6. B

The primary focus of this question is Objective 0007:

Understand how to structure and manage a classroom to create a safe, healthy, and secure learning environment.

This is a priority-setting question—you must select Ms. Piazza's primary purpose for creating the model. Eliminate (A) because the question stem does not support it— Ms. Piazza is not gathering information about socioeconomic backgrounds. Eliminate (C) because, whereas Ms. Piazza's model might delineate classroom friendships, it wouldn't tell her how to redirect those friendships. That is something she would have to come up with after studying the model. Perhaps she would want, for some activities, to pair students who do not ordinarily play together so that they could get to know each other better. Eliminate (D) because it describes information that would best be obtained from direct observation of the children's classroom performance. By constructing a model of the friendship and interaction patterns of the students in her class, Ms. Piazza would be clarifying the peer relationships in the class, and such information would be an excellent supplement to her own observations of classroom interaction. Choice (B) is the correct response.

7. A

The primary focus of this question is Objective 0005:

Understand diverse student populations and use knowledge of diversity within the school and the community to address the needs of all learners, to create a sense of community among students, and to promote students' appreciation of and respect for individuals and groups.

This question concerns a common problem in modern education: how *best* to deal with a class in which students come from diverse backgrounds. The basic principle to remember is that classroom activities should nurture a sense of community and foster in all learners an appreciation of their own and others' cultures. Eliminate (B) because, whereas it does provide students with information about each other, it does so in a humdrum manner. Eliminate (C) because, although students learn better when they find information themselves, this activity is not the most effective way to nurture a sense of community in the class. Eliminate (D) because, whereas it may be an appropriate starting point, it provides no depth. The best activity to use with the class is given in (A). Because the entire class will be reading and discussing a story, all the students will learn about the achievements and cultural uniqueness of the background represented. Choice (A) is the correct response.

8. C

The primary focus of this question is Objective 0009:

Understand the interrelationship between assessment and instruction and how to use formal and informal assessment to learn about students, plan instruction, monitor student understanding in the context of instruction, and make effective instructional modifications.

Eliminate (A) because there is no factual basis for assuming this. Eliminate (B) because students who say little in class may in fact be just as competent as more talkative students. They may have reasons other than lack of proficiency in English for not speaking up more often. Eliminate (D) because this would shortchange the ESL learners and send the message that Mr. Libdeh considers them less able than their non-ESL peers. The varied cultural backgrounds of students who are English-language learners makes assessing their grasp of spoken English difficult. It may simply be that the culture in which they acquired their first language mandates silence or reticence in a wider range of social situations. Choice (C) is the correct response.

9. B

The primary focus of this question is Objective 0017:

Understand how to reflect productively on one's own teaching practice and how to update one's professional knowledge, skills, and effectiveness.

Eliminate (A) because students do not give up their rights as citizens, just because they are in school. They are entitled to the civil rights guaranteed to all citizens, including the right to due process as mentioned in the question stem. When these rights are violated, the federal government does have the right to step in. Eliminate (C) and (D) because they simply do not explain the rationale for states having the say over the use of physical force upon students. Whereas New York State has chosen to forbid the use of corporal punishment in New York public schools, the state does allow the use of "reasonable physical force" to prevent injury to people or damage to property. Each state, as the question stem reminds you, has the right to adopt measures permitting corporal punishment. This right sustains the basic doctrine articulated by the Supreme Court that common law recognizes that "teachers may impose reasonable, but not excessive, force to discipline a child." Choice (B) is the correct response.

10. A

The primary focus of this question is Objective 0019:

Understand reciprocal rights and responsibilities in situations involving interactions between teachers and students, parents/guardians, community members, colleagues, school administrators, and other school personnel.

This question takes up the issue of a student's right to refuse to salute the flag. The Supreme Court has ruled that no student may be required to take part in a flag salute ceremony as a condition of attendance, making (A) the correct answer. The court felt that a flag salute such as the Pledge of Allegiance cannot be required by the school, just as a prayer cannot be required by the school and for the same reason. The school cannot choose a belief, whether it's a matter of nationalism, religion, politics, or whatever, and tell its students to believe it or face the consequences. Choice (B) correctly says that the student is within her rights to refuse to salute the flag but gives the wrong reason. The due process clause does not apply to this situation. Eliminate (C) because it directly contradicts the Supreme Court decision. Eliminate (D) because it is an out-of-focus answer. The student is not asking the school to support her beliefs. She simply does not want to participate in an activity that apparently does not correspond with her beliefs, and she is entitled to do so. Choice (A) is the correct response.

11. D

The primary focus of this question is Objective 0009:

Understand the interrelationship between assessment and instruction and how to use formal and informal assessment to learn about students, plan instruction, monitor student understanding in the context of instruction, and make effective instructional modifications.

This is a multiple-response question. Read the statements and try to identify one with which you strongly agree or one with which you strongly disagree, whichever seems easier. Teachers should evaluate the uses and limitations of assessment techniques for meeting various instructional needs. Eliminate Statement II because a teacher-made test is not a standardized test and so would not have national norms for comparisons. Eliminate (A) and (B) because they contain Statement II. Choices (C) and (D) both contain Statements III and IV, so you need only decide whether Statement I should be included in the correct response. Statement I is correct because Ms. Estrada's test will likely reflect the success of her instructional materials and teaching methods. Eliminate (C). Statement III is correct because this is information to be gained from the test (given that it is aligned with the unit objectives as it should be). Statement IV is correct because information about individual students is readily determined based on their individual tests. Choice (D) is the correct response.

12. A

The primary focus of this question is Objective 0008:

Understand curriculum development and apply knowledge of factors and processes in curricular decision making.

In designing curriculum, educators should select appropriate materials and resources that are responsive to students' characteristics and needs. Eliminate (B) because, even if a publishing company is speaking in good faith, it cannot be an objective judge of bias in its materials because it is trying to sell them. A money-back guarantee is really no help. Once students have been insulted or made to feel bad, it's not going to make them feel better to know that the school is getting its money back. Eliminate (C) because it is not the school librarian's responsibility to perform this function. Eliminate (D) because approval by the Regents certainly allows Mr. Wechsler to use the books, but it doesn't tell him that they meet his criteria. It is Mr. Wechsler's responsibility to form this determination. He knows his students better than anyone else and presumably would have a better sense of what might be offensive to them. Choice (A) is the correct response.

13. B

The primary focus of this question is Objective 0016:

Understand the history, philosophy, and role of education in New York State and the broader society.

Eliminate (A) because, whereas evaluation of teachers providing instructional services includes the teacher's conduct and competence in the classroom, it is not limited to those factors and must by law include other factors (e.g., the teacher's content knowledge). Furthermore, the Supreme Court has ruled that it finds "no requirement in the federal Constitution that a teacher's classroom conduct be the sole basis for determining fitness." Eliminate (C) because the district is entitled to take the teacher's outside activities into account when making an employment decision but state law does not require the district to do so. Eliminate (D) because state law does not support it. In New York State, whereas the professional performance review plan for districts specifies eight criteria that district must use to evaluate its teachers, the district is not limited to these criteria and is entitled to include the teacher's personal behavior outside the classroom as part of its evaluation. Choice (B) is the correct response.

14. D

The primary focus of this question is Objective 0007:

Understand how to structure and manage a classroom to create a safe, healthy, and secure learning environment.

Eliminate (A) and (B) because a negative attitude about the subject matter or inability to concentrate does not warrant removal from class. Whereas (C) may make Ms. Cavuto quite uncomfortable, it is not a sufficient reason to remove a student from class. Further, the hostility is described as "suppressed," which suggests that the student is not acting overtly hostile toward anyone. The key principle to keep in mind is that a student has a right to an education but loses that right if the student interferes with the other students' right to an education. Choice (D) is the correct response.

15. A

The primary focus of this question is Objective 0018:

Understand the importance of and apply strategies for promoting productive relationships and interactions among the school, home, and community to enhance student learning.

This is a multiple-response question. Read the statements and try to identify one with which you strongly agree or one with which you strongly disagree, whichever seems easier. Eliminate Statement III because discipline at home is a private matter that in general the school should not get involved in. Eliminate (C) and (D) because they contain Statement III. (A) and (B) both contain Statement I. You must decide whether to include Statement II or IV in your answer choice. Eliminate Statement IV because the school has no guarantee that this will happen just because the parents have been informed about the suspension. Eliminate (B). Informing parents of impending internal suspensions will make them partners in their child's discipline (Statement I) and make them accountable for knowledge of their child's behavior (Statement II). Choice (A) is the correct response.

16. D

The primary focus of this question is Objective 0009:

Understand the interrelationship between assessment and instruction and how to use formal and informal assessment to learn about students, plan instruction, monitor student understanding in the context of instruction, and make effective instructional modifications.

This is a priority-setting question. You must select the answer choice that should *most* concern Mr. O'Grady. Eliminate (A) because learning at a slower pace isn't abnormal in itself. As long as the child is learning, Mr. O'Grady has no reason to be alarmed about a child who learns at a slower pace than the other students do. Eliminate (B) because differences in learning styles are not a cause for concern. Whereas (C) may be frustrating for Mr. O'Grady, it is not abnormal and is certainly no cause for serious concern. All of the situations presented in the answer choices are situations that could very well happen in any classroom, but only one of them is a cause for serious concern, and that's (D). If a teacher has taught particular concepts in class, yet a student can't apply those concepts, then something has apparently gone wrong. Perhaps the student is able to deal with the concepts at the procedural level of understanding, following directions and rules correctly, but has not yet developed conceptual understanding. The point is that a student who has trouble applying the concepts needs some sort of help, and the teacher should take the time and concern to come up with that help. Choice (D) is the correct response.

17. A

The primary focus of this question is Objective 0002:

Understand learning processes and use this understanding to promote student development and learning.

This is a priority-setting question. You must select the answer choice that is *most* likely to promote higher-order thinking skills. Eliminate (B) because naming the characters simply involves knowledge-level learning. Eliminate (C) because writing a thank-you letter can be done entirely by rote. Eliminate (D) because writing a recipe involves sequencing skills (putting things down one after another) but not higher-order thinking skills. Filling in missing components of a pattern requires the higher-order thinking skills of analysis (involving the ability to examine relationships of the parts of the pattern to one another) and synthesis (involving the ability to predict what part is missing). Choice (A) is the correct response.

18. B

The primary focus of this question is Objective 0007:

Understand how to structure and manage a classroom to create a safe, healthy, and secure learning environment.

This is a priority-setting question—you must select which one of the answer choices is *most* important. The spatial arrangement of the room has a great deal to do with the interaction among the students and between the students and the teacher. Eliminate (A), (C), and (D) because these factors tend to be relatively irrelevant. Notice that (C) is a little tricky. You might think that the more windows there are, the more students may be distracted by gazing out of them. But even if that factor were particularly relevant, it would have to do with the overall amount of window space, not the number of windows. Choice (B) is the correct response.

19. C

The primary focus of this question is Objective 0011:

Understand various instructional approaches and use this knowledge to facilitate student learning.

This is a multiple-response question. Read the statements and try to identify one with which you strongly agree or one with which you strongly disagree, whichever seems easier. Eliminate Statement II because Mr. O'Grady is not asking the children to deal with values or feelings (i.e., affective learning). Eliminate (A), (B), and (D) because they contain Statement II. Statements I and III are correct because the students are engaged in brainstorming and divergent thinking—they've asked to come up with a variety of new ideas. Statement IV is correct because the students are engaged in cooperative learning in that the children within each group are cooperating toward a common goal. Choice (C) is the correct response.

20. D

The primary focus of this question is Objective 0005:

Understand diverse student populations and use knowledge of diversity within the school and the community to address the needs of all learners, to create a sense of community among students, and to promote students' appreciation of and respect for individuals and groups.

Eliminate (B) and (C) because they are essentially the same answer. Because there is only one correct answer choice, neither of these can be the correct response. Middle school boys and girls behave differently socially and academically, and biological and cultural factors in combination play a role in these differences. For example, in terms of biological factors, girls mature earlier than boys, emotionally and mentally. On the other hand, we know that all sorts of cultural variables intervene to stereotype the behavior of boys and girls. Eliminate (A) because it deals with only one of the major factors, so it is an insufficient response. Choice (D) is the correct response.

21. B

The primary focus of this question is Objective 0006:

Understand the characteristics and needs of students with disabilities, developmental delays, and exceptional abilities (including gifted and talented students) and use this knowledge to help students reach their highest levels of achievement and independence.

Eliminate (A), (C), and (D) because it is the teacher's responsibility to define learning objectives for his or her classroom. The resource teacher has the training and expertise to choose particular strategies that will help the student attain those objectives. Choice (B) is the correct response.

22. A

The primary focus of this question is Objective 0018:

Understand the importance of and apply strategies for promoting productive relationships and interactions among the school, home, and community to enhance student learning.

Eliminate (B) because it suggests that Ms. Rudovsky should take the position that the parent is wrong. The teacher who starts arguing with the parent about the book is automatically suggesting that she is right and the parent is wrong. What about listening to what the parent has to say? Eliminate (C) because it goes in the opposite direction, saying that Ms. Rudovsky should simply give in to the parent and excuse from the assignment any student who finds it objectionable. This isn't a good idea either because Ms. Rudovsky has made no effort at all to get the parent to understand her point of view. Whereas it's wise to listen to the parent, it's also wise to talk with the parent a bit about the value of the assignment and the goals Ms. Rudovsky expects to meet by studying the book. Eliminate (D) because this would remove Ms. Rudovsky from the situation completely. The problem concerns what is going on in her classroom, so she ought to be involved in the solution to the problem. Ms. Rudovsky should arrange a conference with the parents and the school principal. If the parents are still convinced at the end of the conference that the book is objectionable, Ms. Rudovsky should assign their child a different book. Think about the value of this approach. Ms. Rudovsky gives the parents full opportunity to voice their objections. She's had a chance to present her point of view. The principal has been present to assist the teacher and to reassure the parents about the school's concern. The parents and Ms.Rudovsky are most likely to walk away from the situation satisfied that the educational process can be carried out in a cooperative manner. Choice (A) is the correct response.

23. C

The primary focus of this question is Objective 0016:

Understand the history, philosophy, and role of education in New York State and the broader society.

In theory, federal regulations should not affect New York State public schools because the power to regulate education is a power granted under the Constitution to the states, not to the federal government. Federal regulations enter the picture because federal funds are available to public education. The catch is that the schools accepting federal funds must comply with federal laws and regulations. Eliminate (A) because the Constitution grants the regulation of education to the states. Eliminate (B) because it is too narrow an answer. Whereas the laws about civil rights must be obeyed in the schools, other laws must be obeyed as well. Eliminate (D) because, as mentioned earlier for instance, the federal government can require school districts to comply with federal regulations when the district is accepting federal monies. Choice (C) is the correct response.

24. B

The primary focus of this question is Objective 0016:

Understand the history, philosophy, and role of education in New York State and the broader society.

This question involves an understanding of the "chain of command." In a New York State school district, teachers answer to the principal, who, in turn, answers to the superintendent, whose actions are subject to the approval of the school board. Mr. Johnson does have to go along with what Ms. Rhodes asks. If she wants his lesson plans two months in advance, he has to give her the lesson plans two months in advance. Eliminate (C) because finding out what the other teachers are doing will not be particularly helpful because Mr. Johnson has no choice but to do what the principal asks. Eliminate (D) because refusing to comply is not an option. Eliminate (A) because complying with the principal's request by writing cursory lesson plans may backfire on Mr. Johnson and make him seem insubordinate. He should comply with Ms. Rhodes's request. It's perfectly reasonable to explain to her that he's constantly revising his plans as things change in the classroom and offer to provide her with such changes. This approach will demonstrate his willingness to work cooperatively with Ms. Rhodes to accomplish educational goals. Choice (B) is the correct response.

25. B

The primary focus of this question is Objective 0005:

Understand diverse student populations and use knowledge of diversity within the school and the community to address the needs of all learners, to create a sense of community among students, and to promote students' appreciation of and respect for individuals and groups.

This is a multiple-response question. Read the statements and try to identify one with which you totally agree or one with which you totally disagree, whichever seems easier. Eliminate Statement IV because the goal of bilingual education is not to get rid of the native language. The idea is to provide a transition from the native language into English. Eliminate (C) and (D) because they contain Statement IV. Both (A) and (B) contain Statements I and III, so you need decide only on whether to include Statement II in your answer choice. Statement II is correct because another goal of bilingual education is to maintain academic skills that are not directly involved with language, such as math or science, while the student is learning English. Other goals of bilingual education are to increase proficiency in the native language (Statement I) and to foster pride in the student's native background (Statement III). The idea is to help the student to become bilingual and to feel good about both languages. Choice (B) is the correct response.

26. C

The primary focus of this question is Objective 0005:

Understand diverse student populations and use knowledge of diversity within the school and the community to address the needs of all learners, to create a sense of community

among students, and to promote students' appreciation of and respect for individuals and groups.

Eliminate (A) because failure to discuss racial or ethnic issues openly may allow conflict between groups to develop unchecked, thus working against group harmony. Eliminate (B) because competitive activities might contribute to group disharmony. Eliminate (D) because this would isolate the English language learners, denying them the opportunity to work with and get to know their classmates. Research indicates that cooperative-learning methods using groups that are culturally mixed improve intergroup relations. Mr. Sato should use cooperative groups that are racially and ethnically balanced. This will allow his students the opportunity to get to know each other and cooperate with one another, thereby developing harmonious relations. Choice (C) is the correct response.

27. B

The primary focus of this question is Objective 0003:

Understand how factors in the home, school, and community may affect students' development and readiness to learn and use this understanding to create a classroom environment within which all students can develop and learn.

Eliminate (A) because it is an out-of-focus answer choice that contains tempting terminology related to *developmentally appropriate practices* (Objective 0001). Eliminate (C) because it is an out-of-focus answer choice that contains tempting terminology related to *diversity* (Objective 0005). Eliminate (D) because it is an out-of-focus answer choice that contains tempting terminology related to *students with special needs* (Objective 0006). By holding high expectations of success for all his students, Mr. Sato illustrates that he understands how classroom factors, such as teacher expectations, may affect students' self-concepts and learning. He is aware that his expectations about a student can eventually lead that student to behave or achieve in ways that confirm his expectations; in other words, what he expects from students, he will probably get. Choice (B) is the correct response.

28. C

The primary focus of this question is Objective 0001:

Understand human development, including developmental processes and variations, and use this understanding to promote student development and learning.

Eliminate (A), (B), and (D) because research studies support the self-fulfilling prophecy hypothesis that teacher expectations affect student achievement and behavior. In general, good or bad, what teachers expect, they get. With regard to middle school children, peer relations and peer influences tend to be relatively impervious to the impact of teachers. This circumstance is probably due to the great concern that adolescents have for peer acceptance. Choice (C) is the correct response.

29. B

The primary focus of this question is Objective 0017:

Understand how to reflect productively on one's own teaching practice and how to update one's professional knowledge, skills, and effectiveness.

Notice that the question is asking about Ms. Ruiz's *decision* to meet with the counselor to discuss her concerns about Abbe. Eliminate (A) because its focus is Abbe's writing problems, not Ms. Ruiz's decision. Eliminate (C) because it is an out-of-focus answer that uses tempting terminology related to *classroom management* (Objective 007). Eliminate (D) because it is not supported by the question—there is no indication that Ms. Ruiz is trying to promote a sense of community in the school. Ms. Ruiz's decision reflects her desire to take advantage of various resources (e.g., the counselor) and opportunities to enhance her effectiveness in the classroom. She understands that she is a member of a learning community and should work with other members of the community to enhance her own effectiveness. Choice (B) is the correct response.

30. D

The primary focus of this question is Objective 0011:

Understand various instructional approaches and use this knowledge to facilitate student learning.

Eliminate (A) because worksheets address low-level objectives (i.e., facts and knowledge). (For this reason, by the way, having students complete worksheets is unlikely to be a correct answer on the ATS-W.) Eliminate (B) because it is teacher directed with students as passive recorders. Eliminate (C) because the students who are listening are passive participants. Ms. Akhtar knows that allowing students to discover properties of light in a cooperative-group setting will help them to develop a deeper understanding of the scientific principles involved. Choice (D) is the correct response.

31. C

The primary focus of this question is Objective 0002:

Understand learning processes and use this understanding to promote student development and learning.

This is a multiple-response question. Read the statements and try to identify one with which you totally agree or one with which you totally disagree, whichever seems easier. Eliminate Statement I because this type of environment would be likely to result in less risk taking and less higher-level thinking and to discourage active inquiry. Eliminate (A) because it contains Statement I. Eliminate Statement III because metacognitive strategies should be practiced as students are learning, not memorized and recited in isolation. Eliminate (B) and (D) because they contain Statement III. Critical thinking is the mental process of acquiring information, then evaluating it to make a rational decision, reach a logical conclusion, or form an opinion or belief. Encouraging students to discuss their conclusions with each other (Statement II) and to justify the reasoning behind their conclusions (Statement IV) will force students to analyze critically their and each other's thinking and, further, help them to clarify their own thinking. Choice (C) is the correct response.

32. C

The primary focus of this question is Objective 0011:

Understand various instructional approaches and use this knowledge to facilitate student learning.

Eliminate (A) and (B) because ability grouping may negatively affect the attitudes, achievement, and opportunities of low-ability learners. Eliminate (D) because it disagrees with research indicating that students benefit from working in small groups. Some evidence suggests that high-ability learners may gain from ability grouping, but removing them from interaction with their peers may be problematic. Most authorities agree that mixed-ability grouping benefits all learners, as long as there is group interdependence and individual accountability. These two conditions mitigate against the higher-ability students doing most of the work or one or more students being shut out of group interactions because they are thought to have little to contribute. Choice (C) is the correct response.

33. C

The primary focus of this question is Objective 0007:

Understand how to structure and manage a classroom to create a safe, healthy, and secure learning environment.

Eliminate (A) and (D) because, in most scholastic situations, it's not appropriate for students to call teachers by their first names. Eliminate (B) because telling Alex in front of the class that the behavior is inappropriate will probably embarrass him. Because he did not intend to be disrespectful, this approach is unnecessarily punishing toward him. Ms. Ramon does need to tell Alex that they cannot interact in class the same way they did in the basketball league. It's important that Ms. Ramon point this out to him as soon as possible, but privately so as not to embarrass him. Choice (C) is the correct response.

34. B

The primary focus of this question is Objective 0007:

Understand how to structure and manage a classroom to create a safe, healthy, and secure learning environment.

Eliminate (A) because it is not supported by the question—Ms. Fatemah is working only with her students, *not* with members of the school community in general. Eliminate (C) because this is something Ms. Fatemah can do without calling a class meeting. Eliminate (D) because it is an out-of-focus answer that uses tempting terminology related to *motivation* (Objective 0013). Ms. Fatemah's action illustrates her understanding that providing an opportunity for the students to recognize the problem and suggest solutions is likely to promote ownership in a smoothly functioning learning community. Choice (B) is the correct response.

35. A

The primary focus of this question is Objective 0001:

Understand human development, including developmental processes and variations, and use this understanding to promote student development and learning.

Eliminate (B) because, in general, adolescents are rebellious toward adult authority and place high regard on their peer group (*not* adult authorities) as a source of ideas and values. Eliminate (C) because most adolescents have reached Piaget's stage of formal operational thought and so *are* capable of reasoning hypothetically about a situation contrary to fact. Eliminate (D) because adolescents assume that they will not have to face the consequences of their behavior. In fact, they feel invincible and believe that bad things happen to other people, not to them. Choice (A) is the correct response.

36. C

The primary focus of this question is Objective 0003:

Understand how factors in the home, school, and community may affect students' development and readiness to learn and use this understanding to create a classroom environment within which all students can develop and learn.

This is a priority-setting question—you must select the *most* effective answer choice. Eliminate (A) because this approach may negatively affect Ellen's self-esteem if she is not successful after having been urged to try harder. Eliminate (B) and (D) because while these measures might positively impact Ellen's self-esteem, would not be as effective as the approach given in (C). Mr. Nestor can most effectively enhance Ellen's self-esteem by planning activities that are challenging for her but for which she can achieve success through her own efforts. By successfully coping with difficult tasks, Ellen likely will be convinced of her own abilities and come to appreciate herself and her inherent worth. Choice (C) is the correct response.

37. B

The primary focus of this question is Objective 0002:

Understand learning processes and use this understanding to promote student development and learning.

Eliminate (A) and (D) because these approaches focus on a narrow aspect of the metric system; that is, conversion of units. Further, they emphasize students doing math in a rote fashion, whether they have conceptual understanding of what they are doing or not. Eliminate (C) because whereas previewing what they will be doing later may help orient students to the lesson, doing worksheets is seldom a productive way for students to spend their time in math class. Ms. Spagnola should recognize the importance of previous knowledge in the learning process. By writing down and discussing in small groups what they already know about the metric system, the students will review their previous knowledge on the topic. This will make it easier for them to link new knowledge encountered to their previous understandings. Choice (B) is the correct response.

38. C

The primary focus of this question is Objective 0019:

Understand reciprocal rights and responsibilities in situations involving interactions between teachers and students, parents/guardians, community members, colleagues, school administrators, and other school personnel.

Notice that the question is about the armbands, *not* about Frederic's vandalism. Eliminate (A) because such measures have been held to be unconstitutional. Eliminate (B) because this would encourage future action in a similar vein. Eliminate (D) because the students are already voicing their protests and (D) only provides an additional forum. Students have a right to free speech and are permitted to express their opinions by wearing distinctive apparel as long as the apparel does not represent a health hazard or disrupt orderly learning. Because the armbands do neither, at this point, the best course of action for the teachers is to do nothing. Choice (C) is the correct response.

39. C

The primary focus of this question is Objective 0012:

Understand principles and procedures for organizing and implementing lessons and use this knowledge to promote student learning and achievement.

The key to answering this question correctly is in the phrase *a literature unit introducing the story and characters of Shakespeare's* Romeo and Juliet. Eliminate (A) because inspiring students to read more Shakespeare is not one of the instructional objectives described in the question stem. The same is true of (B). If this were among the instructional objectives for the unit, (B) would make sense, but as the question is written, (B) doesn't apply. Eliminate (D) because whereas it may sadden the teacher that the students prefer great literature in the form of a movie, that's not a reason to reteach the unit. Choice (C) says that fewer than half of the students can explain why Juliet commits suicide. In other words, fewer than half of the students understand a crucial part of the story. This outcome is a cause for concern and is a compelling reason to reteach the unit. Choice (C) is the correct response.

40. D

The primary focus of this question is Objective 0009:

Understand the interrelationship between assessment and instruction and how to use formal and informal assessment to learn about students, plan instruction, monitor student understanding in the context of instruction, and make effective instructional modifications.

This is a multiple-response question. Read the statements and try to identify one with which you totally agree or one with which you totally disagree, whichever seems easier. Eliminate Statement I because any comparison with the other social studies classes would be misguided. Among other things, students in the other classes may have different levels of ability, different backgrounds, and different motivational levels. Eliminate (A) and (C) because they contain Statement I. Choices (B) and (D) both contain Statement II, so you now must decide whether to include Statements III and IV as well. The students' scores on the state social studies assessment will certainly provide Mr. Jingjoy useful information about his students' performance in social studies (Statement II), as will their pre- and postgain scores on a unit mastery test (Statement III). The cumulative class anecdotal records (Statement IV) should, if they've been kept properly, yield information as to how students have been doing on a day-to-day basis. That's certainly useful information. Choice (D) is the correct response.

41. D

The primary focus of this question is Objective 0014:

Understand communication practices that are effective in promoting student learning and creating a climate of trust and support in the classroom and how to use a variety of communication modes to support instruction.

Eliminate (A) because when a teacher points out all the errors in writing assignments, students tend to be overwhelmed, and when the teacher assigns an overall grade, the students don't receive any specific information. Eliminate (B) because, whereas it is a better choice than (A), assigning an overall grade is problematic for the students. Is the grade for the ideas, the expression, or the grammar? Eliminate (C) because it has the same problem—it is too vague. It doesn't tell the students on what specific areas (grammar? spelling? organization?) they need to focus. Choice (D) gives the students feedback on what they're doing right and gives the individual student a strategy for improving his or her work. Choice (D) is the correct response.

42. C

The primary focus of this question is Objective 0013:

Understand the relationship between student motivation and achievement and how motivational principles and practices can be used to promote and sustain student cooperation in learning.

Eliminate (A) because praise should give students feedback on the quality of their work. Eliminate (B) because some research suggests giving tangible rewards to students for doing what they wanted to do anyway works against intrinsic motivation. Further, this approach likely would cause resentment toward the students who receive the rewards. Eliminate (D) because the topics Ms. Kirby finds interesting may "turn off" some, or possibly, all of her students. Intrinsic motivation is shown to increase when students are given a measure of control over their learning activities. Allowing students to select their own writing topics will prompt students to relate classroom activities to their own interests and experiences. Choice (C) is the correct response.

43. D

The primary focus of this question is Objective 0008:

Understand curriculum development and apply knowledge of factors and processes in curricular decision making.

This is a multiple-response question. Read the statements and try to identify one with which you totally agree or one with which you totally disagree, whichever seems easier. Statement I is correct because the teachers on the team will have opportunities to share ideas and resources. Eliminate (C) because it does not contain Statement I. Statements II and IV are correct because interdisciplinary teams work together to create integrated lessons for their students. Eliminate (A) and (B) because they do not contain Statement IV. Statement III is correct because through integrated lessons—for instance, a math-science activity where students graph real-life data—students have opportunities for realistic problem solving. Choice (D) is the correct response.

44. D

The primary focus of this question is Objective 0002:

Understand learning processes and use this understanding to promote student development and learning.

Eliminate (A) because the visual learner would probably benefit *most* from reading-related activities. Eliminate (B) because the tactile learner would probably benefit most from handling plastic alphabet letters and similar manipulatives. The aural learner would develop language skills by listening and speaking more than by the activity described in the question. A kinesthetic learner (D) learns best through movement and activity. Of course, the great majority—if not all—children learn through a combination of these modalities. In some people, one particular modality predominates. The activity in the question stem would help those children whose primary learning modality is kinesthetic because they would connect the song words with the dance movements. Choice (D) is the correct response.

45. B

The primary focus of this question is Objective 0002:

Understand learning processes and use this understanding to promote student development and learning.

This is a multiple-response question. Read the statements and try to identify one with which you totally agree or one with which you totally disagree, whichever seems easier. Eliminate Statement III because rote learning is strictly memorization without comprehension—not particularly effective in improving learning and memory. Eliminate (C) and (D) because they contain Statement III. Both (A) and (B) contain Statements I and II, so you need only decide whether to include Statement IV. Mnemonics (Statement I), chunking (Statement II), and rehearsal (Statement IV) are all basic memorization techniques. Mnemonics are used to simplify memorization; they are "tricks" you use to memorize things—for example, "*i* before *e* except after *c* or when sounded like *a*, as in *neighbor* or *weigh*." Chunking involves grouping or clustering more than one particular piece of data or more than one stimulus in some meaningful way in order to remember it. For example, when you remember telephone numbers, you remember them as two chunks of information, the first three digits and the last four digits, rather than as seven separate digits. Rehearsal is a process that you constantly use to remember things. It's the process of repeating information, either aloud or silently, as a means of holding it in short-term memory and preparing it for long-term memory. Choice (B) is the correct response.

46. C

The primary focus of this question is Objective 0014:

Understand communication practices that are effective in promoting student learning and creating a climate of trust and support in the classroom and how to use a variety of communication modes to support instruction.

The key to answering questions about convergent and divergent thinking is to remember that questions encouraging convergent thinking have a clear right answer—a word, a number, a list, etc.—whereas questions that encourage divergent thinking have a variety of answers, none of which can be described as the "right" answer. Eliminate (A) and (D) because there is only one right answer for these questions. Eliminate (B) because the correct answer is a list. The question in (C) is not meant to elicit one specific answer. It's meant to encourage students to think of all the different ways of traveling across the country, and no answer is going to be more correct than another. The point of asking such a question is to get as wide a variety of responses as possible. Choice (C) is the correct response.

47. D

The primary focus of this question is Objective 0009:

Understand the interrelationship between assessment and instruction and how to use formal and informal assessment to learn about students, plan instruction, monitor student understanding in the context of instruction, and make effective instructional modifications.

Eliminate (A) because the question stem does not indicate that Mr. Honea will use different strategies when he reteaches the unit. (Remember, don't read too much into a question.) If the students didn't learn it the first time, why should he expect them to learn it the second time if he doesn't try a different approach? Eliminate (B) and (C) because piling on extra work while the students are trying to master the material in the new unit is going to lead to additional disappointing results. Further, (B) focuses the extra work on students who have done poorly, which seems punitive. Also, these students may have done poorly because of failures in the instructional strategies. The students who have done poorly will likely become frustrated and discouraged. Rather than going through everything again, Mr. Honea should analyze what the students need and reteach that material but use different strategies. Choice (D) is the correct response.

48. C

The primary focus of this question is Objective 0010:

Understand instructional planning and apply knowledge of planning processes to design effective instruction that promotes the learning of all students.

This is a priority-setting question. You must select the strategy that would be *most* in accord with inclusion. The success of meeting the needs of all students in general education environments requires thoughtful planning and openness to adapting instructional methods to ensure that students with disabilities are afforded meaningful participation in the classroom. Eliminate (A) because ability grouping will likely decrease the opportunities for interaction between students with learning disabilities and their nondisabled peers. Eliminate (B) and (D) because these methods tend to isolate students from each other and so are not as supportive of inclusion as the method given in (C), cooperative learning. Research indicates that, in particular, children with physical or mental disabilities benefit academically and socially from involvement in cooperative-learning instruction because of the opportunities to explore their abilities and interests in the same context as their nondisabled classmates. Choice (C) is the correct response.

49. D

The primary focus of this question is Objective 0006:

Understand the characteristics and needs of students with disabilities, developmental delays, and exceptional abilities (including gifted and talented students) and use this knowledge to help students reach their highest levels of achievement and independence.

This is a multiple-response question. Read the statements and try to identify one with which you strongly agree or one with which you strongly disagree, whichever seems easier. Eliminate Statement I because a child with a disability is entitled to the least restrictive environment. Setting aside a special area of the classroom violates that by separating the child from the rest of the class. In addition, it makes the child feel stigmatized and makes the students more likely to treat the child in an unacceptable way. Eliminate (A) and (B) because they contain Statement I. Choices (C) and (D) both contain Statements II and III, so you need only decide whether to include Statement IV in your answer choice. Statement IV is correct because modifying instructional techniques and materials is one way to ensure meaningful participation of the child in the classroom. It is also appropriate to consult with the child's parents regarding the child's IEP (Statement II) because the parents are by law involved in the process of their child's education. Explaining to the other children the nature of the child's disability (Statement III) is a wise action because kindergarten children are likely to be very curious about a child with a disability and an explanation would help them understand the special nature of the new student. Further, it would communicate to them that their curiosity is natural and acceptable. Preparing the other children for the arrival of a child with a disability will help make the transition easier for everyone involved. If the other children understand the problems and needs of a child with a disability, there's much less chance that they will be frightened by the child or treat the child in an unacceptable way. Choice (D) is the correct response.

50. A

The primary focus of this question is Objective 0010:

Understand instructional planning and apply knowledge of planning processes to design effective instruction that promotes the learning of all students.

This is a priority-setting question—you must select which of the answer choices is *most* important for Ms. Cooper to consider. When teachers have students with special needs in their classroom, the teachers should make it a priority to ensure that these children participate to the greatest extent possible in all instructional activities. Eliminate (D) because it is contrary to this principle. Eliminate (B) and (C) because, whereas these are things Ms. Cooper will likely think about, they are not as important as making sure children with special needs are included in the field trip by considering the accessibility for children with disabilities. Choice (A) is the correct response.

51. A

The primary focus of this question is Objective 0001:

Understand human development, including developmental processes and variations, and use this understanding to promote student development and learning.

Mr. Fuesdon needs to take Christine's complaint seriously because children at this age are insecure and fear rejection. Eliminate (B) because, even if it does seem to Mr. Fuesdon that Christine is imagining her problem, he should not just say so and dismiss the whole issue. Instead, he might try to convince Christine that she really is well liked by reminding her of times when her classmates showed their fondness for her. Eliminate (C) because this approach is likely to make the situation worse. When other children are scolded and told to treat a certain child better, it reinforces the perception that there's something wrong with the child. Further, middle school children tend to be even harder on students that the teacher singles out for protection. Eliminate (D) because this action is too extreme. Further, general education teachers should avoid "diagnosing" a student who is having problems because they do not hold credentials to perform this function. The challenge for Mr. Fuesdon is to help Christine with her problem without further stigmatizing her in her own eyes or in the eyes of her classmates. By arranging a time to talk with Christine about the problem, Mr. Fuesdon is showing his concern. Giving Christine a chance to talk is very important because she is already feeling bad about herself. Mr. Fuesdon's concern might be the first step in restoring her self-image. In the course of the conversation, he can let Christine know that he cares about her problem and help her to think of ways to solve it. By working with Christine to come up with ways she can solve her problem, Mr. Fuesdon is helping her take charge of her situation, rather than letting her assume the role of a helpless victim. This approach will help Christine handle future unpleasant situations with more confidence. Choice (A) is the correct response.

52. B

The primary focus of this question is Objective 0012:

Understand principles and procedures for organizing and implementing lessons and use this knowledge to promote student learning and achievement.

Notice that the question is asking about Ms. Washington's *decision* to use a computer simulation. Eliminate (A) because it is an out-of-focus answer choice that contains tempting terminology related to *instructional approaches* (Objective 0011). Eliminate (C) because it's an out-of-focus answer choice that contains tempting terminology related to *classroom management* (Objective 0007). Eliminate (D) because it's an out-of-focus answer choice that contains tempting terminology related to *school-community interactions* (Objective 0018). Teachers should evaluate various instructional resources in relation to achieving intended outcomes. To this end, they must analyze the advantages and disadvantages of having students acquire information through a variety of modes and formats, as Ms. Washington likely did when making her decision to use a computer simulation activity. Choice (B) is the correct response.

53. D

The primary focus of this question is Objective 0011:

Understand various instructional approaches and use this knowledge to facilitate student learning.

Eliminate (A) because simulations usually take more time than expository teaching methods. Eliminate (B) because it is not supported by the question—there is no mention of community awareness. Eliminate (C) because it is not supported by the question stem—you don't know that the students will be role-playing. Teachers should use an array of instructional strategies to engage students actively in learning. Ms. Washington is aware that, during the simulation activity, the students will need to seek out knowledge actively so they can plan their strategies and make decisions. Choice (D) is the correct response.

54. D

The primary focus of this question is Objective 0011:

Understand various instructional approaches and use this knowledge to facilitate student learning.

Eliminate (A) because students learn from their mistakes, so Ms. Washington should not control the activities to the extent that she does not allow the students to make errors or think illogically. Eliminate (B) because it is teacher directed rather than student centered. Students should assume responsibility for and direct their own learning. Eliminate (C) because it is likely to create resentment among students. Further, teams should be given sufficient time to complete tasks without being pressured. Ms. Washington needs to be aware of the important role the teacher must assume in collaborative learning situations. She should apply procedures for promoting positive and productive small-group interactions by monitoring each team and assessing and guiding individual and team collaborative skills. Choice (D) is the correct response.

55. B

The primary focus of this question is Objective 0014:

Understand communication practices that are effective in promoting student learning and creating a climate of trust and support in the classroom and how to use a variety of communication modes to support instruction.

Evaluation-level thinking requires students to use criteria or standards to form judgments or opinions about the value of a topic or phenomenon being considered. Eliminate (A), (C), and (D) because these require lower-level thinking in which students are not asked to form judgments or opinions. A class discussion in which students evaluate the merits of the stimulation activity would work best for engaging students in evaluation-level thinking. Choice (B) is the correct response.

56. A

The primary focus of this question is Objective 0011:

Understand various instructional approaches and use this knowledge to facilitate student learning.

Eliminate (B) and (D) because they are not supported by the question stem—there is no indication that Ms. Crowfoot is emphasizing using concrete objects as problem-solving tools or responding to the specific interests and needs of individual students. Eliminate (C) because Ms. Crowfoot's instructional strategy does not emphasize the presentation of content through a mix of approaches that might appeal to students with different learning styles and preferences. Ms. Crowfoot's instructional strategy is an especially good one because it places an emphasis on student initiative and self-directed learning, thus fostering student ownership and responsibility in relation to their own learning. Choice (A) is the correct response.

57. B

The primary focus of this question is Objective 0014:

Understand communication practices that are effective in promoting student learning and creating a climate of trust and support in the classroom and how to use a variety of communication modes to support instruction.

Eliminate (A) because the question stem does not support it—there is no indication that Ms. Crowfoot intends for individual students to critically assess their own strengths and weaknesses. Eliminate (C) and (D) because these reasons reflect a negative attitude about lower-achieving learners—an inappropriate attitude for teachers to adopt. Ms. Crowfoot understands the value of students' verbal interactions in the classroom. She knows that when students explain and discuss their ideas with each other, they clarify their own thinking and, at the same time, have the opportunity to help and encourage each other. Choice (B) is the correct response.

58. D

The primary focus of this question is Objective 0005:

Understand diverse student populations and use knowledge of diversity within the school and the community to address the needs of all learners, to create a sense of community

among students, and to promote students' appreciation of and respect for individuals and groups.

This is a priority-setting question. You're presented with a situation that requires you to decide which of the four responses offered would *best* dispel stereotypical impressions about women and mathematics—that is, change the opinions of the students with regard to women and mathematics. Eliminate (A) because while this is an action Ms. Crowfoot should take, it is unlikely to change the opinions of the students. Research about prejudice and learning shows that simply telling students that a stereotypical opinion is false is likely to result in few, if any, students changing what they think. Eliminate (B) because, whereas this may foster an appreciation that women are capable of doing mathematics, this approach is not the most effective option. Eliminate (C) because, whereas it may heighten students' awareness of the importance of mathematics in general, it does not directly address the issue of stereotypical opinions about women and mathematics. From what we know from research about prejudice and learning, long-term interventions work best for changing attitudes. By bringing in both men and women to talk about how they use math, Ms. Crowfoot will provide opportunities for students to hear for themselves from real people that math is useful to women and men alike, which will likely result in more lasting impressions and changes in attitude. Further, the guests will provide positive role models for all Ms. Crowfoot's students. Choice (D) is the correct response.

59. C

The primary focus of this question is Objective 0018:

Understand the importance of and apply strategies for promoting productive relationships and interactions among the school, home, and community to enhance student learning.

This is a priority-setting question—you must select the *most* probable answer choice. Eliminate (B) because it would be inappropriate for volunteers to assume such roles. Eliminate (A) and (D) because these may occur incidentally but you have no reason to believe they would be most probable. Because community members, especially parents and grandparents, have a vested interest in the schools, they are a valuable resource for teachers. By using community volunteers, the school is cultivating strong community-school partnerships, thus fostering positive ties between the school and the community. Choice (C) is the correct response.

60. B

The primary focus of this question is Objective 0018:

Understand the importance of and apply strategies for promoting productive relationships and interactions among the school, home, and community to enhance student learning.

This is a priority-setting question—you must select the *most* important answer choice. Field trips are an effective way for teachers to involve students in learning; however, careful planning, including preparing the parent volunteers who will be going on the trip, is an essential component of a successful field trip. Because parent volunteers will be supervising students, it is most important that they know what actions to take if students misbehave. Volunteers should be made aware that, the same as in the classroom, they are not in charge of discipline. Although, minor incidents, such as inattention or excessive talking, can be handled by a stern look or a firm command, any major misbehavior such as hitting another student should be brought to the attention of Ms. Drew, who will deal with it. Eliminate (A) because it is not as important as (B). Eliminate (C) because training and monitoring volunteers is something teachers should do but going so far as to teach them their lesson objectives is not necessary. Eliminate (D) because the brochure may not be printed in the home language of some of the volunteers so they likely would be unable to read it. Choice (B) is the correct response.

61. C

The primary focus of this question is Objective 0003:

Understand how factors in the home, school, and community may affect students' development and readiness to learn and use this understanding to create a classroom environment within which all students can develop and learn.

The roles used in cooperative learning are designed to promote responsibility and leadership for all students. Ms. Chertoff should model respect for all learners and encourage them to feel capable of taking on demanding and leadership roles. Eliminate (A), (B), and (D) because they conflict with the ideal that teachers should create classroom environments within which all students feel valued and capable. Over time, each group member should have the opportunity to experience a variety of group roles—some easy and some more demanding—including leadership roles. Choice (C) is the correct response.

62. A

The primary focus of this question is Objective 0010:

Understand instructional planning and apply knowledge of planning processes to design effective instruction that promotes the learning of all students.

Eliminate (B) because it is unlikely that simply posting the rules will ensure learners' compliance. Eliminate (C) because it is false: Most children are "social animals" and enjoy working with other students more than working in isolation. Eliminate (D) because having children memorize rules out of context is not a recommended teaching strategy and should be avoided. Children need to be helped to show consideration for others. When planning for cooperative-learning activities, Ms. Chertoff needs to consider that she will need to spend time in class teaching students the desired behaviors. Choice (A) is the correct response.

63. C

The primary focus of this question is Objective 0019:

Understand reciprocal rights and responsibilities in situations involving interactions between teachers and students, parents/guardians, community members, colleagues, school administrators, and other school personnel.

Because the district receives federal monies, it must adhere to federal law. Title IX forbids the district to discriminate on the basis of sex. This law has been interpreted to mean that the district must supply equal access to athletic activities for boys and girls alike. The question stem states that the district is attempting to save money by eliminating girls' softball. This is illegal because it violates Title IX. The girls should write a letter to the school board citing pertinent provisions of the Title IX legislation. That course of action is reflected in (C). Eliminate (A) because, whereas it is not illegal to organize a boycott and it may even arouse a great deal of attention, it's unnecessary in light of the fact that the board must adhere to federal regulations or lose federal funds. In other words, the boycott may have an effect, but the best course of action is still given in (C). Eliminate (B) and (D) because they suggest alternatives to school softball. However, the girls are entitled by law to the same school sports programs that are offered to boys and are certainly within their legal rights to demand change. Choice (C) is the correct response.

64. B

The primary focus of this question is Objective 0006:

Understand the characteristics and needs of students with disabilities, developmental delays, and exceptional abilities (including gifted and talented students) and use this knowledge to help students reach their highest levels of achievement and independence.

This is a multiple-response question. Read the statements and try to identify one with which you strongly agree or one with which you strongly disagree, whichever seems easier. Eliminate Statement II because impulsive behavior and noticeable hyperactivity in a child that is *persistent over time* may more likely be an indication of attention-deficit/hyperactivity disorder, which is not a type of learning disability. Eliminate (A), (C), and (D) because they contain Statement II. Difficulty in understanding social cues (Statement I), poor reading comprehension coupled with word recognition errors when reading (Statement III), and inability to apply what is learned in one setting to another (Statement IV) are all indications of learning disabilities. Students with learning disabilities are often served in the general education classroom, so teachers need to know about these students because they likely will address the needs of one or more of them in classes they teach. Choice (B) is the correct response.

65. A

The primary focus of this question is Objective 0001:

Understand human development, including developmental processes and variations, and use this understanding to promote student development and learning.

Eliminate (B) because other teachers might be able to tell the teacher about the student but only if the fear or phobia is one that would be expressed and/or noticed in the school situation. Eliminate (C) for a similar reason. A student who is terrified of insects might very well have shown that in the classroom, but what about a student who is terrified of the dark? Other teachers or students would have little opportunity to observe such a problem during the school day. Eliminate (D) because talking with the student is unreliable. Because of the tendency of children at this age to be self-conscious, a middle school student is unlikely to be willing to admit a fear or phobia to a teacher even if the teacher is very kind and sympathetic. If the student is embarrassed about the fear or doesn't know the teacher very well, it is unlikely that the student will admit the problem. The most accurate source of information about a middle school student's fears or phobias is the parents. The parents are the most probable individuals to have noticed such a fear and to be able and willing to describe it in an accurate way. Choice (A) is the correct response.

66. B

The primary focus of this question is Objective 0018:

Understand the importance of and apply strategies for promoting productive relationships and interactions among the school, home, and community to enhance student learning.

Eliminate (A); because he is the person who is most familiar with the contents of the unit, Mr. Lozek should assume primary responsibility for convincing the parents that the unit is appropriate. He would be forsaking his professional principles and responsibility if he does nothing. Eliminate (C) because involving students at this point only escalates tension. Releasing the results of the poll probably will not change the parents' minds. In fact, it could even heighten their opposition to the unit. Eliminate (D) because in the real world, few things are accomplished without leadership. Choice (D) almost guarantees that the unit is going to continue to be an issue. The most professional course of action and the one with the best chance of successfully resolving the problem with the parents' group is given in (B). First, Mr. Lozek would be observing protocol by consulting with the principal. It is the principal's role to call this meeting, and the principal must be involved in every step of the process to ensure a smooth resolution to the situation. Second, the approach in (B) permits parents to express their views and gives Mr. Lozek the opportunity to communicate the benefits of the unit as he sees them. It also provides a forum in which to work out differences and find a plan with which everyone feels comfortable. Choice (B) is the correct response.

67. B

The primary focus of this question is Objective 0014:

Understand communication practices that are effective in promoting student learning and creating a climate of trust and support in the classroom and how to use a variety of communication modes to support instruction.

Eliminate (A) because it doesn't go far enough. If Mr. Blum doesn't give the question the respect it deserves, he would not be setting a good example or encouraging Akina to continue her interest in DNA. Eliminate (C) because in certain circumstances it might be the kind of message that a teacher would want to send in a nicer way but it's not appropriate for this occasion. Eliminate (D) because, whereas admitting he doesn't know the answer is good and he's offering a specific suggestion on how Akina can find the answer, Mr. Blum is not setting a good example. The best reaction is for Mr. Blum to admit that he doesn't know the answer and then suggest ways that both he and Akina can find out and inform the class. The message sent would be "This is an important question. I don't know the answer, but I'd like to learn it. Here's how we can both find the answer and share it with the class." Choice (B) is the correct response.

68. A

The primary focus of this question is Objective 0002:

Understand learning processes and use this understanding to promote student development and learning.

This is a multiple-response question. Read the statements and try to identify one with which you totally agree or one with which you totally disagree, whichever seems easier. Eliminate Statement III because webs are not intended to develop skill in using descriptive language. Eliminate (C) and (D) because both include Statement III. Choices (A) and (B) both include Statement I. Thus, you need to decide only whether Statement II or Statement IV should be included in the answer choice. Eliminate Statement IV because in the webbing process To'nuel is brainstorming, not making predictions. Eliminate (B). The webbing process will help To'nuel to organize what he knows about pandas (Statement I) and prompt him to think about what he already knows about them—so he can connect new information to this previous knowledge (II). Choice (A) is the correct response.

69. D

The primary focus of this question is Objective 0018:

Understand the importance of and apply strategies for promoting productive relationships and interactions among the school, home, and community to enhance student learning.

Ms. Freeman should understand basic principles of conducting parent-teacher conferences, such as beginning and ending on a positive note. Eliminate (A) because it begins the conference on a negative note. Eliminate (B) because it is inappropriate and unprofessional for Ms. Freeman to do this. Teachers should avoid diagnosing a child without the proper credentials to do so. Eliminate (C) because this is also inappropriate and unprofessional. Ms. Freeman should not discuss other students' performance, even if not by name, with Chera's parents. Ms. Freeman should end the conference on a positive note by sharing some information about Chera's accomplishments in the class. Choice (D) is the correct response.

70. C

The primary focus of this question is Objective 0005:

Understand diverse student populations and use knowledge of diversity within the school and the community to address the needs of all learners, to create a sense of community among students, and to promote students' appreciation of and respect for individuals and groups.

Eliminate (A) because this would send a negative message to Ling about her home language. Eliminate (B) because Mr. Nejad should not second-guess the outcome of the screening procedure that resulted in Ling's placement in his classroom. It would be inappropriate and unprofessional for him to approach Ling's parents about having her removed from his class. Eliminate (D) because it is not supported by the question—Mr. Nejad has no basis for assuming Ling is behind in science. Ling should receive instruction at the same level in science as the other students. It is appropriate for Mr. Nejad to address Ling's academic needs by using drawings, demonstrations, concrete objects, and other visuals to reinforce spoken explanations of concepts. Choice (C) is the correct response.

71. C

The primary focus of this question is Objective 0014:

Understand communication practices that are effective in promoting student learning and creating a climate of trust and support in the classroom and how to use a variety of communication modes to support instruction.

Eliminate (A), (B), and (D) because these strategies would exclude Ling from full participation in class activities at the same level as the other students. Further, such treatment would probably not go unnoticed by Ling's classmates. They may resent that she is not being challenged as much as they are. Mr. Nejad should know how to apply strategies for adjusting communication to enhance student understanding. By addressing questions to Ling using body language and gestures (e.g., pantomiming actions when giving instructions) to enhance meaning, Mr. Nejad will not only be involving Ling more fully but also modeling to the other students how to enhance their communication with Ling. Choice (C) is the correct response.

72. D

The primary focus of this question is Objective 0014:

Understand communication practices that are effective in promoting student learning and creating a climate of trust and support in the classroom and how to use a variety of communication modes to support instruction.

This is a multiple-response question. Read the statements and try to identify one with which you strongly agree or one with which you strongly disagree, whichever seems easier. Eliminate Statement III because feedback is especially important during initial learning, when children's basic patterns of learning are set. Eliminate (B) and (C) because they contain Statement III. Both (A) and (D) contain Statement I, so it is correct. Feedback should be immediate. Immediate feedback allows students to make adjustments in what they are doing or in their understandings before they get too off track. You need now to decide whether Statements II and IV are also correct. Feedback should be specific (Statement II) and should be about what is correct and incorrect (Statement IV). Students learn from their mistakes, and they also learn from knowing what they did right. Choice (D) is the correct response.

73. B

The primary focus of this question is Objective 0010:

Understand instructional planning and apply knowledge of planning processes to design effective instruction that promotes the learning of all students.

Eliminate (A) because this is an out-of-focus answer choice related to *assessment* (Objective 0009). Furthermore, students should not be stressing about assessment during the scientist's presentation. Eliminate (C) because the question stem does not support it—the discussion is not about society. Eliminate (D) because the question stem does not support it—there is no indication Mr. Naughton will be outlining the scientist's presentation during the discussion. The discussion beforehand will serve to activate the students' previous understandings about the causes of global warming and encourage them to make predictions they can test during the scientist's presentation. Choice (B) is the correct response.

74. A

The primary focus of this question is Objective 0013:

Understand the relationship between student motivation and achievement and how motivational principles and practices can be used to promote and sustain student cooperation in learning.

Eliminate (B) because the question stem does not support this answer choice; Ms. Martin is not making a point about why it is important to know about the planets. Eliminate (C) because tangible incentives, like stickers or redeemable tokens, can enhance motivation in given situations but the question stem does not support this answer choice—there is no mention of tangible incentives. Eliminate (D) because, whereas this, too, is an effective motivational strategy, the question stem does not support this answer choice either—there is no mention of the workplace. One effective means of arousing interest in the material in a lesson is to introduce the lesson by relating it to something in the students' cultural experiences—for instance, popular television programs. Choice (A) is the correct response.

75. C

The primary focus of this question is Objective 0017:

Understand how to reflect productively on one's own teaching practice and how to update one's professional knowledge, skills, and effectiveness.

This is a priority-setting question. You must decide which of the four responses offered would *most* help Ms. Twomey. Effective teachers should constantly monitor and adjust their classroom practices. A very natural and effective way teachers can do this is to keep a reflective journal in which they write about, among other things, what they liked about what they did in a lesson, what didn't work, and what they will do differently next time. This course of action is given in (C). Choices (A) and (B) are also ways to improve teaching effectiveness, but these are not as effective as the approach given in (C). Eliminate (D) because, whereas it may be acceptable to observe a colleague one or two times, it would likely become annoying to the other teacher if done on a regular basis. Ms. Twomey should keep a reflective journal in which she deliberates on the quality of her teaching and is responsive to what she determines. Choice (C) is the correct response.

76. A

The primary focus of this question is Objective 0008:

Understand curriculum development and apply knowledge of factors and processes in curricular decision making.

Educators should design curriculum that is responsive to students' developmental characteristics and needs at different grade levels. Eliminate (B) and (C) because in general, middle school children have a well-developed ability to reverse observable physical actions mentally and to reason logically in reference to actions, objects, and properties that are familiar. Eliminate (D) because this is characteristic of older learners, not middle school children. Generally speaking, middle school children have a strong curiosity about the world around them and are interested in investigating realistic problems and situations. Choice (A) is the correct response.

77. C

The primary focus of this question is Objective 0009:

Understand the interrelationship between assessment and instruction and how to use formal and informal assessment to learn about students, plan instruction, monitor student understanding in the context of instruction, and make effective instructional modifications.

Eliminate (A) because there is no indication in the question that they will be noting the relevance of problem solving to other subjects. Eliminate (B) because when students are explaining and justifying their solutions, they are not simply recording results. Eliminate (D) because it is not supported by the question—there is no mention of real-life concerns. When students explain and defend their solutions in writing, they spend time reflecting on the validity of their results and will often make revisions as they organize their thoughts and clarify their thinking about the mathematical concepts. Ms. Qiyue is aware that children must be active participants in their own understanding to construct meaning from classroom experiences. Choice (C) is the correct response.

78. B

The primary focus of this question is Objective 0002:

Understand learning processes and use this understanding to promote student development and learning.

Eliminate (A) because it is not supported by the question; there is no indication that students will be accessing information. Eliminate (C) because journals are vehicles for communication, not evaluation. To grade journal writing defeats its purpose as a means of learning about students' ideas and monitoring their understanding of concepts. Eliminate (D) because it is not supported by the question; there is no indication the students will be working in varied contexts. Having students write in journals is a natural and very effective way to help them reflect on what they are learning. Journals are a place for students to write about, among other things, what they learned and how they learned it, what they may still need help with, and how they feel about aspects of math and their own understanding of it. Choice (B) is the correct response.

79. D

The primary focus of this question is Objective 0016:

Understand the history, philosophy, and role of education in New York State and the broader society.

In ruling on the issue of teaching creationism as the sole explanation for the origins of life, the Supreme Court took the position that creationism is drawn from a book of religious teaching, the Old Testament. They concluded that if it were taught in the public schools as the only explanation for the beginnings of life, this would amount to teaching one particular religious doctrine over all others. For one thing, it would infringe on the rights of students who do not believe in a Supreme Being. This is unacceptable under the Court's interpretation of the separation of church and state, and that's why (D) is correct. Eliminate (A) because the Supreme Court is there to interpret the Constitution, not to pass judgment on various theories of our origins. Eliminate (B) because it has the same problem as (A). Eliminate (C) because it's not a sound basis for a Supreme Court decision. The Court is not interested in pedagogy. It's interested in extending the rights and privileges outlined in the Constitution to all Americans. Choice (D) is the correct response.

80. C

The primary focus of this question is Objective 0006:

Understand the characteristics and needs of students with disabilities, developmental delays, and exceptional abilities (including gifted and talented students) and use this knowledge to help students reach their highest levels of achievement and independence.

The Individuals with Disabilities Education Act (IDEA) guarantees access to appropriate education for all children. As more and more children with special needs are placed in general education classrooms, teachers face increasing challenges to ensure that these children, like their classmates, are an integral part of the class and participate to the greatest extent possible in all classroom activities. For many youngsters with visual impairments, the social benefits of inclusion do not occur unless teachers specifically direct their efforts toward this end. Eliminate (A) and (B) because these are exclusionary approaches. Eliminate (D) because this approach would make Carlos dependent on the sighted student during the activity, which would hinder Carlos's ability to participate fully and contribute equally. Students with low vision, like their sighted classmates, learn through meaningful involvement in activities from beginning to end. Ms. Clooney can best fulfill her legal and ethical responsibilities toward Carlos by making sure he has access to adapted equipment that will allow him to participate fully in the group activity. Choice (C) is the correct response.

SCORING YOUR WRITTEN ASSIGNMENT

The official scorers will evaluate your written assignment using the following performance characteristics as a guide.

Purpose	Did you fulfill the charge of the assignment?
Application of Content	Did you accurately and effectively apply the relevant knowledge and skills in your writing?
Support	Did you support your response with appropriate examples and/or sound reasoning that reflects an understanding of the relevant knowledge and skills?

ATS-W Scoring Scale

The written assignment is scored according to the following scale:

Score Point	Score Point Description
4	**The "4" response reflects a thorough command of the relevant knowledge and skills.** • The response completely fulfills the purpose of the assignment by responding fully to the given task. • The response demonstrates an accurate and highly effective application of the relevant knowledge and skills. • The response provides strong support with high-quality, relevant examples and/or sound reasoning.
3	**The "3" response reflects a general command of the relevant knowledge and skills.** • The response generally fulfills the purpose of the assignment by responding to the given task. • The response demonstrates a generally accurate and effective application of the relevant knowledge and skills. • The response provides support with some relevant examples and/or generally sound reasoning.

2	**The "2" response reflects a partial command of the relevant knowledge and skills.** • The response partially fulfills the purpose of the assignment by responding in a limited way to the given task. • The response demonstrates a limited, partially accurate and partially effective application of the relevant knowledge and skills. • The response provides limited support with few examples and/or some flawed reasoning.
1	**The "1" response reflects little or no command of the relevant knowledge and skills.** • The response fails to fulfill the purpose of the assignment. • The response demonstrates a largely inaccurate and/or ineffective application of the relevant knowledge and skills. • The response provides little or no support with few, if any, examples and/or seriously flawed reasoning.

Practice ATS-W—Elementary Written Assignment Sample Response

Remember, this written assignment is assessing your understanding of the role of the teacher in relation to the following:

- Knowledge of the Learner

- Instructional Planning and Assessment

- Instructional Delivery

- The Professional Environment

You'll want to use the prompt itself as the skeleton of your essay.

Let's review the prompt. It asks you to do the following:

- Identify a level/subject. You can do this before you begin the essay or work it into the introduction. Just don't forget to include it.

- Explain the importance of the goal. This becomes paragraph 1, the introduction to your essay.

- Describe two strategies. Each strategy that you describe should be a paragraph in the body of your essay.

- Explain why each strategy would be effective. Your essay should include one paragraph that explains the effectiveness of the first strategy you described and another paragraph that explains the effectiveness of the second strategy you described.

Using the template suggested in chapter 3, you can produce an essay similar to the following sample.

Grade level/subject area: 7th grade, mathematics

As a seventh-grade mathematics teacher, it is my responsibility that every student in my class is taught in a well-managed classroom environment that fosters and supports his or her active engagement in learning. This goal is important because all students, no matter their differences, have the right to have learning experiences in school that will provide them the opportunity to achieve their greatest potential. In my classroom, I want to create a risk-free and accepting environment in which every student is actively involved in learning.

One strategy that I would use to accomplish this goal is to use cooperative-learning groups. Cooperative learning is an instructional strategy in which students at various performance levels work together in small groups to accomplish a collective task. The students are expected to complete the assigned task without direct or immediate teacher intervention. The focus is on students actively engaged in learning, rather than on the teacher telling and explaining. The basic purpose underlying cooperative learning is to motivate students to help each other learn. Group members take responsibility for their own learning and for the learning of each other. In order for these cooperative-learning groups to be effective, I would set up both group goals and individual accountability.

Cooperative learning is an effective strategy because it helps to create a community of learners in the classroom. Small-group work provides a low-risk environment in which students can engage in realistic and meaningful learning. Furthermore, group goals and individual accountability combine to create an incentive for all students, even those who usually perform poorly, to succeed. Studies show that when cooperative learning is used, students benefit academically, as well as personally and socially. Shared learning gives students an opportunity to further develop their critical thinking, reasoning, and problem-solving skills in an atmosphere of intergroup responsibility, collaboration, and mutual respect.

Another strategy I would use to achieve the goal of providing a well-managed classroom environment that fosters and supports active engagement in learning is to set up learning centers in my classroom. A learning center is a well-defined space in the classroom where materials are organized in such a way that children can learn with limited teacher supervision. I would provide a variety of learning centers—which reflect students' interests and suggestions—for students to choose from. The centers will contain an assortment of materials and media that show knowledge of and support for the varied characteristics of students in my classroom.

This strategy would be effective because it would allow the students' learning to be hands-on, experienced based, and individualized to meet particular needs, interests, learning styles, and abilities. Furthermore, using learning centers creates an environment that conveys a message to students about their active roles as learners. When learning centers are available in the classroom, students are expected to make decisions about and assume a measure of control of their own learning. This allows students to develop positive feelings about themselves and about their learning.

Again, the goal that every student in my class is taught in a well-managed classroom environment that fosters and supports his or her active engagement in learning is important because all students, no matter their differences, have the right to have learning experiences in school that will provide them the opportunity to achieve their greatest potential. Cooperative learning and learning centers are two strategies that will ensure quality learning opportunities for all students in my seventh-grade mathematics class.

This essay is one of thousands of possible responses to the prompt. There is no one "correct" or "best" answer. Let's check it as suggested in chapter 3:

Check against the prompt:

- ☑ I explained the importance of the educational goal in paragraph 1.

- ☑ I described two strategies in paragraphs 2 and 4.

- ☑ I explained the effectiveness of my two strategies in paragraphs 3 and 5.

- ☑ I included my grade level and subject area in my response.

Check for organization:

- ☑ My essay begins with an introductory sentence that (1) identifies the grade level and subject I teach and (2) restates the educational goal presented in the prompt.

- ☑ Each paragraph in the body of my essay begins with a topic sentence that clearly addresses one aspect of the prompt.

- ☑ My essay includes a short conclusion in which (1) I state that the educational goal is important and (2) I state that my two strategies are effective.

Check the content:

- *Does your writing reflect your understanding of the role of the teacher in relation to learner characteristics, instructional design and delivery, and the professional environment?* Yes, the response is learner centered and sensitive to students' varied characteristics and interests.

- *Based on your experience and your understanding of the ATS-W test objectives, have you included the best strategies, resources, and general teaching practices that could fit into this essay?* Yes, the essay includes instructional strategies, cooperative learning, and learning centers that promote critical thinking and active engagement in learning—a test-maker-friendly response that is strongly consistent with a constructivist philosophy (the ATS-W Mindset).

Finally, read through your response one more time:

- ☑ Complete sentences: Does every sentence express a complete thought?

- ☑ Agreement: Make sure singular subjects have singular verbs. Make sure pronouns agree with the nouns they replace.

- ☑ Check that apostrophes replace the correct letters in contractions.

- ☑ Check that each sentence ends with a correct end mark.

- ☑ Watch out for misused homonyms.

- ☑ Look for common misspellings and errors.

CHAPTER 13: PRACTICE ATS-W—SECONDARY

Before taking this practice test, find a quiet room where you can work uninterrupted for 4 hours. Make sure you have a comfortable desk and several No. 2 pencils.

Use the answer sheet provided to record your answers.

Once you start this practice test, don't stop until you've finished. Remember, you can complete the sections of the test in any order you wish.

You will find an answer key and explanations following the test.

Good luck!

SAMPLE DIRECTIONS

This test booklet contains a multiple-choice section and a single written assignment section. You may complete the sections of the test in the order you choose.

Each question in the first section of this booklet is a multiple-choice question with four answer choices. Read each question CAREFULLY and choose the ONE best answer. Record your answer on the answer document in the space that corresponds to the question number. Completely fill in the space having the same letter as the answer you have chosen. *Use only a No. 2 lead pencil.*

Sample Question
1. What is the capital of New York?

    A. Buffalo

    B. New York City

    C. Albany

    D. Rochester

The correct answer to this question is (C). You would indicate that on the answer document as follows:

1. (A)   (B)   ●   (D)

You should answer all questions. Even if you are unsure of an answer, it is better to guess than not to answer a question at all. You may use the margins of the test booklet for scratch paper, but you will be scored only on the responses on your answer document.

The directions for the written assignment appear later in this test booklet.

FOR TEST SECURITY REASONS, YOU MAY NOT TAKE NOTES OR REMOVE ANY OF THE TEST MATERIALS FROM THE ROOM.

The words "End of Test" indicate that you have completed the test. You may go back and review your answers, but be sure you have answered all questions before raising your hand for dismissal. Your test materials must be returned to a test administrator when you finish the test.

If you have any questions, please ask them now before beginning the test.

STOP

DO NOT GO ON UNTIL YOU ARE TOLD TO DO SO.

KAPLAN

ATS-W Answer Sheet

1. Ⓐ Ⓑ Ⓒ Ⓓ
2. Ⓐ Ⓑ Ⓒ Ⓓ
3. Ⓐ Ⓑ Ⓒ Ⓓ
4. Ⓐ Ⓑ Ⓒ Ⓓ
5. Ⓐ Ⓑ Ⓒ Ⓓ
6. Ⓐ Ⓑ Ⓒ Ⓓ
7. Ⓐ Ⓑ Ⓒ Ⓓ
8. Ⓐ Ⓑ Ⓒ Ⓓ
9. Ⓐ Ⓑ Ⓒ Ⓓ
10. Ⓐ Ⓑ Ⓒ Ⓓ
11. Ⓐ Ⓑ Ⓒ Ⓓ
12. Ⓐ Ⓑ Ⓒ Ⓓ
13. Ⓐ Ⓑ Ⓒ Ⓓ
14. Ⓐ Ⓑ Ⓒ Ⓓ
15. Ⓐ Ⓑ Ⓒ Ⓓ
16. Ⓐ Ⓑ Ⓒ Ⓓ
17. Ⓐ Ⓑ Ⓒ Ⓓ
18. Ⓐ Ⓑ Ⓒ Ⓓ
19. Ⓐ Ⓑ Ⓒ Ⓓ
20. Ⓐ Ⓑ Ⓒ Ⓓ
21. Ⓐ Ⓑ Ⓒ Ⓓ
22. Ⓐ Ⓑ Ⓒ Ⓓ
23. Ⓐ Ⓑ Ⓒ Ⓓ
24. Ⓐ Ⓑ Ⓒ Ⓓ
25. Ⓐ Ⓑ Ⓒ Ⓓ
26. Ⓐ Ⓑ Ⓒ Ⓓ
27. Ⓐ Ⓑ Ⓒ Ⓓ

28. Ⓐ Ⓑ Ⓒ Ⓓ
29. Ⓐ Ⓑ Ⓒ Ⓓ
30. Ⓐ Ⓑ Ⓒ Ⓓ
31. Ⓐ Ⓑ Ⓒ Ⓓ
32. Ⓐ Ⓑ Ⓒ Ⓓ
33. Ⓐ Ⓑ Ⓒ Ⓓ
34. Ⓐ Ⓑ Ⓒ Ⓓ
35. Ⓐ Ⓑ Ⓒ Ⓓ
36. Ⓐ Ⓑ Ⓒ Ⓓ
37. Ⓐ Ⓑ Ⓒ Ⓓ
38. Ⓐ Ⓑ Ⓒ Ⓓ
39. Ⓐ Ⓑ Ⓒ Ⓓ
40. Ⓐ Ⓑ Ⓒ Ⓓ
41. Ⓐ Ⓑ Ⓒ Ⓓ
42. Ⓐ Ⓑ Ⓒ Ⓓ
43. Ⓐ Ⓑ Ⓒ Ⓓ
44. Ⓐ Ⓑ Ⓒ Ⓓ
45. Ⓐ Ⓑ Ⓒ Ⓓ
46. Ⓐ Ⓑ Ⓒ Ⓓ
47. Ⓐ Ⓑ Ⓒ Ⓓ
48. Ⓐ Ⓑ Ⓒ Ⓓ
49. Ⓐ Ⓑ Ⓒ Ⓓ
50. Ⓐ Ⓑ Ⓒ Ⓓ
51. Ⓐ Ⓑ Ⓒ Ⓓ
52. Ⓐ Ⓑ Ⓒ Ⓓ
53. Ⓐ Ⓑ Ⓒ Ⓓ
54. Ⓐ Ⓑ Ⓒ Ⓓ

55. Ⓐ Ⓑ Ⓒ Ⓓ
56. Ⓐ Ⓑ Ⓒ Ⓓ
57. Ⓐ Ⓑ Ⓒ Ⓓ
58. Ⓐ Ⓑ Ⓒ Ⓓ
59. Ⓐ Ⓑ Ⓒ Ⓓ
60. Ⓐ Ⓑ Ⓒ Ⓓ
61. Ⓐ Ⓑ Ⓒ Ⓓ
62. Ⓐ Ⓑ Ⓒ Ⓓ
63. Ⓐ Ⓑ Ⓒ Ⓓ
64. Ⓐ Ⓑ Ⓒ Ⓓ
65. Ⓐ Ⓑ Ⓒ Ⓓ
66. Ⓐ Ⓑ Ⓒ Ⓓ
67. Ⓐ Ⓑ Ⓒ Ⓓ
68. Ⓐ Ⓑ Ⓒ Ⓓ
69. Ⓐ Ⓑ Ⓒ Ⓓ
70. Ⓐ Ⓑ Ⓒ Ⓓ
71. Ⓐ Ⓑ Ⓒ Ⓓ
72. Ⓐ Ⓑ Ⓒ Ⓓ
73. Ⓐ Ⓑ Ⓒ Ⓓ
74. Ⓐ Ⓑ Ⓒ Ⓓ
75. Ⓐ Ⓑ Ⓒ Ⓓ
76. Ⓐ Ⓑ Ⓒ Ⓓ
77. Ⓐ Ⓑ Ⓒ Ⓓ
78. Ⓐ Ⓑ Ⓒ Ⓓ
79. Ⓐ Ⓑ Ⓒ Ⓓ
80. Ⓐ Ⓑ Ⓒ Ⓓ

Use the information below to answer the five questions that follow.

Carol Harrison is a new middle school social studies teacher in a large, urban school district. Ms. Harrison's eighth-grade class is highly diverse ethnically and culturally, and several students have only recently moved to the United States. Ms. Harrison wants to create an environment in which every child feels comfortable, secure, and valued.

1. To help her students extend their understanding and appreciation of diversity, it would be most beneficial for Ms. Harrison to have the students:

    A. put up posters and photographs in the classroom of people from various countries and cultures.

    B. watch a video about the holiday traditions of people from a variety of cultures.

    C. in mixed groups, do activities related to the different cultural backgrounds represented in the class.

    D. participate in a class discussion about the variety of languages spoken in the community.

2. Ms. Harrison is concerned because in her eighth-grade social studies class she has several students who seem especially unmotivated. These students rarely participate in class discussions and regularly fail to turn in completed homework assignments. Ms. Harrison can increase motivation to learn in her classroom by:

    I. selecting content that is relevant to the students' lives.

    II. encouraging students to assist in planning instructional activities.

    III. using "I" messages when dealing with student misbehavior.

    IV. using simulations and role-play.

    A. I and II only

    B. I, II, and IV only

    C. II, III and IV only

    D. I, II, III, and IV

3. Given the developmental characteristics of students in this age group, Ms. Harrison should expect the greatest amount of variation among her students in terms of their:

   A. ability to remain on task during assigned activities.

   B. sense of what is fair and unfair behavior in a game situation.

   C. ability to understand and follow verbal instructions.

   D. attitudes toward and interactions with opposite-sex peers.

4. Perry, one of Ms. Harrison's students, is a special education student who has been diagnosed as emotionally disturbed. Perry is rarely on task and appears to have an inability to learn. With regard to Perry, Ms. Harrison should:

   A. discuss with Perry's parents the need for him to have stricter discipline at home.

   B. give Perry poor grades and require him to remain until all work is done.

   C. decide whether placement in a general education classroom is appropriate.

   D. ensure that planned lessons and activities are in compliance with Perry's IEP.

5. Ms. Harrison is beginning an interdisciplinary unit in which students will read about and explore the theme of citizenship in many different contexts. To help the students make connections with the theme, which of the following would probably be the most effective introductory activity to the unit?

   A. asking them to read a biography of a historical or contemporary person who demonstrated civic values

   B. suggesting they write a research paper about the Bill of Rights

   C. having them participate in a class discussion in which they share personal and family stories about actions that showed good citizenship

   D. asking them to research the rights of citizens in other major countries

Use the information below to answer the three questions that follow.

Ashley Loving, a high school science teacher, is beginning an instructional unit on erosion. She has assigned students in her classroom to mixed-ability groups. During the course of the unit, the groups will do a variety of experiments to explore and discover concepts related to erosion and report their findings to the rest of the class.

6. Ms. Loving can best prepare her students for the unit on erosion by:

   A. asking them to make a chart in which they write down what they already know and what they want to learn about erosion.

   B. distributing a list of key vocabulary words from the text for them to look up in the dictionary.

   C. having them read photocopied articles about erosion and make notes on the key ideas.

   D. asking them to preview a worksheet on erosion that they will be expected to complete after they have finished the unit.

7. Ms. Loving's grouping practice is probably intended:

   A. to provide opportunities for peers with various levels of academic ability to work together.

   B. to provide opportunities for students to manage conflict in a group situation.

   C. to enhance students' self-esteem by ensuring that each student's contribution to the group is recognized and celebrated.

   D. to provide an environment in which students' ideas are validated by others.

8. Ms. Loving's use of group activities in her classroom best reflects an awareness that adolescent students are likely to benefit from:

   A. peer support in unfamiliar social contexts.

   B. doing their own work and feeling self-reliant.

   C. receiving positive and negative reinforcement for responses to environmental stimuli.

   D. interacting with peers during instructional activities.

9. Liam Bradshaw is a high school art teacher. He notes that a few students sometimes make hurtful remarks to others who are less artistically inclined. Which of the following approaches would be most appropriate for Mr. Bradshaw to use to help less tolerant students become more accepting of students who are not as able artistically as they are?

   A. providing activities that will allow all students to perform competently and have fun

   B. assigning less tolerant students to work one-on-one as peer helpers with students who are less artistically inclined

   C. having students who make hurtful remarks stay after class to clean up the work area

   D. implementing each activity as a series of distinct skills or steps, each of which is worked on simultaneously by the entire class until all students are successful

10. Heather O'Connor has a student who is being a chronic behavior problem in her class. She has talked with the student but has not been successful in curtailing the student's misbehavior. Upon examining the student's cumulative file, Ms. O'Connor finds this student has a history of misbehaving in school. What should be Ms. O'Connor's next step to find out information that would help her deal with this student?

    A. talk with the student's friends

    B. talk with the counselor

    C. talk with the principal

    D. talk with the student's parents

Use the information below to answer the two questions that follow.

Markeith Campbell teaches speech communication in a large urban school located in a disadvantaged neighborhood. Mr. Campbell's learners have been reading and discussing the advantages and disadvantages of living in various regions of New York State.

11. To connect this activity to a lesson on persuasive speech, it would be most effective for Mr. Campbell to assign students to groups based on their favorite region and ask them to:

    A. role-play geologists presenting a description of the group's favorite region at a make-believe geological conference.

    B. write an oral report explaining the advantages of living in the group's favorite region.

    C. develop and present to the class a "television commercial" designed to promote tourism in the group's favorite region.

    D. use creative drama to depict the original discovery of the group's favorite region.

12. Mr. Campbell arranges for senior citizens to serve as volunteer tutors for at-risk students in his class. Which of the following would be a likely outcome of this arrangement?

    A. It will promote a sense of community and neighborhood.

    B. It will ensure that community members will be made aware of school-based problems.

    C. It will allow the students, while at school, the opportunity to discuss their problems with a sympathetic outsider.

    D. It will reduce student vandalism in the community.

13. During the first week of school, Ryan Dubose, a middle school science teacher, has each of his classes participate in an activity in which the success of the activity depends upon the cooperation and participation of the entire group working as a team. Mr. Dubose's primary purpose for the activity is:

    A. to foster a view of learning as a purposeful pursuit.

    B. to encourage students to assume responsibility for their own learning.

    C. to encourage student-initiated activities.

    D. to promote student ownership in a safe and productive learning environment.

14. Every Monday, Rebekah Sopko, a middle school social studies teacher, spends individual time with each of her students. What is Ms. Sopko's primary purpose for this practice?

    A. She is aware that spending time with students increases self-esteem.

    B. She wants to help the students recognize areas of personal strength and weakness.

    C. She realizes that stress from home can affect a student's schoolwork.

    D. She wants to model listening skills for her students.

15. Vanessa Rice, a high school mathematics teacher, observes that girls in her class are reluctant to participate in class discussions. To ensure greater female participation, Ms. Rice should:

    A. ask the girls easier questions so they will get the answers right and thus be more willing to participate in the future.

    B. call on students using a classroom grid that will ensure she calls on all students on an equal basis.

    C. have a meeting with the girls in which she assures them that they are just as capable in science as the boys are.

    D. give no critical feedback to the girls who give incorrect answers so they will not be embarrassed in front of their peers.

Use the information below to answer the two questions that follow.

Stephanie Rollins is a first-year teacher who has taken a teaching position in a small, rural community. The school where Ms. Rollins is assigned does not have a mentoring program for new teachers. Although it is a relatively small school, Ms. Rollins feels isolated and insecure about how to cope with her new situation.

16. On her first day of inservice training, a colleague comments, "You have to really watch yourself in this town—it's a gossip's paradise. Even when you are not in school, everyone keeps up with your business." Ms. Rollins is concerned, so she asks the principal how she should conduct herself when she is not in school. It would be most appropriate for the principal to advise Ms. Rollins that:

    A. this is a free country—she has the right to conduct herself any way she wants.

    B. she should conduct herself as she would when she is in school.

    C. she should conduct herself just like any other member of the community.

    D. she should obey the laws and stand out in the community as a positive role model.

17. Ms. Rollins decides she should get to know another teacher with whom she can exchange ideas and turn to for professional advice. The best approach for her to take for this purpose is to:

    A. ask another new teacher in the school if they can meet regularly after school to discuss mutual problems.

    B. show interest in the faculty in general by spending time visiting in the faculty lounge.

    C. show some interest in the work of a teacher she respects and ask for help.

    D. tell all her problems to the teacher next door.

Use the information below to answer the two questions that follow.

Linda Nethery, an Algebra I teacher, prepares for a parent-teacher conference with Mr. and Mrs. Mahaffey who are very concerned because their son Brent has been struggling in Ms. Nethery's class. Ms. Nethery is aware that although Brent can perform algebraic manipulation quite well, he usually gives up when it comes to problem solving using algebraic approaches.

18. Which of the following would be appropriate actions for Ms. Nethery to take during the conference?

    A. Eliminate opening remarks so as not to waste valuable time that should be spent conveying important information.

    B. Start off on a positive note by assuring the parents that, although Brent probably has a learning disability, he is able to deal with basic algebraic manipulation quite well.

    C. Alleviate the parents' concerns by making sure they are aware that other students in Ms. Nethery's class are having difficulty with problem solving.

    D. Suggest ways the parents can help Brent with problem solving at home.

19. As the parent-teacher conference is ending, Mr. and Mrs. Mahaffey tell Ms. Nethery that they are thinking about rewarding Brent for good grades in algebra. They ask Ms. Nethery for her opinion about whether they should do this. How should Ms. Nethery respond?

    A. She should not give her opinion because it is a personal family matter that the school should not get involved in.

    B. She should give her opinion, but tell the parents they should make their own decision.

    C. She should not give an opinion, but should give the parents information about intrinsic and extrinsic motivation to help them make an informed decision.

    D. She should tell them it's a bad idea and they shouldn't do it.

20. Amanda Quinn, a high school physical education teacher, has noticed that Nicole, a student in her class, frequently has bruises on her face and arms. When she asks Nicole about the bruises, Nicole says only that she runs into things a lot and does not offer any other information. Ms. Quinn doubts Nicole's explanation about the bruises; she suspects instead that Nicole is being physically abused. At this point, Ms. Quinn has a legal obligation to:

    A. contact Nicole's parents to set up a conference to discuss her concerns.

    B. report her suspicions immediately to the local police department.

    C. inform the principal immediately about her suspicions.

    D. ask the counselor to report the abuse to the proper legal authorities.

Use the information below to answer the three questions that follow.

Richard Welch, a middle school teacher, has several students with special needs in his classroom. Two of his students have limited English proficiency (LEP), and three students have been identified as having a learning disability. Both Ms. Hardy, the ESL teacher, and Ms. Fryman, the special education teacher, are working closely with Mr. Welch to assist these students in his class.

21. Which of the following would be appropriate for Mr. Welch to do when working with the ESL teacher?

    A. Ask her to come in and watch him teach.

    B. Provide her copies of his lesson plans.

    C. Recommend that she have the LEP students tested to see if they should be in a special education class.

    D. Suggest that she modify the curriculum for the LEP students so that it is not as challenging.

22. When would be the best time for Ms. Fryman to come into Mr. Welch's class to work with the special education students?

    A. when the special education students are working in a group by themselves

    B. when all the students are working in groups and centers

    C. when the whole class is working silently and individually

    D. when the whole class is engaged in a variety of activities

23. Mr. Welch decides to ask Ms. Hardy and Ms. Fryman for suggestions about materials he could read to learn more about how to help the special needs students in his class. This decision best illustrates which of the following principles?

    A. The teacher understands the relationship between careful planning and student success in the classroom.

    B. The teacher knows how to use different sources of support to enhance his own professional skills and knowledge.

    C. In designing instruction, the teacher takes account of factors relevant to instructional planning.

    D. As a member of a collaborative team, the teacher identifies and uses group processes to make decisions and solve problems.

24. Ms. Ecker asks her mentor Mr. Krieg for assistance in establishing guidelines for homework assignments. Mr. Krieg is quick to share information and offer guidance. Mr. Krieg's response to Ms. Ecker best illustrates which of the following principles?

    A. Teachers should know the value of cultivating positive interpersonal relationships with colleagues.

    B. Teachers should know how to work effectively with their colleagues to accomplish educational goals.

    C. Teachers should know how to use different sources of information and guidance to enhance student achievement.

    D. Teachers should recognize personal factors that affect their role as professionals.

25. Erika Ramirez has been using cooperative-learning groups in her classroom. One morning in the middle of a group activity, a parent, Mr. Risk, appears at the door. Mr. Risk is the father of Valerie, one of Ms. Ramirez high-achieving students. Mr. Risk, in a loud voice, informs Ms. Ramirez that he is very upset that Valerie is working in groups in her class. He complains that Valerie tells him she does all the work and the other kids copy off her. Which of the following should be Ms. Ramirez's immediate response in dealing with Mr. Risk?

    A. Let Mr. Risk know that she is willing to talk with him, but that she cannot do it right at the moment.

    B. Tell Mr. Risk that he should see the principal to discuss his concerns.

    C. Inform Mr. Risk that Valerie is misrepresenting the facts.

    D. Take this opportunity to explain the value of cooperative-learning groups to Mr. Risk in order to allay his concerns.

26. Joshua Grindle, a middle school teacher, begins a lesson in social studies by helping the learners make connections between important concepts and their own homes and families. Mr. Grindle's way of introducing the lesson is an especially good one for his students because it should foster their social studies learning by:

    I. promoting their higher-order thinking.

    II. helping them become aware of ways their home environments relate to their learning.

    III. capitalizing on sociological experiences they bring to the classroom.

    IV. teaching them about their own homes and families.

    A. I and IV only

    B. II and III only

    C. I, II, and III only

    D. I, III, and IV only

Use the information below to answer the two questions that follow.

Kimberly Landrum teaches an Earth science class that contains many ESL learners. She recognizes the importance of addressing the needs of all her learners, including students from homes where English is not the primary language.

27. Ms. Landrum asks Mr. Patterson, the ESL teacher, for advice on how she can best meet the needs of ESL learners when they are in her classroom. Mr. Patterson's response is likely to include which of the following?

    I. seat them in the front of the room

    II. seat them where they can see the teacher

    III. support instruction with hands-on activities

    IV. use frequent repetition of key terms during class discussion

    A. I and III only

    B. I, II, and IV only

    C. II and III only

    D. II, III, and IV only

28. Ms. Landrum tells Mr. Patterson that she wants to have a weekly newsletter in her class and asks for his guidance about how she can best accommodate the parents/guardians/caregivers whose primary language is other than English when she sends home the newsletter. Mr. Patterson probably will suggest that she should:

    A. have the students write, in the primary language of their home, a description of what they have been doing in class to take home with the newsletter.

    B. have the students role-play how to help their parents/guardians/caregivers understand the newsletter.

    C. make every effort to ensure the newsletter is written in the primary language of the parents/guardians/caregivers.

    D. make every effort to have an interpreter make home visits to explain the newsletter to the parents/guardians/caregivers.

29. Micah Pate is a high school mathematics teacher. He introduces the topic of quadrilaterals by leading a class discussion and creating on the chalkboard the semantic map shown below.

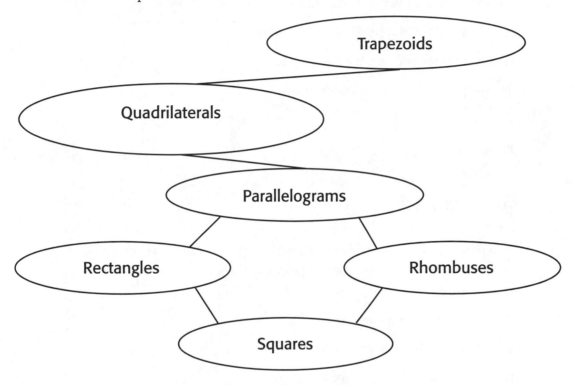

As an introductory activity, this strategy is helpful to learners primarily because it:

  I. provides them with detailed information in concise form.

  II. provides an opportunity to evaluate relevant concepts.

  III. activates their prior knowledge.

  IV. allows them to develop or review key concepts and vocabulary.

A. I and II only

B. I, III, and IV only

C. II and III only

D. III and IV only

30. Public education in the United States has historically operated in an environment influenced by the social contexts of:

  I. the home and family environment.

  II. the ethnic composition of the community.

  III. the presence of violence and crime.

  IV. the political nature of education.

  A. I, II, and III only

  B. I and IV only

  C. II, III, and IV only

  D. I, II, III, and IV

31. When designing curriculum for the middle school, educators should be aware that it is developmentally appropriate that early adolescents be given opportunities to:

  A. do concrete problems, but at a higher level.

  B. grapple with complex problems.

  C. receive knowledge passively.

  D. reverse physical actions mentally.

32. When designing curriculum for the early high school years, educators should be aware that, at this stage of development:

  A. adolescents have an increased capacity for abstract reasoning.

  B. adolescents have a strong interest in the future.

  C. adolescents have a limited ability to use speech to express one's self.

  D. adolescents learn best by absorbing carefully structured knowledge transferred directly from the teacher.

Use the information below to answer the three questions that follow.

Before school starts, Tasha Moore, a new English language arts teacher, has received her class rosters for the upcoming school year. She notes that the students in her classes are culturally diverse and that among them are several children who have physical or learning disabilities.

33. In planning her classroom layout, it is most important for Ms. Moore to consider:

    A. the materials and resources available in her room.

    B. the materials and resources available in her school.

    C. the instructional approaches she is planning to use with her learners.

    D. the cultural diversity of the students she will have in the classroom.

34. Ms. Moore plans to begin the school year with assigned seats in all her classes. When making seat assignments, which of the following should Ms. Moore consider:

    A. the value of seating learners near peers with similar academic ability.

    B. the importance of seating learners with limited English proficiency in the front of the room.

    C. the types of friendships that are likely to be formed among the students.

    D. the special needs of the students with physical or learning disabilities.

35. Ms. Moore wants to initiate and maintain effective communication with the parents/guardians/caregivers of her students. Which of the following would be best for keeping parents/guardians/caregivers regularly informed about class activities?

    A. a detailed letter once a month

    B. a brief weekly newsletter

    C. a note sent home with report cards

    D. weekly phone calls home

Use the information below to answer the four questions that follow.

Po-Chun Tang, a government teacher, has set up two computer stations in the corner of the classroom as a research area where students can go to search the Internet for information, especially current events, about topics they are currently studying in class.

36. Before the students start using the Internet, it is most important that Mr. Tang make sure that:

    A. the students have the necessary computer skills to access information.

    B. software that blocks access to inappropriate sites is in place.

    C. software that assists students in writing reports is available.

    D. students know how to store favorite Web page addresses for quick access at a later time.

37. One day, in Mr. Tang's freshman class, several students go to the research area at the same time and begin arguing over the use of the computers. The best strategy for Mr. Tang to adopt in response to this situation would be to:

    A. tell the students that, because of their misbehavior, no one in their class will be allowed to go to the research area for the rest of the week.

    B. talk with the principal to request additional computers for the research area.

    C. hold a class meeting to explain the problem to the students and ask for their help in finding a solution.

    D. suggest that the students develop their own methods for resolving conflicts among themselves.

38. Students are likely to benefit most from which of the following methods of assessing their use of the research area?

    I. multiple-choice testing with teacher feedback

    II. informal teacher observation with feedback

    III. short quizzes over how to access relevant information with teacher feedback

    IV. self-assessment journal entries

    A. I, II, and III only

    B. I and III only

    C. II and III only

    D. II and IV only

39. Mr. Tang has observed that Jena, one of his students, is rushing through her other work so that she can go to the research area. How should Mr. Tang deal with this situation?

    A. Use a form that Jena must check to see if her work is complete before she can go to the research area.

    B. Give Jena a grade of incomplete for work not finished properly.

    C. Have Jena bring her work to Mr. Tang to look over before she can go to the research area.

    D. Grade Jena on the quality of her work.

40. Mr. Crump, the father of one of Whitney DeWitt's students, is a police officer. He has offered to come to Ms. DeWitt's classroom to talk with the students about drugs. What should Ms. DeWitt do in response to this parent's offer?

   A. She should accept the offer, but contact all parents first and inform them about the topic of the presentation; some parents may object to exposing their child to information about drugs.

   B. She should accept the offer, but tell the officer to only give facts about drugs and to not let the students ask questions during the presentation; students might give information about their families' possible drug use, and the school could be sued.

   C. She should decline the offer; the classroom is not the place for such a discussion.

   D. She should decline the offer, but suggest that the officer provide a packet of information on drugs that can be sent home for the child and parents to look at together.

Use the information below to answer the five questions that follow.

Victor Rivera, an English language arts teacher, plans a unit designed to strengthen students' skills in reading comprehension and critical thinking. Throughout the unit, students, working in cooperative-learning groups, critically analyze a variety of literature including poems, short stories, plays, and chapters from books. Student groups complete a report for each literature selection.

41. As part of the initial planning process, Mr. Rivera's first step in defining learning objectives for the new unit should be to:

   A. select appropriate instructional strategies for fostering growth in reading comprehension and critical thinking.

   B. analyze the benefits and limitations of using cooperative-learning groups.

   C. determine students' strengths and needs in the areas of reading comprehension and critical thinking.

   D. apply procedures for promoting positive and productive small-group interactions.

42. As students work in groups, Mr. Rivera circulates from table to table, answering questions, soliciting information, and monitoring student progress. Mr. Rivera has designed a checklist, shown below, that he uses to record his informal observations of students during small-group activities.

GROUP CHECKLIST

Student Name _____ Date _____

Activity Observed _____

Student Behavior	Yes	Somewhat	No	No Opportunity to Observe
1. Is prepared for activity.				
2. Participates in discussions.				
3. Demonstrates understanding of the selection.				
4. Shows enthusiasm for activity.				
5. Cooperates with peers.				
6. Treats peers with respect.				

Mr. Rivera could most appropriately use student information from the checklist for which of the following purposes?

   I. guarding against the "free rider" effect, in which some group members fail to be active participants

  II. grouping students according to their academic ability

 III. planning or adjusting lessons and activities

  IV. emphasizing students' use of self-assessment in evaluating their progress in reading comprehension and critical thinking

  A. I and II only

  B. I and III only

  C. II and III only

  D. III and IV only

43. Items 4 and 5 on the checklist demonstrate Mr. Rivera's understanding that teachers who use cooperative-learning groups should:

    A. assess interpersonal skills during group activities.

    B. make expectations of group behavior clear.

    C. communicate task expectations.

    D. follow up with informal evaluation after each activity.

44. As a final individual project for the unit, Mr. Rivera assigns the students to write an original poem or short story. When the students are working on this assignment, Crystal comments, "Boys are no good at this are they, Mr. Rivera? Girls are much better writers than boys." In his immediate response to Crystal, Mr. Rivera should consider it most important to:

    A. explain to Crystal that such attitudes make it difficult for him to create a classroom climate that fosters a safe and productive learning environment.

    B. make it clear to Crystal that her words can hurt and will not be tolerated.

    C. explain to Crystal that boys can write as well as girls.

    D. assure the class that all students can be effective writers.

45. In confronting the incident with Crystal, Mr. Rivera should first:

    A. check himself to make sure he is not modeling any gender stereotyping.

    B. meet with the boys and girls separately to discuss the situation.

    C. check the textbook to make sure it does not contain gender stereotyping.

    D. attend a workshop about gender differences in academic performance.

46. Midway through the grading period, Martha Goldsberry, a health education teacher, notices that one of her better students, Jeremy, has been frequently off-task recently. He has not been very engaged in classroom activities and has failed to turn in several homework assignments. She has tried talking privately with Jeremy, but he insists he is fine. Which of the following will be most effective for Ms. Goldsberry to use with Jeremy?

    A. Meet with him before or after class about assignments.

    B. Have him journal back and forth with her on a weekly basis.

    C. Reward him for effort as well as for achievement.

    D. Give him a "timeout" every time he is off-task.

47. Madai Redon, a middle school language arts teacher, begins a lesson by showing her students the picture below.

    Which of the following questions should Ms. Redon ask the class to encourage higher-order thinking?

    A. How many people are in the car?

    B. How fast do you think the car is traveling?

    C. Where is the person in the car going?

    D. Why is the person in the car in a hurry?

48. Alan Sowards, a high school science teacher, is planning a field trip to a science museum for his students. He is concerned because Beverly, a student in one of his classes, is physically disabled and uses a wheelchair for mobility. What should Mr. Sowards do to accommodate this special needs student?

    A. Ask a special education teacher to accompany Beverly on the field trip.

    B. Pair Beverly with a peer buddy who will assist her during the field trip.

    C. Go to the museum beforehand to check out problems that need to be addressed.

    D. Provide an alternative assignment for Beverly.

49. Naomi García, a high school mathematics teacher, has her students interview professional people in the community to ask how they use mathematics in their careers. This practice demonstrates Ms. García's understanding that motivation to learn can be enhanced when:

    A. students are given public recognition for their efforts.

    B. learning is connected to meaningful situations beyond the classroom.

    C. students are able to experience concrete, observable phenomena.

    D. prior knowledge is used as a basis for understanding new content.

50. J'Nal Reneau, a high school government teacher, begins a unit on citizenship by having the students brainstorm about a time they witnessed someone being a good citizen in school or in the community. This practice demonstrates Ms. Reneau's understanding that motivation to learn can be enhanced by:

    A. encouraging students to participate in student-initiated activities.

    B. prompting students to recognize that concepts presented in the classroom relate to their everyday experiences.

    C. promoting students' critical thinking about a topic of interest.

    D. improving students' ability to recall factual information.

51. The mathematics faculty in an inner-city high school collaboratively plans a unit designed to strengthen students' skills in problem solving and critical thinking. This practice illustrates which of the following principles?

    A. Teachers should use effective communication techniques to shape the classroom into a community of learners.

    B. Teachers should work cooperatively with others to design effective instruction.

    C. Teachers should work with colleagues to establish a vision that reflects students' need for higher-level thinking skills.

    D. Teachers should apply strategies for developing interdisciplinary curricula.

Use the information below to answer the two questions that follow.

Clint Hammack, a middle school physical education teacher, wants to promote the concept of wellness in his school. He approaches the science and mathematics teachers, who agree to collaborate with him in developing a unit on health and fitness. For instance, the students will develop menus for healthful meals in Mr. Hammack's class, perform nutritional experiments in science class, and figure menu calories and percent fat content in mathematics class.

52. Mr. Hammack's decision to involve other teachers in developing the unit illustrates his understanding that:

    A. teachers should employ collaborative planning processes to evaluate cross-disciplinary curricula.

    B. teachers should develop curricula to promote healthy lifestyles for students as they progress through school.

    C. teachers should work with colleagues to develop interdisciplinary curricula.

    D. teachers should practice active listening and encourage open communication.

53. Which of the following developmental characteristics of middle school students would be most important for Mr. Hammack and the other teachers to consider when planning this unit?

    A. adolescents' sensitivity to the many changes they are experiencing as they develop physically

    B. adolescents' inability to sit for long periods of time

    C. adolescents' tendency to be introspective and reflective

    D. adolescents' intense concern for peer approval

54. Ms. Ling teaches in a high school located in a low-income neighborhood. She worries that some of her students may have low self-esteem due to their disadvantaged environment. In general, which of the following is likely to contribute most to a student's sense of self-esteem?

    A. being praised for being a good student

    B. receiving free time for doing good work

    C. being singled out in front of classmates for his or her achievements

    D. meeting and mastering a new challenge

55. Tracy Chaviers, a high school mathematics teacher, has her students write daily in their learning logs in response to the following prompts:

> What did I learn today?
> How did I learn it?

Writing in their learning logs in response to these prompts is likely to benefit students most by:

    A. fostering a sense of ownership in their own learning.

    B. encouraging them to set short- and long-term learning goals.

    C. providing a means for the teacher to assess their learning.

    D. promoting their ability to recognize effective methods for enhancing communication.

Use the information below to answer the four questions that follow.

During an activity, Rachel Werner, a middle school art teacher, overhears the following conversation between two of her students, Shawn and Carlos.

Shawn: What are you drawing?

Carlos: It's a picture of my dog. He's a Dalmatian.

Shawn: That doesn't look like a Dalmatian. *(laughing)* It looks like a cow!

Carlos: Does not! *(looking very upset)*

Shawn: That's a cow if I ever saw one!

(Shawn walks away laughing, leaving Carlos almost in tears.)

56. Immediately following the exchange between Shawn and Carlos, Ms. Werner approaches the two boys. Which of the following should Ms. Werner make a priority of her intervention?

    A. Talk with both boys about how their words could hurt.

    B. Tell Carlos that Shawn did not mean what he said.

    C. Talk with Shawn about how his words could hurt Carlos.

    D. Get Carlos to explain to Shawn how he feels about Shawn's comments.

57. After the exchange between Shawn and Carlos, Ms. Werner decides to spend time in class teaching social skills such as treating others with respect and praising, showing sensitivity, and encouraging others. When a skill is introduced, a brainstorming session is held to list examples of what might be said (e.g., "Nice work") or done (e.g., "Thumbs-up") to show the skill, as well as nonexamples of the skill (e.g., laughing, making fun, rolling eyes). Ms. Werner's decision demonstrates her ability to:

    A. analyze how classroom environments that respect diversity foster positive student experiences.

    B. reflect productively on her own practice.

    C. establish and maintain high expectations for all students.

    D. use students' prior knowledge as a basis for understanding new content.

58. Ms. Werner plans to teach social skills directly to her students (e.g., through activities designed to promote prosocial behavior). This decision demonstrates her understanding that students at this developmental stage:

   A. have a limited ability to use speech to express themselves.

   B. generally see rules as fixed and unchangeable.

   C. are not aware that certain social skills are important in their lives.

   D. are not yet capable of understanding the perspective of others.

59. The day following the incident with Shawn and Carlos, Ms. Werner consults with the school counselor to seek advice on handling similar situations. The counselor suggests that Ms. Werner attend an upcoming workshop on conflict resolution. Ms. Werner's decision to consult the school counselor demonstrates her ability to:

   A. apply strategies for assessing her own teaching strengths and weaknesses.

   B. use resources and opportunities for enhancing her professional development.

   C. recognize ways in which school personnel can work together to promote a sense of community.

   D. recognize issues related to the creation of a safe and productive learning climate.

60. A few weeks into the school year, Kristin Kamiguchi is having difficulty with Tony, a student in her mathematics class. Tony is easily distracted and has difficulty sustaining attention in class. At this point, how should Ms. Kamiguchi deal with Tony?

   A. Engage him in more hands-on activities.

   B. Give him step-by-step instructions.

   C. Have him tested for attention deficit hyperactivity disorder.

   D. Seat him in the front of the room.

Use the information below to answer the three questions that follow.

Aaron Barrett begins a unit on weather in his middle school science class with a brainstorming activity in which the students create a semantic map around the topic of weather. Next Mr. Barrett plans to invite Jerry Peltier, the meteorologist from a local television station, to visit the class and talk with the students about weather forecasting. Over the course of the unit, the students will collect weather data and make observations of weather conditions.

61. Mr. Barrett can promote the success of Mr. Peltier's presentation by:

    A. giving him photocopies of material about weather from the science textbook to look over before the presentation.

    B. listening to his presentation beforehand and giving him feedback on it.

    C. sharing with him what the students already know about weather.

    D. asking him to recommend instructional activities related to weather.

62. To help his students learn from the presentation, Mr. Barrett should:

    A. before Mr. Peltier comes, supply students with reading material about the weather to stimulate their interest in the presentation.

    B. before Mr. Peltier comes, have the students work in small groups to create a list of questions to ask Mr. Peltier.

    C. take notes himself during the presentation, then ask students questions when Mr. Peltier leaves.

    D. select certain students to ask prepared questions during the presentation.

63. When the students begin collecting weather data, one girl complains, "I don't like doing science. I think it's boy stuff." Mr. Barrett notices agreement on the faces of other students in the class—both male and female. Which of the following would be the most effective way for Mr. Barrett to counter gender stereotyping?

   A. Have the students do research papers on female scientists.

   B. Show a video about famous female scientists.

   C. Have a day in which the class learns about and celebrates women in science.

   D. Invite a variety of male and female guests who have science-related careers to visit the class throughout the year.

Use the information below to answer the two questions that follow.

Students from one of Lindsay Kline's ninth-grade science classes will be going to the nearby elementary school to do science activities with fifth graders in Troy Jarboe's classroom. Ms. Kline has never taught fifth grade, so she invites Mr. Jarboe to visit her class to discuss some guidelines for interacting effectively with the younger students.

64. What should be the teachers' main concern in regard to the activity?

   A. making sure the lesson objectives are clearly stated

   B. making sure students are paying attention when instructions are given

   C. making sure the fifth graders are not exposed to anything inappropriate

   D. making sure the ninth graders are not bored during the activity

65. Which of the following is an effective way for Ms. Kline to prepare her students for the activity beforehand?

    A. In groups, have students role-play how to do the activity with a fifth grader.

    B. In groups, have the students read to each other about how to do the activity.

    C. Individually, have the students learn the names of all the fifth graders in the class.

    D. Individually, have the students write a summary of how to do the activity and memorize it.

66. Students in Anna Diaz's government class are designing a questionnaire to survey students in the school about safety issues. The students work in small groups to compose questions for the questionnaire. Allowing the students to compose their own questions for the questionnaire is likely to enhance their interest in the survey project by:

    A. relating their learning to world issues and community concerns.

    B. enabling them to pursue topics of personal interest.

    C. helping them to set their own goals.

    D. giving them a sense of control over their learning experiences.

Use the information below to answer the two questions that follow.

Tamara Heard invites Ira Irvine, who is physically disabled and uses a motorized wheelchair for mobility, to visit her seventh-grade health class and talk with her students about his everyday life. Ms. Heard prepares her students for Mr. Irvine's visit by having them brainstorm questions they might want to ask Mr. Irvine. One student wants to know if Mr. Irvine has a job; others are interested in how he gets dressed, prepares meals, and so on. Ms. Heard assures the students that these questions are appropriate and encourages them to think of additional questions.

67. Ms. Heard's primary purpose for inviting Mr. Irvine is to:

   I. help her students realize that people are more alike than different.

  II. help her students see the diversity among themselves.

 III. help her students relate concepts presented in class to everyday experiences.

 IV. help her students realize that for some people life is very difficult and hard to manage.

  A. I only

  B. II and III only

  C. III and IV only

  D. IV only

68. Which of the following does bringing in Mr. Irvine most probably promote?

  A. students' critical thinking

  B. students' natural curiosity

  C. students' creativity

  D. students' autonomy

69. During a parent-teacher conference, Shironda's mother, Mrs. LeBoulan, informs Ms. Kendall, Shironda's sixth-grade classroom teacher, that Shironda is a better dancer than student and Ms. Kendall should not expect too much homework to get done on ballet nights. Shironda is an underachieving student, and Ms. Kendall does not want to see her fall behind in class. In order to establish a balance between Shironda's school work and ballet, Ms. Kendall should:

   A. accept Mrs. LeBoulan's reasoning—after all, she is Shironda's mother and knows her daughter best.

   B. explain to Mrs. LeBoulan that school work is more important and Shironda should limit her involvement in ballet until her grades improve.

   C. offer Shironda an extension on her homework the nights that she attends ballet class.

   D. volunteer to assist Shironda and her mother in setting up a schedule for completing regularly assigned homework.

70. In middle school, the use of student journals for instructional purposes is most effective when:

   A. students are assured that what they reveal in their journals will be kept confidential.

   B. students are encouraged to write freely about feelings related to self-awareness and personal relationships that may affect their learning.

   C. students complete a daily story prompt as directed by the teacher in order to prepare better for the written part of the New York State English Language Arts test.

   D. students have the opportunity to write before and after the lesson to reflect on their own learning.

71. Mohsen is a sixth grader who consistently and enthusiastically participates in classroom discussion and does well answering questions. He listens attentively to his teacher, Ms. Mintz, and to his classmates and is acknowledged as a personable leader in extracurricular activities. Nonetheless, since the beginning of the school year, he has performed poorly on written tests and homework. Since Mohsen's difficulty with written performances has persisted over an extended period of time, Ms. Mintz should:

   A. initiate a parent-teacher conference in order to suggest that Mohsen's parents need to help Mohsen study more at home.

   B. take measures to curtail Mohsen's involvement in extracurricular activities until his performance on tests and homework shows marked improvement.

   C. remove Mohsen from the classroom during written tests and have a classroom aide administer an oral test covering the same material.

   D. seek assistance from a special education colleague with regard to Mohsen.

72. Roxy Enrico is a high school science teacher in a working-class suburban community. She wants to assign a research project to her ninth-grade students, but she is concerned that many of them will not have adequate resources at their disposal. The school library is small and growing, but it does not have the necessary books and online resources that are needed for the project. When she surveys her class to find out what they have available, the resources ranged from being very limited to having CD-ROM encyclopedias and Internet access at home. The most efficient way for Ms. Enrico to ensure that all her students can complete the research assignment is to:

   A. send a letter home, advising parents that Internet access will be required for all students during the next grading period.

   B. take her students to the local public library once a week for research sessions.

   C. ask her students who have Internet access at home to print off materials to share around the classroom.

   D. assemble the required materials herself and make them available in her classroom for students' use.

73. Michael Krugman teaches U.S. history in a high school where the students come from a wide range of ethnic backgrounds. Which of the following activities could Mr. Krugman organize that would most effectively familiarize students in his classes with each other's backgrounds while promoting the pride and self-respect of each student?

    A. Plan a class trip to a museum that features art or artifacts from around the world.

    B. Prepare a handout about each ethnic group represented in the class and have the students discuss the information in class.

    C. Plan a unit of study in which students work in groups to research and report on the contributions of each ethnic group in U.S. history.

    D. Give students the assignment of going to the library and individually researching information about their respective backgrounds.

74. Nejad, a high school student with strong political views, organized a demonstration in the school hallways during class hours. The demonstration consisted of 30 participants loudly shouting slogans and banging on noisemakers to attract the attention of the students in class. Dr. Vernerio, the principal, stopped the demonstration. The principal's action was:

    A. an infringement of Nejad's right to speech as described by the First Amendment.

    B. within her duties as the school principal because she stopped a disruption to students' class time.

    C. contrary to Nejad's right to a hearing before disciplinary action is taken.

    D. within her duties as the school principal because the protest was not supervised by a teacher.

75. Murray Porter is a new high school geometry teacher. He is excited about teaching geometry and has many ideas for keeping students actively engaged in learning. He understands that there are many factors that may impact a student's engagement in learning on a given day. He is likely aware that a high school student's active engagement in learning is probably least affected by:

   A. the differences in past achievement scores among class members.

   B. the individual's student's preferred learning style.

   C. an upsetting incident that occurred before school that morning.

   D. the teacher's skill in organizing appropriate learning materials and activities.

76. An English department of 12 English, speech, drama, and writing teachers is meeting to discuss the purchasing of new novels for the upcoming school year. The department's budget will allow for only four sets of novels to be purchased. During this process of deciding which novels to purchase with the available funds, it would be most important for the teachers to:

   I. review the state learning standards to determine which novels align with the state-required knowledge and skills for English language arts.

   II. determine which teachers chose last year's novels and give this year's choice to other teachers, in order to be fair.

   III. evaluate the suggested novels for the purpose of identifying how they meet standards published by the National Council of Teachers of English.

   IV. select novels with contemporary themes that will appeal to adolescent readers.

   A. I, II, and III only

   B. III and IV only

   C. I and III only

   D. II and III only

77. Lilia DeFoe, an experienced high school teacher, transfers from one school district to another district, which is nearer to her home. In planning her course for the next year, Ms. DeFoe would be best advised to design an instructional sequence based primarily on:

    A. the lesson plans published in conjunction with the textbook used in the district.

    B. her instructional objectives in the course based on learning standards set for by the district and state and on her new students' past performance on state assessments.

    C. the lesson materials used by her predecessor at the school, with some changes to take advantage of her own unique strengths in the subject area.

    D. the units of instruction she found to be most effective in her previous district.

78. Chuck Meshkini is a ninth-grade social studies teacher. Students in his class have a wide range of academic abilities, from those with reading disabilities to students identified as gifted and talented. Mr. Meshkini wants to design an end-of-semester assessment that provides an opportunity for students to showcase what they have learned during the course. Which of the following projects is best suited for this purpose?

    A. cooperative group presentations to the class in the form of oral reports, television-show formats, dramatizations, or computer-generated "slide shows" that highlight the most important things learned in class

    B. an in-class essay written in response to the open-ended prompt: "The most important thing I learned in this class . . . "

    C. a multiple-choice posttest that is graded on score improvement from the same test given to all students at the beginning of the semester as a pretest

    D. individual portfolios of student work compiled throughout the term and submitted to the teacher to show what the student feels represents his or her best work in the class

79. Federal laws and regulations must be complied with in a New York State school district:

   A. because the U.S. Congress has a constitutional mandate to regulate education in the United States.

   B. at no time and in no situation because the power to regulate education in a state is constitutionally the province of that individual state.

   C. only in cases that involve the civil rights of students.

   D. whenever the school district accepts and receives federal monies.

80. Students in Calley Capacio's eighth-grade social studies class are extremely reticent when it comes to discussion. Apparently, most of the class has had little experience with discussion-oriented activities. What is Ms. Capacio's best strategy for dealing with this problem?

   A. Break the class into small groups, assign a problem to be solved, and later reconvene as a whole to discuss it.

   B. Explain that she understands their lack of experience.

   C. Lay down the law that she expects each student to participate more fully.

   D. Assign students a series of oral reports.

SAMPLE DIRECTIONS FOR THE WRITTEN ASSIGNMENT

This section of the test consists of a written assignment. You are asked to prepare a written response of about 300–600 words on the assigned topic. *The assignment can be found on the next page.* You should use your time to plan, write, review, and edit what you have written for the assignment.

Read the assignment carefully before you begin to write. Think about how you will organize what you plan to write. You may use any blank space provided on the following pages to make notes, write an outline, or otherwise prepare your response. *However, your score will be based solely on the response you write in the written response booklet.*

Your response will be evaluated on the basis of the following criteria:

- **PURPOSE:** Fulfill the charge of the assignment.
- **APPLICATION OF CONTENT:** Accurately and effectively apply the relevant knowledge and skills.
- **SUPPORT:** Support the response with appropriate examples and/or sound reasoning reflecting an understanding of the relevant knowledge and skills.

The ATS written assignment is intended to assess teaching knowledge and skills, not writing ability. However, candidates' responses must be communicated clearly enough to permit valid judgment of these factors by scorers. Candidates should present a thoughtful, reasonable response to the assignment, supported by detail, argument, and evidence. The final version of the response should conform to the conventions of edited American English. This should be your original work, written in your own words, and not copied or paraphrased from some other work.

Be sure to write about the assigned topic and use multiple paragraphs. Please write legibly. You may not use any reference materials during the test. Remember to review what you have written and make any changes you think will improve your response.

Practice Written Assignment—Secondary ATS-W

Reading and writing in the content areas are important skills that students need to develop. Imagine that the principal and teachers of your school have determined that reading and writing across the content areas will be a major focus of instruction for the coming year. To underscore this effort, the following goal has been established as part of the school's instructional mission.

GOAL: In English language arts, social studies, mathematics, and science classes, students will read and write a variety of texts for a number of different purposes and audiences.

Examples of teaching objectives:

- Students will learn specific strategies for reading and understanding English language arts content, social studies content, mathematics content, and science content.

- Students will write in a variety of formats and styles to convey their understanding of content knowledge (e.g., summaries, reports, letters to the editor).

- Students will use reflective writing to delineate and understand their own thinking processes in relation to literary interpretation, historical research, mathematical problem solving, and scientific inquiry.

In an essay written for a group of New York State educators, frame your response by identifying a grade level/subject area for which you are prepared to teach. Then:

- explain the importance of providing valuable reading and writing opportunities to all students in your classroom;

- describe two strategies you would use to achieve this goal; and

- explain why the strategies you describe would be effective in achieving this educational goal.

Be sure to specify a grade level/subject area in your essay and frame your ideas so that an educator certified at your level (i.e., elementary or secondary) will be able to understand the basis for your response.

CHAPTER 14: PRACTICE ATS-W— SECONDARY ANSWERS AND EXPLANATIONS

Answer Key

1. C	21. B	41. C	61. C
2. B	22. D	42. B	62. B
3. D	23. B	43. A	63. D
4. D	24. B	44. B	64. C
5. C	25. A	45. A	65. A
6. A	26. C	46. B	66. D
7. A	27. D	47. D	67. A
8. D	28. C	48. C	68. B
9. A	29. D	49. B	69. D
10. B	30. D	50. B	70. D
11. C	31. B	51. B	71. D
12. A	32. A	52. C	72. D
13. D	33. C	53. A	73. C
14. C	34. D	54. D	74. B
15. B	35. B	55. A	75. A
16. D	36. B	56. D	76. C
17. C	37. C	57. B	77. B
18. D	38. D	58. C	78. A
19. B	39. A	59. B	79. D
20. C	40. A	60. A	80. A

Answers and Explanations

1. C

The primary focus of this question is Objective 0005:

Understand diverse student populations and use knowledge of diversity within the school and the community to address the needs of all learners, to create a sense of community among students, and to promote students' appreciation of and respect for individuals and groups.

This is a priority-setting question—you must select the answer choice that is *most* beneficial. Eliminate (A) and (B) because these approaches are too general and too passive. Eliminate (D) because it is probably too general as well; that is, not necessarily specific to the cultures represented in the classroom. Adolescents are usually focused on themselves, so they would be more interested in learning about the cultures represented in their classroom. Having them work in mixed groups to do culture-related activities likely will promote interaction and foster students' understanding and appreciation of diversity. Choice (C) is the correct response.

2. B

The primary focus of this question is Objective 0013:

Understand the relationship between student motivation and achievement and how motivational principles and practices can be used to promote and sustain student cooperation in learning.

This is a multiple-response question. Read the statements and try to identify one with which you totally agree or one with which you totally disagree, whichever seems easier. Eliminate Statement III because it deals with *classroom management* (Objective 0007), not motivation. Eliminate (C) and (D) because they both include Statement III. Choices (A) and (B) both include Statement I and Statement II. Thus, you need only decide whether Statement IV is an appropriate strategy for increasing motivation. Simulations and role-play can increase motivation by making the learning more relevant to students' lives. Teachers should apply procedures for enhancing student interest and helping students find their own motivation (e.g., relating concepts presented in the classroom to students' everyday experiences, allowing students to have choices in their learning, encouraging student-initiated activities) and recognize factors and situations that tend to promote or diminish student motivation. They can increase motivation to learn in their classrooms by selecting content that is relevant to the students' lives (Statement I), encouraging students to assist in planning instruction (Statement II), and using simulations and role-playing (Statement IV). Choice (B) is the correct response.

3. D

The primary focus of this question is Objective 0001:

Understand human development, including developmental processes and variations, and use this understanding to promote student development and learning.

Eliminate (A) and (C) because most students at this age are able to stay on task and to understand verbal instructions. Eliminate (B) because most students at this age have strong, but similar, beliefs about fairness. During early adolescence, teenagers tend to exhibit substantial variation with regard to their relationships with peers of the opposite sex. Choice (D) is the correct response.

4. D

The primary focus of this question is Objective 0006:

Understand the characteristics and needs of students with disabilities, developmental delays, and exceptional abilities (including gifted and talented students) and use this knowledge to help students reach their highest levels of achievement and independence.

Eliminate (A) because this is very inappropriate. Teachers should collaborate with parents of students with emotional disturbances, not criticize what they do or don't do at home. Eliminate (B) because these measures probably will be ineffective with Perry. Perry would more likely benefit from a curriculum designed around his own strengths and interests and from a motivational reward system for completed tasks. Eliminate (C) because Ms. Harrison cannot legally do this. Only the IEP team can make the decision about the appropriate placement for a special education student. Ms. Harrison is legally obligated to follow Perry's IEP, so it is acutely important that Ms. Harrison ensure that planned lessons and activities are in compliance with Perry's IEP. Choice (D) is the correct response.

5. C

The primary focus of this question is Objective 0002:

Understand learning processes and use this understanding to promote student development and learning.

This is a priority-setting question—you must select the answer choice that is the *most* effective activity. Teachers should analyze processes by which students construct meaning and apply strategies for facilitating learning in instructional situations (e.g., by building connections between new information and prior knowledge, by relating learning to world issues and community concerns, by making learning purposeful). Eliminate (A), (B), and (D) because these activities would be too passive, and further probably would fail to activate prior knowledge—an important step toward learning and understanding a topic. By having a class discussion in which learners share personal and family stories, the teacher is helping students connect their new learning to prior understandings. Choice (C) is the correct response.

6. A

The primary focus of this question is Objective 0002:

Understand learning processes and use this understanding to promote student development and learning.

Eliminate (B), (C), and (D) because these measures are too passive—in other words, these strategies fail to promote students' active engagement in learning. Teachers should analyze processes by which students construct meaning and apply strategies for facilitating learning in instructional situations (e.g., by building connections between new information and prior knowledge, by relating learning to world issues and community concerns, by making learning purposeful). They also should recognize effective strategies for fostering students' sense of ownership and responsibility in relation to their own learning. Ms. Loving can best prepare her students for new learning by having them write down (1) what they already know about erosion—to facilitate linking new information to prior knowledge—and (2) what they want to learn about erosion—to give them ownership in their own learning and make it purposeful. These are steps in the K-W-L strategy that effective teachers use to enable students to focus their learning in an interactive setting. The strategy involves three categories of information:

> K—What the learner Knows (before the interactive learning)
>
> W—What the learner Wants to find out (during the interactive learning)
>
> L—What the learner Learned (as a result of the interactive learning)

Choice (A) is the correct response.

7. A

The primary focus of this question is Objective 0011:

Understand various instructional approaches and use this knowledge to facilitate student learning.

Eliminate (B), (C), and (D) because these choices are not supported by the information given—be careful, don't read too much into a question! You are not told anything about what will be happening in the groups, so you cannot assume that learners will have opportunities to manage conflict (B), that each learner's contribution will be recognized and celebrated (C), or that students' ideas will be validated by others (D). By assigning students to mixed-ability groups, Ms. Loving is providing opportunities for peers with various levels of academic ability to work together. Experts on cooperative learning agree that groups will be stronger and, generally, more beneficial for students if they are of mixed abilities. Choice (A) is the correct response.

8. D

The primary focus of this question is Objective 0011:

Understand various instructional approaches and use this knowledge to facilitate student learning.

Eliminate (A) because it is not supported by the information in the question. The students will be working in the classroom, not in an unfamiliar social situation. Eliminate (C) because it is not supported by the information in the question—there are no instances of positive or negative reinforcement indicated, and besides, it is inconsistent with the philosophical framework of the ATS-W, which de-emphasizes a behaviorist approach. Teachers should analyze the benefits or limitations of a specific instructional approach (e.g., cooperative learning) in relation to given purposes or learners. Eliminate (B) because this is a benefit of students working *individually*, not in groups. By using group activities, Ms. Loving capitalizes on the increased importance that adolescent students place on peer relationships; furthermore, and more significantly, this practice reflects her awareness that when students work in groups—among other things—they receive group feedback and support, they are exposed to a variety of ideas and opinions, and they have an opportunity to learn and practice appropriate social behaviors needed to work successfully with others. Choice (D) is the correct response.

9. A

The primary focus of this question is Objective 0003:

Understand how factors in the home, school, and community may affect students' development and readiness to learn and use this understanding to create a classroom environment within which all students can develop and learn.

Teachers should analyze ways in which peer interactions may promote or hinder a student's success in school and determine effective strategies for dealing with peer-related issues in given classroom situations. Eliminate (B) because this may prompt the less able student to compare his or her work to that of the more artistically inclined student, rather than valuing his or her own effort and progress. Eliminate (C) because it is likely to cause resentment toward the less artistically inclined students. Eliminate (D) because this measure forces instruction into a lockstep mode that fails to recognize the importance of designing instruction that recognizes the individual talents, learning styles, and prior learning experiences of the students. The question describes a situation in which highly artistic students are acting negatively toward those whose level of ability is not as high. In this situation, an effective technique for encouraging a greater sense of equity and acceptance among all students is to provide activities in which all students can perform successfully (e.g., have them make collages, rather than draw pictures), making differences in student performance levels less important and apparent. Choice (A) is the correct response.

10. B

The primary focus of this question is Objective 0019:

Understand reciprocal rights and responsibilities in situations involving interactions between teachers and students, parents/guardians, community members, colleagues, school administrators, and other school personnel.

This is a priority-setting question—you must select what Ms. O'Connor should do *next*. Eliminate (A) because it would be inappropriate and a violation of the student's right to privacy to discuss the student's behavior with other students. Eliminate (D) because Ms. O'Connor should exhaust appropriate resources at school before talking with parents. You must now decide which is the better answer choice: (B) or (C)? Eliminate (C) because Ms. O'Connor may talk with the principal, but the counselor is the best resource on campus for information about students. Furthermore, it is the counselor's job to assist Ms. O'Connor with her problem and to offer suggestions on how best to deal with the students' misbehavior. He or she likely will know which previous teachers Ms. O'Connor might consult if that becomes an option. Some previous teachers may have given up on the student, so they would not be helpful to Ms. O'Connor. Also, the counselor probably will know whether the student's parents would be helpful. Choice (B) is the correct response.

11. C

The primary focus of this question is Objective 0010:

Understand instructional planning and apply knowledge of planning processes to design effective instruction that promotes the learning of all students.

This is a priority-setting question. You must select the strategy that would be *most* effective. Successful teachers understand the relationship between careful planning and student success in the classroom. In designing instruction, the teacher takes account of key factors (e.g., students' characteristics and prior experiences) relevant to instructional planning. Eliminate (A) because it is related to *descriptive* speech, not persuasive speech. Eliminate (D) because it doesn't include persuasion. Eliminate (B) because it could be an appropriate activity but would not be as effective as developing and presenting a "television commercial," something that most students, even those from disadvantaged neighborhoods, are very familiar with and know a lot about. Choice (C) is the correct response.

12. A

The primary focus of this question is Objective 0018:

Understand the importance of and apply strategies for promoting productive relationships and interactions among the school, home, and community to enhance student learning.

This is a priority-setting question—you must select the *most* likely outcome. Eliminate (C) because it would be inappropriate for volunteer tutors to assume such a role and teachers should guard against it by training the volunteers before they work with the students. Eliminate (B) and (D) because these may occur unintentionally but would not be most likely. Since community members have a vested interest in the schools, they are a valuable resource to teachers. Teachers should apply strategies for using community resources, such as volunteers, to enrich learning experiences, and they should recognize various ways in which the school and local citizens can work together to promote a sense of neighborhood and community. By using grandparent volunteers, Mr. Campbell is cultivating strong community-school partnerships, thereby fostering positive ties between the school and the community, which will likely establish a sense of community ownership of the school. Choice (A) is the correct response.

13. D

The primary focus of this question is Objective 0007:

Understand how to structure and manage a classroom to create a safe, healthy, and secure learning environment.

This is a priority-setting question—you must select the *primary* purpose of the activity. When you read the stimulus, two aspects that should catch your attention are that Mr. Dubose's whole-group activity is conducted during the *first week* of school and that the success of the activity depends on the class *working as a team*. Teachers typically plan activities during the first week of school that will help their classrooms become places where learning can occur—where students are responsible, cooperative, purposeful, and mutually supportive. They should recognize issues related to the creation of a productive classroom climate (e.g., with regard to shared values, shared experiences, patterns of communication). These ideas are related to classroom management, which is clearly the primary focus of this question. Eliminate (A) and (B) because they deal with *learning processes* (Objective 0002) and (C) because it deals with *motivational principles* (Objective 0013)—all of which undoubtedly will receive Mr. Dubose's attention *after* he has established a suitable climate for learning. Mr. Dubose encourages the students to work as a team during the class activity. Clearly, during this *first* week of school, he wants to promote student ownership in a safe and productive learning environment. Choice (D) is the correct response.

14. C

The primary focus of this question is Objective 0003:

Understand how factors in the home, school, and community may affect students' development and readiness to learn and use this understanding to create a classroom environment within which all students can develop and learn.

This is a priority-setting question—you must select the *primary* purpose of the practice. When you read the stimulus, one important aspect that should catch your attention is that Ms. Sopko spends time with the students every *Monday*. Monday is the day after students have spent a weekend at home. Keep this in mind as you read the answer choices. Eliminate (A) because spending time with students may positively impact self-esteem but experts suggest that other measures, such as providing opportunities for students to meet and master meaningful challenges work better. Eliminate (B) because it is not supported by the question—you are not told she will be discussing students' strengths and weaknesses, and besides, why is it important to do it on Mondays? Eliminate (D) because this may be something that will occur incidentally, but Ms. Sopko's primary purpose for spending individual time with her students every *Monday* is that she realizes that stress from home can affect a student's performance at school. Choice (C) is the correct response.

15. B

The primary focus of this question is Objective 0014:

Understand communication practices that are effective in promoting student learning and creating a climate of trust and support in the classroom and how to use a variety of communication modes to support instruction.

Teachers should be aware how gender differences can affect communication in the classroom and recognize effective methods for enhancing communication. Eliminate (A) and (D) because these measures would be demeaning to the female students. Eliminate (C) because a "pep talk" is unlikely to change the girls' reluctance to participate during math discussions. Ms. Rice can increase female participation by creating a system in which she calls on all students on an equal basis. Choice (B) is the correct response.

16. D

The primary focus of this question is Objective 0019:

Understand reciprocal rights and responsibilities in situations involving interactions between teachers and students, parents/guardians, community members, colleagues, school administrators, and other school personnel.

As educators, teachers work within a clearly defined framework of professional and ethical conduct. Eliminate (A) because teachers should not conduct themselves any way they want; for example, they shouldn't commit crimes. Eliminate (B) because they should not conduct themselves outside of school as they would in school; for example, they shouldn't correct other people's children when they are shopping in a store. Eliminate (C) because they shouldn't conduct themselves like those community members who are not law-abiding citizens. Teachers should exhibit the highest standard of professionalism and base their daily decisions on ethical principles.

They should obey the laws and stand out in the community as positive role models. Choice (D) is the correct response.

17. C

The primary focus of this question is Objective 0017:

Understand how to reflect productively on one's own teaching practice and how to update one's professional knowledge, skills, and effectiveness.

Teachers should apply strategies for working effectively with members of the immediate school community (e.g., colleagues) to increase their knowledge or skills in a given situation. Eliminate (A) because forming a support group with another new teacher is probably a good idea but a new teacher will unlikely be the best source for professional advice. Eliminate (B) because this might work but also could backfire on Ms. Rollins, because some teachers go to the faculty lounge to relax and would rather not "talk shop" there. Eliminate (D) because this may alienate the teacher next door who may tire of Ms. Rollins's complaining. As members of a learning community, the teachers at Ms. Rollins's school should recognize their obligation to serve as mentors for the new faculty. Ms. Rollins should feel comfortable approaching a teacher she respects and asking for help. Choice (C) is the correct response.

18. D

The primary focus of this question is Objective 0018:

Understand the importance of and apply strategies for promoting productive relationships and interactions among the school, home, and community to enhance student learning.

Teachers should apply strategies for initiating and maintaining effective communication between themselves and parents or other caregivers and recognize factors that may facilitate or impede communication in given situations (including parent-teacher conferences). Eliminate (A) because opening remarks are important for establishing the tone of the conference and helping the parents to feel at ease. Eliminate (B) because regular education teachers should avoid "diagnosing" a student who is not doing well since they do not hold credentials to perform this function. Eliminate (C) because teachers should avoid discussing other students in parent-teacher conferences. Ms. Nethery should encourage Brent's parents' involvement in his in-school learning by suggesting ways they can help Brent with problem solving at home (e.g., working math puzzles and brain teasers). Choice (D) is the correct response.

19. B

The primary focus of this question is Objective 0018:

Understand the importance of and apply strategies for promoting productive relationships and interactions among the school, home, and community to enhance student learning.

Ms. Nethery should recognize the importance of maintaining effective communication with parents. Eliminate (A) and (C) because the parents have asked for her opinion. She risks making them feel reluctant to seek her opinion on other matters in the future if she doesn't give one this time; besides, teachers should feel comfortable about offering their professional opinion when it is solicited. Another problem with (C) is that, depending on their educational backgrounds, Mr. and Mrs. Mahaffey may have difficulty evaluating the merits of intrinsic versus extrinsic motivation. Eliminate (D) because it is inappropriate. Teachers should be sensitive to parents and caregivers and avoid being pejorative about their ideas. Ms. Nethery can keep communication open, while at the same time showing respect and consideration for Mr. and Mrs. Mahaffey, by offering her professional opinion about their rewarding Brent for good grades in algebra, then telling them that, nevertheless, they should make their own decision in the matter. Choice (B) is the correct response.

20. C

The primary focus of this question is Objective 0019:

Understand reciprocal rights and responsibilities in situations involving interactions between teachers and students, parents/guardians, community members, colleagues, school administrators, and other school personnel.

Teachers should apply their knowledge of their rights and legal responsibilities in various situations (e.g., in relation to students who may be abused). According to Title 6 of the New York State Social Services Law, a teacher who has reasonable cause to suspect that a child is an abused or maltreated child shall "immediately notify the person in charge" of the school, which means Ms. Quinn is *legally* mandated to notify the building principal. Eliminate (A) because Ms. Quinn is not *legally* mandated to discuss her concerns with Nicole's parents. Eliminate (B) because Ms. Quinn is not *legally* mandated to report to the police. In fact, child abuse cases are usually handled through the Child Protective Service, not through police departments. Eliminate (D) because Ms. Quinn *must* notify the principal, not the counselor. Choice (C) is the correct response.

21. B

The primary focus of this question is Objective 0017:

Understand how to reflect productively on one's own teaching practice and how to update one's professional knowledge, skills, and effectiveness.

Teachers should apply strategies for working effectively with members of the immediate school community (e.g., special needs professionals) to enhance learning for students with special needs. Eliminate (A) because this would reflect a failure on Mr. Welch's part to recognize the time constraints of the ESL teacher and, more importantly, that she is a professionally trained individual who does not need to come in and watch him teach. Eliminate (C) and (D) because these measures are inappropriate. Mr. Welch should not question the placement of the LEP students in an ESL program, nor should he suggest that they be placed in special education or have a less challenging curriculum. Teachers should hold high expectations for all students, including those with limited English proficiency. Mr. Welch should provide the ESL teacher copies of his lesson plans so that she can design her instruction to build on his to strengthen the ESL learners' understandings. Choice (B) is the correct response.

22. D

The primary focus of this question is Objective 0006:

Understand the characteristics and needs of students with disabilities, developmental delays, and exceptional abilities (including gifted and talented students) and use this knowledge to help students reach their highest levels of achievement and independence.

Teachers should apply strategies to ensure that students with special needs and exceptionalities are an integral part of the class and participate to the greatest extent possible in all classroom activities. Eliminate (A) because it would be inappropriate for Mr. Welch to separate the special education students into a group by themselves. Special education students should be authentic members of the classroom, not isolated. Eliminate (B) because special education students should not be interrupted or disturbed when they are given opportunities to interact with and work closely with their nondisabled peers. Eliminate (C) because the whole class working silently and individually is contrary to the philosophical framework of the ATS-W, which enjoins that classrooms should be active, challenging learning environments. The best time for the special education teacher to come in and work with the special education students is when the whole class is engaged in a variety of activities. This way, the special education students are less likely to feel they are in the spotlight when receiving assistance. Choice (D) is the correct response.

23. B

The primary focus of this question is Objective 0017:

Understand how to reflect productively on one's own teaching practice and how to update one's professional knowledge, skills, and effectiveness.

This question describes a situation where a teacher asks other teachers for assistance in identifying resources he can use for professional growth. Clearly, the primary focus of this question is professional development and effectiveness. Eliminate (A) and (C) because they relate to *instructional planning* (Objective 0010). Eliminate (D) because it is not supported by the information in the question. Mr. Welch's decision to consult Ms. Hardy and Ms. Fryman best illustrates that he knows how to use different sources of support to enhance his own professional skills and knowledge. Choice (B) is the correct response.

24. B

The primary focus of this question is Objective 0016:

Understand the history, philosophy, and role of education in New York State and the broader society.

This is a priority-setting question—you must select the *best* answer choice. Eliminate (C) because Mr. Krieg is acting as a resource, not using a resource. Eliminate (D) because it is not supported by the information in the question: Mr. Krieg is not examining his role as a professional. You must now decide which is the better answer choice: (A) or (B)? Eliminate (A) because by helping Ms. Ecker, Mr. Krieg may be cultivating a positive relationship with Ms. Ecker, but Mr. Krieg's actions best illustrate that he recognizes he is a member of a learning community and knows how to work with all members of that community (for instance, by mentoring) to accomplish educational goals. Choice (B) is the correct response.

25. A

The primary focus of this question is Objective 0018:

Understand the importance of and apply strategies for promoting productive relationships and interactions among the school, home, and community to enhance student learning.

Teachers should apply strategies for initiating and maintaining effective communication between themselves and parents or other caregivers and recognize factors that may facilitate or impede communication in given situations. Eliminate (B) because Ms. Ramirez should talk with this parent when she has time to do so, rather than pawn him off on the principal. Eliminate (C) and (D) because these are defensive actions that might escalate the confrontation. Ms. Ramirez should not stop her lesson to spend time discussing the matter with Mr. Risk at the moment. She should let him know that she is willing to talk with him and should do so as soon as possible. Choice (A) is the correct response.

26. C

The primary focus of this question is Objective 0012:

Understand principles and procedures for organizing and implementing lessons and use this knowledge to promote student learning and achievement.

This is a multiple-response question. Read the statements and try to identify one with which you totally agree or one with which you totally disagree, whichever seems easier. Eliminate Statement IV because it is not supported by the question—Mr. Grindle is helping the students apply their current knowledge from their home environments, not teaching them about their home environments. Eliminate (A) and (D) because both include Statement IV. Choices (B) and (C) both include Statement II and Statement III. Thus, you need decide only whether Statement I should be included in the answer choice. Statement I is correct because making connections between two concepts that may appear unrelated requires application of several types of higher-order thinking, including analysis, synthesis, and evaluation. Eliminate (B) because it does not contain Statement I. Statement II is correct because helping learners apply information they have gained from their home life to content they study in school will help them recognize their home environments as valuable resources in their learning. Statement III is correct because the strategy that Mr. Grindle uses recognizes that learners come to school with knowledge and experiences on which they can build as they construct meaningful understandings. Choice (C) is the correct response.

27. D

The primary focus of this question is Objective 0005:

Understand diverse student populations and use knowledge of diversity within the school and the community to address the needs of all learners, to create a sense of community

among students, and to promote students' appreciation of and respect for individuals and groups.

This is a multiple-response question. Read the statements and try to identify one with which you totally agree or one with which you totally disagree, whichever seems easier. Eliminate Statement I because ESL learners need to be authentic members of the classroom community, not seated in a special part of the classroom; besides, "in the front of the room" is a vague place—you are not given any information about it, so you don't know what awaits students who are seated there. Eliminate (A) and (B) because both include Statement I. Choices (C) and (D) both include Statement II and Statement III. Thus, you need decide only whether Statement IV should be included in the answer choice. Statement IV is correct because frequent repetition of key terms during class discussion reinforces the spoken language. Statement II is correct because the teacher can use gestures and body language to enhance meaning. Statement III is correct because hands-on activities enhance comprehension. Choice (D) is the correct response.

28. C

The primary focus of this question is Objective 0005:

Understand diverse student populations and use knowledge of diversity within the school and the community to address the needs of all learners, to create a sense of community among students, and to promote students' appreciation of and respect for individuals and groups.

This is a priority-setting question—you must select the answer choice that will *best* accommodate the parent/guardians/caregivers whose primary language is other than English. Read all the answer choices and eliminate any that you are sure are not good responses. Eliminate (A) because this approach would make the newsletter superfluous in the homes where English is not the primary language. Eliminate (D) because this approach is not as expedient and simple as the approaches described in (B) and (C). You must now decide which is the better answer choice: (B) or (C)? Eliminate (B) because this is something that a teacher might do to help the parent/guardians/caregivers understand the newsletter but it would not be as effective as having the newsletter translated into the primary language of the home. Choice (C) is the correct response.

29. D

The primary focus of this question is Objective 0012:

Understand principles and procedures for organizing and implementing lessons and use this knowledge to promote student learning and achievement.

This is a multiple-response question. Read the statements and try to identify one with which you totally agree or one with which you totally disagree, whichever seems easier. Eliminate Statement I because it is not supported by the question—semantic maps are not intended to provide detailed information. Eliminate (A) and (B) because both include Statement I. Choices (C) and (D) both include Statement III. Thus, you need decide only whether Statement II or Statement IV should be included in the answer choice. Eliminate Statement II because the students are not evaluating (i.e., making value judgments) about concepts during the activity. Eliminate (C). Statements III and IV are correct because having a class discussion to create a semantic map prompts learners to think about what they already know about a topic and also provides an opportunity for reviewing and developing important vocabulary in a meaningful context. Choice (D) is the correct response.

30. D

The primary focus of this question is Objective 0016:

Understand the history, philosophy, and role of education in New York State and the broader society.

This is a multiple-response question. Read the statements and try to identify one with which you totally agree or one with which you totally disagree, whichever seems easier. Schools do not operate, nor do they change, in a vacuum. Statements I, II, and III are correct because factors in the home (e.g., latchkey children) and community (e.g., ethnic pluralism, violence and crime) shape the educational process and provide a context in which schools carry out their mission. Statement IV is correct because historically schools operate within a political climate, where stakeholders exercise pressure and influence on education. Choice (D) is the correct response.

31. B

The primary focus of this question is Objective 0008:

Understand curriculum development and apply knowledge of factors and processes in curricular decision making.

Educators should design curriculum that is responsive to students' developmental characteristics and needs at different grade levels. Eliminate (C) because this approach is contrary to the idea that teachers should promote students' active engagement in learning (Objective 0002)—no passive observers allowed. Eliminate (D) because most early adolescents have achieved the ability to reverse physical actions mentally, usually between the ages of 5 and 7. You must now decide which is the better answer choice: (A) or (B)? Eliminate (A) because these activities may occur in the middle school curriculum but would fail to provide what, developmentally, early adolescents need more—opportunities to grapple with complex problems. Children in middle school are in the process of moving from the concrete operational stage of cognitive development into formal operational thinking, which occurs at about age 11 or 12. Experts suggest that experience with complex problems is necessary for formal operational reasoning to develop. Choice (B) is the correct response.

32. A

The primary focus of this question is Objective 0008:

Understand curriculum development and apply knowledge of factors and processes in curricular decision making.

Educators should design curriculum that is responsive to students' developmental characteristics and needs at different grade levels. Eliminate (B) because early high school adolescents are interested in the present and have limited thoughts of the future. Eliminate (C) because early high school adolescents have an improved ability to use speech to express one's self. Eliminate (D) because it is a teacher centered approach. Generally, early high school adolescents are beginning to develop formal operational thought and, with it, the ability to reason abstractly. Educators should design curriculum that encourages the development of this emerging ability to think and reason abstractly. Choice (A) is the correct response.

33. C

The primary focus of this question is Objective 0007:

Understand how to structure and manage a classroom to create a safe, healthy, and secure learning environment.

This is a priority-setting question—you must select the answer choice that is *most* important for Ms. Moore to consider. Read all the answer choices and eliminate any that you are sure are not good responses. Eliminate (A) and (B) because materials and resources should not be a limiting factor for teachers. In other words, Ms. Moore should decide upon a spatial arrangement based on what she thinks would provide the most effective learning environment for her students, not on what materials and resources are available. Eliminate (D) because this may be a factor that Ms. Moore might consider but it is not as important as considering the instructional approaches she is planning to use with her students. Her spatial arrangement should support her instructional approaches. Choice (C) is the correct response.

34. D

The primary focus of this question is Objective 0006:

Understand the characteristics and needs of students with disabilities, developmental delays, and exceptional abilities (including gifted and talented students) and use this knowledge to help students reach their highest levels of achievement and independence.

Eliminate (A) and (B) because Ms. Moore should strive to mix students academically and culturally to foster peer interaction. Eliminate (C) because Ms. Moore has no way of determining this, and besides, it shouldn't be a consideration. Ms. Moore needs to consider the special needs of the children with physical or learning disabilities to ensure that they are an integral part of the class and participate to the greatest extent possible in all classroom activities. Choice (D) is the correct response.

35. B

The primary focus of this question is Objective 0018:

Understand the importance of and apply strategies for promoting productive relationships and interactions among the school, home, and community to enhance student learning.

This is a priority-setting question—you must select the *best* answer choice. Eliminate (A) and (C) because the time period in between letters/notes is too long. You must now decide which is the better answer choice: (B) or (D)? Eliminate (D) because this is one way a teacher might communicate regularly with parents/guardians/caregivers but there could be problems, such as a language barrier or not being able to catch all parties at home. A brief weekly newsletter—which could be produced and published by the students themselves—would be best for keeping them regularly informed about class activities, provided of course, that the newsletter is written in the home language of the parents/guardians/caregivers. Choice (B) is the correct response.

36. B

The primary focus of this question is Objective 0011:

Understand various instructional approaches and use this knowledge to facilitate student learning.

This is a priority-setting question—you must select the answer choice that is *most* important. Read all the answer choices and eliminate any that you are sure are not good responses. Teachers should analyze the uses, benefits, and limitations of a specific instructional approach (e.g., technology-based approach) in relation to given purposes or learners. Eliminate (C) because the students will be researching on the Internet, not writing reports while in the research area. Eliminate (A) and (D) because these are skills that students will likely need but *safety* is the most important issue when students are using the Internet. Mr. Tang needs to make sure that his students are prevented from accessing sites with inappropriate content. Choice (B) is the correct response.

37. C

The primary focus of this question is Objective 0007:

Understand how to structure and manage a classroom to create a safe, healthy, and secure learning environment.

Eliminate (A) because this measure is something Mr. Tang might do as part of a group contingency plan but, in the situation described in the question, it is a punitive and arbitrary reaction to the misbehavior. Eliminate (B) because this is a step Mr. Tang may want to take later but it will not help with the present situation. Eliminate (D) because the answer is too broad—the problem is how to deal with the present conflict, not about resolving conflicts in general—and further, this approach places too much responsibility on the students. By involving the whole class and letting them work out a fair way (e.g., make a sign-up sheet) for accessing the computers, Mr. Tang will be fostering an atmosphere of mutual responsibility and recognizing that when students are involved in developing guidelines for appropriate behavior, they are more likely to agree to observe them. Choice (C) is the correct response.

38. D

The primary focus of this question is Objective 0009:

Understand the interrelationship between assessment and instruction and how to use formal and informal assessment to learn about students, plan instruction, monitor student understanding in the context of instruction, and make effective instructional modifications.

This is a multiple-response question. Read the statements and try to identify one with which you totally agree or one with which you totally disagree, whichever seems easier. Eliminate Statement I because this method of assessment is too formal for the situation. Eliminate (A) and (B) because both contain Statement I. Choices (C) and (D) both contain Statement II. Thus, you need decide only whether to include Statement III or Statement IV. Eliminate Statement III because this method would not be as beneficial as the more learner-centered, reflective approach of self-assessment journal entries. Statement II is correct because informal observation while the students are in the research area would be a more authentic assessment than tests or quizzes. Choice (D) is the correct response.

39. A

The primary focus of this question is Objective 0007:

Understand how to structure and manage a classroom to create a safe, healthy, and secure learning environment.

Eliminate (B) and (D) because these measures would penalize Jena for her enthusiasm about the research area. Eliminate (C) because it is too teacher centered. Teachers should analyze relationships between classroom management strategies (e.g., in relation to discipline, student decision making, establishing and maintaining standards of behavior) and student learning, attitudes, and behavior. Mr. Tang can encourage Jena to be self-managed by providing a form that she must check to see if her work is complete before she can go to the research area. Choice (A) is the correct response.

40. A

The primary focus of this question is Objective 0012:

Understand principles and procedures for organizing and implementing lessons and use this knowledge to promote student learning and achievement.

Teachers should evaluate various instructional resources (e.g., textbook, guest speaker, film) in relation to given learners or goals. Eliminate (C) and (D) because Ms. DeWitt should recognize the instructional value of having an expert come in and talk with the students. Eliminate (B) because the students are naturally going to be curious and want to ask questions and this should not be discouraged. Because the topic of drugs can be a controversial issue for many parents, Ms. DeWitt should accept the offer but make sure the parents are informed beforehand. Choice (A) is the correct response.

41. C

The primary focus of this question is Objective 0010:

Understand instructional planning and apply knowledge of planning processes to design effective instruction that promotes the learning of all students.

This is a priority-setting question—you must select the answer choice that should be done *first*. Eliminate (A), (B), and (D) because these measures are related to *instructional delivery* (Subarea III) and should come *after* objectives have been determined. The purpose of instruction is to improve performance. In order to create clearly defined objectives, Mr. Rivera needs to have a sound basis by which success can be measured—by *first* determining students' strengths and needs in the areas of reading comprehension and critical thinking. Choice (C) is the correct response.

42. B

The primary focus of this question is Objective 0009:

Understand the interrelationship between assessment and instruction and how to use formal and informal assessment to learn about students, plan instruction, monitor student understanding in the context of instruction, and make effective instructional modifications.

This is a multiple-response question. Read the statements and try to identify one with which you totally agree or one with which you totally disagree, whichever seems easier. Eliminate Statement II because it is contrary to cooperative learning principles, of which mixed-ability grouping is an essential component. Eliminate (A) and (C) because they both include Statement II. Choices (B) and (D) both include Statement III. Thus, you need decide only whether Statement I or Statement IV should be included in the answer choice. Eliminate Statement IV because it is not supported by the information in the question—the teacher, not the students, is using the checklist. Statement I is correct because items 1 and 2 on the checklist assess whether a student is contributing to the success of the group. This guards against the "free rider" effect, an important pitfall of cooperative learning that must be avoided. Statement III is correct because results from item 3 can be used to make instructional adjustments, if needed. Choice (B) is the correct response.

43. A

The primary focus of this question is Objective 0009:

Understand the interrelationship between assessment and instruction and how to use formal and informal assessment to learn about students, plan instruction, monitor student understanding in the context of instruction, and make effective instructional modifications.

Mr. Rivera uses the observation checklist to assess individual student participation in group activities. Eliminate (B) and (C) because these choices deal with *communication* (Objective 0014), not assessment. Eliminate (D) because the checklist is being used during the activity, not afterwards. Teachers should recognize that placing students in learning groups and expecting them to cooperate and successfully work together is unrealistic and likely to lead to disappointing results. Teachers should monitor groups to ensure that students are practicing the interpersonal skills needed for high-quality group work. Choice (A) is the correct response.

44. B

The primary focus of this question is Objective 0003:

Understand how factors in the home, school, and community may affect students' development and readiness to learn and use this understanding to create a classroom environment within which all students can develop and learn.

This is a priority-setting question—you must select the answer choice that is *most* important. Eliminate (A) because it is a teacher-focused response. Eliminate (C) and (D) because research about learning and prejudice suggests that telling someone (Crystal and those in the class who agree with her) that his or her stereotypical opinion is incorrect is unlikely to change that person's opinion. Teachers should analyze ways peer interactions may hinder a student's success in school and determine strategies for dealing with peer-related issues in given classroom situations. It is important that Mr. Rivera immediately deal with this problem so as not to leave the impression that Crystal's remarks are acceptable. He should make it clear to Crystal that her words can hurt and will not be tolerated. Choice (B) is the correct response.

45. A

The primary focus of this question is Objective 0005:

Understand diverse student populations and use knowledge of diversity within the school and the community to address the needs of all learners, to create a sense of community among students, and to promote students' appreciation of and respect for individuals and groups.

This is a priority-setting question—you must select the answer choice that is *most* important. Eliminate (B) because this strategy would probably compound the problem by focusing the students' attention on gender as a dividing mechanism for the class. Eliminate (D) because this is something that Mr. Rivera might do but it is not as important or necessary as the approach given in choice (A). Eliminate (C) because this is something Mr. Rivera should do but he should *first* examine his own personal beliefs and feelings about male students' abilities in language arts. Even though Mr. Rivera is a male teacher, he may have unconscious biases and prejudices about the boys in this regard. Choice (A) is the correct response.

46. B

The primary focus of this question is Objective 0014:

Understand communication practices that are effective in promoting student learning and creating a climate of trust and support in the classroom and how to use a variety of communication

This is a priority-setting question—you must select the answer choice that will be *most* effective. Eliminate (C) because this strategy is used when a student has a history of academic failure and has developed an expectation of failure. This is not the case with Jeremy since, until recently, he was one of Ms. Goldsberry's better students and, besides, he isn't putting forth much effort for which to be rewarded. Eliminate (D) because "timeout" is a punitive procedure that is used for students who are "acting up" in class in order to get attention from their peers and/or the teacher—this is not the case with Jeremy. You must now decide which is the better answer choice: (A) or (B)? Eliminate (A) because it is a teacher-centered approach. But by having Jeremy journal back and forth with her on a weekly basis, Ms. Goldsberry will be establishing a line of communication with Jeremy and fostering a measure of trust and support in their teacher-student interactions. This should lead to Jeremy's eventually opening up to Ms. Goldsberry about his lack of engagement in her class. Choice (B) is the correct response.

47. D

The primary focus of this question is Objective 0014:

Understand communication practices that are effective in promoting student learning and creating a climate of trust and support in the classroom and how to use a variety of communication modes to support instruction.

Teachers should recognize effective questioning methods for specific purposes (e.g., facilitating factual recall, encouraging higher-order thinking). Eliminate (A), (B), and (C) because these questions are convergent—soliciting one-word responses. To encourage higher-order thinking, teachers should ask divergent, open-ended questions that solicit multiple and varied responses. Choice (D) is the correct response.

48. C

The primary focus of this question is Objective 0006:

Understand the characteristics and needs of students with disabilities, developmental delays, and exceptional abilities (including gifted and talented students) and use this knowledge to help students reach their highest levels of achievement and independence.

Eliminate (A) because this approach would reflect a failure on Mr. Sowards's part to recognize the time constraints of the special education faculty. Eliminate (D) because special needs students should be an integral part of the class and should participate to the greatest extent possible in all classroom activities. Eliminate (B) because a student should not be given the responsibility of a special needs student on a field trip since the student helper may not be able to handle unanticipated occurrences. To accommodate Beverly, Mr. Sowards should go to the museum beforehand to check out problems (e.g., wheelchair access) that need to be addressed. Choice (C) is the correct response.

49. B

The primary focus of this question is Objective 0013:

Understand the relationship between student motivation and achievement and how motivational principles and practices can be used to promote and sustain student cooperation in learning.

Eliminate (A) because it is not supported by the information in the question— the students are going out into the public arena, not receiving public recognition. Eliminate (C) because it relates to *instructional approaches* (Objective 0011)—students learn best from working with concrete objects and phenomena. Eliminate (D) because it relates to *learning processes* (Objective 0002)—students learn best when they can connect new learning to prior understandings. Teachers should apply procedures for enhancing student interest and helping students find their own motivation. By highlighting connections between academic learning and the workplace, Ms. Garcîa is enhancing motivation by connecting learning to meaningful situations beyond the classroom. Choice (B) is the correct response.

50. B

The primary focus of this question is Objective 0013:

Understand the relationship between student motivation and achievement and how motivational principles and practices can be used to promote and sustain student cooperation in learning.

Eliminate (A) because it is not supported by the information in the question; the teacher, not the students, initiated the brainstorming activity. Eliminate (C) because critical thinking involves using analysis, synthesis, and/or evaluation—thinking skills that require a deeper understanding of content then the students have at the start of a unit. Eliminate (D) because recalling factual information does not tend to promote motivation. Teachers should apply procedures for enhancing motivation such as prompting students to recognize that concepts presented in the classroom relate to their everyday experiences. Choice (B) is the correct response.

51. B

The primary focus of this question is Objective 0010:

Understand instructional planning and apply knowledge of planning processes to design effective instruction that promotes the learning of all students.

Notice that the question is asking which principle the practice of collaboratively planning a unit illustrates. Eliminate (A) because it deals with *communication* (Objective 0014), not collaboration. Eliminate (C) because it is not supported by the question—the teachers are not establishing a vision; they are planning instruction, a more mundane yet vital activity that comes after visions have been established. Eliminate (D) because it relates to *curriculum development* (Objective 0008) and it is not supported by the question—the teachers are planning a mathematics unit, not an interdisciplinary unit. The teachers are working together to design effective instruction. Choice (B) is the correct response.

52. C

The primary focus of this question is Objective 0008:

Understand curriculum development and apply knowledge of factors and processes in curricular decision making.

Notice that the question is asking what Mr. Hammack's *decision* to involve other teachers in developing the unit illustrates. Eliminate (A) because it is not supported by the question—the teachers are developing the unit, not evaluating (judging the worth or value of) the unit. Eliminate (B) because it's not about Mr. Hammack's decision to involve other teachers; it's about his decision to do the unit. Eliminate (D) because it's not about Mr. Hammack's decision to involve other teachers, it's about *communication* (Objective 0014). Mr. Hammack's decision to involve the science and mathematics teachers illustrates his understanding that teachers should work with colleagues to develop interdisciplinary curricula. Choice (C) is the correct response.

53. A

The primary focus of this question is Objective 0001:

Understand human development, including developmental processes and variations, and use this understanding to promote student development and learning.

Eliminate (B), (C), and (D) because these are characteristics of middle school students that the teachers may consider but it is *most* important—for a unit on health and fitness—that the teachers keep in mind that adolescents are self-conscious about the physical changes they are undergoing as their bodies develop. Choice (A) is the correct response.

54. D

The primary focus of this question is Objective 0003:

Understand how factors in the home, school, and community may affect students' development and readiness to learn and use this understanding to create a classroom environment within which all students can develop and learn.

This is a priority-setting question—you must select the answer choice that is likely to contribute the *most*. Eliminate (A), (B), and (C) because these approaches involve reinforcing students with praise, rewards, or recognition—all of which are more closely related to *motivation* (Objective 0013). Choice (A) is incorrect also because praise should be given for a specific desirable behavior, not for generally "being good."

Choices (B) and (C) may contribute in some indirect way to self-esteem, but these approaches are not as likely to contribute to self-esteem as the approach given in (D). Furthermore, the approach in (B) should be used cautiously since some research suggests that extrinsic rewards may work against intrinsic motivation for tasks that are intrinsically motivating. Choice (C) should be used with caution as well because some adolescents are shy and would not enjoy being singled out in front of their peers. Experts suggest that self-esteem improves as a child grows more competent in school tasks. To facilitate this process, learning experiences should be developmentally appropriate and meaningful for the child, making it more likely that the he or she will succeed. Ms. Ling can enhance the self-esteem of her students by providing opportunities for them to meet and master new challenges. Choice (D) is the correct response.

55. A

The primary focus of this question is Objective 0002:

Understand learning processes and use this understanding to promote student development and learning.

This is a priority-setting question—you must select the answer choice that is likely to benefit students *most*. Notice that the prompts encourage students to process their learning for the day. The question is asking how *responding* to these prompts is likely to benefit students. Keep this in mind as you read the answer choices. Eliminate (B) because it is not supported by the question—the prompts address current learning, not future goals. Eliminate (D) because it is about *communication* (Objective 0014), not learning processes. Eliminate (C) because the learning logs may be used as an assessment tool by the teacher but the benefit to the students comes from processing their learning and reflecting on their own learning strategies, which in turn fosters a sense of ownership in their own learning. Choice (A) is the correct response.

56. D

The primary focus of this question is Objective 0003:

Understand how factors in the home, school, and community may affect students' development and readiness to learn and use this understanding to create a classroom environment within which all students can develop and learn.

This is a priority-setting question—you must select the answer choice that should be a *priority*. Teachers should analyze ways in which peer interactions may hinder a student's success in school and determine effective strategies for dealing with peer-related issues. Eliminate (A) because it is not supported by the question—Carlos did not say hurtful words to Shawn. Eliminate (B) because it is not supported by the question—Ms. Werner doesn't know that Shawn didn't mean what he said. You must now decide which is the better answer choice: (C) or (D)? Eliminate (C) because this is something that Ms. Werner should do but she needs to help Carlos deal with his feelings *first*. Victims *always* take priority over perpetrators in conflict resolution. Choice (D) is the correct response.

57. B

The primary focus of this question is Objective 0017:

Understand how to reflect productively on one's own teaching practice and how to update one's professional knowledge, skills, and effectiveness.

Notice that the question is asking what Ms. Werner's decision to teach social skills demonstrates. Keep this in mind as you read the answer choices. Eliminate (A), (C), and (D) because they do not respond to the question being asked. Choice (A) is also incorrect because it relates to *diversity* (Objective 0005), which is not mentioned in the question, and *you should not assume it based on students' names (e.g., Carlos)*. Choice (C) is also incorrect because it relates to *motivation* (Objective 0013). Choice (D) is also incorrect because it relates to *learning processes* (Objective 0002). Teachers should be reflective practitioners who use observed student needs to guide instructional planning. By deciding to teach social skills based on the interaction between Shawn and Carlos, Ms. Werner is reflecting productively on her own practice. Choice (B) is the correct response.

58. C

The primary focus of this question is Objective 0001:

Understand human development, including developmental processes and variations, and use this understanding to promote student development and learning.

Eliminate (A), (B), and (D) because these characteristics are typical of younger children, not adolescents. Many middle school students are not aware that certain social skills are important in their lives, so Ms. Werner cannot expect them to develop the skills without assistance. Most adolescents need help in learning how, for example, to show consideration for others. Choice (C) is the correct response.

59. B

The primary focus of this question is Objective 0017:

Understand how to reflect productively on one's own teaching practice and how to update one's professional knowledge, skills, and effectiveness.

Notice that the question is asking what Ms. Werner's decision to consult the school counselor demonstrates. Keep this in mind as you read the answer choices. Eliminate (A) because Ms. Werner will have done this prior to her decision to consult the counselor. Eliminate (C) and (D) because they do not respond to the question being asked. Choice (C) is also incorrect because it relates to *school-community interactions* (Objective 0018), and choice (D) is also incorrect because it relates to *classroom management* (Objective 0007). Ms. Werner's decision to consult the school counselor demonstrates her ability to use different resources and opportunities (e.g., other educators) to enhance her professional development. Choice (B) is the correct response.

60. A

The primary focus of this question is Objective 0006:

Understand the characteristics and needs of students with disabilities, developmental delays, and exceptional abilities (including gifted and talented students) and use this knowledge to help students reach their highest levels of achievement and independence.

Eliminate (B) because this approach would be used for a child who has a specific learning disability, which Ms. Kamiguchi should not assume is the cause of Tony's inability to pay attention. Eliminate (C) because Ms. Kamiguchi cannot legally do this. Evaluation of students under the Individuals with Disabilities Education Act (IDEA) is surrounded with safeguards, including parent's written consent, before testing can take place. Eliminate (D) because this may make Tony feel different and isolated and, besides, "in the front of the room" is a vague place—you are not told what awaits a child there. At this point, Ms. Kamiguchi should explore ways to help Tony become more attentive in her class by, for instance, engaging him in more hands-on activities. Choice (A) is the correct response.

61. C

The primary focus of this question is Objective 0018:

Understand the importance of and apply strategies for promoting productive relationships and interactions among the school, home, and community to enhance student learning.

Teachers should know how to take advantage of community resources to foster student growth, while at the same time establishing strong and positive ties with the community. Eliminate (A) and (B) because these approaches might offend Mr. Peltier and they would inconvenience him as well. Eliminate (D) because it is inappropriate to ask Mr. Peltier (or any noneducator guest speaker) to perform the function of an educator. Choice (C) is the correct response.

62. B

The primary focus of this question is Objective 0002:

Understand learning processes and use this understanding to promote student development and learning.

Teachers should analyze processes by which students construct meaning and apply strategies for facilitating learning in instructional situations (e.g., by building connections between new information and prior knowledge, by relating learning to world issues and community concerns, by making learning purposeful). Eliminate (A) because this approach would be too passive for the learners. Eliminate (C) because it is teacher focused. Eliminate (D) because it singles out certain students and may cause resentment. Mr. Barrett can make the learning relevant and personally meaningful for his students by having them create their own list of questions to ask Mr. Peltier (Remember, K-W-L.) Choice (B) is the correct response.

63. D

The primary focus of this question is Objective 0005:

Understand diverse student populations and use knowledge of diversity within the school and the community to address the needs of all learners, to create a sense of community among students, and to promote students' appreciation of and respect for individuals and groups.

This is a priority-setting question—you must select the answer choice that would be *most* effective. Eliminate (A) because this approach has limited effectiveness in countering gender stereotyping. Eliminate (B) and (C) because these approaches may send the message that recognizing and celebrating the accomplishments of women need attention only for the day. Research indicates that by age 9, children have well-established prejudices that are highly resistant to change; therefore, Mr. Barrett must go beyond brief and superficial measures to counter gender stereotyping in these older learners—a long-term intervention is warranted. Bringing in both male and female guests who have science-related careers throughout the year will provide positive role models in science for all of Mr. Barrett's students. Choice (D) is the correct response.

64. C

The primary focus of this question is Objective 0011:

Understand various instructional approaches and use this knowledge to facilitate student learning.

Teachers should analyze the uses, benefits, and limitations of a specific instructional approach (e.g., cross-age tutoring) in relation to given learners. This is a priority-setting question—you must select the answer choice that should be the *main* concern of using the cross-age activity. Eliminate (A), (B), and (D) because these are concerns the teachers may have but their main concern must be the safety of the children in their care. It is very important that the teachers ensure that the fifth graders are not exposed to anything inappropriate when interacting with the older students. Choice (C) is the correct response.

65. A

The primary focus of this question is Objective 0011:

Understand various instructional approaches and use this knowledge to facilitate student learning.

Eliminate (B), (C), and (D) because these do not actively engage the learners. Having the ninth graders role-play the activity beforehand will give them an opportunity to practice the activity and appropriate behavior in a meaningful context. Furthermore, it will promote their understanding of the typical characteristics of the younger students and encourage them to monitor their own conduct during the planned activity. Choice (A) is the correct response.

66. D

The primary focus of this question is Objective 0013:

Understand the relationship between student motivation and achievement and how motivational principles and practices can be used to promote and sustain student cooperation in learning.

Teachers should apply procedures for enhancing student interest and helping students find their own motivation. Notice the question is asking why the act of composing their own questions is motivational for the students. Eliminate (A) because it does not respond to the question—the questions in the survey may relate to world issues and community concerns, but the *act* of composing the questions does not. Eliminate (B) and (C) because these choices are not supported by the question—the students are composing questions, not pursuing topics of personal interests or setting their own goals. Ms. Diaz understands that intrinsic motivation is enhanced when students are given a measure of control over their learning experiences. Choice (D) is the correct response.

67. A

The primary focus of this question is Objective 0005:

Understand diverse student populations and use knowledge of diversity within the school and the community to address the needs of all learners, to create a sense of community among students, and to promote students' appreciation of and respect for individuals and groups.

This is a multiple-response question *and* a priority-setting question. Read the statements and try to identify one with which you totally agree or one with which you totally disagree, whichever seems easier. Eliminate Statement IV because this would be counter to the idea of appreciating the uniqueness of individuals and celebrating (not pointing out the hardships of) differences. Eliminate (C) and (D) because they both include Statement IV. Eliminate III because it is not supported by the question: The students will be asking Mr. Irvine questions, not relating concepts to everyday experiences. Eliminate (B) because it contains Statement III. Statement II is incorrect because this may occur incidentally but it would not be a primary purpose. Teachers should apply strategies for fostering students' understanding and appreciation of diversity and for using diversity that exists within the community to enhance all students' learning. By inviting Mr. Irvine and having the students ask him questions about his everyday life, Ms. Heard is helping her students realize that people are more alike than different. Choice (A) is the correct response.

68. B

The primary focus of this question is Objective 0002:

Understand learning processes and use this understanding to promote student development and learning.

Eliminate (A) and (C) because these choices are not supported by the question—the students will be obtaining information, not using the higher-level thinking (analysis, synthesis, and evaluation) associated with critical thinking and creativity. Eliminate (D) because it is not supported by the question—students will be obtaining information, not learning to be self-managed/self-directed. By bringing in Mr. Irvine, Ms. Heard is promoting her students' natural curiosity about things that are strange and different to them. Choice (B) is the correct response.

69. D

The primary focus of this question is Objective 0003:

Understand how factors in the home, school, and community may affect students' development and readiness to learn and use this understanding to create a classroom environment within which all students can develop and learn.

Eliminate (A) because this response reinforces Mrs. LeBoulan's lack of confidence in Shironda's potential academic achievement. Eliminate (B) and (C) because they both send the message that Ms. Kendall feels that Shironda is incapable of doing both her schoolwork and ballet. Teachers should be aware that students in middle school have the natural desire to gain competence and skills that allow them to feel successful and have greater control over their environment. There are many factors that may influence how this desire is expressed in any one child. A major factor is how the parent views and expresses beliefs regarding the child's abilities. If a parent is confident about the child's school success and offers encouragement, it makes it easier for the child to strive to achieve academically. Yet, if a parent makes it known that the parent lacks confidence in the child's academic ability, a teacher may see that lack of confidence mirrored in the child. It is to Shironda's benefit for Ms. Kendall and Mrs. LeBoulan to work together to help Shironda attain her goals in both school and ballet. Choice (D) is the correct response.

70. D

The primary focus of this question is Objective 0002:

Understand learning processes and use this understanding to promote student development and learning.

This is a priority-setting question. While teachers use journals in a variety of ways, you must select the answer choice that is *most* effective. Eliminate (A) because the teacher's purpose in assigning journal writing is to monitor what learning is being documented and to respond appropriately to this valuable feedback. Eliminate (B) because students' academic journals are not intended to be personal diaries. This is something that can be implemented with the school counselor if need be. Eliminate (C) because while story prompts are excellent tools to use when students have difficulty generating writing ideas, use of this method exclusively for the purpose of standardized test preparation is contrary to a constructivist perspective—testing should not dictate classroom intercourse. When students have the opportunity to write in a journal before and after a lesson, they are afforded the opportunity to document their prior knowledge and then to reflect on what they learned as well as to monitor the progress of their own work. Choice (D) is the correct response.

71. D

The primary focus of this question is Objective 0006:

Understand the characteristics and needs of students with disabilities, developmental delays, and exceptional abilities (including gifted and talented students) and use this knowledge to help students reach their highest levels of achievement and independence.

Eliminate (A) because while a parent-teacher conference would probably be a good idea, Ms. Mintz should not assume that Mohsen's problem is due to lack of help at home. Eliminate (B) because this is a punitive measure that could negatively affect Mohsen's attitude toward school. Eliminate (C) because it would be inappropriate for Ms. Mintz to make this kind of modification for a student who has not been identified by credentialed specialists as needing such an accommodation. At this point, Ms. Mintz should confer with a special education specialist concerning Mohsen to explore ways in which Mohsen might overcome his difficulty with written performance. Choice (D) is the correct response.

72. D

The primary focus of this question is Objective 0003:

Understand how factors in the home, school, and community may affect students' development and readiness to learn and use this understanding to create a classroom environment within which all students can develop and learn.

Teaching students from diverse socioeconomic backgrounds presents a challenge where research projects are concerned and demands a leveling of the playing field in terms of access to resources. Eliminate (A) because demanding that parents supply expensive or technical resources is inappropriate and doing so may well be impossible for some of them. Eliminate (B) because middle school schedules and the availability of additional adults to supervise a weekly trip to the library usually make such a solution difficult or implausible. Eliminate (C) because, while students should be encouraged to bring in anything that will help with the project, asking students to contribute the bulk of the necessary materials is inappropriate, invites comparisons, and may make some students feel uncomfortable. Further, asking students to supply the resources for the rest of the class puts an inappropriate burden on those students who have access to resources and places them in an uncomfortable position in relation to their classmates. No student should be penalized because he or she cannot use certain educational resources that other students have available. Teachers must assure that every student has access to needed materials. Taking students to the resources or bringing resources to the students can do this. In this case, the most efficient solution is to bring the resources to the students. Ms. Enrico should assemble the required materials herself and make them available in her classroom for students' use. Choice (D) is the correct response.

73. C

The primary focus of this question is Objective 0005:

Understand diverse student populations and use knowledge of diversity within the school and the community to address the needs of all learners, to create a sense of community among students, and to promote students' appreciation of and respect for individuals and groups.

This is a priority-setting question. You must choose which activity would be *most* effective. Teachers must make themselves aware of and capitalize on the cultural backgrounds of their students. How they do this depends in part upon the academic content of the course or courses they teach. Eliminate (A) because a trip to a museum is a worthwhile activity when it serves clear instructional goals but it is not the most effective way to familiarize students with each others' backgrounds—the information is impersonal and limited. Eliminate (B) because a handout is impersonal and puts the teacher in the role of dispenser of knowledge. Eliminate (D) because this is an ideal topic and body of content for students to explore together, learning from each other rather than in isolation. Mr. Krugman has the perfect opportunity to connect students' personal prior knowledge of their own cultures with new information about the roles of these cultures in U.S. history. Small-group research projects would allow students to search out information, analyze it, synthesize it into a form for reporting back, and to build on the contributions of each member of the group. Choice (C) is the correct response.

74. B

The primary focus of this question is Objective 0019:

Understand reciprocal rights and responsibilities in situations involving interactions between teachers and students, parents/guardians, community members, colleagues, school administrators, and other school personnel.

Eliminate (A). Nejad is certainly entitled to free speech, but only so long as he doesn't deprive other students of the education to which they're entitled. Since the demonstration was disruptive, the principal was within her rights to stop it. Eliminate (C) because it is not supported by the question. The principal simply stopped the demonstration; the principal did not take disciplinary action—no hearing is warranted. Eliminate (D) because it brings up an irrelevant issue. Whether or not a teacher was supervising the demonstration, the demonstration was disrupting the learning environment and had to be stopped. Once a student or group of students becomes so disruptive that they disrupt the learning environment for others, that activity has to stop. Even though Nejad is entitled to express his opinions because he is entitled to free speech just as everyone else is, he and the other demonstrators are not entitled to disrupt the classes of the other student, and that's why the principal was within her rights to stop the demonstration. Choice (B) is the correct response.

75. A

The primary focus of this question is Objective 0003:

Understand how factors in the home, school, and community may affect students' development and readiness to learn and use this understanding to create a classroom environment within which all students can develop and learn.

This is a priority-setting question in reverse. You must determine which factor would *least* affect the student's learning. Eliminate (B) because the individual's learning style has a direct bearing on the kinds of activities he or she feels comfortable experiencing. Eliminate (C) because environmental factors, like an upsetting incident before school, have an impact on a student's mindset to engage in learning activities. Eliminate (D) because the teacher's skill in organizing appropriate learning materials and activities has a major effect on student engagement in learning. Past achievement scores will vary in any class and bear little relationship to the day-to-day forward progress of the curriculum and of student engagement in the present. Standardized achievement test scores are affected by a variety of influences such as test anxiety, prior educational opportunity, and "test-wiseness." A class in which some have test scores lower than others is not necessarily a class in which the learning will be slowed down or speeded up. It's up to the teacher to offer a challenging curriculum for all! Choice (A) is the correct response.

76. C

The primary focus of this question is Objective 0008:

Understand curriculum development and apply knowledge of factors and processes in curricular decision making.

This is a multiple-response priority-setting question. You must identify what is *most* important. Read the statements and try to identify one with which you totally agree or one with which you totally disagree, whichever seems easier. Eliminate Statement II because, while colleagues in a school might seek to accommodate each others' needs by taking turns with purchasing choices, actual decisions about which materials to purchase must be based on how well these materials align with state standards and the standards of professional organizations in the field. Eliminate (A) and (D) because they contain Statement II. Choices (B) and (C) both include Statement III. Thus, you need decide only whether Statement I or Statement IV should be included in the answer choice. Eliminate Statement IV. Although choosing novels with contemporary themes that will appeal to adolescent readers is positive because it represents a learner-centered approach, it is more important that the novels selected be in alignment with state standards and standards of professional organizations; otherwise, scarce budgetary resources should not be spent on them. Choice (C) is the correct response.

77. B

The primary focus of this question is Objective 0010:

Understand instructional planning and apply knowledge of planning processes to design effective instruction that promotes the learning of all students.

One multiple-choice question certainly cannot reference everything a teacher takes into account when planning what to teach, but this question isn't looking for an extensive listing of considerations. It's looking for a basic way of thinking about planning instructional objectives in a new situation. Eliminate (A) because textbooks are created at a general level and don't take into account features of a specific district or classroom. Eliminate (C) because you are given no information to ascertain the quality of the predecessor's lesson materials. Eliminate (D) because Ms. DeFoe's previous instructional units may not be appropriate for her new students. Ms. DeFoe must consider the abilities and backgrounds of her current students while designing instructional objectives that comply with the learning standards set forth by the district where she is currently employed and by the state. Choice (B) is the correct response.

78. A

The primary focus of this question is Objective 0009:

Understand the interrelationship between assessment and instruction and how to use formal and informal assessment to learn about students, plan instruction, monitor student understanding in the context of instruction, and make effective instructional modifications.

Eliminate (B), (C), and (D) because these assessments do not fulfill Mr. Meshkini's purpose to provide "an opportunity for students to showcase what they have learned during the course." Choice (D) is a tempting distractor because your training has taught you that teachers should use portfolio assessments; however, the question stem doesn't indicate that the student portfolios will have a wider audience than the student and Mr. Meshkini. While a teacher must keep track of each individual student's progress, students are often better able to synthesize and retain their new understandings through creating a new form (e.g., dramatization) for expressing what they've learned, rather than by merely recalling or reciting information in a form generated by the teacher. Choice (A) is the correct response.

79. D

The primary focus of this question is Objective 0016:

Understand the history, philosophy, and role of education in New York State and the broader society.

Eliminate (A) because the Constitution grants the regulation of education to the states. Eliminate (C) because it's too narrow an answer. While the laws about civil rights must be obeyed in the schools, other federal laws must be obeyed also. This answer choice doesn't mention them. In theory, federal regulations should not affect the schools because the power to regulate education is a power granted to the states, not to the federal government. Federal regulations enter the picture because federal funds are available to public education. The catch is that the schools accepting federal monies must comply with federal laws and regulations as a condition for receiving them. Eliminate (B) since it contradicts this reality. Choice (D) is the correct response.

80. A

The primary focus of this question is Objective 0014:

Understand communication practices that are effective in promoting student learning and creating a climate of trust and support in the classroom and how to use a variety of communication modes to support instruction.

Eliminate (B) because simply explaining to the class that she, as a teacher, understands their lack of experience doesn't tell them what to do or help them feel more comfortable in doing it. Eliminate (C) because laying down the law would likely increase tension and would be counterproductive. Eliminate (D) because this may, over time, make it somewhat easier for students to speak up in class but not necessarily to participate in discussions. In small groups, students tend to speak up and voice their opinions. Then when the class reconvenes, students are often more willing to speak up because they have already done so and survived it. Choice (A) is the correct response.

SCORING YOUR WRITTEN ASSIGNMENT

The official scorers will evaluate your written assignment using the following performance characteristics as a guide.

Purpose	Did you fulfill the charge of the assignment?
Application of Content	Did you accurately and effectively apply the relevant knowledge and skills in your writing?
Support	Did you support your response with appropriate examples and/or sound reasoning that reflects an understanding of the relevant knowledge and skills?

ATS-W Scoring Scale

The written assignment is scored according to the following scale:

Score Point	Score Point Description
4	**The "4" response reflects a thorough command of the relevant knowledge and skills.** • The response completely fulfills the purpose of the assignment by responding fully to the given task. • The response demonstrates an accurate and highly effective application of the relevant knowledge and skills. • The response provides strong support with high-quality, relevant examples and/or sound reasoning.
3	**The "3" response reflects a general command of the relevant knowledge and skills.** • The response generally fulfills the purpose of the assignment by responding to the given task. • The response demonstrates a generally accurate and effective application of the relevant knowledge and skills. • The response provides support with some relevant examples and/or generally sound reasoning.

2	**The "2" response reflects a partial command of the relevant knowledge and skills.**
	• The response partially fulfills the purpose of the assignment by responding in a limited way to the given task.
	• The response demonstrates a limited, partially accurate and partially effective application of the relevant knowledge and skills.
	• The response provides limited support with few examples and/or some flawed reasoning.
1	**The "1" response reflects little or no command of the relevant knowledge and skills.**
	• The response fails to fulfill the purpose of the assignment.
	• The response demonstrates a largely inaccurate and/or ineffective application of the relevant knowledge and skills.
	• The response provides little or no support with few, if any, examples and/or seriously flawed reasoning.

Practice ATS-W—Secondary Written Assignment Sample Response

Remember, this written assignment is assessing your understanding of the role of the teacher in relation to the following:

- Knowledge of the Learner

- Instructional Planning and Assessment

- Instructional Delivery

- The Professional Environment

You'll want to use the prompt itself as the skeleton of your essay.

Let's review the prompt. It asks you to do the following:

- Identify a level/subject. You can do this before you begin the essay or work it into the introduction. Just don't forget to include it.

- Explain the importance of the goal. This becomes paragraph 1, the introduction to your essay.

- Describe two strategies. Each strategy that you describe should be a paragraph in the body of your essay.

- Explain why each strategy would be effective. Your essay should include one paragraph that explains the effectiveness of the first strategy you described and another paragraph that explains the effectiveness of the second strategy you described.

Using the template suggested in chapter 3, you can produce an essay similar to the following sample.

Grade level/subject area: 8th grade, social studies

As an eighth-grade social studies teacher, it is important that I help students develop their reading and writing skills. Reading and writing across the content areas are important for the development of critical thinking and reasoning skills. By reading and writing in all subjects, in addition to English language arts, students become aware of the value of these skills and their relevance to the world outside of school.

One strategy I would use to achieve this educational goal is a "Letters Project." As part of an interdisciplinary unit on the Civil War, students will read excerpts from historical novels, such as Steven Crane's *Red Badge of Courage*, Irene Hunt's *Across Five Aprils*, and Michael Shaara's *Killer Angels*, along with nonfictional accounts of the war written by soldiers who served. While they read, students will respond to specific questions in their journals. Next, I will briefly review the friendly-letter format. Finally, I will have students write letters from the point of view of a soldier in the Civil War. In letters written to a family member, students demonstrate their knowledge of Civil War facts and their understanding of the reasons behind the war, the general conditions under which the soldiers fought, and the feelings that the soldiers experienced. Students are graded on their content knowledge, writing mechanics, and creativity as specified in a predetermined scoring rubric.

The Letters Project is effective because it incorporates reading and writing into the social studies curriculum. Reading accounts of what happened during the Civil War reinforces what students have learned from classroom instruction and from the required textbook. It helps them see the effects of the Civil War on the individual rather than just on the country at large. Writing the letters gives them practice writing from a particular point of view and writing for a specific audience. In a creative and meaningful way, students demonstrate their understanding of the ideas and concepts they've learned.

Another strategy I will use to achieve the goal of reading and writing across the curriculum is a Reading/Writing Workshop. At the beginning of every unit, I will provide students with a list of outside reading books and articles that relate to the topic we are studying. Throughout the unit, students will read and respond to questions in reading logs. Every Tuesday, class time will be used to share their outside reading experiences. Using a roundtable format, I will ask general questions to generate discussion on the topic we are studying. Students will be encouraged to listen to each other and make connections between what they have read, what other students in the class have read, and what we have been doing in class. Greater understanding of the event or time period being studied likely will come out of these discussions. At the end of class on Tuesdays, students will be given time to reflect on the class discussion and record what they have learned.

Reading/Writing Workshop is effective because it reinforces the value of reading in classes other than English language arts. It allows students to choose genres they enjoy and make connections to their own lives. In addition to reading and writing skills, the roundtable discussion emphasizes listening and critical thinking skills. Students enjoy the informal setting of the "book chat" and freely share their enthusiasm about the books they've chosen.

Reading and writing across the curriculum teaches students the value of both of these lifelong skills. As an eighth-grade social studies teacher, it is important that I support the English language arts teacher and encourage students to read and write in my classroom and at home. The Letters Project and Reading/Writing Workshop are both effective strategies that strengthen these skills and, at the same time, achieve my content objectives.

This essay is one of thousands of possible responses to the prompt. There is no one "correct" or "best" answer. Let's check it as suggested in chapter 3.

Check against the prompt:

☑ I explained the importance of the educational goal in paragraph 1.

☑ I described two strategies in paragraphs 2 and 4.

☑ I explained the effectiveness of my two strategies in paragraphs 3 and 5.

☑ I included my grade level and subject area in my response.

Check for organization:

- ☑ My essay begins with an introductory sentence that (1) identifies the grade level and subject I teach and (2) restates the educational goal presented in the prompt.

- ☑ Each paragraph in the body of my essay begins with a topic sentence that clearly addresses one aspect of the prompt.

- ☑ My essay includes a short conclusion in which (1) I state that the educational goal is important and (2) I state that my two strategies are effective.

Check the content:

- *Does your writing reflect your understanding of the role of the teacher in relation to learner characteristics, instructional design and delivery, and the professional environment?* Yes, the response is learner centered and sensitive to students' varied characteristics and interests.

- *Based on your experience and your understanding of the ATS-W test objectives, have you included the best strategies, resources, and general teaching practices that could fit into this essay?* Yes, the essay describes instructional strategies—a Letters Project and Reading/Writing Workshop—that promote interdisciplinary instruction, critical thinking, and active engagement in learning. It is a test-maker-friendly response that is strongly consistent with a constructivist philosophy (the ATS-W Mindset).

Finally, read through your response one more time:

- ☑ Complete sentences: Does every sentence express a complete thought?

- ☑ Agreement: Make sure singular subjects have singular verbs. Make sure pronouns agree with the nouns they replace.

- ☑ Check that apostrophes replace the correct letters in contractions.

- ☑ Check that each sentence ends with a correct end mark.

- ☑ Watch out for misused homonyms.

- ☑ Look for common misspellings and errors.

THE MULTI-SUBJECT CST

CHAPTER 15: WHAT YOU NEED TO KNOW: THE MULTI-SUBJECT CST OBJECTIVES

The purpose of the Multi-Subject CST is to assess knowledge and skills of prospective teachers in New York State in eight subareas. The Multi-Subject CST is comprised of 90 multiple-choice questions and one constructed-response (written) assignment. The approximate percentage of the test that corresponds to each subarea is listed in the following chart:

SUBAREA	PERCENTAGE
I: English Language Arts	21%
II: Mathematics	18%
III: Science and Technology	13%
IV: Social Studies	15%
V: The Fine Arts	8%
VI: Health and Fitness	8%
VII: Family and Consumer Science and Career Development	7%
VIII: Foundations of Reading: Constructed-Response Assignment	10%

THE MULTI-SUBJECT CST OBJECTIVES

The Multi-Subject CST test objectives are listed in this chapter. Each objective is followed by focus statements that provide examples of the range, type, and level of content that may appear on the test.

Be sure to access our exclusive online review guide for each of the following objectives, found at **kaptest.com/Education/NYSTCE/Practice-for-the-NYSTCE**.

SUBAREA I: ENGLISH LANGUAGE ARTS

Objective 0001: Understand the foundations of reading development.

- Demonstrating knowledge of the developmental progression from prereading to conventional literacy, with individual variations, and analyzing how literacy develops in multiple contexts through reading, writing, and oral language experiences

- Defining phonological awareness and phonemic awareness and analyzing their role in reading development

- Demonstrating knowledge of concepts about print (e.g., book-handling skills, awareness that print carries meaning, recognition of directionality, ability to track print, ability to recognize and name letters)

- Demonstrating knowledge of the alphabetic principle and analyzing how emergent readers use this principle to master letter-sound correspondence and to decode simple words

- Demonstrating knowledge of a variety of word identification strategies, including use of phonics, use of semantic and syntactic cues, context clues, syllabication, analysis of word structure (e.g., roots, prefixes, suffixes), and sight-word recognition

- Analyzing factors that affect a reader's ability to construct meaning from texts (e.g., word recognition, reading fluency, vocabulary development, context clues, visual cues, prior knowledge and experience)

Objective 0002: Understand skills and strategies involved in reading comprehension.

- Demonstrating knowledge of literal comprehension skills (e.g., the ability to identify the sequence of events in a text, the ability to identify explicitly stated main ideas, details, and cause-and-effect patterns in a text)

- Demonstrating knowledge of inferential comprehension skills (e.g., the ability to draw conclusions or generalizations from a text; the ability to infer ideas, details, and cause-and-effect relationships that are not explicitly stated in a text)

- Demonstrating knowledge of evaluative comprehension skills (e.g., the ability to distinguish between facts and opinions in a text, the ability to detect faulty reasoning in a text, the ability to detect bias and propaganda in a text)

- Applying knowledge of strategies to use before, during, and after reading to enhance comprehension (e.g., developing and activating prior knowledge, connecting texts to personal experience, previewing a text, making predictions about a text, using K-W-L charts and other graphic organizers, taking notes on a text, discussing a text)

- Demonstrating knowledge of methods for helping readers monitor their own comprehension as they read (e.g., think-alouds, self-questioning strategies)

- Demonstrating knowledge of various methods for assessing comprehension of a text (e.g., questioning the reader, having the reader give an oral or written retelling, asking the reader to identify the theme(s) or to paraphrase or summarize the main idea)

Objective 0003: Understand and apply reading skills and strategies for various purposes (including information and understanding, critical analysis and evaluation, literary response, and social interaction).

- Recognizing how to vary reading strategies for different texts and purposes (e.g., skimming, scanning, in-depth reading, rereading) and for different types and genres of written communication (e.g., fiction, nonfiction, poetry)

- Applying knowledge of techniques for gathering, interpreting, and synthesizing information when reading a variety of printed texts and electronic sources

- Recognizing how to analyze and assess a writer's credibility or objectivity when reading printed and electronic texts

- Analyzing and interpreting information from texts containing tables, charts, graphs, maps, and other illustrations

- Demonstrating knowledge of strategies to promote literary response skills (e.g., connecting the text to personal experience and prior knowledge, citing evidence from a text to support an interpretation, using reading logs or guided reading techniques)

- Identifying effective ways of modeling independent reading for enjoyment and encouraging participation in a community of readers (e.g., book clubs, literature circles)

Objective 0004: Understand processes for generating, developing, revising, editing, and presenting/publishing written texts.

- Applying knowledge of prewriting strategies (e.g., brainstorming, prioritizing and selecting topics including clustering and other graphic organizers)

- Identifying effective techniques of note taking, outlining, and drafting

- Revising written texts to improve unity and logical organization (e.g., formulating topic sentences, reordering paragraphs or sentences, adding transition words and phrases, eliminating distracting sentences)

- Editing written work to ensure conformity to conventions of standard English usage (e.g., eliminating misplaced or dangling modifiers, eliminating sentence fragments, correcting errors in subject-verb agreement and pronoun-antecedent agreement)

- Editing and proofreading written work to correct misspellings and eliminate errors in punctuation and capitalization

- Applying knowledge of the uses of technology to plan, create, revise, edit, and present/publish written texts and multimedia works

Objective 0005: Understand and apply writing skills and strategies for various purposes (including information and understanding, critical analysis and evaluation, literary response and personal expression, and social interaction).

- Analyzing factors a writer should consider when writing for a variety of audiences and purposes (e.g., informative, persuasive, expressive), including factors related to selection of topic and mode of written expression

- Recognizing how to incorporate graphic representations (e.g., diagrams, graphs, time lines) into writing for various purposes

- Applying knowledge of skills involved in writing a research paper (e.g., generating ideas and questions, posing problems, evaluating and summarizing data from a variety of print and nonprint sources)

- Identifying techniques for expressing point of view, using logical organization, and avoiding bias in writing for critical analysis, evaluation, or persuasion

- Demonstrating knowledge of strategies for writing a response to a literary selection by referring to the text, to other works, and to personal experience

- Demonstrating awareness of voice in writing for personal expression and social interaction

Objective 0006: Understand skills and strategies involved in listening and speaking for various purposes (including information and understanding, critical analysis and evaluation, literary response and expression, and social interaction).

- Recognizing appropriate listening strategies for given contexts and purposes (e.g., interpreting and analyzing information that is presented orally, appreciating literary texts that are read aloud, understanding small-group and large-group discussions)

- Analyzing factors that affect the ability to listen effectively and to construct meaning from oral messages in various listening situations (e.g., using prior knowledge, recognizing transitions, interpreting nonverbal cues, using notetaking and outlining) and applying measures of effective listening (e.g., the ability to repeat instructions, the ability to retell stories)

- Analyzing how features of spoken language (e.g., word choice, rate, pitch, tone, volume) and nonverbal cues (e.g., body language, visual aids, facial expressions) affect a speaker's ability to communicate effectively in given situations

- Recognizing how to vary speaking strategies for different audiences, purposes, and occasions (e.g., providing instructions, participating in group discussions, persuading or entertaining an audience, giving an oral presentation or interpretation of a literary work)

- Recognizing the effective use of oral communication skills and nonverbal communication skills in situations involving people of different ages, genders, cultures, and other personal characteristics

- Applying knowledge of oral language conventions appropriate to a variety of social situations (e.g., informal conversations, job interviews)

Objective 0007: Understand and apply techniques of literary analysis to works of fiction, drama, poetry, and nonfiction.

- Analyzing similarities and differences between fiction and nonfiction

- Demonstrating knowledge of story elements in works of fiction (e.g., plot, character, setting, theme, mood)

- Applying knowledge of drama to analyze dramatic structure (e.g., introduction, rising action, climax, falling action, conclusion) and identify common dramatic devices (e.g., soliloquy, aside)

- Applying knowledge of various types of nonfiction (e.g., informational texts, newspaper articles, essays, biographies, memoirs, letters, journals)

- Analyzing the use of language to convey style, tone, and point of view in works of fiction and nonfiction

- Recognizing the formal elements of a poetic text (e.g., meter, rhyme scheme, stanza structure, alliteration, assonance, onomatopoeia, figurative language) and analyzing their relationship to the meaning of the text

Objective 0008: Demonstrate knowledge of literature, including literature from diverse cultures and literature for children/adolescents.

- Demonstrating awareness of ways in which literary texts reflect the time and place in which they were written

- Demonstrating awareness of the ways in which literary works reflect and express cultural values and ideas

- Recognizing major themes and characteristics of works written by well-known authors

- Demonstrating knowledge of important works and authors of literature for children and adolescents

- Analyzing themes and elements of traditional and contemporary literature for children and adolescents

SUBAREA II: MATHEMATICS

Objective 0009: Understand formal and informal reasoning processes, including logic and simple proofs, and apply problem-solving techniques and strategies in a variety of contexts.

- Using models, facts, patterns, and relationships to draw conclusions about mathematical problems or situations

- Judging the validity or logic of mathematical arguments

- Drawing a valid conclusion based on stated conditions and evaluating conclusions involving simple and compound sentences

- Applying inductive reasoning to make mathematical conjectures

- Using a variety of problem-solving strategies to model and solve problems and evaluating the appropriateness of a problem-solving strategy (e.g., estimation, mental math, working backward, pattern recognition) in a given situation

- Analyzing the usefulness of a specific model or mental math procedure for exploring a given mathematical, scientific, or technological idea or problem

Objective 0010: Use mathematical terminology and symbols to interpret, represent, and communicate mathematical ideas and information.

- Using mathematical notation to represent a given relationship

- Using appropriate models, diagrams, and symbols to represent mathematical concepts

- Using appropriate vocabulary to express given mathematical ideas and relationships

- Relating the language of ordinary experiences to mathematical language and symbols

- Translating among graphic, numeric, symbolic, and verbal representations of mathematical relationships and concepts

- Using mathematical representations to model and interpret physical, social, and mathematical phenomena

Objective 0011: Understand skills and concepts related to number and numeration and apply these concepts to real-world situations.

- Selecting the appropriate computational and operational method to solve a given mathematical problem

- Demonstrating an understanding of the commutative, distributive, and associative properties

- Using ratios, proportions, and percents to model and solve problems

- Comparing and ordering fractions, decimals, and percents

- Solving problems using equivalent forms of numbers (e.g., integer, fraction, decimal, percent, exponential and scientific notation) and problems involving number theory (e.g., primes, factors, multiples)

- Analyzing the number properties used in operational algorithms (e.g., multiplication, long division)

- Applying number properties to manipulate and simplify algebraic expressions

Objective 0012: Understand patterns and apply the principles and properties of linear algebraic relations and functions.

- Recognizing and describing mathematical relationships

- Using a variety of representations (e.g., manipulatives, figures, numbers, calculators) to recognize and extend patterns

- Analyzing mathematical relationships and patterns using tables, verbal rules, equations, and graphs

- Deriving an algebraic expression or function to represent a relationship or pattern from the physical or social world

- Using algebraic functions to describe given graphs, to plot points, and to determine slopes

- Performing algebraic operations to solve equations and inequalities

- Analyzing how changing one variable changes the other variable for linear and nonlinear functions

Objective 0013: Understand the principles and properties of geometry and trigonometry and apply them to model and solve problems.

- Identifying relationships among two- and three-dimensional geometric shapes

- Applying knowledge of basic geometric figures to solve real-world problems involving more complex patterns (e.g., area and perimeter of composite figures)

- Applying the concepts of similarity and congruence to model and solve problems

- Applying inductive and deductive reasoning to solve problems in geometry

- Using coordinate geometry to represent and analyze properties of geometric figures

- Applying transformations (e.g., reflections, rotations, dilations) and symmetry to analyze properties of geometric figures

Objective 0014: Understand concepts, principles, skills, and procedures related to the customary and metric systems of measurement.

- Demonstrating knowledge of fundamental units of customary and metric measurement

- Selecting an appropriate unit to express measures of length, area, capacity, weight, volume, time, temperature, and angle

- Estimating and converting measurements using standard and nonstandard measurement units within customary and metric systems

- Developing and using formulas to determine the perimeter and area of two-dimensional shapes and the surface area and volume of three-dimensional shapes

- Solving measurement problems involving derived measurements (e.g., velocity, density)

- Applying the Pythagorean theorem and right triangle trigonometry to solve measurement problems

Objective 0015: Understand concepts and skills related to data analysis, probability, and statistics and apply this understanding to evaluate and interpret data and to solve problems.

- Demonstrating the ability to collect, organize, and analyze data using appropriate graphic and nongraphic representations

- Displaying and interpreting data in a variety of different formats (e.g., frequency histograms, tables, pie charts, box-and-whisker plots, stem-and-leaf plots, scatterplots)

- Computing probabilities using a variety of methods (e.g., ratio and proportion, tree diagrams, tables of data, area models)

- Using simulations (e.g., spinners, multisided dice, random number generators) to estimate probabilities

- Applying measures of central tendency (mean, median, mode) and spread (e.g., range, percentiles, variance) to analyze data in graphic or nongraphic form

- Formulating and designing statistical experiments to collect, analyze, and interpret data

- Identifying patterns and trends in data and making predictions based on those trends

SUBAREA III: SCIENCE AND TECHNOLOGY

Objective 0016: Understand and apply the principles and processes of scientific inquiry and investigation.

- Formulating hypotheses based on reasoning and preliminary results or information

- Evaluating the soundness and feasibility of a proposed scientific investigation

- Applying mathematical rules or formulas (including basic statistics) to analyze given experimental or observational data

- Interpreting data presented in one or more graphs, charts, patterns, or relationships

- Evaluating the validity of a scientific conclusion in a given situation

- Applying procedures for the safe and appropriate use of equipment and the care and humane treatment of animals in the laboratory

Objective 0017: Understand and apply concepts, principles, and theories pertaining to the physical setting (including earth science, chemistry, and physics).

- Analyzing interactions among the earth, the moon, and the sun (e.g., seasonal changes, the phases of the moon)

- Analyzing the effects of interactions among components of air, water, and land (e.g., weather, volcanism, erosion)

- Distinguishing between physical and chemical properties of matter and between physical and chemical changes in matter

- Distinguishing among forms of energy and identifying the transformations of energy observed in everyday life

- Analyzing the effects of forces on objects in given situations

- Inferring the physical science principle (e.g., effects of common forces, conservation of energy) illustrated in a given situation

Objective 0018: Understand and apply concepts, principles, and theories pertaining to the living environment.

- Recognizing the characteristics of living things and common life processes

- Analyzing processes that contribute to the continuity of life (e.g., reproduction and development, inheritance of genetic information)

- Analyzing the factors that contribute to change in organisms and species over time

- Comparing the ways a variety of organisms carry out basic life functions and maintain dynamic equilibrium (e.g., obtaining nutrients, maintaining water balance)

- Analyzing the effects of environmental conditions (e.g., temperature, availability of water and sunlight) on living organisms and the relationships between plants and animals within a community

- Inferring the life science principle (e.g., adaptation, homeostasis) illustrated in a given situation

Objective 0019: Apply knowledge of technology and the principles of engineering design.

- Demonstrating an understanding of technological systems (e.g., transportation system) and the principles on which technological systems are constructed (e.g., the use of component subsystems)

- Analyzing the roles of modeling and optimization in the engineering design process

- Evaluating a proposed technological solution to a given problem or need

- Applying criteria for selecting tools, materials, and other resources to design and construct a technological product or service

- Recognizing appropriate tests of a given technological solution

- Analyzing the positive and negative effects of technology on individuals, society, and the environment

Objective 0020: Understand the relationships among and common themes that connect mathematics, science, and technology and the application of knowledge and skills in these disciplines to other areas of learning.

- Making connections among the common themes of mathematics, science, and technology (e.g., systems, models, magnitude and scale, equilibrium and stability, patterns of change)

- Applying principles of mathematics, science, and technology to model a given situation (e.g., the movement of energy and nutrients between a food chain and the physical environment)

- Applying principles of mathematics, science, and technology to explore phenomena from other areas of learning (e.g., applying statistical methodologies to examine census data)

- Designing solutions to problems in the physical and social worlds using mathematical, scientific, and technological reasoning and procedures

- Analyzing the effects of human activities (e.g., burning fossil fuels, clear-cutting forests) on the environment and evaluating the use of science and technology in solving problems related to these effects

SUBAREA IV: SOCIAL STUDIES

Objective 0021: Understand major ideas, eras, themes, developments, and turning points in the history of New York State, the United States, and the world.

- Defining important conceptual terms (e.g., racism, nation-state, nationalism, feudalism) and using them to analyze general historical phenomena and specific historical events

- Analyzing the social effects of major developments in human history (e.g., the agricultural revolution, the scientific revolution, the industrial revolution, the information revolution)

- Understanding major political, social, economic, and geographic characteristics of ancient civilizations and the connections and interactions among these civilizations

- Examining reasons for organizing periods of history in different ways and comparing alternative interpretations of key events and issues in New York State, U.S., and world history

- Analyzing the effects of European contact with indigenous cultures and the effects of European settlement on New York State and the Northeast

- Analyzing how the roles and contributions of individuals and groups helped shape U.S. social, political, economic, cultural, and religious life

Objective 0022: Understand geographic concepts and phenomena and analyze the interrelationships of geography, society, and culture in the development of New York State, the United States, and the world.

- Defining important geographic terms and concepts (e.g., habitat, resource, cultural diffusion, ecology) and using them to analyze various geographic issues, problems, and phenomena

- Demonstrating an understanding of the six essential elements of geography: the world in spatial terms, places and regions, physical settings, human systems, environment and society, and the use of geography

- Recognizing physical characteristics of the earth's surface and the continual reshaping of it by physical processes (e.g., how weather, climate, and the water cycle influence different regions)

- Analyzing the development and interaction of social, political, cultural, and religious systems in different regions of New York State, the United States, and the world

- Examining ways in which economic, environmental, and cultural factors influence demographic change and interpreting geographic relationships, such as population density and spatial distribution patterns

- Analyzing the impact of human activity on the physical environment (e.g., industrial development, population growth, deforestation)

Objective 0023: Understand concepts and phenomena related to human development and interactions (including anthropological, psychological, and sociological concepts).

- Using concepts, theories, and modes of inquiry drawn from anthropology, psychology, and sociology to examine general social phenomena and issues related to intercultural understanding

- Evaluating factors that contribute to personal identity (e.g., family, group affiliations, socialization processes)

- Recognizing how language, literature, the arts, media, architecture, traditions, beliefs, values, and behaviors influence and/or reflect the development and transmission of culture

- Analyzing the roles and functions of social groups and institutions in the United States (e.g., ethnic groups, schools, religions) and their influence on individual and group interactions

- Analyzing why individuals and groups hold different or competing points of view on issues, events, or historical developments

- Understanding the processes of social and cultural change

Objective 0024: Understand economic and political principles, concepts, and systems and relate this knowledge to historical and contemporary developments in New York State, the United States, and the world.

- Defining important economic and political terms and concepts (e.g., scarcity, opportunity cost, supply and demand, productivity, power, natural rights, checks and balances) and using them to analyze general phenomena and specific issues

- Analyzing the basic structure, fundamental ideas, accomplishments, and problems of the U.S. economic system

- Recognizing and comparing basic characteristics of major models of economic organization (e.g., traditional, market, command) and various governmental systems (e.g., democratic, authoritarian)

- Analyzing values, principles, concepts, and key features of American constitutional democracy (e.g., individual freedom, separation of powers, due process, federalism)

- Comparing different perspectives regarding economic and political issues and policies in New York State and the United States (e.g., taxing and spending decisions)

- Analyzing ways in which the United States has influenced other nations (e.g., in the development of democratic principles and human rights) and how other nations have influenced U.S. politics and culture

Objective 0025: Understand the roles, rights, and responsibilities of citizenship in the United States and the skills, knowledge, and attitudes necessary for successful participation in civic life.

- Analyzing the personal and political rights guaranteed in the Declaration of Independence, the U.S. Constitution, the Constitution of the State of New York, and major civil rights legislation

- Recognizing the core values of the U.S. democratic system (e.g., justice, honesty, the rule of law, self-discipline, due process, equality, majority rule, respect for minority rights)

- Demonstrating an understanding of the U.S. election process and the roles of political parties, pressure groups, and special interests in the U.S. political system

- Explaining what citizenship means in a democratic society and analyzing the ways in which citizens participate in and influence the political process in the United States (e.g., the role of public opinion and citizen action groups in shaping public policy)

- Examining the rights, responsibilities, and privileges of individuals in relation to family, social group, career, community, and nation

- Analyzing factors that have expanded or limited the role of the individual in U.S. political life during the twentieth century (e.g., female suffrage, Jim Crow laws, growth of presidential primaries, role of the media in political elections)

Objective 0026: Understand and apply skills related to social studies, including gathering, organizing, mapping, evaluating, interpreting, and displaying information.

- Evaluating the appropriateness of various resources and research methods for meeting specified information needs (e.g., atlas, bibliography, almanac, database, survey, poll) and applying procedures for retrieving information using traditional resources and current technologies (e.g., CD-ROM, the Internet)

- Demonstrating an understanding of concepts, tools, and technologies for mapping information about the spatial distribution of people, places, and environments (e.g., mapping grids, latitude and longitude, the advantages and limitations of different types of maps and map projections)

- Analyzing information in social studies materials (e.g., identifying central themes in important historical speeches or documents, distinguishing fact from opinion, evaluating multiple points of view in policy debates)

- Interpreting information presented in one or more graphic representations (e.g., graph, table, map) and translating written or graphic information from one form to the other

- Summarizing the purpose or point of view of a historical narrative

SUBAREA V: THE FINE ARTS

Objective 0027: Understand the concepts, techniques, and materials of the visual arts; analyze works of visual art; and understand the cultural dimensions and contributions of the visual arts.

- Identifying basic elements (e.g., line, color) and principles (e.g., unity, balance) of art and recognizing how they are used to communicate meaning in works of art

- Analyzing two-dimensional and three-dimensional works of art in terms of their visual and sensory characteristics

- Applying knowledge of the characteristics of various art media (e.g., two-dimensional, three-dimensional, electronic) to select a medium appropriate for a given artistic purpose or intent

- Applying knowledge of basic tools and techniques for working with various materials (e.g., clay, textiles, wood)

- Analyzing how works of art reflect the cultures in which they were produced (e.g., materials or techniques used, subject matter, style)

- Comparing works of art of different cultures, eras, and artists in terms of characteristics such as theme, imagery, and style

Objective 0028: Understand concepts, techniques, and materials for producing, listening to, and responding to music; analyze works of music; and understand the cultural dimensions and contributions of music.

- Comparing various types of instruments (e.g., strings, percussion, woodwind, brass, electronic) in terms of the sounds they produce

- Defining and applying common musical terms (e.g., pitch, tempo)

- Using basic scientific concepts to explain how music-related sound is produced, transmitted through air, and received by listeners

- Relating characteristics of music (e.g., rhythm, beat) to musical effects produced

- Recognizing basic technical skills that musicians must develop to produce an aesthetically acceptable performance (e.g., manual dexterity, breathing techniques, knowledge of musical notation)

- Analyzing how different cultures have created music reflective of their histories and societies (e.g., call-and-response songs, ballads, work songs, folk songs)

Objective 0029: Understand concepts, techniques, and materials related to theater and dance; analyze works of drama and dance; and understand the cultural dimensions and contributions of drama and dance.

- Comparing dramatic and theatrical forms and their characteristics (e.g., pantomime, improvisation)

- Relating types of dance (e.g., ballet, folk, modern) to their characteristic forms of movement, expressive qualities, and cultural origins

- Analyzing how technical aspects of performance (e.g., costumes, props, lighting) affect the message or overall impression created by a performance

- Recognizing how language, voice, gesture, and movement are used to develop character and create interaction among performers in theatrical productions

- Analyzing ways in which different cultures have used drama and dance (e.g., to teach moral lessons, to preserve cultural traditions, to affirm the sense of community, to entertain)

SUBAREA VI: HEALTH AND FITNESS

Objective 0030: Understand basic principles and practices of personal, interpersonal, and community health and safety and apply related knowledge and skills (e.g., decision making, problem solving) to promote personal well-being.

- Identifying common health problems and explaining how they can be prevented, detected, and treated

- Recognizing the basic knowledge and skills necessary to support positive health choices and behaviors

- Applying decision-making and problem-solving skills and procedures in individual and group situations (e.g., situations related to personal well-being, self-esteem, and interpersonal relationships)

- Recognizing basic principles of good nutrition and using them to plan a diet that accommodates nutritional needs, activity level, and optimal weight

- Analyzing contemporary health-related issues (e.g., HIV, teenage pregnancy, suicide, substance abuse) in terms of their causes, effects, and significance for individuals, families, and society and evaluating strategies for their prevention

- Interpreting advertising claims for health care products and services and distinguishing between valid and invalid health information

- Analyzing environmental conditions and their impact upon personal and community health and safety

Objective 0031: Understand physical education concepts and practices related to the development of personal living skills.

- Recognizing sequences and characteristics of physical development throughout the various developmental levels

- Demonstrating knowledge of activities that promote the development of motor skills (e.g., locomotor, manipulative, body mechanics) and perceptual awareness skills (e.g., body awareness, spatial and directional awareness)

- Applying safety concepts and practices associated with physical activities (e.g., doing warm-up exercises, wearing protective equipment)

- Understanding skills necessary for successful participation in given sports and activities (e.g., spatial orientation, eye-hand coordination, movement)

- Analyzing ways in which participation in individual or group sports or physical activities can promote personal living skills (e.g., self-discipline, respect for self and others, resource management) and interpersonal skills (e.g., cooperation, sportsmanship, leadership, teamwork, communication)

Objective 0032: Understand health-related physical fitness concepts and practices.

- Recognizing components, functions, and common disorders of the major body systems

- Demonstrating knowledge of basic components of physical fitness (e.g., strength, endurance, flexibility) and applying principles of training

- Applying strategies for developing a personal fitness plan based on self-assessment, goal setting, and an understanding of physiological changes that result from training

- Analyzing the relationship between lifelong physical activity and the prevention of illness, disease, and premature death

- Applying knowledge of principles and activities for developing and maintaining cardio-respiratory endurance, muscular strength, flexibility, and levels of body composition that promote good health

SUBAREA VII: FAMILY AND CONSUMER SCIENCE AND CAREER DEVELOPMENT

Objective 0033: Understand concepts and practices related to child development and care and apply knowledge of family and interpersonal relationships.

- Recognizing stages and characteristics of physical, cognitive, social, and emotional development during infancy, childhood, and adolescence

- Demonstrating knowledge of children's physical, dietary, and hygienic needs (e.g., nutritional guidelines, dental care, proper washing procedures) and applying developmentally appropriate methods for promoting self-care during childhood

- Identifying causes of common childhood accidents and health care emergencies and applying physical care and safety guidelines for caregivers of infants, toddlers, and preschool and school-age children

- Analyzing factors that affect decisions about whether and when to have children and recognizing ways to prepare for the responsibilities of parenthood

- Demonstrating knowledge of family structure (e.g., extended, blended, single-parent, dual-career), roles and responsibilities of family members, and the functions of families in society

- Recognizing the types and characteristics of interpersonal relationships and analyzing decision-making processes related to interpersonal relationships

- Examining social and cultural influences on interpersonal communication and analyzing factors affecting the formation of positive relationships in the family, workplace, and community

Objective 0034: Understand skills and procedures related to consumer economics and personal resource management.

- Recognizing rights and responsibilities of consumers in various purchasing situations (e.g., rights in relation to product and service warranties and guarantees)

- Demonstrating knowledge of types and characteristics of consumer fraud and applying procedures for seeking redress and registering consumer complaints

- Applying knowledge of procedures for making major purchases (e.g., comparison shopping, negotiation, interpreting labels or contract terminology)

- Analyzing considerations involved in selecting and maintaining housing and motor vehicles, obtaining credit and insurance, and making investments

- Examining steps and considerations involved in planning and maintaining a personal or family budget and applying money management guidelines appropriate for various situations

- Demonstrating knowledge of personal and family resources (e.g., time, skills, energy) and applying decision-making and goal-setting procedures for managing personal and family resources in various situations

Objective 0035: Understand basic principles of career development; apply processes and skills for seeking and maintaining employment; and demonstrate knowledge of workplace skills, behaviors, and responsibilities.

- Demonstrating knowledge of the relationship of personal interests, skills, and abilities to successful employment and recognizing the relationship between the changing nature of work and educational requirements

- Recognizing factors to consider when evaluating careers and applying procedures for conducting career research

- Demonstrating knowledge of steps involved in searching for a job and recognizing factors affecting the success of a job search (e.g., writing an effective letter of application, résumé preparation)

- Applying skills and procedures for job interviews (e.g., personal appearance and demeanor, communicating effectively during an interview)

- Applying knowledge of effective communication principles, work etiquette, interpersonal skills, and techniques for handling stress or conflict in the workplace

- Recognizing rights and responsibilities in relation to employment (e.g., protection from harassment and discrimination, employer's performance expectations)

SUBAREA VIII: FOUNDATIONS OF READING: CONSTRUCTED-RESPONSE ASSIGNMENT

The content to be addressed by the constructed-response assignment is described in Subarea I, Objectives 0001 and 0002, found on pages 428–429.

PREPARING FOR THE MULTI-SUBJECT CST

As you can see, the Multi-Subject CST objectives cover a broad range of topics that test the knowledge and skills necessary for teaching grades preK–9 in New York State. The New York State Education Department created this test to ensure that its multi-subject teachers posses the ability to:

- communicate effectively (understand and apply language skills used in acquiring and transmitting information, responding to literature, expressing feelings and attitudes, evaluating ideas, and maintaining social relationships).

- apply mathematical concepts and procedures to solve a variety of problems.

- draw on knowledge of principles and relationships in the life and physical sciences for scientific inquiry.

- understand the interconnectedness of science, mathematics, and technology.

- employ the perspectives of the social sciences to analyze historical events and the contemporary world.

- interpret works of art using knowledge of a variety of forms, techniques, and cultural contexts.

- understand the principles and practices essential to personal health, fitness, and safety.

- apply skills and concepts related to child development, family and interpersonal relationships, personal resources management, and career development.

- apply factual information and intellectual skills in an interdisciplinary approach to analyze the natural phenomena, historical developments, social dynamics, and individual expressions of the human experience that have shaped out society and the world around us.

The best way to prepare for the Multi-Subject CST exam is by carefully reviewing the objectives and taking time to do extra research on those topics that are problematic for you. Once you feel comfortable with your skills and knowledge relating to the objectives, and after taking the Multi-Subject CST practice test and reviewing the answers and explanations, you will be one step closer to attaining your goal of passing the NYSTCE exam.

CHAPTER 16: **PRACTICE MULTI-SUBJECT CST**

Before taking this practice test, find a quiet room where you can work uninterrupted for 4 hours. Make sure you have a comfortable desk and several No. 2 pencils.

Use the answer sheet provided to record your answers.

Once you start this practice test, don't stop until you've finished. Remember, you can complete the sections of the test in any order you wish.

You will find an answer key and explanations following the test.

Good luck!

SAMPLE DIRECTIONS

This test booklet contains a multiple-choice section and a single written assignment section. You may complete the sections of the test in the order you choose.

Each question in the first section of this booklet is a multiple-choice question with four answer choices. Read each question CAREFULLY and choose the ONE best answer. Record your answer on the answer document in the space that corresponds to the question number. Completely fill in the space having the same letter as the answer you have chosen. *Use only a No. 2 lead pencil.*

Sample Question

1. What is the capital of New York?

    A.   Buffalo

    B.   New York City

    C.   Albany

    D.   Rochester

The correct answer to this question is (C). You would indicate that on the answer document as follows:

1.   D

You should answer all questions. Even if you are unsure of an answer, it is better to guess than not to answer a question at all. You may use the margins of the test booklet for scratch paper, but you will be scored only on the responses on your answer document.

The directions for the written assignment appear later in this test booklet.

FOR TEST SECURITY REASONS, YOU MAY NOT TAKE NOTES OR REMOVE ANY OF THE TEST MATERIALS FROM THE ROOM.

The words "End of Test" indicate that you have completed the test. You may go back and review your answers, but be sure you have answered all questions before raising your hand for dismissal. Your test materials must be returned to a test administrator when you finish the test.

If you have any questions, please ask them now before beginning the test.

DO NOT GO ON UNTIL YOU ARE TOLD TO DO SO.

KAPLAN

MULTI-SUBJECT CST ANSWER SHEET

1. Ⓐ Ⓑ Ⓒ Ⓓ	31. Ⓐ Ⓑ Ⓒ Ⓓ	61. Ⓐ Ⓑ Ⓒ Ⓓ
2. Ⓐ Ⓑ Ⓒ Ⓓ	32. Ⓐ Ⓑ Ⓒ Ⓓ	62. Ⓐ Ⓑ Ⓒ Ⓓ
3. Ⓐ Ⓑ Ⓒ Ⓓ	33. Ⓐ Ⓑ Ⓒ Ⓓ	63. Ⓐ Ⓑ Ⓒ Ⓓ
4. Ⓐ Ⓑ Ⓒ Ⓓ	34. Ⓐ Ⓑ Ⓒ Ⓓ	64. Ⓐ Ⓑ Ⓒ Ⓓ
5. Ⓐ Ⓑ Ⓒ Ⓓ	35. Ⓐ Ⓑ Ⓒ Ⓓ	65. Ⓐ Ⓑ Ⓒ Ⓓ
6. Ⓐ Ⓑ Ⓒ Ⓓ	36. Ⓐ Ⓑ Ⓒ Ⓓ	66. Ⓐ Ⓑ Ⓒ Ⓓ
7. Ⓐ Ⓑ Ⓒ Ⓓ	37. Ⓐ Ⓑ Ⓒ Ⓓ	67. Ⓐ Ⓑ Ⓒ Ⓓ
8. Ⓐ Ⓑ Ⓒ Ⓓ	38. Ⓐ Ⓑ Ⓒ Ⓓ	68. Ⓐ Ⓑ Ⓒ Ⓓ
9. Ⓐ Ⓑ Ⓒ Ⓓ	39. Ⓐ Ⓑ Ⓒ Ⓓ	69. Ⓐ Ⓑ Ⓒ Ⓓ
10. Ⓐ Ⓑ Ⓒ Ⓓ	40. Ⓐ Ⓑ Ⓒ Ⓓ	70. Ⓐ Ⓑ Ⓒ Ⓓ
11. Ⓐ Ⓑ Ⓒ Ⓓ	41. Ⓐ Ⓑ Ⓒ Ⓓ	71. Ⓐ Ⓑ Ⓒ Ⓓ
12. Ⓐ Ⓑ Ⓒ Ⓓ	42. Ⓐ Ⓑ Ⓒ Ⓓ	72. Ⓐ Ⓑ Ⓒ Ⓓ
13. Ⓐ Ⓑ Ⓒ Ⓓ	43. Ⓐ Ⓑ Ⓒ Ⓓ	73. Ⓐ Ⓑ Ⓒ Ⓓ
14. Ⓐ Ⓑ Ⓒ Ⓓ	44. Ⓐ Ⓑ Ⓒ Ⓓ	74. Ⓐ Ⓑ Ⓒ Ⓓ
15. Ⓐ Ⓑ Ⓒ Ⓓ	45. Ⓐ Ⓑ Ⓒ Ⓓ	75. Ⓐ Ⓑ Ⓒ Ⓓ
16. Ⓐ Ⓑ Ⓒ Ⓓ	46. Ⓐ Ⓑ Ⓒ Ⓓ	76. Ⓐ Ⓑ Ⓒ Ⓓ
17. Ⓐ Ⓑ Ⓒ Ⓓ	47. Ⓐ Ⓑ Ⓒ Ⓓ	77. Ⓐ Ⓑ Ⓒ Ⓓ
18. Ⓐ Ⓑ Ⓒ Ⓓ	48. Ⓐ Ⓑ Ⓒ Ⓓ	78. Ⓐ Ⓑ Ⓒ Ⓓ
19. Ⓐ Ⓑ Ⓒ Ⓓ	49. Ⓐ Ⓑ Ⓒ Ⓓ	79. Ⓐ Ⓑ Ⓒ Ⓓ
20. Ⓐ Ⓑ Ⓒ Ⓓ	50. Ⓐ Ⓑ Ⓒ Ⓓ	80. Ⓐ Ⓑ Ⓒ Ⓓ
21. Ⓐ Ⓑ Ⓒ Ⓓ	51. Ⓐ Ⓑ Ⓒ Ⓓ	81. Ⓐ Ⓑ Ⓒ Ⓓ
22. Ⓐ Ⓑ Ⓒ Ⓓ	52. Ⓐ Ⓑ Ⓒ Ⓓ	82. Ⓐ Ⓑ Ⓒ Ⓓ
23. Ⓐ Ⓑ Ⓒ Ⓓ	53. Ⓐ Ⓑ Ⓒ Ⓓ	83. Ⓐ Ⓑ Ⓒ Ⓓ
24. Ⓐ Ⓑ Ⓒ Ⓓ	54. Ⓐ Ⓑ Ⓒ Ⓓ	84. Ⓐ Ⓑ Ⓒ Ⓓ
25. Ⓐ Ⓑ Ⓒ Ⓓ	55. Ⓐ Ⓑ Ⓒ Ⓓ	85. Ⓐ Ⓑ Ⓒ Ⓓ
26. Ⓐ Ⓑ Ⓒ Ⓓ	56. Ⓐ Ⓑ Ⓒ Ⓓ	86. Ⓐ Ⓑ Ⓒ Ⓓ
27. Ⓐ Ⓑ Ⓒ Ⓓ	57. Ⓐ Ⓑ Ⓒ Ⓓ	87. Ⓐ Ⓑ Ⓒ Ⓓ
28. Ⓐ Ⓑ Ⓒ Ⓓ	58. Ⓐ Ⓑ Ⓒ Ⓓ	88. Ⓐ Ⓑ Ⓒ Ⓓ
29. Ⓐ Ⓑ Ⓒ Ⓓ	59. Ⓐ Ⓑ Ⓒ Ⓓ	89. Ⓐ Ⓑ Ⓒ Ⓓ
30. Ⓐ Ⓑ Ⓒ Ⓓ	60. Ⓐ Ⓑ Ⓒ Ⓓ	90. Ⓐ Ⓑ Ⓒ Ⓓ

1. Choosing a topic, considering the audience, and setting the purpose are items included in which stage of the writing process?

    A. revising

    B. editing

    C. prewriting

    D. drafting

2. Historians who are interested in studying the beginnings of democracy would most likely examine

    A. ancient China.

    B. classical Greece and Rome.

    C. Europe during the French Revolution.

    D. the United States at its founding.

3. If there are 2.54 centimeters in 1 inch, how many centimeters, to the nearest hundredth, are in a yard?

    A. 30.48

    B. 101.6

    C. 91.44

    D. 39.37

4. Potential factors that may affect school safety include

    A. the existing school safety plan.

    B. the social climate of the school.

    C. employee selection, training, and supervision.

    D. all of the above.

5. The purpose of *invented spelling* is

    A. to help children become better spellers in the future.

    B. to encourage students to use proper grammar and spelling when they write.

    C. to allow students to express themselves in writing before they have mastered the conventions of grammar and spelling.

    D. to require students to make attempts to spell words that the teacher then corrects.

6. Which of the following is not a member of the Mollusca phylum?

    A. abalone

    B. sea snail

    C. sea urchin

    D. oyster

7. In a science laboratory, you should be cautious of

    A. long, loose hair.

    B. dangling jewelry.

    C. loose clothing.

    D. all of the above.

8. As geographers use the concept, *cultural diffusion* can best be defined as

    A. changes in a population due to birth rate, death rate, and migration.

    B. a shared way of living among a group of people that develops over time.

    C. the spread of one or more aspects of one group's customs and language to another group.

    D. the changes that occur within a society's belief systems and language over time.

9. Which of the following instruments uses a reed?

    A. cello

    B. oboe

    C. French horn

    D. trombone

10. Which major body system protects the body's vital organs?

    A. respiratory

    B. circulatory

    C. digestive

    D. skeletal

11. What is the *primary purpose* of modeling reading for students?

    A. to ensure that students are paying attention

    B. to allow students to demonstrate their fluency

    C. to demonstrate how fluent readers read for meaning

    D. to encourage cooperative learning in the classroom

12. Use the graph below to answer the question that follows.

Time and Distance

The graph above shows the time and distance for a car that is traveling. Which of the following statements is true?

A. The car traveled at a constant speed from 9 A.M. to 8 P.M.

B. The car drove at a faster speed from 3 P.M. to 5 P.M.

C. The car was increasing its speed from 9 A.M. to 12 P.M., then traveled at a constant speed from 12 P.M. to 1 P.M.

D. At 8 P.M., the car was 300 miles from its starting point.

13. Which of the following phenomena was NOT introduced by northeastern indigenous tribes to European settlers?

A. cultivated crops like bean plants and squash

B. wild foods like maple sugar, blueberries, lobsters, and clams

C. spread of disease

D. light, strong canoes

14. Your supervisor tells you that a coworker has accused you of improper workplace conduct. You cannot recall saying or doing anything to have made her so upset. You should

    A. ignore the problem and hope it goes away.

    B. confront the coworker.

    C. follow the protocol for conflict resolution in your employee handbook.

    D. hire a lawyer to settle the case for you.

15. Which of the following changes is not a physical change of matter?

    A. evaporation

    B. decomposition of old leaves

    C. painting wood

    D. cutting a copper wire

16. A teacher has a student read a story, then has her answer comprehension questions about what she has just read. This is which stage of the reading process?

    A. pre-reading

    B. responding

    C. exploring

    D. applying

17. What distinguishes *farce* from *tragedy*?

    A. imitation, usually of a serious work

    B. actors inventing lines and scenarios off the tops of their heads

    C. lines arranged in a metrical pattern

    D. a happy ending

18. Which of the answer choices below shows the correct order for the following numbers, from least to greatest?

$$\frac{3}{4}, 40\%, 2^5, 20, \frac{5}{8}$$

   A. $2^5, 20, \frac{3}{4}, \frac{5}{8}, 40\%$

   B. $\frac{5}{8}, \frac{3}{4}, 20, 2^5, 40\%$

   C. $40\%, \frac{5}{8}, \frac{3}{4}, 2^5, 20$

   D. $40\%, \frac{5}{8}, \frac{3}{4}, 20, 2^5$

19. Which of the following is NOT considered one of the seven optimal conditions for literacy learning?

   A. Students have immersion in language.

   B. There are high expectations for students.

   C. All students are taught at exactly the same level.

   D. Students are evaluated and given feedback as they gain literacy skills.

20. In a board game, if you roll doubles, you double your points. Using two standard dice, what is the probability that you will roll exactly one set of doubles in three attempts?

   A. $\frac{1}{6}$

   B. $\frac{1}{2}$

   C. $\frac{1}{216}$

   D. $\frac{1}{18}$

21. Four specimens of three species of plants were exposed to different amounts of sunlight over the period of a week. At the end of the week, the number of new leaves on each plant was recorded.

Hours of sunlight per day	New leaves on Species A	New leaves on Species B	New leaves on Species C
0	0	0	0
1	0	1	4
3	0	4	8
6	4	7	5

Which of the following conclusions is best supported by information in the table above?

A. Species A requires 6 hours of sunlight per day to produce new leaves.

B. No plants can grow without exposure to sunlight.

C. To optimize growth, Species B should be exposed to more than 6 hours of sunlight per day.

D. To optimize growth, Species C should be exposed to between 2 and 5 hours of sunlight per day.

22. An activity that promotes the development of elementary locomotor skills is

A. playing hopscotch.

B. catching.

C. balancing on one foot.

D. tossing a ball underhanded.

23. The president vetoes a recent law passed by Congress. Congress overrides the president's veto in a two-thirds vote. This scenario embodies which of the following principles of U.S. democracy?

A. executive privilege

B. majority rule

C. rule of law

D. checks and balances

24. When a teacher introduces a leveled book to a small group, then encourages the members of the group to read quietly to themselves while she provides scaffolding, the process taking place is called

    A. interactive reading.

    B. cooperative learning grouping.

    C. guided reading.

    D. direct instruction.

25. Which of the following subsystems is NOT part of the transportation system for an automobile?

    A. lubrication system

    B. fuel system

    C. suspension system

    D. All of the above are part of an automobile's transportation system.

26. Which geographic factor most likely contributed to the development of New York City as an economic power in the late 18th century?

    A. temperate climate

    B. coal reserves

    C. forest land

    D. natural water routes

27. In music, the term *timbre* refers to the _____ of sounds.

    A. interval

    B. speed

    C. quality

    D. volume

28. Read the passage below from the First Amendment of the U.S. Constitution and then answer the following question.

"Congress shall make no law respecting an establishment of religion, or prohibiting the free exercise thereof; or abridging the freedom of speech, or of the press; or the right of the people peaceably to assemble, and to petition the Government for a redress of grievances."

[excerpted from www.archives.gov]

Which of the following situations illustrates a right protected by the First Amendment?

A. A U.S. citizen applies for a license to own a handgun.

B. A police officer informs a suspect that he or she has "the right to remain silent."

C. A white supremacist group is denied a permit to stage a rally because of its inflammatory views.

D. A student refuses to participate in reciting the Pledge of Allegiance.

"The young girl wore a kimono. It was made of a shiny golden silk with large red flowers adorning it. It was cinched at the girl's waist with a tightly drawn red sash."

29. If, after reading the above passage, a child states that the girl is probably Japanese, she is coming to that conclusion based on

A. reader-based information.

B. text-based information.

C. both reader-based and text-based information.

D. metacognition.

J. F. Francis, *Three Children;* The New York Public Library

30. What can the viewer understand about the social status of the children pictured in this painting, *Three Children* by J. F. Francis?

    A. The ruffles on the children's clothing indicate that they come from an impoverished family.

    B. The child in the center is missing a shoe, indicating that the child is neglected by its hardworking parents.

    C. The children's formal style of dress indicates that they come from a family of privilege.

    D. The room in which they are pictured is far too ornate to be their residence, so they must be posed in front of a backdrop.

31. Which of the following words contains a consonant blend?

    A. bait

    B. bland

    C. foil

    D. phone

32. Use the problem situation below to answer the question that follows.

    At Videos Plus rental store, every seventh customer receives a free candy bar. Every 12th customer receives a free rental. What is the first numbered customer who will receive both a free candy bar and a free rental?

    The problem situation above could be used to illustrate what mathematical concept?

    A. probability

    B. mean

    C. least common multiple

    D. division

33. Which of the following characteristics are typical of an adolescent child?

    A. enjoys challenging intellectual and social authorities

    B. possesses a high interest in politics, social justice, current events, and pop culture

    C. works well in small groups, including peer conferencing, lab partners, and partner projects

    D. all of the above

34. During summer in New York State, the days are longer and warmer because

    A. the sun gets warmer and cooler, causing the different seasons.

    B. the earth gets closer to the sun.

    C. the amount of the sun's energy hitting the surface of the earth varies due to regular fluctuations in the amount of energy the sun releases.

    D. the earth tilts on its axis, varying the length of the days and the angle of the sunlight.

35. A student is asked to draw a picture. After drawing the picture, the teacher has the student describe what he has drawn. If the teacher is employing the Language Experience Approach, she will then

  A. help the child write the words he has just dictated.

  B. write the words on the paper for the child.

  C. write the words on the board so the child can copy them.

  D. praise the child for having drawn a good picture.

36. Joining a team sport is a good way to enhance interpersonal skills because

  A. team success depends on teammates listening carefully to their coaches and to each other.

  B. teammates must learn to depend on each other to be successful and to get the job done.

  C. teammates must learn to articulate their thoughts to others as they work together toward a common goal.

  D. all of the above.

37. For a set of quadrilaterals, which of the following logical statements is true?

  A. If a polygon is a rhombus, then it is a square.

  B. If a polygon is a square, then it is a parallelogram.

  C. If a polygon is a parallelogram, then it is a square.

  D. If a polygon is a rectangle, then it is a rhombus.

38. Which of the following is most closely related to the process of dialysis?

  A. osmosis

  B. radioactivity

  C. heat

  D. acidity

39. According to Piaget and his constructivist collaborators, students

    A. create cognitive structures in the brain based on schemata they construct through their interactions with the world.

    B. use executive function to make decisions based on what a teacher tells them.

    C. need to be taught how to be social because it goes against their basic nature.

    D. work best in a teacher-centered classroom.

40. You must hand out a permission slip for next week's field trip to your first graders. When explaining that it must be signed by their guardians and returned as soon as possible, you should say,

    A. "Make sure your mom and dad sign this permission slip. You won't be able go on the trip unless they do."

    B. "Have the grownup at home who takes care of you sign this and return it so you can come on the field trip."

    C. "Have your mom or dad sign the permission slip and return it so you can come on the field trip."

    D. You don't need to explain the handout; just tell them to put it in their backpack.

41. In order to make a clay vessel more durable, you would

    A. glaze the vessel with an opaque glaze.

    B. fire the vessel in a kiln.

    C. throw the vessel on a wheel.

    D. build the vessel as a coil pot.

42.

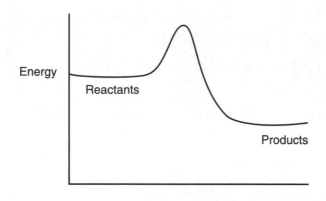

Reaction Pathway

The above graph depicts the energy associated with a specific reaction. In the overall reaction, is energy released into the environment or absorbed?

A. Energy is released because the products are at a lower energy state.

B. Energy is absorbed because the reactants are at a higher energy state.

C. Energy is neither released nor absorbed.

D. Energy is absorbed because the reactants are at a lower energy state.

43. When a teacher reads a chapter book to students even though it is above their actual reading level, she knows that the children can comprehend through her scaffolding. This displays her understanding of

A. the reading process.

B. the zone of proximal development.

C. Piaget's stages of social development.

D. aesthetic stance and efferent stance.

44. Keisha is ordering some merchandise from a catalog. Shipping and handling is based on the weight of the shipment. It is $5.00 for the first 10 ounces and then $0.75 for each additional ounce. Which algebraic expression below would represent the shipping and handling charge for a shipment weighing x ounces, where $x > 10$ ounces?

    A. $5.00 + 0.75x$

    B. $5.00 + 0.75(x - 10)$

    C. $5.00(10) + 0.75(x - 10)$

    D. $5.00 + 10(0.75x)$

45. Which of the following depicts a chemical process?

    A. Helium is combined with neon.

    B. Iron forms rust.

    C. Water causes soil erosion.

    D. Ice melts.

"The waiter handed me the special entree."

46. In the above sentence, which baseline structure is employed?

    A. subject/verb

    B. subject/verb/direct object

    C. subject/verb/predicate nominative

    D. subject/verb/predicate adjective

47. Which of the following statements best expresses the value of due process in the U.S. democratic system?

    A. "No State shall make or enforce any law which shall abridge the privileges or immunities of citizens of the United States; . . . nor deny to any person within its jurisdiction the equal protection of the laws."

    B. "Neither slavery nor involuntary servitude, except as a punishment for crime whereof the party shall have been duly convicted, shall exist within the United States . . ."

    C. "A well regulated Militia, being necessary to the security of a free State, the right of the people to keep and bear Arms, shall not be infringed."

    D. "The Congress shall have power to lay and collect taxes on incomes . . ."

    [excerpted from www.archives.gov]

48. According to the U.S. Department of Agriculture's Food Guide Pyramid, one healthy serving from the Meat, Poultry, Fish, Dry Beans, Eggs, and Nuts Group (also known as the Meat and Beans Group) consists of

    A. 1–2 ounces of cooked lean meat, poultry, or fish.

    B. 2–3 ounces of cooked lean meat, poultry, or fish.

    C. 2 tablespoons of peanut butter.

    D. 1 cup of raw leafy greens.

49. If each dimension of a 3 cm by 3 cm by 3 cm cube is doubled, which of the following statements will be true?

    A. Surface area and volume will increase by a factor of 6.

    B. Surface area will increase by a factor of 2, and volume by a factor of 4.

    C. Surface area will increase by a factor of 4, and volume by a factor of 8.

    D. Surface area and volume will double.

50. Which of the following best describes a fundamental quality of the process of socialization?

    A. the movement of a group of people from one place to another

    B. passing on a community's customs and values to the next generation

    C. the differences in customs and values between two generations

    D. giving equal respect to the diverse cultures within a society

51. What do health professionals and the Center for Disease Control recommend as the best way to avoid getting sick?

    A. Stay in bed for at least a week if you have the flu.

    B. Frequently wash your hands.

    C. Get a yearly checkup from your doctor.

    D. Take prophylactic antibiotics.

52. The final line of a book a teacher is reading to her students is "And the dog rolled over and wagged his tail." She reads the first part of each page aloud but has the children join in to read the final line of each page. This is called

    A. guided reading.

    B. shared reading.

    C. interactive reading.

    D. independent reading.

53. Liz lives 150 miles away from her favorite beach. This beach is 200 miles away from the nation's capital. What is a possible distance from Liz's residence to the capital? Distance is considered the shortest distance between two points.

    A. 60 miles

    B. 360 miles

    C. 25 miles

    D. 700 miles

54. Which line in the table below best matches a goal with the appropriate fitness plan?

Line	Goal	Fitness Plan
1	Tighten and tone core muscles to improve strength and flexibility.	Add abdominal crunches, back-strengthening exercises, and balancing activities to your fitness routine.
2	Increase endurance for the fall football season.	Add an upper-body weight-lifting program to your fitness routine.
3	Build upper-body strength to improve swimming endurance.	Add one half-hour of aerobic activity three times a week to your fitness routine.
4	Improve posture.	Sprint for 30 seconds, jog for 2 minutes, repeat.

A. Line 1

B. Line 2

C. Line 3

D. Line 4

55. Years ago, the most common color for a certain type of moth was light gray; dark gray moths existed, but were rare. The light gray color camouflaged the moths from predatory birds. Then, an industrial plant moved into the area, spewing soot and other industrial waste into the air. Now, the most common color for this type of moth is dark gray. Light gray moths are rare because darker moths are better camouflaged given the introduction of pollution to the environment.

The name for this process is

A. distribution.

B. stabilization.

C. selection.

D. continuation.

56. Use the diagram below to answer the question that follows.

The diagram above represents the first four triangular numbers. The 3rd triangular number is 6, as shown by 6 dots. What is 7th triangular number?

A. 21

B. 28

C. 22

D. 36

57. Preschoolers must learn several concepts in order to be able to read. When they have learned that words on a page are read from left to right, one line at a time, from top to bottom, they have mastered the concept of

A. directionality.

B. book orientation.

C. phonemic awareness.

D. phonics.

58. Which of the following describes the similarities between Japanese Noh and British Shakespearean theatrical forms?

A. Both included between 8 and 20 different acts, ranging from singers to silent pantomime, comedy acts, animal tricks, contortionists, and monologues.

B. Both were first performed exclusively in monasteries.

C. Both were originally performed only by males and contain allegorical generalizations about the human condition.

D. In both countries, the acting profession was regarded with respect, and there was no objection to women being employed on the stage.

59. Given that rectangle *ABCD* has coordinates of *A*(−2,−1), *B*(−2,4), *C*(4,4), and *D*(4,−1), what is the slope of one of the diagonals of the rectangle?

   A. $\frac{3}{2}$

   B. $\frac{5}{6}$

   C. $\frac{5}{2}$

   D. 0

60. Elkonin Boxes are used to help a child

   A. segment sounds.

   B. segment the letters in the word.

   C. isolate the syllables in a word.

   D. write the letter a sound makes.

61. Use the box and whisker plot below to answer the question that follows.

Percent Grades for Final Examination

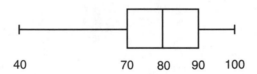

Which of the following statements is true about the plot of grades above?

   A. The median is a score of 70 and the range is 60.

   B. The median is a score of 80 and the range is 20.

   C. The median is a score of 70 and the range is 20.

   D. The median is a score of 80 and the range is 60.

62. You have carefully planned out a family budget based on your income and expenses. Which of the following is the least appropriate money management decision?

    A. taking your family out to dinner for a special occasion

    B. buying a flat-screen TV with your credit card

    C. going over your monthly budget to pay for emergency healthcare

    D. buying a suit for work when it is on sale

63. In order to support their voices properly, singers must be sure to

    A. breathe from their diaphragm.

    B. lock their knees.

    C. open their mouths wide.

    D. enunciate carefully.

64. Use the frequency table below to answer the question that follows.

Height, in inches	Frequency
60	1
61	0
62	4
63	5
64	3
65	3
66	4
67	2
68	1
69	2

Which of the following statements is true?

    A. The median height is 63 inches, and the mean height is 64.56 inches.

    B. The median height is 64.5 inches, and the mean height is 64.5 inches.

    C. The median height is 64 inches, and the mean height is 64.56 inches.

    D. The median height is 63 inches, and the mean height is 64.5 inches.

65. When we are discussing *morphemes*, we are discussing the

    A. phonological system.

    B. syntactic system.

    C. semantic system.

    D. pragmatic system.

66. A bear is chasing a woman through the forest. The enormous mass of the bear is extremely intimidating. If the woman runs through the woods in a zigzag pattern, she will be able to use the large mass of the bear to her own advantage because

    A. bears have poor peripheral vision so the bear won't be able to keep the woman in its field of vision as she zigzags through the forest

    B. the woman will be able to change her state of motion more easily than the bear because she has a smaller inertia

    C. the bear cannot run fast because it is so heavy and will tire quickly

    D. all of the above

67. The difference between an *environmental print* and a *print-rich classroom* is that

    A. the teacher causes the print-rich classroom but environmental print occurs naturally.

    B. classrooms in poor schools do not contain environmental print.

    C. environmental print can be read by children but the labels in print-rich classrooms are simply decorative.

    D. the teacher designs the environmental print but the print-rich classroom occurs naturally.

68. Since first appearing in 1952, television political ads have become an influential tool in presidential politics. Which of the following is NOT one of the goals of television advertising in presidential campaigns?

    A. to distill a candidate's message in a brief segment

    B. to reach out to voters who may be undecided

    C. to present both sides of important issues

    D. to use filmmaking techniques to create powerful images

69. When you are participating in a sport such as skateboarding or rollerblading, the best way to prevent injury is to

    A. move slowly to avoid harsh impact.

    B. avoid surfaces such as hard pavement and gravel.

    C. practice falling.

    D. wear appropriate protective equipment that fits well.

70. When students have been exposed to a word several times and can recognize it, say it without decoding it, and know it's meaning, the students have developed

    A. phonemic awareness of that word.

    B. phonic analysis.

    C. morphemic analysis.

    D. automaticity.

71. A certain trail mix contains seeds, raisins, and nuts in a ratio of 2 : 3 : 5, respectively. How many ounces of nuts are there in 5 pounds of mix?

    A. 5

    B. 8

    C. 16

    D. 40

72. A roller coaster car is at the top of a hill. At this point in the ride it is at its maximum

    A. potential energy.

    B. kinetic energy.

    C. potential and kinetic energy.

    D. speed.

73. Use the chart below to answer the following question.

	New York	United States
Population, 2000	18,976,457	281,421,906
Population, percent change, 1990 to 2000	5.5%	13.1%
Persons under 5 years old, percent, 2000	6.5%	6.8%
Persons under 18 years old, percent, 2000	24.7%	25.7%
Persons 65 years old and over, percent, 2000	12.9%	12.4%
Female persons, percent, 2000	51.8%	50.9%

[Source U.S. Census Bureau: State and County QuickFacts. Data derived from Population Estimates, 2000 Census of Population and Housing, 1990 Census of Population and Housing]

Which of the following conclusions is best supported by the information presented in the table?

    A. New York's population increased at a faster rate than that of the United States as a whole over the last decade.

    B. New York State is the third most populous state in the nation, following California and Texas.

    C. In New York State in 2000, people over age 65 outnumbered children under 5.

    D. In 2000, males outnumbered females in the United States.

74. When two words have different onsets but the same rime in their final syllable, these words

   A. have the same onsets.

   B. rhyme.

   C. are homophones.

   D. are morphemic pairs.

75. The rise in global temperature, by decreasing the desert water supply and thereby reducing the quantity of desert plant life, has affected a decrease in the population of small mammals in this climate. According to the food web below, which of the following statements describes accurately which group(s) would be most affected by the ecological changes to this climate?

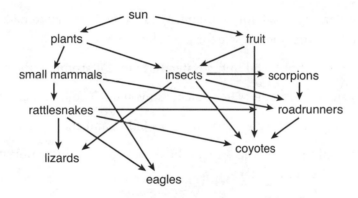

   A. All organisms in the food web would suffer sharp declines as their main food sources become increasingly scarce.

   B. The population of insects would increase because fewer small mammals would be eating them.

   C. The population of eagles would be adversely affected because one of their main food sources is becoming increasingly scarce.

   D. The population of rattlesnakes would increase since fewer small mammals would eat them.

"The runners were very tired as they approached the aid station. They had been running for over four miles at that point, and they had six more miles to go. Suddenly, one of the runners jogged to the edge of the road and sat down, grabbing his knee and rubbing it.

'What's wrong, Joe?' a red-headed runner called out."

76. After a student reads the above passage, the teacher asks the student, "Who is Joe?" Which of the following would be the best answer?

    A. a fellow runner with red hair

    B. a helper at the aid station

    C. the injured runner

    D. It cannot be determined from this passage.

77. You are preparing a bath for an infant. What is the best way to make sure the temperature of the water is safe for the baby?

    A. Place your whole hand in the water and move it around for several seconds.

    B. Dip your finger in the water quickly so you don't contaminate the bath.

    C. Make sure the bath has equal amounts of hot and cold water.

    D. Set the baby's feet in the water. If he or she appears uncomfortable, remove the baby from the water.

78. Solve: $3x + 5(x - 3) = 49$

    A. $x = 8$

    B. $x = \dfrac{52}{15}$

    C. $x = \dfrac{49}{5}$

    D. $x = \dfrac{35}{8}$

79. In an attempt to walk across a frozen lake, a skier tries to determine the best method for getting across the ice without cracking it. She takes into account pressure and force. Which of the following methods would most likely help the skier get across the lake without cracking the ice? (*Hint:* Pressure = Force/Area)

    A. tiptoeing

    B. walking upright

    C. standing on one foot

    D. crawling

80. The breakdown of the number of phonemes in the following word set is

my	*sleep*	*hog*

    A. two have three, and one has four.

    B. one has two, and two have three.

    C. one had two, one has three, one has four.

    D. the number of phonemes cannot be determined unless one hears how each person pronounces the words

81. You have just finished your teaching credential while working as a firefighter. You have no previous experience working with children aside from your assigned student teaching. What is the best way to parlay your experience as a firefighter into marketable teaching skills?

    A. Offer to write the school safety plan since you have experience in the public safety field.

    B. Explain how the communication skills you built on the job will help you communicate well with the families and faculty with which you would be working.

    C. Explain how the intense physical training prepared you for the strenuous life of teaching.

    D. Explain how every child loves firefighters so they will really enjoy being in your class.

KAPLAN

82. Which of the following words or phrases describes a characteristic theme of art for both the Harlem Renaissance and the works of *Los Tres Grandes*, the Mexican muralists Diego Rivera, José Clemente Orozco, and David Alfaro Siqueiros?

    A. despair

    B. hope for the future

    C. religion

    D. nature

83. A pickup truck can hold at most 2 tons of weight. The truck must haul a saw weighing 60 pounds and bricks weighing 3 pounds each. Which inequality below would be used to find the maximum number of bricks that can be hauled?

    A. $2,000 \geq 3(x + 60)$

    B. $4,000 \geq 3x + 60$

    C. $4,000 \leq 3x + 60$

    D. $2,000 \leq 3(x + 60)$

84. Which of the following best illustrates a social effect of the Industrial Revolution in the United States?

    A. population growth in rural areas

    B. the creation of the division of labor

    C. increased autonomy for workers

    D. the strengthening of the traditional family unit

85. The half-life of a substance is the time required for 50% of the substance to decay. The half-life of a certain element is 25 minutes. How much of a 4.0 mg sample is still active after 75 minutes?

    A. 0.50 mg

    B. 1.0 mg

    C. 2.0 mg

    D. 0.25 mg

86. What is the equation of the graph below?

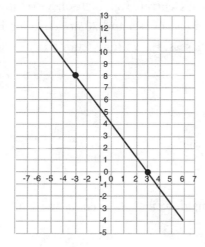

    A. $y = -4x + 3$

    B. $y = 3x + 4$

    C. $y = \frac{4}{3}x + 3$

    D. $y = -\frac{4}{3}x + 4$

87. Which of the following is the best example of the concept of isolationism?

    A. President Kennedy's naval blockade during the Cuban Missile Crisis

    B. the North American Foreign Trade Agreement (NAFTA), which removed trade barriers on goods produced and sold in Canada, Mexico, and the United States

    C. George Washington's Farewell Address, in which he states that the United States should pursue a neutral foreign policy

    D. the U.S. Congress's declaration of war on Germany on April 6, 1917

88. There are 300 seniors at Central High School. Two hundred of the seniors are enrolled in a mathematics course, and 70 are enrolled in a physics class. Fifty are enrolled in both classes. How many students take neither math nor physics?

    A. 100

    B. 30

    C. 80

    D. 150

89. Which of the following describes the role of political parties in the U.S. political system?

     I. to promote candidates

     II. to create consensus in Congress

    III. to form voting blocs in Congress

    IV. to represent the views of all of the electorate

    A. I and III only

    B. II and IV only

    C. II and III only

    D. III and IV only

90. You are writing a cover letter for a job in which you are very interested. The spell-check function on your computer isn't working, and you're unsure of the spelling of a few words. You should

    A. trust your best guess and send the letter.

    B. call a friend you trust and ask them to check over the letter.

    C. look the words up in a dictionary before you send the letter.

    D. wait until you get your computer repaired and then use the spell-check feature on the letter.

SAMPLE DIRECTIONS FOR THE WRITTEN ASSIGNMENT

This section of the test consists of a written assignment. You are asked to prepare a written response of approximately 150–300 words on the assigned topic. The assignment can be found on the next page. You should use your time to plan, write, review, and edit what you have written for the assignment.

Read the assignment carefully before you begin to write. Think about how you will organize what you plan to write. You may use any blank space provided on the following pages to make notes, write an outline, or otherwise prepare your response. However, your score will be based solely on the response you write on the lined pages of your answer document.

Your response will be evaluated on the basis of the following criteria:

- PURPOSE: Fulfill the charge of the assignment.
- APPLICATION OF CONTENT: Accurately and effectively apply the relevant knowledge and skills.
- SUPPORT: Support the response with appropriate examples and/or sound reasoning reflecting an understanding of the relevant knowledge and skills.

Your response will be evaluated based on the content above, not on your writing ability. The final version of the response should conform to the conventions of edited American English. This should be your original work, written in your own words, and not copied or paraphrased from some other work.

Be sure to write about the assigned topic. Please write legibly. You may not use any reference materials during the test. Remember to review what you have written and make any changes you think will improve your response.

Practice Written Assignment—Multi-Subject CST

There are five elements of literature. Delineate and define each element and, using a popular children's story (i.e., *Little Red Riding Hood*), give an example of each element from the story.

_____

_____

_____

_____

_____

_____

_____

_____

_____

_____

_____

_____

_____

_____

_____

_____

_____

_____

_____

CHAPTER 17: **PRACTICE MULTI-SUBJECT CST ANSWERS AND EXPLANATIONS**

Answer Key

1. C	24. C	47. A	70. D
2. B	25. D	48. B	71. D
3. C	26. D	49. C	72. A
4. D	27. C	50. B	73. C
5. C	28. D	51. B	74. B
6. C	29. C	52. B	75. C
7. D	30. C	53. A	76. C
8. C	31. B	54. A	77. A
9. B	32. C	55. C	78. A
10. D	33. D	56. B	79. D
11. C	34. D	57. A	80. B
12. B	35. B	58. C	81. B
13. C	36. D	59. B	82. B
14. C	37. B	60. A	83. B
15. B	38. A	61. D	84. B
16. B	39. A	62. B	85. A
17. D	40. B	63. A	86. D
18. D	41. B	64. C	87. C
19. C	42. A	65. B	88. C
20. B	43. B	66. B	89. A
21. D	44. B	67. A	90. C
22. A	45. B	68. C	
23. D	46. B	69. D	

Answers and Explanations

1. C

The primary focus of this question is Objective 0004:

Understand processes for generating, developing, revising, editing, and presenting/publishing written texts.

The writing process involves five stages. The first of these is the prewriting stage. This is the stage when a student decides what to write about and determines the audience and purpose of the piece. Thus, (C) is the correct answer. Choice (A) is not correct because in the revising step, the student changes the piece in order to improve it. Choice (B) is not correct because in the editing step, the student proofreads the work (or has another person proofread it) and then determines what changes need to be made. Choice (D) is not correct because in the drafting step, the student simply gets words written down on paper (in other words, creates a "first draft").

2. B

The primary focus of this question is Objective 0024:

Understand economic and political principles, concepts, systems and relate this knowledge to historical and contemporary developments in New York State, the United States, and the world.

Democracy did not begin in the United States, (D), nor did it begin with the French Revolution, (C). The concept of democracy dates back to ancient Greece and Rome, (B)—the word *democracy* comes from Greek, meaning "government by the people." Choice (A) is incorrect—a succession of dynasties ruled China from ancient times to the twentieth century.

3. C

The primary focus of this question is Objective 0014:

Understand concepts, principles, skills, and procedures related to the customary and metric systems of measurement.

In the question you are told that there are 2.54 centimeters in an inch. There are 36 inches in a yard, so there are $2.54 \times 36 = 91.44$ centimeters in a yard. Choice (A) is the number of centimeters in a foot. If your choice was (B), you may have mistakenly thought that there are 40 inches in a yard. Choice (D) is incorrect.

4. D

The primary focus of this question is Objective 0030:

Understand basic principles and practices of personal, interpersonal, and community health and safety and apply related knowledge and skills (e.g., decision making, problem solving) to promote personal well-being.

Each of the factors above can affect school safety. A school's safety plan, (A), helps a school respond quickly and safely in an emergency situation. The social climate, (B), (i.e., a school's policy regarding bullying, violence prevention and tolerance, and so on) affects the safety of children, families, and workers. In addition, the employee hiring, training, and supervision process affects safety because the better prepared and knowledgeable about child development, education, and safety employees are, the better they can help keep schools safe, (C). So, (D), all of the above, is the correct answer.

5. C

The primary focus of this question is Objective 0005:

Understand and apply writing skills and strategies for various purposes (including information and understanding, critical analysis and evaluation, literary response and personal expression, and social interaction).

Choice (C) is the correct choice because *invented spelling* (also called approximated spelling) allows young children to get their words down on paper and experience the joy of writing before they have fully learned correct grammar and spelling. It does not help them become better spellers in the future, (A). To do that, students need word study and repeated exposure to words. The purpose of *invented spelling* is not about testing proper grammar and spelling, (C). Choice (D) is not correct because the teacher does not correct the spelling on invented spelling assignments.

6. C

The primary focus of this question is Objective 0018:

Understand and apply concepts, principles, and theories pertaining to the living environment.

The sea urchin, (C), is the only animal listed that is not a mollusk; it is an echinoderm, characterized by living only in the sea (never in fresh water), the ability to regenerate (e.g., starfish can grow a lost arm), and tube feet. Mollusks are characterized by soft bodies usually protected by a shell, a muscular foot, and a special tongue called a radula. Abalones, (A), snails, (B), and oysters, (D), are all mollusks.

7. D

The primary focus of this question is Objective 0016:

Understand and apply the principles and processes of scientific inquiry and investigation.

Long, loose hair, dangling jewelry, and loose clothing are all dangerous in a science laboratory because they are safety hazards. Loose clothing or hair could catch on fire, and dangling jewelry could get caught on something or catch fire as well. Some general safety tips for the science lab are to wear safety goggles, tie back hair, wear closed-toed shoes, make sure a fire extinguisher is handy, and wear clothes that cover the maximum amount of skin to prevent chemical burns or other injuries.

8. C

The primary focus of this question is Objective 0023:

Understand concepts and phenomena related to human development and interactions (including anthropological, psychological, and sociological concepts).

Cultural diffusion, (C), is the term used by geographers to describe the adoption of one or more parts of one society's culture by another society. Choice (A) is incorrect because it describes the concept of demography. Choice (B) is too general—it defines the concept of culture, but does not describe the spread of culture from one group to another. Choice (D) is also incorrect because although a society's culture does change over time, this is not what is meant by the term *cultural diffusion*.

9. B

The primary focus of this question is Objective 0028:

Understand concepts, techniques, and materials for producing, listening to, and responding to music; analyze works of music; and understand the cultural dimensions and contributions of music.

An oboe is the only instrument listed that uses a reed and is, therefore, a woodwind. Choice (A) is incorrect because a cello is a string instrument. Choices (C) and (D) are incorrect because a French horn and a trombone are brass instruments.

10. D

The primary focus of this question is Objective 0032:

Understand health-related physical fitness concepts and practices.

The skeletal system (the 206 bones in the human body) protects vital organs such as the brain, heart, and lungs. The respiratory system, (A), supplies the blood with oxygen so that oxygen is delivered to all parts of the body. The heart, lungs, and blood vessels work together to pump blood through the circulatory system, (B). The digestive system, (C), breaks down food from larger molecules to smaller molecules so it may be used by the body.

11. C

The primary focus of this question is Objective 0003:

Understand and apply reading skills and strategies for various purposes (including information and understanding, critical analysis and evaluation, literary response, and social interaction).

The main reason that teachers read aloud to students is to demonstrate the correct usage of inflection and chunking that allows a student to add meaning to what he or she is reading. People who read this way are fluent. Choice (A) is incorrect because when a teacher models reading, she really can't know whether students are paying attention or just appearing to pay attention. Choice (B) is incorrect because students show *their* fluency when *they* read, not when a teacher is modeling how to read. Choice (D) is incorrect because modeling reading has nothing to do with cooperative learning (working in groups).

12. B

The primary focus of this question is Objective 0015:

Understand concepts and skills related to data analysis, probability, and statistics and apply this understanding to evaluate and interpret data and to solve problems.

In the interval from 3 P.M. to 5 P.M., the car covered the largest distance, 120 miles, in the shortest period of time, 2 hours. This is a speed of 60 miles per hour, which is the fastest speed of the time intervals shown. Speed is measured in miles per hour in this example. Speed is indicated on the graph as the slope of the line segment—the steeper the line, the greater the speed. Because the steepness of these segments is not the same for every time interval, there is not a constant speed from 9 A.M. to 8 P.M, so (A) is incorrect. The horizontal line on the graph from 12 P.M. to 1 P.M. indicates a slope of 0, meaning the car was not moving during this hour, so (C) is incorrect. Choice (D) is also incorrect because at 8 P.M., the car is only 120 miles from its starting point of 9 A.M.

13. C

The primary focus of this question is Objective 0021:

Understand major ideas, eras, themes, developments, and turning points in the history of New York State, the United States, and the world.

Choice (C) describes the spreading of disease, a devastating effect that European settlers had on native people. Among northeastern tribes and native tribes throughout the continent, the spread of disease resulted in significant loss of life. Conversely, (A), (B), and (D) are examples of products introduced to European settlers by indigenous cultures.

14. C

The primary focus of this question is Objective 0035:

Understand basic principles of career development; apply processes and skills for seeking and maintaining employment; and demonstrate knowledge of workplace skills, behaviors, and responsibilities.

Employers create employee handbooks to help in difficult situations like these. It's best to follow the protocol for conflict resolution, (C), rather than ignoring the problem, (A); confronting your coworker, (B), which could escalate the conflict; or hiring a lawyer to settle the case, (D), which is unnecessary at the early stage of the conflict outlined in the question.

15. B

The primary focus of this question is Objective 0017:

Understand and apply concepts, principles, and theories pertaining to the physical setting (including earth science, chemistry, and physics).

A physical change is a change that does not result in the production of a new substance. Evaporation, (A), the painting of wood, (B), and the cutting of a copper wire, (C), are all physical changes. Other examples of physical changes are melting, freezing, condensing, bending, crushing, and breaking. The only change that is not a physical change of matter is (B), the decomposition of old leaves, which is a chemical change (one that results in the production of another substance).

16. B

The primary focus of this question is Objective 0002:

Understand skills and strategies involved in reading comprehension.

There are five stages of the reading process. The responding stage, (B), is the stage in which students react to what they have read and answer questions showing they have understood what they have read. In the pre-reading stage, (A), students look at a book and consider its organization and topic. The teacher may give them anticipatory set questions during this time. In the exploring stage, (C), students look at other things they have just read about. In the applying stage, (D), students use the information they have just read in another context. Thus, (B) is the correct answer.

17. D

The primary focus of this question is Objective 0007:

Understand and apply techniques of literary analysis to works of fiction, drama, poetry, and nonfiction.

A farce is a type of *comedy*, a light, often humorous drama with a happy ending, as opposed to *tragedy*, which dramatizes the downfall and misery of a great character. Choice (A) is incorrect because *parody* is the term for a work that imitates another serious work. Choice (B) is incorrect because *improvising* is the term used when actors extemporaneously invent and perform scenarios. Choice (C) is incorrect because the term for lines arranged in a metrical pattern is *verse*.

18. D

The primary focus of this question is Objective 0011:

Understand skills and concepts related to number and numeration and apply these concepts to real-world situations.

To compare the choices, change each number to its decimal equivalent. By inspection of the decimals, you will see that 40% is the smallest number and 2^5 is the largest number.

$$\frac{3}{4} = 4\overline{)3.00}^{.75} = 0.75$$

$$40\% = \frac{40}{100} = 0.40$$

$$2^5 = 2 \times 2 \times 2 \times 2 \times 2 = 32.0$$

$$20 = 20.0$$

$$\frac{5}{8} = 8\overline{)5.000}^{.625} = 0.625$$

Beware of the trap: (A) displays numbers that are ordered correctly, but they are ordered from greatest to least. The question asks for the correct order from least to greatest; therefore, (D) is correct.

19. C

The primary focus of this question is Objective 0001:

Understand the foundations of reading development.

The seven optimal conditions for literacy learning are these: 1) Children are immersed in language. 2) Children and teachers are actively involved in meaningful demonstrations of language in action. 3) Language is employed for real-life purposes. 4) Children assume responsibility for their own learning. 5) Adults hold expectations that all children will learn. 6) Approximation is encouraged. 7) Feedback is given to the learner as an ongoing process. Therefore, the only choice that is not a condition is (C), all students are taught at exactly the same level.

20. B

The primary focus of this question is Objective 0015:

Understand concepts and skills related to data analysis, probability, and statistics and apply this understanding to evaluate and interpret data and to solve problems.

Probability is calculated with this ratio: $\dfrac{\text{\# of favorable outcomes}}{\text{\# total outcomes}}$. Make a table to show all the possible outcomes of rolling two dice:

1,1	2,1	3,1	4,1	5,1	6,1
1,2	2,2	3,2	4,2	5,2	6,2
1,3	2,3	3,3	4,3	5,3	6,3
1,4	2,4	3,4	4,4	5,4	6,4
1,5	2,5	3,5	4,5	5,5	6,5
1,6	2,6	3,6	4,6	5,6	6,6

The probability of rolling doubles with a standard set of dice is $\dfrac{6}{36} = \dfrac{1}{6}$. You are asked for the probability of rolling exactly one set of doubles in three attempts. This is represented as P(doubles) OR P(doubles) OR P(doubles). The OR function means to add the probabilities. Therefore, $\dfrac{1}{6} + \dfrac{1}{6} + \dfrac{1}{6} = \dfrac{3}{6} = \dfrac{1}{2}$, making (B) the correct answer. Incorrect choice (A) represents the probability of rolling doubles in one attempt. If you chose incorrect choice (C), you multiplied the probabilities instead of adding them.

21. D

The primary focus of this question is Objective 0016:

Understand and apply the principles and processes of scientific inquiry and investigation.

Only (D) is a valid conclusion. Since Species C had the most new leaves at 3 hours of sunlight and demonstrated a drop-off by 6 hours of sunlight, the conclusion that optimal growth occurs for Species C between 2 and 5 hours of sunlight is reasonable. Because the table does not record the number of new leaves produced with exposure to 4 or 5 hours of sunlight, (A) is invalid. (B) is too extreme.

22. A

The primary focus of this question is Objective 0031:

Understand physical education concepts and practices related to the development of personal living skills.

Playing hopscotch is the only activity listed that involves moving from place to place. Catching, (B), and tossing underhand, (D), are manipulative, not locomotor skills. Balancing on one foot, (C), is a body mechanics skill.

23. D

The primary focus of this question is Objective 0025:

Understand the roles, rights, and responsibilities of citizenship in the United States and the skills, knowledge, and attitudes necessary for successful participation in civic life.

In the system of checks and balances, the three branches of government—legislative, executive, and judicial—limit the power of each other so no one branch dominates. The president's power to veto laws and the legislature's ability to override the veto by a two-thirds vote are examples of this system. Executive privilege, (A), refers to the right of the president and his or her administration to keep documents confidential if revealing them would interfere with their ability to govern. Majority rule, (B), is the principle that the majority of a group can make decisions for the whole group. Rule of law, (C), refers to the doctrine that the law, enforced by the courts, governs all citizens, including members of government.

24. C

The primary focus of this question is Objective 0003:

Understand and apply reading skills and strategies for various purposes (including information and understanding, critical analysis and evaluation, literary response, and social interaction).

The question includes the actual definition of guided reading. Choice (A) is not correct because interactive reading refers to two (or more) students taking turns reading and responding to one another. Choice (B) is not correct because cooperative learning grouping has to do with students working together in groups to seek a common goal. Choice (D) is not correct because direct instruction is simply the process of a teacher standing in front of the classroom and giving out information and directions for the students to follow.

25. D

The primary focus of this question is Objective 0019:

Apply knowledge of technology and the principles of engineering design.

Choices (A), (B), and (C) are incorrect because lubrication, fuel, and suspension systems are smaller subsystems that constitute an automobile's transportation system. Choice (D), all of the above, is correct.

26. D

The primary focus of this question is Objective 0022:

Understand geographic concepts and phenomena and analyze the interrelationships of geography, society, and culture in the development of New York State, the United States, and the world.

The most significant factor in much of the city's increase in economic power came from its value as an ocean port and its access to the Hudson River, an inland water route that facilitated trade. The city also benefited from its geographic location between the ports of New England and Maryland, helping make it a center of commerce. Neither a temperate climate, (A), access to coal reserves, (B), nor the presence of forest land, (C), influenced the city's economic growth more than its natural water routes. Therefore, (D) is correct.

27. C

The primary focus of this question is Objective 0028:

Understand concepts, techniques, and materials for producing, listening to, and responding to music; analyze works of music; and understand the cultural dimensions and contributions of music.

Timbre refers to the quality that makes a particular instrument or voice distinctive; for example, a woodwind has a different timbre than a string. Choice (A), *interval*, refers to the distance of pitch between two tones; for example, the distance between the notes C to D is a second, C to E is a third, and C to F is a fourth. Choice (B) is incorrect because the musical term for speed is *tempo*. The term *volume*, (D), is incorrect because *volume* refers to how loud or intense a sound is.

28. D

The primary focus of this question is Objective 0025:

Understand the roles, rights, and responsibilities of citizenship in the United States and the skills, knowledge, and attitudes necessary for successful participation in civic life.

According to a 1943 Supreme Court decision, the freedom of speech granted by the First Amendment prohibits the government from compelling a citizen to salute the American flag or say the Pledge of Allegiance, (D). Choices (A) and (B) are protected by constitutional amendments other than the First Amendment. "The right to bear arms," illustrated by (A), is protected by the Second Amendment, and the Fifth

Amendment guarantees citizens "the right to remain silent," (B), if accused of a crime. In the situation posed by (C), the First Amendment should protect, not deny, the right of assembly and the freedom of speech.

29. C

The primary focus of this question is Objective 0002:

Understand skills and strategies involved in reading comprehension.

Reader-based information is the information (prior knowledge) a person who is reading brings to the piece. Text-based information is the information actually found in the reading. In this case, the reader gains information from the text (the girl is wearing a kimono), but also brings prior knowledge (the fact that kimonos are often worn by Japanese people) to the reading experience, making (C) the correct answer. Choice (A) is not correct because a reader must gain some information from the text. Choice (B) is not correct because the text does not include information on the race of the girl wearing the kimono. Choice (D) is not correct because metacognition is the process of thinking about one's thinking.

30. C

The primary focus of this question is Objective 0027:

Understand the concepts, techniques, and materials of the visual arts; analyze works of visual art; and understand the cultural dimensions and contributions of the visual arts.

The children's formal dress, paired with the painting's elaborate and ornate setting, indicates that these are children born of a wealthy family (C). Choice (A) is not correct because it states the opposite of the correct answer. Choice (B) is incorrect because to infer that a child is neglected based on a missing shoe would be extreme. Choice (D) is incorrect because the children's formal style of dress does indeed match the ornate setting in which they are pictured.

31. B

The primary focus of this question is Objective 0001:

Understand the foundations of reading development.

A *consonant blend* is a situation where two or more consonants appear next to each other within a word and each of the individual consonant sounds are audible. The *bl–* and *–nd* in the word *bland* are both consonant blends. Choice (A) contains a vowel digraph but no blend. Choice (C) contains a diphthong (*–oi*) but no blend. Choice (D) contains a consonant digraph (*ph–*) but no blend.

32. C

The primary focus of this question is Objective 0010:

Use mathematical terminology and symbols to interpret, represent, and communicate mathematical ideas and information.

This problem situation illustrates the concept of least common multiple. The first customer to receive both the candy bar and the free rental is determined by examining the multiples of both 7 and 12 until a common multiple is revealed:

Multiples of 7: 7, 14, 21, 28, 35, 42, 49, 56, 63, 70, 77, 84

Multiples of 12: 12, 24, 36, 48, 60, 72, 84

The first customer to receive both is the 84th customer. Probability, (A), is not illustrated by this problem; probability deals with the number of favorable outcomes divided by the number of total possible outcomes, and it takes the form of a fraction. Mean, (B), is the average of a group of data elements, a concept that is not part of the problem situation. Choice (D), division, is not illustrated by this problem.

33. D

The primary focus of this question is Objective 0033:

Understand concepts and practices related to child development and care and apply knowledge of family and interpersonal relationships.

The cognitive characteristics listed in (A), (B), and (C) are typical of adolescent children. Their emerging independence and quest for their own identity sets this group apart as they (sometimes rather forcefully) distance themselves from adults. Their interest in and enjoyment of their peers should be tapped into in order to strengthen their cognitive development.

34. D

The primary focus of this question is Objective 0022:

Understand geographic concepts and phenomena and analyze the interrelationships of geography, society, and culture in the development of New York State, the United States, and the world.

Because the Earth is tilted as it orbits around the sun, where and how much sunlight strikes a particular portion of the Earth varies. The angle at which the Sun's light strikes Earth affects the temperature; the Sun's energy is more concentrated when the Sun is high in the sky. Weather is also warmer in summer because the Sun, being higher, provides more hours of light as it travels a greater distance across the sky. This longer exposure to sunlight gives the land, seas, and air masses more time to warm during the day. Choices (A) and (C) are incorrect because the Sun's temperature does not change significantly between the seasons, nor does the amount of energy it releases. Choice (B) is incorrect because the Earth does not get any closer or any further away from the Sun while orbiting around it. The Earth maintains a near-circular orbit around the Sun and remains about the same distance from it at all times.

35. B

The primary focus of this question is Objective 0001:

Understand the foundations of reading development.

In the Language Experience Approach (LEA), students are encouraged to illustrate and then come up with words to describe their illustration. This approach is used with children who cannot write fluently yet. It encourages students to be creative (drawing) and to express themselves verbally. It also shows them that pictures and words are related. Choices (A) and (C) are both strategies that can be used, but they are not included in the LEA. Choice (D) is not correct because whether the painting is good is irrelevant to the LEA.

36. D

The primary focus of this question is Objective 0031:

Understand physical education concepts and practices related to the development of personal living skills.

Building a team depends on good communication—listening to others and voicing personal ideas and opinions—and trust. These cooperation, communication, and teamwork skills extend beyond athletics into successful personal and professional lives. Therefore, since all of the choices are correct, (D) is the best answer choice.

37. B

The primary focus of this question is Objective 0009:

Understand formal and informal reasoning processes, including logic and simple proofs, and apply problem-solving techniques and strategies in a variety of contexts.

All squares are parallelograms. So if a polygon is a square, it is necessarily also a parallelogram. Parallelograms have 2 pairs of opposite sides that are both congruent and parallel, which is true of all squares. Some rhombuses are squares (those with 4 right angles), but not all rhombuses are squares, so (A) is incorrect. It is possible for a quadrilateral to be a rhombus and not a square. Some parallelograms are squares (those with 4 right angles and 4 congruent sides), but not all parallelograms are squares, so (C) is incorrect. Only one type of rectangle is a rhombus, and that is the square. All other rectangles are not rhombuses, so (D) is also incorrect.

38. A

The primary focus of this question is Objective 0018:

Understand and apply concepts, principles, and theories pertaining to the living environment.

Osmosis is the passive transport of water based on cell membrane selectivity. Dialysis is most similar to osmosis because it uses what is called a dialyzing membrane to permit small molecules and ions to pass through but retain larger molecules, thereby filtering out certain toxic material from the blood.

39. A

The primary focus of this question is Objective 0033:

Understand concepts and practices related to child development and care and apply knowledge of family and interpersonal relationships.

Constructivists believe that students "construct" their knowledge. It is their belief that the brain is pliable and that, through exposure, students cause their brain structures to grow. Thus, (A) is the correct answer. Choice (B) is not correct because while executive function refers to the idea of using the brain to make sense of the world (a concept with which the constructivists would agree), the constructivists would not agree that executive function only occurs under a teacher's guidance. Choice (C) is not correct because constructivists believe that humans are naturally social creatures.

Choice (D) is not correct—in fact, constructivists believe the opposite: a student-centered classroom is the most effective learning environment.

40. B

The primary focus of this question is Objective 0033:

Understand concepts and practices related to child development and care and apply knowledge of family and interpersonal relationships.

Families are made up all sorts of combinations other than mom, dad, and kids. Today it is common for extended family—grandparents, aunts, uncles, or cousins—to act as legal guardians. Some of your students may have families with two moms, two dads, or divorced parents. Families can be blended and/or include adopted or foster children. Be careful not to marginalize students who might not live with mom and/or dad; it's best to refer to the "grown-up at home who takes care of you" instead of using "mom" and "dad." Based on this, you can eliminate (A) and (C). Choice (D) is also incorrect because a teacher should always explain important information to students so they understand what's going on and can explain it to their families.

41. B

The primary focus of this question is Objective 0017:

Understand and apply concepts, principles, and theories pertaining to the physical setting (including earth science, chemistry, and physics).

A *kiln* is a special oven or furnace used to fire, harden, and dry clay and other materials. Firing the vessel in a kiln would make the clay more durable. Glazing the vessel, (A), would not make the vessel stronger, as this process simply creates a smooth, glossy surface on the pot. "Throw the vessel on a wheel," (C), means to use a potter's wheel to make the vessel; therefore, (C) is incorrect. A coil pot is a ceramic pot that is made by a series of stacked coils or "snakes." Building the vessel as a coil pot, (D), would not necessarily make the pot more durable.

42. A

The primary focus of this question is Objective 0017:

Understand and apply concepts, principles, and theories pertaining to the physical setting (including earth science, chemistry, and physics).

As the graph depicts, the energy level of the reactants is greater than that of the products, illustrating that energy was lost during the reaction. Thus, the products are at a lower energy level. The only choice that corresponds to the graph is (A). Choice (B) is incorrect because energy is not absorbed. If it were, the graph would show a higher peak on the products side. Choice (D) is incorrect because the reactants are at a higher energy state.

43. B

The primary focus of this question is Objective 0003:

Understand and apply reading skills and strategies for various purposes (including information and understanding, critical analysis and evaluation, literary response, and social interaction).

Vygotsky's zone of proximal development suggests that students can comprehend and perform at a significantly higher level that their individual ability level if someone helps them. Thus, with scaffolding (someone helping), students can perform skills that they could not perform alone. Choice (A) is not correct because the reading process in and of itself does not involve levels. Choice (C) is not correct because Piaget did not develop stages of social development. Piaget developed stages of cognitive development that do not include the ideas of scaffolding or teaching above one's ability level. Choice (D) refers to how one absorbs information and has nothing to do with levels of comprehension.

44. B

The primary focus of this question is Objective 0012:

Understand patterns and apply the principles and properties of linear algebraic relations and functions.

Shipping and handling is a flat $5.00 for the first 10 ounces. If x represents the total weight of the order, $(x - 10)$ represents the additional ounces. Each of these additional ounces is multiplied by $0.75. So the correct expression is (B): $5.00 + 0.75(x - 10)$. Choice (A) represents a cost that would be $5.00 plus $0.75 for every ounce, including the first 10 ounces. Choice (C) represents a cost that would be $5.00 for each one of the first 10 ounces, plus $0.75 for each additional ounce. Choice (D), after multiplying, represents a cost of $5.00 plus $7.50 for every ounce of weight, including the first 10.

45. B

The primary focus of this question is Objective 0017:

Understand and apply concepts, principles, and theories pertaining to the physical setting (including earth science, chemistry, and physics).

Iron forms rust when water (or an even better electrolyte) turns iron and oxygen into iron oxide (Fe_2O_3), a chemical process. Helium and neon are both inert, so they do not react chemically. Water causing soil erosion may or may not incur a chemical change, and ice melting does not alter the chemistry of H_2O.

46. B

The primary focus of this question is Objective 0004:

Understand processes for generating, developing, revising, editing, and presenting/publishing written texts.

The subject of the sentence is *waiter*. The verb of the sentence is *handed*. The direct object (the word receiving the action of the verb) is *entree*. Thus, (B) is the only possible answer. An example of a sentence that only has a subject and a verb, (A), is "The boy jumped." Predicate nominatives, (C), rename the subject (e.g., "My *father* is a kind *man*.") Predicate adjectives, (D), describe the subject (e.g., "That *horse* is *fast*.")

47. A

The primary focus of this question is Objective 0024:

Understand economic and political principles, concepts, systems and relate this knowledge to historical and contemporary developments in New York State, the United States, and the world.

A core value of U.S. democracy, due process, is the principle that all people be treated equally in accordance with the law. The correct choice, (A), an excerpt from Amendment 14 of the U.S. Constitution ratified in 1868, states this right. Choices (B), (C), and (D) are also excerpts from constitutional amendments, but none explicitly addresses the principle of due process. Choice (B) is an excerpt from Amendment 13, abolishing slavery; (C) is from Amendment 2, granting the right to bear arms; (D) is from Amendment 16, authorizing the implementation of income tax.

48. B

The primary focus of this question is Objective 0030:

Understand basic principles and practices of personal, interpersonal, and community health and safety and apply related knowledge and skills (e.g., decision making, problem solving) to promote personal well-being.

According to the Food Guide Pyramid, one healthy serving from the Meat and Beans Group consists of 2–3 ounces of cooked lean meat, poultry, or fish. Choices (A) and (C) are less than one serving, while (D) is part of the vegetable group.

49. C

The primary focus of this question is Objective 0014:

Understand concepts, principles, skills, and procedures related to the customary and metric systems of measurement.

If all the dimensions of a cube are doubled, the dimensions have increased by a factor of 2. The surface area of the original cube is $6 \times (3 \times 3) = 54$ square centimeters, as there are 6 equal 3 by 3 faces. The surface area of the new cube is $6 \times (6 \times 6) = 216$ square centimeters, and $216 \div 54 = 4$, which illustrates a growth by a factor of 4. The original volume is $3 \times 3 \times 3 = 27$ cubic centimeters. The new volume is $6 \times 6 \times 6 = 216$ cubic centimeters, and $216 \div 27 = 8$, a growth factor of 8. Therefore (C) is correct. The concept tested here is that doubling the sides of a geometric figure causes the area and volume of a figure to grow by a factor larger than 2 (double).

50. B

The primary focus of this question is Objective 0023:

Understand concepts and phenomena related to human development and interactions (including anthropological, psychological, and sociological concepts).

Socialization is the process in which individuals learn the customs and values of a social group. By socializing children and other members of a community through social institutions such as family, school, and peer groups, a society can pass on its culture to the next generation, making (B) the correct answer. Choice (A) describes the term *migration*, whereas (C) describes a "generation gap," in which two generations, separated by age, do not share the same values. Choice (D) describes the value of multiculturalism.

51. B

The primary focus of this question is Objective 0030:

Understand basic principles and practices of personal, interpersonal, and community health and safety and apply related knowledge and skills (e.g., decision making, problem solving) to promote personal well-being.

Washing your hands often and thoroughly is the most important thing you can do to avoid getting sick. When you touch contaminated surfaces, you pick up germs that can lead to infection when you rub your eyes or touch your nose or mouth. Frequent hand washing will reduce your risk of contracting diseases as common as a cold or as serious as meningitis. Staying in bed for a week if you have the flu, (A), will not necessarily prevent illness. A yearly checkup from your doctor, (C), is important for maintaining good health; however, certain illnesses, such as colds and the flu, cannot be avoided by seeing your doctor. Choice (D), taking prophylactic (preventative) antibiotics only applies to certain people, as antibiotics must be prescribed by a doctor.

52. B

The primary focus of this question is Objective 0002:

Understand skills and strategies involved in reading comprehension.

Shared reading, (B), is the process of the teacher and the students reading aloud together. Typically, the teacher reads a few lines, and then the students join in. This process is employed in the primary grades, especially in kindergarten. Choice (A) is not correct because guided reading is the process of a teacher introducing a leveled book to a small group and then encouraging the members of the group to read quietly to themselves while she provides scaffolding. Choice (C) is not correct because interactive reading is the process of two or more students taking turns reading while helping one another as needed. Choice (D) is not correct because independent reading is the process of having students read individually and silently to themselves.

53. A

The primary focus of this question is Objective 0013:

Understand the principles and properties of geometry and trigonometry and apply them to model and solve problems.

Of the choices listed, 60 miles is the only possible distance from Liz's house to the capital. To understand this problem, draw a picture similar to the following figure.

Indicate the distance from Liz's house to the beach (150 miles) as a line segment. The capital is 200 miles from the beach. A circle with a radius of 200 miles with the beach as the center shows all possible locations of the capital.

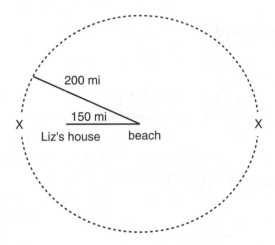

This configuration results in a triangle being formed by the three locations, with the exception of the two locations marked above with X's. The figure below shows a possible triangle formed.

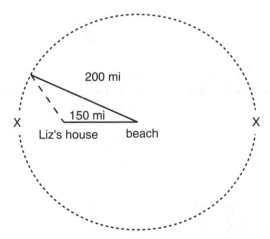

In all triangles, the sum of any two sides must be larger than the third side. Thus, the third side of the triangle, representing the distance from the house to the capital, must be between 50 miles and 350 miles. Sixty miles, (A), is a possible distance, while 360 miles, (B), is not a possible distance because the other two sides of the triangle, 200 and 150, result in a sum of 350, which is smaller than 360 miles. Likewise, 25 miles, (C), is not a possible distance because the sum of the sides of 25 and 150 is 175, which is smaller than the third side of 200 miles. (D), 700 miles, is not a possible distance because the sum of sides 200 and 150 is 350, which is smaller than 700 miles.

54. A

The primary focus of this question is Objective 0032:

Understand health-related physical fitness concepts and practices.

Line 1 is the only line that appropriately matches a fitness plan to a goal. Adding abdominal crunches, back-strengthening exercises, and balancing activities to your fitness routine will improve strength and flexibility and tighten and tone core muscles. A good fitness plan to increase endurance for the fall football season, (B), is adding wind sprints to a fitness routine, thereby improving anaerobic fitness. In order to build upper-body strength for improved swimming endurance, you would want to add an upper-body weight-lifting program to your fitness routine, (C). To improve posture, your fitness plan would be similar to the correct answer; you would want to add abdominal crunches, back-strengthening exercises, and balancing activities to your fitness routine. These activities would strengthen your core muscles, thus improving posture.

55. C

The primary focus of this question is Objective 0020:

Understand the relationships among and common themes that connect mathematics, science, and technology and the application of knowledge and skills in these disciplines to other areas of learning.

Selection, (C), is the process by which species can inherit certain characteristics that make them more likely to survive. Choice (A), *distribution*, is incorrect because it means the natural geographic range of an organism. Choice (B), *stabilization*, is incorrect because it means the act of being unchanging. *Continuation*, (D), is also incorrect because it means the act of staying the same.

56. B

The primary focus of this question is Objective 0012:

Understand patterns and apply the principles and properties of linear algebraic relations and functions.

To answer this questions, look for a pattern in the diagram. The numbers represented by the dots are 1, 3, 6, 10... Look at the difference between successive elements. $3 - 1 = 2$; $6 - 3 = 3$; $10 - 6 = 4$. From this pattern, you are able to deduce that the next triangular number will be 5 larger than 10, or 15. The sixth number will be 6 larger than 15, or 21. The seventh number will be 7 larger than 21, or 28. Choice (B) is correct.

57. A

The primary focus of this question is Objective 0001:

Understand the foundations of reading development.

The question defines *directionality*, (A). Young children do not instinctively know that words begin at the top of the page and run from left to right. They gain this information by being read to or by observing others reading. Choice (B), book orientation, is a child's understanding of how to hold, open, and turn the pages of a book. Phonemic awareness, (C), is the understanding that words are broken into sounds. Choice (D), phonics, is the understanding that letters represent sounds.

58. C

The primary focus of this question is Objective 0007:

Understand and apply techniques of literary analysis to works of fiction, drama, poetry, and nonfiction.

Japanese Noh and Shakespearean dramas were both based on timeless truths about the human condition, and neither allowed women to perform. Choice (A) refers to vaudeville theater, (B) refers to Russian mysteries, and (D) refers to ancient Hindu dramas.

59. B

The primary focus of this question is Objective 0012:

Understand patterns and apply the principles and properties of linear algebraic relations and functions.

Draw a set of coordinate axes and graph the rectangle. Also draw in one of the diagonals, such as $\overline{AC}$ as shown below:

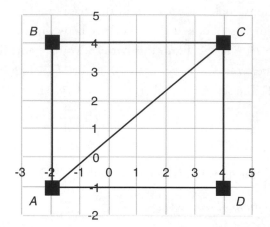

The slope of the diagonal $\overline{AC}$ is found by calculating the change in the y-coordinates divided by the change in x-coordinates. The slope of $\overline{AC} = \dfrac{4 - (-1)}{4 - (-2)} = \dfrac{5}{6}$. To answer this question correctly, it is important to know how to calculate the slope of a line and how to do positive and negative arithmetic. If you chose (D), you may have thought that the question asked for the slope of one of the sides, $\overline{AD}$ or $\overline{BC}$. These sides have a slope of 0.

60. A

The primary focus of this question is Objective 0001:

Understand the foundations of reading development.

Elkonin Boxes are used with young children and in remedial classes to help children dissect a word into its sounds. It is not concerned with letters, so (B) is not correct. It does not work with syllables (in fact, they are used mostly with one-syllable words), so (C) is not correct. Choice (D) is not correct because students don't write the letters. They often move letters into the boxes instead of writing them.

61. D

The primary focus of this question is Objective 0015:

Understand concepts and skills related to data analysis, probability, and statistics and apply this understanding to evaluate and interpret data and to solve problems.

The median is shown on a box and whisker plot as the centerline that divides the box part of the plot. This line is at the score of 80. The range of data on a box and whisker plot is the difference between the upper extreme, 100, minus the lower extreme, 40; $100 - 40 = 60$. Choice (D) is correct.

62. B

The primary focus of this question is Objective 0034:

Understand skills and procedures related to consumer economics and personal resource management.

The only answer choice that does not fall within a practical family budget is (B), buying an expensive TV with your credit card. A purchase such as this is not an essential purchase, and putting an expensive item on a credit card will add to the total cost because credit cards often charge high interest rates. The other answer choices would be acceptable money management decisions because they are not extravagant or particularly expensive purchases.

63. A

The primary focus of this question is Objective 0028:

Understand concepts, techniques, and materials for producing, listening to, and responding to music; analyze works of music; and understand the cultural dimensions and contributions of music.

Good breathing technique, deep breaths supported by the diaphragm (the muscle that connects the chest and abdominal cavities in mammals), is essential to proper and strong support of a singer's voice. Choice (B) is incorrect because locking the knees does not help a singer support his or her voice. Choice (C), opening the mouth wide, would help the vocal tone resonate; however, it does not help a singer *support* his or her voice. Choice (D) is incorrect because while it is important to enunciate (speak clearly), enunciating doesn't help singers support their voices.

64. C

The primary focus of this question is Objective 0015:

Understand concepts and skills related to data analysis, probability, and statistics and apply this understanding to evaluate and interpret data and to solve problems.

To solve this problem, calculate the median and mean, remembering to take into consideration the frequency and the amount of each data item. The median is the middle data element when the data is arranged in increasing or decreasing order.

The actual data is 60, 62, 62, 62, 62, 63, 63, 63, 63, 63, 64, 64, 64, 65, 65, 65, 66, 66, 66, 66, 67, 67, 68, 69, 69. There are 25 actual data items; the median is the thirteenth element, or 64. To find the mean, add up the individual elements shown above and divide by 25 to get 64.56. The data element of 63 is the mode of the data (the data that occur most frequently). Given the median, mean, and mode, choice (C) is the only true statement.

65. B

The primary focus of this question is Objective 0001:

Understand the foundations of reading development.

Morphemes are the smallest units of language to which a meaning is attached. In other words, morphemes are words or affixes. The syntactic cueing system, (B), encompasses the structural organization of language and involves morphemes, making it the correct choice. Choice (A) is not correct because the phonological system refers to the usage of phonemes (the smallest unit of sound) and their symbols (i.e., letters). Choice (C) is not correct because the semantic system refers to the meaning system (of which vocabulary is the major component). Choice (D) is not correct because the pragmatic system refers to the social aspects of how language is used.

66. B

The primary focus of this question is Objective 0016:

Understand and apply the principles and processes of scientific inquiry and investigation.

Inertia is every object's resistance to changing its speed and direction of travel. Things naturally want to keep going the way they were going. Furthermore, the more mass an object has, the more inertia it has, and the more it tends to resist changes in its state of motion. Therefore, because the bear has a larger inertia than the woman, the bear will have more difficulty changing direction rapidly, so (B) is correct. Choices (A), (C), and (D) are incorrect because the question is asking about using the mass of the bear to the woman's advantage, not about its vision or physical fitness.

67. A

The primary focus of this question is Objective 0002:

Understand skills and strategies involved in reading comprehension.

Print-rich means that the teacher labels items in her room, creates bulletin boards with words on them, and hangs up posters with words on them. Thus, a print-rich environment is created by the teacher. *Environmental print* involves words that occur in a child's life naturally. Examples include signs in bathrooms, names on stores, product labels, titles on books, street signs, newspaper headlines, words on billboards, etc. Choice (B) is not correct because there is environmental print in classrooms, even in underfunded schools. Choice (C) is not correct because labels in print-rich classrooms are not simply decorative; they exist to help children create relationships between objects and the symbolic code. Choice (D) is not correct because it is the opposite of the correct answer.

68. C

The primary focus of this question is Objective 0025:

Understand the roles, rights, and responsibilities of citizenship in the United States and the skills, knowledge, and attitudes necessary for successful participation in civic life.

Political ads do not aim to present an objective perspective on issues, (C). Political ads are meant to promote a candidate or an agenda. Choices (A), (B), and (D) are true statements, so they are *not* the correct choices because the question is asking you to find the *untrue* statement. Because airtime is expensive and ads are short (often only 30 seconds long), ad creators must try to represent a candidate's message in brief segments, (A). Ads aim to influence voters, reaching out to a candidate's base of support and hoping to sway undecided voters, (B). They often try to appeal to viewers' emotions through use of filmmaking techniques, (D), such as editing, music, lighting, text, and powerful images.

69. D

The primary focus of this question is Objective 0031:

Understand physical education concepts and practices related to the development of personal living skills.

The best way to prevent injury while skateboarding or roller skating is to wear protective equipment that fits properly. Even at a slow speed, a person could still take a dangerous spill, (A). Some people cannot avoid skating on hard pavement and gravel, (B), and practicing falling in any situation, (C), is dangerous and ill advised.

KAPLAN

70. D

The primary focus of this question is Objective 0001:

Understand the foundations of reading development.

The root word of *automaticity*, (D), is *automatic*. In education, repetition leads to learning. Reading skills develop when a large number of word meanings are automatic for us. Automaticity comes from repeated exposures to words. Choice (A) is not correct because phonemic awareness of a word simply means that a person recognizes that the word is made up of several sounds. Phonic analysis, (B), means that the person recognizes that the symbols in the words (the letters) represent the sounds in the word. Morphemic analysis, (C), involves looking at the various parts of the word that have meaning (the root, affixes).

71. D

The primary focus of this question is Objective 0011:

Understand skills and concepts related to number and numeration and apply these concepts to real-world situations.

Given the ratio of 2 : 3 : 5, consider this a mix divided into 10 pieces ($2 + 3 + 5 = 10$) of which 2 parts are seeds, 3 parts are raisins, and 5 parts are nuts. Five pounds is equivalent to 80 ounces ($5 \times 16 = 80$). Set up an equation: $10x = 80$. Divide both sides by 10 to get $x = 8$. There are 8×5 ounces of nuts = 40 ounces of nuts in the mix, choice (D).

72. A

The primary focus of this question is Objective 0017:

Understand and apply concepts, principles, and theories pertaining to the physical setting (including earth science, chemistry, and physics).

The law of conservation says that energy cannot be created or destroyed, but it can be converted from one form to another; therefore, in an idealized world without friction, the sum of potential and kinetic energies would remain constant. Potential energy means stored energy. Therefore, at the top of a hill, the roller coaster car has its maximum potential energy because it will speed up going down the hill and a minimum kinetic energy, or energy of motion, because it is moving slowly. As it gains speed moving down the hill, it gains kinetic energy but loses potential energy. Therefore, (B), (C), and (D) are incorrect.

73. C

The primary focus of this question is Objective 0020:

Understand the relationships among and common themes that connect mathematics, science, and technology and the application of knowledge and skills in these disciplines to other areas of learning.

The chart shows the percent of population change in New York State and the United States; it also breaks down the rate of population change by age and gender. According to the table, in New York State, people over 65 made up 12.9 percent of the population, whereas people under 5 made up 6.5 percent in 2000. Clearly, people over the age of 65 outnumbered children under 5, making (C) the correct answer. Choices (A) and (D) are incorrect—the U.S. population increased by 13.1 percent, whereas the New York State population increased by 5.5 percent, and females made up more than half of the New York State population in 2000. Although New York is the third most populous American state, (B), the table does not support this fact, making this choice incorrect.

74. B

The primary focus of this question is Objective 0002:

Understand the foundations of reading development.

Onsets are the beginning sounds in each syllable. *Rime* is the vowel + ending sound (if any) of the syllable. Every syllable has a rime (at least a vowel). Not all syllables have an onset. In the word *relay*, the first syllable has an onset of *ruh* and a rime of *ee*. The second syllable has an onset of *luh* and a rime of *ay*. If the final rime of a word is the same as another, the words rhyme (e.g., *relay* and *decay*). Choice (A) is not correct because the question states that the onsets are different. Homophones, (C), are not correct because homophones are two words with the same sound but with different meanings and usually different spellings. Morphemic pairs, (D), are two words with similar structure.

75. C

The primary focus of this question is Objective 0018:

Understand and apply concepts, principles, and theories pertaining to the living environment.

According to the food web, eagles have only two food sources—small mammals and rattlesnakes. Due to the scarcity of one of their main food sources, their population would most likely decrease, so (C) is correct. Small mammals are the main food source for rattlesnakes, roadrunners, and eagles; therefore, the populations of plants, insects, scorpions, and fruit would barely be affected, making (A) incorrect. The population of insects would not likely be much affected by the decline in the small mammal population because small mammals do not generally eat insects. Therefore, choice (B) is incorrect. It is unlikely that the population of rattlesnakes would increase because one of their food sources decreases, making (D) incorrect.

76. C

The primary focus of this question is Objective 0002:

Understand skills and strategies involved in reading comprehension.

This question determines whether a person can figure out words in context. By asking Joe what is wrong, the assumption can be made that Joe is the injured runner, (C). The person doing the asking is the runner with red hair, (A). A helper at the aid station, (B), could ask the question of Joe, but he would not be Joe. Choice (D) is not correct because there are enough context clues to give us the answer.

77. A

The primary focus of this question is Objective 0033:

Understand concepts and practices related to child development and care and apply knowledge of family and interpersonal relationships.

A caregiver should *always* test the water him- or herself before placing a baby in a bath. Children have thinner skin than adults and can be easily scalded at lower temperatures than adults; water at 140ºF can cause a serious burn in 3 seconds. Even water at 130ºF can produce a burn in 30 seconds—so (D) is an incorrect answer. It's best to place your whole hand in the water and move it around for several seconds, (A); if the water feels even slightly hot, it's too hot for a child. Dipping your finger into the water quickly, (B), wouldn't accurately gauge the temperature of the water. Choice (C), "Make sure the bath has equal amounts of hot and cold water," will not necessarily prevent burns.

78. A

The primary focus of this question is Objective 0010:

Use mathematical terminology and symbols to interpret, represent, and communicate mathematical ideas and information.

To solve this equation, first use the distributive property on the left-hand expression to distribute the 5 to the terms in parentheses: $3x + 5(x − 3)$ becomes $3x + 5 \times x − 5 \times 3 = 3x + 5x − 15$. Next, combine like terms on the left-hand expression: $8x − 15$. Now solve the simplified equation: $8x − 15 = 49$. Add 15 to both sides of the equation to produce $8x = 64$. When you divide both sides by 8, $x = 8$, choice (A).

79. D

The primary focus of this question is Objective 0017:

Understand and apply concepts, principles, and theories pertaining to the physical setting (including earth science, chemistry, and physics).

Because $P = \dfrac{\text{Force}}{\text{Area}}$, the more surface area the skier covers, the lower the pressure exerted on the ice, thereby reducing the possibility of cracking the ice. Standing on one foot, (C), creates the most pressure on the ice because this method provides the least amount of surface area. Tiptoeing, (A), and walking upright, (B), create more surface area than standing on one foot, but crawling, (D), provides the maximum amount of surface area of all the choices. Therefore, (D) is correct.

80. B

The primary focus of this question is Objective 0001:

Understand the foundations of reading development.

Phonemes are the individual sounds in a word. *My* has two sounds (*muh* and long *i*). *Sleep* has three sounds (*sluh*, long *e*, and *puh*). *Hog* has three sounds (*huh*, *ah*, and *guh*). Therefore, (B), one has two and two have three, is correct.

81. B

The primary focus of this question is Objective 0035:

Understand basic principles of career development; apply processes and skills for seeking and maintaining employment; and demonstrate knowledge of workplace skills, behaviors, and responsibilities.

Employers are looking for excellent communication skills—both listening and speaking. Therefore, it's best to demonstrate that you have these skills and are adept at using them, (B). Offering to write the school safety plan, (A), is inappropriate since you are applying for a teaching job, not an administrative job. To highlight your marketable skills, a better explanation for how intense physical training can prepare you for teaching, (C), is to describe how it improved your self-discipline and provided techniques for handling stress on the job. Choice (D), explaining how children love firefighters so they will enjoy being in your class, is an unfounded statement and is not necessarily true.

82. B

The primary focus of this question is Objective 0027:

Understand the concepts, techniques, and materials of the visual arts; analyze works of visual art; and understand the cultural dimensions and contributions of the visual arts.

The art of the Harlem Renaissance was characterized by a feeling of hope for the future and a better life. Similarly, *Los Tres Grandes*, who were working during the cultural revival after the Mexican Revolution, tapped into themes of hope for the future as they created art that educated and portrayed common people. Despair, (A), religion, (B), and nature, (D), are not common themes of the artistic movements mentioned in the question.

83. B

The primary focus of this question is Objective 0010:

Use mathematical terminology and symbols to interpret, represent, and communicate mathematical ideas and information.

One ton is equal to 2,000 pounds; therefore, 2 tons is 4,000 pounds. This is the maximum weight capacity of the truck. The materials hauled must be less than or equal to 4,000 pounds. As such, 4,000 must be greater than or equal to the weight hauled. The weight hauled is 60 pounds to represent one saw, plus 3 times x (the number of bricks), to produce the expression $3x + 60$. Given this set of data, (B) is the only correct choice.

84. B

The primary focus of this question is Objective 0021:

Understand major ideas, eras, themes, developments, and turning points in the history of New York State, the United States, and the world.

The shift from an agricultural to an industrial society in the United States had significant social effects on the nation, including the movement of people to cities, more interdependence and less autonomy for workers, and a disruption of the traditional family as people left the home to work (all opposites of (A), (C), and (D)). Factory jobs also changed the nature of work, creating the system of division of labor in which each worker performs one task of a job, instead of one worker completing all aspects of a job. Therefore, (B) is the only correct response.

85. A

The primary focus of this question is Objective 0017:

Understand and apply concepts, principles, and theories pertaining to the physical setting (including earth science, chemistry, and physics).

As it states in the question, the half-life is the time it takes for 50% of a substance to decay. Because the element in question has a half-life of 25 minutes, the answer equals three half lives (75 ÷ 25 = 3). Therefore, the 4 mg will decay by 50% three consecutive times as shown below:

4 mg   original sample

2 mg   1 half-life

1 mg   2 half-lives

0.5 mg   3 half-lives

Thus, choice (A) is correct.

86. D

The primary focus of this question is Objective 0012:

Understand patterns and apply the principles and properties of linear algebraic relations and functions.

Remember the slope-intercept form of an equation, which is $y = mx + b$, where m represents the slope and b represents the y-intercept. The y-intercept is the value of the y-coordinate where the graph crosses the y-axis, in this case at +4. The slope is calculated as $\frac{\text{rise}}{\text{run}}$. Pick two points on the graph and calculate the rise as the change in the y-values and the run as the change in the x-values. Use the points of (0,4) and (3,0), shown on the graph. Slope $= \frac{4-0}{0-3} = \frac{4}{-3} = -\frac{4}{3}$. Substitute these values into the slope-intercept form of an equation to get the correct equation of $y = -\frac{4}{3}x + 4$, choice (D).

87. C

The primary focus of this question is Objective 0024:

Understand economic and political principles, concepts, and systems and relate this knowledge to historical and contemporary developments in New York State, the United States, and the world.

Isolationism is a national policy of avoiding political and economic relations with other nations and staying out of other nations' conflicts and affairs. In his "Farewell Address," George Washington expressed an isolationist view by advising that the interest of the United States was best served by avoiding European conflicts. The remaining choices are all examples of actions or arrangements in which the United States was either in alliance or conflict with other nations. The Cuban Missile Crisis, (A), was a major confrontation in the Cold War between the United States and the Soviet Union. Choice (B), NAFTA, is an example of a trade arrangement among nations. Choice (D) marked the end of an isolationist period and the entrance of the United States into World War I.

88. C

The primary focus of this question is Objective 0009:

Understand formal and informal reasoning processes, including logic and simple proofs, and apply problem-solving techniques and strategies in a variety of contexts.

The most efficient way to solve this logic problem is by using a Venn diagram.

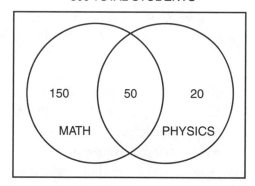

The number of students taking *both* mathematics and physics, 50, is represented by the overlap of the two circles in the diagram. This leaves 150 students who take mathematics and not physics. Likewise, 20 students are taking physics and not mathematics. Add the numbers in the circles, 150 + 50 + 20 = 220, to get the number of students taking one or both of the classes. To find the number of students who are taking neither mathematics nor physics, subtract the number of students who take one or both of the classes from the total number of students: 300 − 220 = 80, choice (C). Choice (D) is incorrect because it considers only students who are not taking both of the classes.

89. A

The primary focus of this question is Objective 0025:

Understand the roles, rights, and responsibilities of citizenship in the United States and the skills, knowledge, and attitudes necessary for successful participation in civic life.

Political parties have had an influential role in American politics, despite the fact that their existence is not referred to in the U.S. Constitution. Among their functions are selecting and supporting candidates who share their point of view (statement I) and creating voting blocs in Congress to back legislation that fits their beliefs (statement III). Choices (B), (C), and (D) are incorrect because in the U.S. political system, in which two political parties dominate, a political party's goal is to garner the majority of congressional votes, not create consensus among all representatives (statement II). Likewise, a political party does not aim to represent the views of all voters (statement IV) but rather to mobilize voters who agree with its political agenda.

KAPLAN

90. C

The primary focus of this question is Objective 0035:

Understand basic principles of career development; apply processes and skills for seeking and maintaining employment; and demonstrate knowledge of workplace skills, behaviors, and responsibilities.

First impressions are extremely important; therefore, it is always important to check resumes, cover letters, and other official paperwork carefully for spelling and other errors before you submit them. It's best to use the spell-check function, proofread the document yourself, *and* have a friend or family member proofread it as well. In the situation outlined in the question, the best choice is to look the words up in the dictionary, (C); it's best to verify with an official source that spelling is correct. You should avoid guessing, (A), or trusting someone else to know how to spell difficult words correctly, (B). Waiting until your computer is repaired, (D), could cost you valuable time, which might cost you the job.

Practice Written Assignment Sample Responses

For the written assignment, you were asked to write an essay that reflects accurately and effectively the skills and knowledge relevant to Objectives 0001 and 0002.

The written assignment is scored according to the following scale:

Score Point	Score Point Description
4	**Reflects a thorough command of the relevant knowledge and skills.** • Completely fulfills the purpose of the assignment by responding fully to the given task. • Demonstrates an accurate and highly effective application of the relevant knowledge and skills. • Provides strong support with high-quality, relevant examples and/or sound reasoning.
3	**Reflects a general command of the relevant knowledge and skills.** • Generally fulfills the purpose of the assignment by responding to the given task. • Demonstrates a generally accurate and effective application of the relevant knowledge and skills. • Provides support with some relevant examples and/or sound reasoning.

2	**Reflects a partial command of the relevant knowledge and skills.**
	• Partially fulfills the purpose of the assignment by responding in a limited way to the given task.
	• Demonstrates a limited, partially accurate and partially effective application of the relevant knowledge and skills.
	• Provides limited support with few examples and/or some flawed reasoning.
1	**Reflects little or no command of the relevant knowledge and skills.**
	• Fails to fulfill the purpose of the assignment.
	• Demonstrates a largely inaccurate and/or ineffective application of the relevant knowledge and skills.
	• Provides little or no support with few, if any, examples and/or seriously flawed reasoning.

Practice CST Written Assignment Sample Response

Prompt: There are five elements of literature. Delineate and define each element, and using a popular children's story (i.e., *Little Red Riding Hood*), give an example of each element from the story.

What follows are two sample responses with scoring explanations.

Poor response:

There are five elements of literature. These include title and author, plot, main characters, setting, and conclusion.

The title, in this case, Little Red Riding Hood, tells what the story is about. Sometimes, it can be misleading. The author is the person who wrote the book. In this case, it is a fairy tale and has been around a long time. Thus, it does not really have an author.

The plot tells what happens in the story. In this story, a child is on a journey to her grandmother's house. She stops to talk to a wolf. The wolf then tricks her. The main characters in the book are the little girl, the wolf, and her grandmother.

The setting is another element. The setting where the story takes place. This story takes place in the woods and at grandma's house. The final element is the conclusion. This is the final even that takes place. In this case, the grandmother is saved and everyone is happy.

Scoring Explanation:

This essay would receive a 2. It has some of the elements correct (the elements are plot, characters, setting, theme, and point of view), but others that are incorrect. Although the essay itself does contain correct grammar and spelling, it does not include transitions. In addition, three things were required for each of the elements. Each element was to be named, defined, and illustrated by an example from the story. In order to receive higher points, the writer would need to make sure all six elements were correct and that each of the three parts for each element was included.

Strong response:

The five elements of literature include plot, characters, setting, theme, and point of view. Each of these elements are present in every story.

The first element is plot. The plot is the action that takes place in a story. In the story, Little Red Riding Hood, the main action centers around Little Red Riding Hood. She is walking through the woods to her grandmother's house when she encounters a wolf. She gives the wolf information and then he uses that information to go to her grandmother's house to trick her. In the end, the grandmother and a woodcutter help destroy the wolf.

The second element involves the characters in the story. In this story, the characters are Little Red Riding Hood, the Big Bad Wolf, the grandmother, and the woodcutter. The characters are the main people (or animals) who are involved in the action of the story.

The third element is the setting. This involves the places where the action takes place in the story. In Little Red Riding Hood, there are two settings. The first is the woods on the way to the grandmother's house. The second is the grandmother's house.

The fourth element is theme. The theme is the moral of the story. It is the main message the story is trying to convey. In this story, the main idea for children to learn is not to talk to strangers. Because the little girl talks to the wolf, there is trouble later. Children reading this story learn not to talk to strangers.

The final element is point of view. This involves what person the story is written in as well as who is telling the story. This story is written in third person. It is, however, written from the point of view of the main character, the little girl.

In conclusion, there are five main elements of literature. Each contributes in its own way to the story. The plot, characters, and setting tell us what is happening to whom and where it is taking place. The theme tells us the moral of the story, and the point of view helps us know who is telling us the story.

Scoring Explanation:

This essay would receive a 4 because it answers the question fully. It includes the five correct elements (plot, characters, setting, theme, point of view), and it gives the three requirements for each element (name it, define it, and give an example from the story of it). The essay is well written and includes transitions. It follows the format of having an introductory paragraph (telling the main points), a body (explaining the main points), and conclusion (wrapping up the main points).

RESOURCES

GLOSSARY OF IMPORTANT NYSTCE TERMS

Ability—the degree of competence present in a student to perform a given physical or mental act.

Ability grouping—the grouping of students for instruction by ability or achievement for the purpose of reducing variability.

Abstract concepts—those concepts that can be acquired only indirectly through the senses or cannot be perceived directly through the senses.

Accountability—a concept in which the school system, and especially teachers, are held responsible for the quality of instruction and the progress of their students.

Accommodation—the process of modifying existing ways of doing things to fit new situations.

Achievement—level of attainment or proficiency.

Achievement motivation—the generalized tendency to strive for success without extrinsic reward.

Achievement test—a standardized test designed to measure levels of knowledge, understanding, abilities, or skills acquired in a particular subject already learned.

Active listening—being in tune with the words and thoughts of the speaker.

Active participation—ongoing involvement of the learner in the learning process both overtly and covertly.

Adaptive equipment—devices, aids, controls, supplies, or appliances that increase the ability of a student with a disability to function in school with independence and safety.

Advance organizers—preview questions, semantic maps, webs, and so forth that provide structure for new information to be presented to increase learners' comprehension.

Affective domain—the realm of feelings, emotions, and attitudes in people.

Affective objectives—behavioral objectives that emphasize changes in interest, attitudes, and values or a degree of adjustment, acceptance, or rejection.

Affiliation motive—the intrinsic desire to be with others.

Analysis—learning that involves the subdividing of knowledge to show how it fits together.

Analytical—dividing principle parts into its basic elements.

Annual Professional Performance Review (APPR)—mandate set forth in Section 100.2 of the Commissioner's Regulations that requires the work of all professional staff members be observed and monitored each year.

Anticipatory set—words or actions used by the teacher to create a mindset for learning in the learner.

Anxiety—a feeling of uneasiness associated with the fear of failure.

Application—learning that requires applying knowledge to produces a results; problem solving.

Assessment—a measure of the degree to which instructional objectives have been attained.

Assimilation—the process of fitting a new experience into existing ways of doing things.

At-risk students—students who have a great chance of dropping out of school before graduation; low-achieving, slower learners who fall between regular and special education, but are identified as possibly having or potentially developing a problem (physical, mental, educational, etc.) requiring further evaluation and/or intervention. Also referred to as "high-risk students."

Attending behavior—use of verbal and nonverbal cues by the listener that demonstrate he or she is listening with concern to what is being said.

Attention deficit hyperactivity disorder (ADHD)—a label applied to individuals who are extremely active, impulsive, distractible, and excitable and have great difficulty concentrating on what they are doing.

Attitude—a predisposition to act in a positive or negative way toward persons, idea, or events.

Attraction—friendship patterns in the classroom area.

Authentic assessment—assessment of students' performances in real-world, knowledge-application tasks; includes, but is not limited to, the use of projects, presentations, hands-on science demonstrations, oral interviews, portfolios, reflective journals, etc.

Base score—a score calculated as a point of comparison with later test scores. Students' base scores are relatively stable indicators of typical performance in a content area.

Behavior—what someone does.

Behavior disorder—a form of behavior that is socially unacceptable.

Behavior modification—the use of learning theory to reduce or eliminate undesirable behavior or to teach new responses.

Behavioral learning theory—explanations of learning that emphasize observable changes in behavior.

Behavioral (instructional) objectives—aims of instruction (or any learning activity) stated in terms of observable behavior.

Behaviorism—school of psychological thought that seeks to explain learning through observable changes in behavior.

Benchmark—a baseline of data.

Between-class ability grouping—a system of grouping in which students are assigned to classes according to achievement and abilities.

Bilingual—capable of using two languages, but usually with differing levels of skills.

Bilingual education—programs designed to help students acquire English proficiency while they continue to learn the subject areas appropriate to their age and grade levels in their native language.

Bloom's taxonomy of the cognitive domain—a hierarchy of six levels of thinking, often referred to as levels of complexity; level one is the easiest. 1) Knowledge (memorizing a fact); 2) Comprehension (understanding); 3) Application (applying concepts); 4) Analysis (breaking down complex information); 5) Synthesis (putting together complex ideas); and 6) Evaluation (judging or forming an opinion).

Board of Regents—the governing body of the University of the State of New York. Established in 1784, it consists of 16 regents elected by the legislature for five-year terms. They exercise legislative functions over the state educational system.

Brainstorming—a teaching strategy in which students generate ideas, judgments of the ideas of others are forbidden, and ideas are used to create a flow of new ideas.

Burnout—the condition of losing interest and motivation in teaching.

Campus committee—a committee or consortium of administrators, teachers, parents, etc. that represents a campus and makes decisions affecting the campus.

Campus leadership—refers to the principal, assistant principal, or the campus leadership team.

Carnegie credits—credits given at the successful completion of a course towards a high school diploma.

Centration—focusing attention on only one aspect of an object or situation.

Chapter 1—a federal program that gives money for education to districts that have a high number of disadvantaged students.

Checking for understanding—ongoing techniques used by a teacher during instruction to verify student comprehension.

Choral response—response to a question made by the whole class in unison; useful when there is only one correct answer.

Chronological age—age in calendar years.

Chunking—memorization technique that involves grouping or clustering more than one particular piece of data or more than one stimuli in some meaningful way in order to remember it. For example, telephone numbers can be remembered as two chunks of information, the first three digits and the last four digits, rather than as seven separate digits.

Classical conditioning—a form of conditioning in which a neutral stimulus (the bell in Pavlov's experiment) comes to elicit a response (salivation) after it is repeatedly paired with reinforcement (food).

Classroom control—the process of influencing student behavior in the classroom.

Classroom management—the teacher's system of establishing a climate for learning, including techniques for preventing and handling student behavior.

Closure—a component in the lesson in which the teacher summarizes the lesson and brings it to an appropriate conclusion.

Coaching—teaching by an "expert" who gives feedback on performance; can be as effective as athletic coaching; results in about 83 percent retention of learning.

Cognition—the mental operations involved in thinking.

Cognitive development—increasing complexity of thought and reasoning.

Cognitive domain—the psychological field of mental activity.

Cognitive objectives—behavioral objectives that emphasize remembering or reproducing something that has presumably been learned or that involve the solving of some intellectual task.

Cohesiveness—the collective feeling that the class members have about the classroom group; the sum of the individual members' feelings about the group.

Comprehension—learning that involves making interpretations of previously learned materials.

Compulsory education—legal mandated education for all students within certain age groups.

Compulsory school age—age at which a child must begin school and the age when a student is required to remain in school.

Computer assisted instruction (CAI)—instruction in which a computer is used to present instructional material.

Concept—an abstract idea common to a set of objects, conditions, events, or processes.

Concept map—a procedure for organizing and graphically displaying and organizing relationships among ideas relevant to a given topic.

Concrete concepts—concepts that can be perceived directly through one of the five senses.

Concrete operations—Piagetian stage (7 to 11 years) in which learners begin to decenter, make inferences about reality, and use inductive reasoning. They can also group items into categories and are capable of conserving, reversing, and putting things in order by size or number.

Conditioned reinforcers—reinforcers that are learned.

Consequence—a condition that follows a behavior, designed to weaken or strengthen the behavior.

Conservation—the logical thinking ability to recognize an invariant property under different conditions.

Constructivism—theory of cognitive development that holds that learners actively build their own understandings by interacting with the environment and adjusting prior knowledge and understandings accordingly.

Content validity—the degree to which the content covered by a measurement device matches the instruction that preceded it.

Continuous reinforcement schedule—a reinforcement schedule in which every occurrence of the desired behavior is reinforced.

Convergent question—a question that has only one correct response.

Convergent thinking—thinking that occurs when the task, or question, is so structured that the number of possible appropriate conclusions is limited (usually one conclusion).

Cooperative learning—teaching strategy that groups together children with differing abilities for them to accomplish a task or solve problems, such as working on a big math puzzle.

Core curriculum—required curriculum for all students.

Corporal punishment—any act of physical force upon a student for the purpose of punishing that student. Corporal punishment is not allowed in New York State public schools. Physical restraint may be used to prevent injury to people or damage to property.

Creation—cognitive learning that entails combining elements and parts in order to form a new or whole or to produce an evaluation based on specified criteria.

Creative thinking—putting together information to come up with new ideas or understandings.

Critical thinking—complex thinking skills that include the ability to evaluate information, generate insights, and come to objective conclusions by logically examining the problem and the evidence.

Cross-age tutoring—peer tutoring in which an older student teachers a younger student; recommended over same-age tutoring; tutor should be two to three grade levels ahead of tutee.

Cues—signals as to what behaviors will be reinforced or punished.

Cultural pluralism—the condition in which all cultural groups are valued components of the society and the language and traditions of each group are maintained.

Culturally fair test—a test designed to reduce cultural bias.

Dangle—a lesson transition during which the teacher leaves a lesson hanging while tending to something else in the classroom.

Decentralization—a term that refers to decision making being done at the lowest possible level rather than, traditionally, at the highest level.

Decision making—the making of well-thought-out choices from among several alternatives.

Deductive learning—learning that proceeds from the general to the specifics.

Deductive reasoning—reasoning that proceeds from general principles to a logical conclusion.

Deficiency needs—Maslow's term for the lower-level needs in his hierarchy: survival, safety, belonging, and self-esteem.

Delayed reinforcement—reinforcement of desired action that took place at an earlier time.

Descriptive data—data that have been organized, categorized, or quantified by an observer but do not involve a value judgment.

Development—growth, adaptation, or change over the course of a lifetime.

Developmentally appropriate—term that applies to providing a child with a program and a learning environment that provides for all areas of the child's development: physical, emotional, social, and cognitive.

Developmental level—level at which a child is performing compared to a given norm.

Diagnostic evaluation—evaluation administered before instruction to determine students' strengths and weaknesses.

Diagnostic procedure—procedures to determine what pupils are capable of doing with respect to given learning tasks.

Diagnostic test—an evaluation that provides information that can be used to identify specific areas of strength and weakness.

Direct instruction—a deductive model of instructional delivery that encourages high engagement of learners and requires structured, accomplishable tasks.

Direct teaching—a frontal model of instruction that has the teacher in control of all class activities.

Disability—any hindrance or difficulty imposed by a physical, mental, or emotional problem.

Discipline—in teaching, the process of controlling student behavior in the classroom.

Discovery learning—instructional approach in which students learn through their own active explorations of concepts and principles.

Disjunctive concepts—concepts that have two or more sets of alternative conditions under which the concept appears.

Distance education—the use of telecommunications to deliver live instruction by content experts to remote geographic settings.

Distributed practice—practice repeated at intervals over a period of time.

Diversity—the condition of having a variety of groups in the same setting.

Divergent thinking—the type of thinking whereby an individual arrives at a new or unique answer that has not been completely determined by information he or she has remembered.

Disabled—the condition of an individual who had lost physical, social or psychological functioning that significantly interferes with normal growth and development.

Drill and practice—learning from repeated performance.

Due process—procedural safeguards afforded students, parents, and teachers that protect individual rights.

Early childhood—the period from the end of infancy to about 5 or 6 years of age; preschool years.

Eclectic—utilizing the best from a variety of sources.

Educational goal—a desired instructional outcome that is broad in scope.

Educational placement—the setting in which a student receives educational services.

Effective school correlates—a body of research identifying the characteristics of effective and ineffective schools: (1) safe and orderly environment, (2) climate of high expectations for success, (3) instructional leadership, (4) clear and focused mission, (5) opportunity to learn and student time on task, (6) frequent monitoring of student progress, and (7) home/school relations.

Effective schools research—educational research focused on identifying unusually effective schools, studying the underlying attributes of their programs and personnel, and designing techniques to operationalize these attributes in less effective schools.

Effective teacher—one who is able to bring about intended learning outcomes.

Egocentric—believing that everyone sees the world as you do.

Egocentrism—Piaget's term for the preoperational child's inability to distinguish between his or her own and one another's perceptions.

Empathy—the ability to understand the feelings of another person.

Empirical questions—questions that require that a judgment be made or a value be put on something.

Engaged time or time on-task—the actual time individual students spend as active participants in the learning process.

English as a second language (ESL)—the teaching of English to a non-English-speaking student; not only includes the teaching of the English language but also cultural adjustment elements.

Enrichment—the process of providing richer and more varied content through strategies that supplement the standard curriculum.

Enrichment activities—assignments or activities designed to broaden or deepen the knowledge of students who master classroom lessons quickly.

Epistemology—the study of how knowledge is acquired.

Equal opportunities for success—in cooperative learning, calculations of team achievement must be designed to ensure that equal individual improvement results in equal individual contribution to the team score, in spite of differences among teammates in absolute achievement.

Equilibration—the process of restoring balance between what is understood and what is experienced.

Essentialism—educational philosophy that holds that a common core of knowledge and ideals should be the focus of curriculum.

Ethnicity—the ethnic identity (Caucasian, African American, Hispanic American, Native American, Asian American, etc.) of an individual or group.

Ethnocentrism—the belief that one's culture is better than any other culture.

Eurocentrism—believing European culture is superior.

Evaluation—the cognitive process of establishing and applying standards in judging materials and methods.

Evaluation questions—questions that require that a judgment be made or a value be put on something.

Evocation—creating something through the power of memory or imagination.

Exceptional child—a child who deviates from the average child in any of the following ways: mental characteristics, sensory ability, neuromotor or physical characteristics, social behavior, communication ability, or multiple handicaps.

Explanation—a component in the lesson cycle that contains what the teacher does to move learning to the student and the way in which the teacher accomplishes this transfer.

Explaining behavior—planned teacher talk designed to clarify any idea, procedure, or process not understood by a student.

Exposition—a statement intended to give information.

Extension—a component in the lesson cycle that involves enlarging or expanding the original objective.

Extinction—the gradual disappearance of a behavior through the removal or the withholding of reinforcement.

Extraneous—not essential or vital.

Extreme—extending far beyond the norm.

Extrinsic motivation—motivation created by events or rewards outside the individual.

Facts—well-grounded, clearly established pieces of information.

Factual questions—questions that require the recall of information through recognition or rote memory.

Feedback—information from the teacher to the student, or vice versa, that provides disclosure about the reception of the intended message.

Field-dependent—learning style in which patterns are perceived as whole.

Field-independent—learning style in which separate parts of a pattern are apparent.

Fine-tuning—making small adjustments in the planned procedures for a lesson during teaching of the lesson.

Fixed-interval reinforcement schedule—a pattern in which reinforcement is given only at certain periodic times; often results in a great deal of work (cramming) at the last minute, just before the reinforcement is given. Ex.: Final exams are fixed-interval reinforcements.

Fixed-ratio reinforcement schedule—a pattern in which reinforcement is given after a desired observable behavior has occurred a fixed number (1, 5, 10, etc.) of times; effective in motivating students to do a great deal of work, but runs the risk of losing its value if the reinforcing is done too frequently. If modified so that reinforcement initially occurs every time, then switches to every second time, then every third time, and so on, the frequency of the behavior increases, and the behavior becomes highly resistant to extinction. Ex.: Giving students stars after they read 10 books is fixed-ratio reinforcement.

Flip-flop—a lesson transition in which the teacher changes back and forth from one subject or activity to another.

Focus—component in the lesson in which the teacher secures the attention of the students and communicates the lesson objectives. Also, a center of interest of activity.

Focusing question—a question used to focus students' attention on a lesson or on the content of a lesson.

Formal operations—Piagetian stage (11 to adulthood) in which learners are ready to engage in logical and abstract thought and to reason hypothetically about situations contrary to fact.

Formative evaluation—evaluation that takes place both before and during the learning process; used to guide the content and pace of lessons.

Free Appropriate Public Education (FAPE)—education and related services provided at public expense, under public supervision and direction, and without charge to the individual.

Frequency measurement—a measure of the number of times specified observable behaviors are exhibited in a constant time interval.

Gender bias—favoring one gender over the other.

Generalization—the carryover of learning from one setting to a different setting.

Gifted—a label applied to students who are exceptionally intelligent, creative, and/or talented.

Goals—extremely broad statements of school or instructional purposes.

Goal structure—the degree to which students have to cooperate or compete for classroom rewards.

Grades—letters, numbers, or symbols used to indicate the quality of work performed by students.

Graphic organizers—visual, hierarchical overviews designed to show relationships among the important concepts of a lesson; types include semantic mapping, webbing, clustering, and structured overviews.

Gross-motor skills—skills that require the use of the large muscles of the body.

Group discussion—verbal interaction with other learners.

Group contingencies—strategies in which the entire class (subgroup of students within the class) is rewarded on the basis of everyone's behavior; removes peer support for misbehavior.

Group-focus behaviors—behaviors that teachers use to maintain a focus on the group rather than on an individual student during individual recitations.

Group investigation—a cooperative-learning strategy in which students brainstorm a set of questions on a subject, form learning teams to find answers to questions, and make presentations to the whole class.

Grouping, heterogeneous—a method of grouping in which students with a broad range of abilities, interests, achievement levels, and backgrounds are grouped together.

Grouping, homogeneous—a method of grouping in which students with similar abilities, interests, achievement levels, and backgrounds are grouped together.

Group process skills—interactive skills needed to function as a team to achieve desired goals.

Growth needs—Maslow's term for the three higher-level needs in his hierarchy: intellectual achievement, aesthetic appreciation, and self-actualization.

Guided practice—a component in the lesson in which the student practices the learning under the direct guidance of the teacher.

Halting time—a teacher's pause in talking, used to give students time to think about presented materials or directions.

Handicap—any hindrance or difficulty imposed by a physical, mental, or emotional problem; preferred term is *disability*.

Hands-on—refers to the firsthand work by students with the tools, processes, procedures, etc.

Hemispheric dominance—attributing of certain specialized abilities to the right or left side of the brain.

Hidden curriculum—pervasive moral atmosphere that characterizes a school.

Holistic evaluation—determination of the overall quality of a piece of work or an endeavor.

Humanistic education—educational system designed to achieve affective outcomes or psychological growth oriented toward improving self-awareness and mutual understanding among people.

Hypothesize—to make an educated guess to explain a phenomenon.

Identity foreclosure—an adolescent's premature choice of a role.

Identity diffusion—inability of an adolescent to develop a clear sense of self.

Imagery—use of mental imagery to improve retention.

"I" messages—clear teacher messages that tell students how the teacher feels about problem situations and implicitly ask for corrected behaviors.

Imitation—carrying out the basic rudiments of a skill when given directions and supervision.

Implied—said or expressed indirectly.

Improvement scores—scores calculated by comparing the entering achievement levels with the performance after instruction.

Impulsivity—the tendency to respond quickly but often without regard to accuracy.

Inclusion—philosophy that believes education should be provided to all students, including those with severe handicaps—as well as equitable opportunities to receive effective educational services with the needed supplementary aids and support services in age-appropriate classes in the neighborhood schools—in order to prepare students for productive lives as full members of the society.

Independent practice—a component in the lesson cycle in which students practices the learning on their own.

Independent practice—practice by the student of the learning without direct supervision (e.g., homework); should occur only when the learner has mastered the learning objective.

Individual accountability—in cooperative learning, making sure each individual is responsible for his or her own learning.

Individual instruction—teaching to meet the needs, interests, and abilities of each learner.

Individuals with Disabilities Act (IDEA)—a federal law that makes it possible for states and localities to receive federal funds to assist in the education of students with disabilities.

Individualized Education Plan (IEP)—a written statement of instruction specially designed to meet the needs of a child with a disability.

Inductive reasoning—the process of drawing a general conclusion based on several examples.

Inference—a conclusion derived from, and bearing some relation to, assumed premises.

Informational objectives—abbreviated instructional objectives in which only the student performance and the product are specified.

Infrastructure—an underlying base or foundation of a building or organization.

Inquiry—obtaining information by asking.

Inquiry/discovery model—an inductive teaching model focusing on student investigation and explanation of a situation and designed to promote problem-solving skills and critical thinking skills; steps involved are defining the problem, developing hypotheses, data gathering, organizing and formulating explanations, and analyzing the process.

Inquiry learning—like discovery learning, except that the learner designs the processes to used in resolving a problem. It requires higher levels of mental operation than does discovery learning.

Instigate—to stir up; to start.

Instruction—any method or procedure used in the school faculty to impart knowledge or develop skills.

Instructional event—any activity or set of activities in which students are engaged (with or without the teacher) for the purpose of learning.

Instructional grouping—dividing a class into small subunits for purposes of teaching.

Instructional strategy—the plan for teaching a lesson, unit, or course. Its two components are the methodology and the procedure.

Instructional teams—a group of teachers who share responsibility for planning, instructing, and evaluating a common group of students.

Instructional time—blocks of class time translated into productive learning activities.

Integrated language arts—teaching reading, writing, and spelling not as separate subjects but as an unsegregated whole.

Intelligence—general ability to learn and understand.

Intelligence quotient (IQ)—a measure of intelligence for which 100 is the score assigned to those of average intelligence.

Interdisciplinary approach—participation or cooperation of two or more disciplines; used for multidisciplinary approach.

Interdisciplinary instruction—teaching by themes or activities that cross subject area boundaries. Most frequently, interdisciplinary instruction involves bringing ideas, concepts, and/or facts from one subject area to bear on issues or problems raised in another.

Interference—a process that occurs when information to be recalled gets mixed up with other information.

Intermittent reinforcement schedule—a pattern in which correct responses are reinforced often but not following each occurrence of the desirable behavior.

Intern teaching—like student teaching, except an intern teacher usually is paid a salary.

Internalization—the extent to which an attitude or value becomes a part of the learner.

Internet—literally, a system of computer networks; used by a community of users to communicate with one another around the planet.

Interval reinforcement schedule—a pattern in which reinforcement is dispensed after desired observable behavior has occurred for a specified length of time.

Intrinsic motivation—an internal source of motivation associated with activities that are rewarding in themselves.

Intuition—knowing without conscious reasoning.

Invented spelling—spelling based on how a word sounds; used when the writer does not know the conventional spelling of the word.

Inventory questions—questions asking individuals to describe their thoughts, feelings, and manifested actions.

Irrelevant—having no application to a specific circumstance.

Judgment—estimate of present conditions or prediction of future conditions; involves comparing information to some referent.

Knowledge learning—cognitive learning that entails the simple recall of learned materials.

Knowledge questions—questions requiring the student to recognize or recall information.

Labeling—assigning a special education category to an individual.

Laboratory learning model—an instructional model focusing on "hands-on" manipulation and firsthand experience.

Language experience approach—an approach to teaching reading and language arts that uses words and stories from the student's own language and experiences.

Large muscle activity—physical movement involving the limbs and large muscles.

Leadership—those behaviors that help the group move toward the accomplishment of its objectives.

Learned helplessness—the learned belief, based on experience, that one is doomed to failure.

Learning—a relatively permanent change in an individual's capacity for performance as a result of experience.

Learning center—a defined space where materials are organized in such a way that children learn without the teacher's constant presence and direction.

Learning disability—a disorder in one or more of the basic psychological processes involved in understanding or in using language, spoken or written, which manifests itself in an imperfect ability to listen, think, speak, read, write, spell, or to do mathematical calculations. A student who exhibits a discrepancy of 50 percent or more between expected achievement and actual achievement determined on an individual basis shall be deemed to have a learning disability.

Learning styles—orientations for approaching learning tasks and processing information in certain ways.

Least restrictive environment (LRE)—requirement that a disabled student must be placed in a setting that enables him or her to function to the fullest capability; one of the principles outlined in the Individuals with Disabilities Education Act (IDEA).

Lecture—planned teacher talk designed to convey important information in an effective and efficient manner.

Limited English proficiency (LEP)—limited mastery of English.

Long-term memory—component of the memory system that can hold a large amount of information for a long periods of time.

Magnet school—a school that focuses on special themes (i.e., science, mathematics, language arts, etc.).

Mainstreaming—including students with special needs in regular education classrooms for some or all of the school day.

Maintenance—the continuation of a behavior.

Mandated time—the set amount of time, established by the state, during which school is in session.

Manipulation—independent performance of a skill.

Massed practice—repeated practice in a concentrated period of time.

Mastery learning—a teaching strategy designed to permit as many students as possible to achieve objectives to a specified level with the assignment of grades based on achievement of objectives at specified levels.

Mastery learning model—a five-step pattern of instruction that emphasizes the mastery of stated objectives by all students by allowing learning time to be flexible.

Measurement—the assignment of numerical values to objects, events, performances, or products to indicate how much of a characteristic being measured they possess.

Melting pot theory—the belief that other cultures should assimilate and blend into the dominant culture.

Mental age—an age estimate of an individual's level of mental development, derived from a comparison of the individual's IQ score and chronological age.

Mental retardation (MR)—condition, usually present at birth, that results in below average intellectual skills and poor adaptive behavior.

Mental set—a student's attitude toward beginning the lesson.

Mentors—experienced teachers who support, guide, and advise the development of younger or less experienced teachers.

Metacognition—thinking about one's own thinking and thought processes.

Metaphor—a figure of speech in which a term is transferred to designate another object.

Methodology—the patterned behaviors that form the definite steps by which the teacher influences learning.

Minority group—an ethnic or racial group that is a minority within a larger society.

Mission statement—a broad statement of the unique purpose for which the organization exists and the specific function it performs.

Mnemonic—a method to aid memory such as keyword association, loci, and so forth.

Mnemonics memorization—techniques that are "tricks" used to remember things—for example, "*i* before *e* except after *c* or when sounded like *a*, as in *neighbor* or *weigh*."

Modeling—the process of providing models to students by teacher or student demonstration or the provision of a finished or completed product or procedure.

Monopoly—exclusive control over a commercial activity.

Mood—an impression on the feelings of an observer.

Motivation—the willingness of drive to accomplish something.

Movement management behaviors—those behaviors that the teacher uses to initiate, sustain, or terminate a classroom activity.

Multicultural education—a structured process designed to foster understanding, acceptance, and constructive relations among people of many different cultures.

National Education Association (NEA)—largest professional educators organization in the United States; its purpose includes working for improved education and enhancing the status of teachers.

Nationalistic—devotion to the interests or culture of a particular nation.

Negative reinforcement—strengthening a behavior by release from an unpleasant situation.

Negligence—lack of ordinary care in one's action; failure to exercise due care.

No-lose tactic—a problem-resolution tactic whereby a teacher and one or more students negotiate a solution such that neither comes out the loser.

Nondiscriminatory testing—assessment that properly takes into account a child's cultural and linguistic diversity.

Noninstructional responsibility—duties assumed by, or assigned to, teachers who are outside of their regular teaching responsibilities.

Nonverbal cues—eye contact, facial expressions, gestures, movement toward someone, placing a hand on someone's shoulder, etc.

Nonverbal reinforcement—using some form of physical action as a positive consequence to strengthen a behavior or event.

Normal curve—bell-shaped curve that describes the distribution of many natural phenomena; approximately 95 percent of the scores fall within two standard deviations of the mean.

Norming group—a large sample of people who are similar to those for whom a particular standardized test is designed and who take the test to establish the group standards. The norming group serves as a comparison group for scoring the test.

Norm-referenced—a standardized test that focuses on a comparison of a student's score to the average of a norm group.

Norms—rules that apply to all members of a group.

Novice—a person who is inexperienced in performing a particular activity.

Objective—a clear and unambiguous description of instructional intent.

Observable behavior—an overt act by an individual.

Observation—the process of looking and listening, noticing the important elements of a performance or a products.

On-task behavior—student behavior that is appropriate to the task.

Outcome-based education (OBE)—an effort designed to focus and organize all of the school's programs and instructional efforts around clearly defined outcomes that students are able to demonstrate.

Overlapping—teacher's ability to attend to disruptions without stopping the lesson.

Overlapping behaviors—those behaviors by which the teacher indicates that he or she is attending to more than one thing when several things are going on at a particular time.

Overlearning—practicing beyond the point of mastery to improve retention.

Pacing—determining the speed of performance of a learning task.

Paired-associate learning—a task involving the linkage of two items in a pair so that when one is presented the other can be recalled.

Paradigm—a pattern or model; sets of rules that establish boundaries.

Paraprofessional—an adult who is not a credentialed teacher but works in the classroom with and under the supervision of a credentialed teacher.

Parenting styles—the different ways parents interact with their children, including (1) authoritarian—parents are restrictive, place limits and controls on the child, and offer very little give-and-take; (2) authoritative—parents are warm and nurturing and encourage the child to be independent, but still place limits, demands, and controls on the child's actions; (3) permissive indulgent—parents allow great freedom to the child and are undemanding, but are responsive and involved in the child's life; (4)

permissive indifferent—parents are neglectful, unresponsive, and highly uninvolved in the child's life.

Pedagogy—the art and science of teaching.

Peers—individual's equal in age and/or status.

Peer tutoring—an instruction practice in which students assist with the instruction of other students needing supplemental instruction; principal types are same-age tutoring, where the tutor is the same age as the tutee, and cross-age tutoring, where the tutor is older than the tutee.

Performance assessment—assessment in which students create an answer or a product that demonstrates their acquisition of knowledge or skill.

Performance-based assessment—testing method other than multiple-choice or true/false that requires students to create an answer or product that demonstrates their knowledge or skills in a subject area.

PINS (Person in Need of Supervision)—a petition that is filed in family court showing that a youth needs more supervision than is being given by the family. The court may require the family to meet certain goals. If the goals are not met, the court has the authority to remove the youth from the home.

Planning—decision-making process in which the teacher decides what, why, when, and how to teach; composed of three elements: task analysis, planning for student behaviors/outcomes, and planning for teacher behaviors/strategies.

Portfolios—a collection of a student's work and achievements that is used to assess past accomplishments and future potential; can include finished work in a variety of media and can contain materials from several courses over a period of time. In one method of portfolio assessment, the teacher or academic team confers and collaborates with the student on the portfolio, reviewing its contents, adding to it, selecting from it, and choosing a best work for review.

Positive reinforcement—strengthening a behavior by giving a desirable reward.

PQ4R—a study strategy where students preview the reading, create questions, read to answer questions, reflect, recite, and review the original material.

Precision—psychomotor ability to perform an act accurately, efficiently, and harmoniously.

Preoperational—Piagetian stage (2 to 7 years) characterized by egocentrism (self-indulgence and greed), semilogical reasoning, and limited social awareness.

Primacy effect—the tendency to be able to recall the first things in a list.

Primary motives—forces and drives, such as hunger, thirst, and the need for security, that are basic and inborn.

Primary reinforcers—questions following a response that requires the respondent to provide more support, be clearer or more accurate, or offer greater specificity or originality.

Principal—administrator in charge of individual schools.

Principle—a rule that explains the relationship between or among factors.

Prior knowledge—information and concepts classified and stored in long-term memory that can be related to new information being taught.

Private speech—children's self-talk.

Probationary teacher—an untenured teacher.

Probing questions—questions that follow a student response and require the student to think and respond more thoroughly than in the initial response.

Procedure—a sequence of steps and activities that have been designed to lead to the acquisition of learning objectives.

Productive questions—broad, open-ended questions with many correct responses that require students to use their imagination, to think creatively, and to produce something unique.

Professional autonomy—freedom of professionals or groups of professionals to function independently.

Professional development—education undertaken by individuals in order to improve themselves. It is a voluntary, lifelong, continuing program of personal and professional growth.

Programmed instruction—a program in which students work through specially constructed print or electronic self-instructional materials at their own pace.

Progressive—making use of or interested in new ideas, findings, or opportunities.

Prompting questions—questions that involve the use of hints and clues to aid students in answering questions or in correcting an initial response.

Puberty—developmental stage at which a person becomes capable of reproduction.

Public Law 94-142—federal law requiring that all schools receiving federal funds provide an education for every handicapped child in the least restrictive environment.

Pull-out programs—programs in which students with special needs are taken out of regular classes for instruction.

Punishment—using unpleasant consequences to weaken or extinguish an undesirable behavior.

Qualified reinforcement—reinforcement of only the acceptable parts of an individual's response or action or of the attempt itself.

Questionnaire—a list of written statements regarding attitudes, feelings, and opinions that are to be read and responded to.

Rating scale—a scale of values arranged in order of quality describing someone or something being evaluated.

Ratio reinforcement schedule—a pattern in which reinforcement is dispensed after a desired observable behavior has occurred a certain number of times.

Reality therapy—therapy in which individuals are helped to become responsible and able to satisfy their needs in the real world.

Receiving—affective learning that involves being aware of, and willing to freely attend to, a stimulus.

Recency effect—the tendency to be able to recall the last things in a list.

Reciprocal teaching—an instructional approach in which the teacher helps the students learn to ask teacher-type questions; designed to help low-achievers learn reading.

Redirecting—the technique of asking several individuals to respond to a question in light of or to add new insight to the previous responses.

Referent—that to which you compare the information you have about an individual to form a judgment.

Reflection—giving direct feedback to individuals about the way their verbal and nonverbal messages are being received; also, quiet thought or contemplation that includes analysis of past experience.

Reflective listening—the act of listening with feeling as well as with cognition.

Reflectivity—examining and analyzing oneself and one's thoughts before taking action.

Regular class—a typical classroom designed to serve students without disabilities.

Rehearsal—the process of repeating information, either aloud or silently, as a means of holding it in short-term memory and preparing it for long-term memory.

Reinforcement—using consequences to strengthen the likelihood of a behavior or event.

Reinforcement schedule—the frequency with which reinforcers are given; common schedules are fixed-ratio, which includes continuous reinforcement; variable-ratio; fixed-interval; and variable-interval.

Relational concepts—concepts that describe relationships between items.

Reliability—the consistency of test scores obtained in repeated administrations to the same individuals on different occasions or with different sets of equivalent items.

Remediation—instruction given to students having difficulty learning that supplements whole-class instruction.

Repertoire—a set of alternative routines or procedures, all of which serve some common purpose and each of which serves some additional, unique purpose.

Reproduced data—data that have been recorded in video, audio, or verbatim transcript form and can be reproduced when desired.

Responding—affective learning that involves freely attending to a stimulus as well as voluntarily reacting to it in some way.

Restructuring—a radically altering reform of schools as organizations and of the way schooling is delivered.

Reteaching—instruction in the original objective that is substantially different from the initial instruction; differences may be reflected in an adjustment or modification of time allocation, practice depth/length, or instructional modality.

Review closure—a type of closure technique whose main characteristic is an attempt to summarize the major points of a presentation or discussion.

Reversibility—the ability to change direction in thinking and go back to a starting point.

Rhetoric—the art of speaking or writing effectively.

Rhetorical—question asked for effect without expecting an answer.

Ripple effect—the spreading of behaviors from one individual to others through imitation.

Role-playing—an activity in which students act out roles.

Routine—an established pattern of behavior.

Rote learning—memorization of facts or associations.

Rubric—guidelines used in determining scores; typically it contains a scale that states the dimensions being assessed and descriptors that summarize the requirements for properly locating each work on the scale.

Salad-bowl theory—the belief that the various cultures should mix but still retain their unique characteristics.

Same-age tutoring—peer tutoring in which one student teaches another student (usually, a classmate) of the same age; runs the risk of being ineffective because resentment toward the same-age tutor (especially if he or she is a classmate) may develop.

Scaffolding—providing support for learning and problem solving, such as giving clues, reminders, encouragement, examples, etc.; needed more during early stages of learning and should be diminished later to allow the learner to become self-directed.

Schema—mental diagrams that guide behavior.

Schizophrenia—abnormal behavior patterns and personality disorganization accompanied by less than adequate contact with reality.

School board—an elected body that oversees and manages a public school district's affairs, personnel, and properties.

School climate—sum total of all the relationships of all the people within the school.

Secondary motives—forces and drives, such as the desire for money or grades, that are learned through association with primary motives.

Section 504—a section of the Rehabilitation Act of 1973 that is a federal civil rights statute prohibiting discrimination against persons with disabilities in programs receiving federal financial assistance.

Self-actualization—reaching one's fullest potential.

Self-concept—how a person thinks of him or herself.

Self-directed learning—learning by designing and directing one's own learning activities.

Self-esteem—the value a person places on what he or she is.

Self-fulfilling prophecy—actions or behaviors that occur because of a belief or prediction that they will occur.

Sensorimotor stage—Piagetian stage (birth to 2 years) characterized primarily through sense and motor activity development.

Set induction—teacher actions and statements at the outset of a lesson to get student attention, to trigger interest, and to establish a conceptual framework.

Short-term memory—component of the memory system that can hold a limited amount of information for a short period of time.

Silent time—the time the teacher waits following a student response before replying or continuing with the presentation.

Simulation—an enactment of an artificial situation or event that represents real life as much as possible, but with most of the risk and complicating factors removed; works best when students are assigned roles and teacher acts as a facilitator but does not become actively involved in the make-believe situation.

Site-based decision making—moving some decisions traditionally made by the central office to the building level and, in turn, allowing staff and community members the opportunity to participate in some decisions formerly made unilaterally by the principal.

Site-based management (SBM)—school-level (campus) governance that has been mandated by state legislation. It mandates input from the community, parents, teachers, and administration on topics concerning the students. Decisions are made by consensus.

Small muscle activity—physical movement involving the fine muscles of the hand.

Social objective—a requirement of the cooperative-learning model dealing with the social skills, roles and relationships, and group processes that students need to accomplish the learning task.

Sociodrama—a form of role-playing that focuses on a group solving a problem.

Socioeconomic status (SES)—a measure of social prestige defined in terms of such things as income, occupation, education, etc.

Special education—individualized education for children and youth with special needs.

Stagnant—not developing.

Standardized test—a commercially developed test that samples behavior under uniform procedures; used to provide accurate and meaningful information on students' levels of performance relative to others at their age or grade levels.

Steering group—a group of pupils within the class who are carefully observed by the teacher to determine whether the class is understanding the content being discussed in the lesson.

Stimulation approach—emphasis on the viewpoint that factors outside the individual account for behaviors.

Structuring the task—a step in the lesson, particularly in inductive-type lessons, that requires the teacher to specify the processes and procedures students are to follow to be successful with the learning experience.

Subtle—difficult to understand.

Success—attainment, achievement, or accomplishment.

Summative evaluation—assessment that follows instruction and evaluates at the end of a unit, semester, etc.; used to guide programs, curricula, etc.

Supervisor—administrator responsible for specific programs in public schools (e.g., supervisor of special education, vocational education supervisor, supervisor of elementary or secondary curriculum).

Symbolic medium—a representational medium for acquiring concepts through symbols such as language.

Synthesis—thinking that involves putting together ideas or elements to form a whole.

Synthesis questions—questions requiring the student to put together elements and parts to form a whole.

Target mistakes—the teacher stopping the wrong students or desisting a less serious misbehavior.

Task analysis—analyzing a task to determine its fundamental subskills.

Taxonomy—a classification system; used here in reference to a classification system of educational objectives or skills.

Teachable moment—a moment when an interruption offers the opportunity to teach more effectively to a different objective.

Teacher empowerment—the concept of putting decision making in the hands of teachers, the school personnel closest to the student.

Teacher expectations—teacher's opinion of a students' abilities to be successful.

Teacher-made test—an assessment instrument developed and scored by a teacher to meet particular classroom needs.

Teaching—the actions of someone who is trying to assist others to reach their fullest potential in all aspects of development.

Teaching style—the way a teacher teaches, that teacher's distinctive mannerisms complemented by his or her choices of teaching behaviors and strategies.

TGT (Teams Games Tournaments)—a cooperative-learning strategy in which teacher presentation is followed by team practice and individual mastery is tested in "tournaments," with two or three students of matched achievement, rather than tests.

Tenure—an employee benefit that makes it difficult to terminate someone; usually provided to teachers after several years of successful teaching experience.

Terminal behavior—that which has been learned as a direct result of instruction.

Terminal goals—goals one can expect to reach at the end of a given learning experience.

Test—a device used to determine if learning objectives have been met.

Test of English as a Foreign Language (TOEFL)—a standardized test used to assess the English language skills of nonnative individuals; frequently required of foreign students applying for admission to colleges and universities in the United States.

Testimonial—letter of recommendation.

Theme—a specific or distinctive quality or characteristic.

Thematic teaching—the organization of teaching and learning around a specific theme or topic. Although themes may be used in a single subject area such as English, sociology, or literature, two or more subject areas may be integrated using a single thematic approach.

Theoretical knowledge—concepts, facts, and propositions that make up much of the content of the disciplines.

Thinking—the act of withholding judgment in order to use past knowledge and experience to find new information, concepts, or conclusions.

Time-out—a form of punishment in which the student is removed for a short while from the rest of the class (sit in the corner, stand out in the hall, etc.); used when the teacher believes the student misbehaves because he or she wants attention.

Token reinforcement system—a system in which students perform actions or behaviors desired by the teacher in order to earn neutral tokens that can be exchanged periodically for rewards.

Tracking—the assigning of students to a curricular track based on perceived ability and performance.

Transfer—the ability to use information learned in one situation in another situation.

Tutoring—an instructional arrangement in which an individual assists with the instruction of another individual.

Transfer—the application of knowledge and skills in a new context.

Truant—a student between the ages of 6 and 16 who willfully does not attend school.

Trust—a value-relationship between and among individuals; includes such subordinate terms as *confidence, reliance, stability, absence of deception*.

Unit plan—a plan for a sequence of several lessons dealing with the same general topic.

Unity—harmony.

Usability—in regard to a test, practical considerations such as cost, time to administer, difficulty, and scoring procedure.

Validity—the ability of a test to measure what it purports to measure.

Valued data—data that involve a value judgment on the part of an observer.

Values clarification—a teaching program that focuses on students understanding and expressing their own values.

Valuing—affective learning that involves voluntarily giving worth to an object, a phenomenon, or a stimulus.

Variable—a characteristic that varies from entity to entity.

Variable-interval reinforcement schedule—a pattern for giving reinforcements, in which the time at which reinforcement will occur is unpredictable; effective for maintaining a high rate of behavior and highly resistant to extinction. Ex.: Teachers checking students' work at random intervals is variable-interval reinforcement.

Variable-ratio reinforcement schedule—a pattern for giving reinforcements, in which the number of desired responses before reinforcement is given, is unpredictable; effective in motivating individuals to work a long time, even after reinforcement has stopped and highly resistant to extinction. Ex.: Teachers checking random samples of students' work is variable-ratio reinforcement.

Verbal component—the actual words and meaning of a spoken message.

Verbal reinforcement—using positive comments as consequences to strengthen a behavior or event.

Vocal component—the meaning attached to a spoken message, resulting from such variables as voice firmness, modulation, tone, tempo, pitch, and loudness.

Wait time—the amount of time a teacher waits for a student to respond to a question before moving on to another student or giving the answer; also, a term used to describe the time a teacher waits before calling on a student to answer after posing a question to the whole class.

Within-class ability grouping—a system for accommodating differences between students by dividing a class into groups for instructional purposes (e.g., reading groups, mathematics groups, science groups).

With-it-ness—a teacher's awareness of what is going on in all parts of the classroom.

Whole-class discussion—a discussion among the whole class with the teacher as moderator; seating arrangements should be U-shaped or in a circle.

Whole-language approach—method of integrating language arts "across the curriculum" that uses the real literature of various age groups and subjects to promote literacy.

Year-round school program—a year-round school program has a calendar that provides for instruction for the entire year with short vacation periods throughout the year.

"You" messages—teacher messages that attack students.

Zone of proximal development—level of development that is one step above current level; learning in this zone requires assistance of peer or adult.

GETTING STARTED: ADVICE FOR NEW TEACHERS

So you've passed the LAST, ATS-W, and CST with flying colors and fulfilled all the requirements for becoming a teacher in New York. Now it's time to put all your learning into practice!

FINDING THE RIGHT POSITION

It is common knowledge that more good teachers are needed across the country. According to the National Center for Education Statistics, approximately 2 million new teachers would be needed in the United States in 2008–2009 (nces.ed.gov). But finding the right job for you can be a daunting process.

1. DO YOUR RESEARCH

First, determine the grade levels and/or subjects you'd like to teach. Make sure you have fulfilled all the qualifications for teaching in New York. These vary according to what type of certificate you are seeking, but the basics include these:

- Bachelor's degree from an accredited college or university
- Completion of an approved teaching program
- Passing scores on the LAST, ATS-W and CST Multi-Subject

Consult the state education department (nysed.gov) for more detailed information on certification.

2. IDENTIFY WHERE YOU WOULD LIKE TO WORK

Make a list of the districts and/or schools where you would most like to work. The NYS Department of Education has a listing of districts at nysed.gov/admin/admindex.html. Many school districts have websites on which they post job openings.

In addition, you should call the district office to find out if any positions are open and what their application procedures are.

Use the Internet as a resource. In addition to the many general websites for job hunters, some websites are devoted solely to teaching jobs. A few listing services charge a subscription fee, but many others are free. Some of these sites are included at the end of this chapter.

3. Attend Job Fairs

Job fairs are a good way to learn about openings and to network with other education professionals. Many schools in the State University of New York system host job fairs for teachers. Several of the websites for job seekers listed at the end of this chapter also have job fair listings by state. When attending a job fair, remember to act as if you were going to a job interview.

Remember that you are assessing potential employers as much as they are assessing you. Consider asking the following:

- What is the first professional development opportunity offered to new teachers?
- What additional duties outside the classroom are expected of teachers?
- When can I expect to meet my mentor?
- What is the top schoolwide priority this year?
- What kinds of materials or resources would be available in my classroom? (if applicable)
- What is your policy on lesson planning?

You may also want to ask about the demographics of the student population and what kinds of unique challenges they present.

4. Sign Up for Substitute Teaching

Substitute teaching can be another good strategy for getting your foot in the door in a particular school or district, even if there are no permanent jobs available. Think of this as an opportunity to impress principals and to learn from other teachers about possible openings. You can even submit your resume to the principals in the schools where you are substitute teaching and give them the chance to observe you in the classroom.

STARTING IN THE CLASSROOM

Don't get disillusioned if you're not immediately comfortable in your role as a teacher. Give yourself time to adjust, and don't hesitate to ask for advice from others. Be persistent about finding a mentor who can provide support during your first year and beyond. Try to find one in your subject area and determine how much experience you would like that person to have. For the sake of convenience, it's best to find someone who has a similar class schedule or daily routine.

TEACH RULES AND RESPECT

With students, be friendly but firm. Establish clear routines and consistent disciplinary measures early on. This way, the students have a firm understanding of what is expected of them and when certain behaviors are appropriate. Have the principal review your disciplinary plan to make certain that he or she will support it and that there aren't any potential legal issues. Be aware of how cliques and social hierarchies impact classroom dynamics, and don't underestimate the power of your own advice.

Although disciplinary issues vary according to grade level, there are some general tips you may find helpful in setting rules in the classroom:

- Often, troublesome students misbehave merely to get your attention. Reduce this negative behavior by paying the least amount of attention when a student is acting out and giving that child your full attention when he or she is behaving.

- When it comes to establishing classroom rules, allow your students to have some input. This will increase their sense of empowerment and respect for the rules.

- Convince all of your students that they are worthwhile and capable. It is easy to assume that struggling students are lazy or beyond help—do not allow yourself to fall into this trap.

- When disciplining students, absolutely avoid embarrassing them in any way, especially in front of their peers.

- Double standards and favoritism will lose you the respect of all your students—always be firm, fair, and consistent. Never talk down to your students.

- Avoid becoming too chummy with your students. Young teachers often feel that they must make "friends" with students, particularly in the older grades.

However, it's important to maintain some professional distance and to establish yourself as an authority figure.

- Admit your mistakes. If you wrongly accuse a student of doing something she did not do, make an inappropriate joke, or reprimand a student more harshly than necessary, be sure to apologize and explain. If a parent or administrator criticizes you for your mistake, calmly explain how you felt at that moment and why. Also, explain how you plan to handle that kind of situation in the future.

Do Your Homework

Any veteran teacher will tell you that you will spend almost as many hours working outside the classroom as you do with your students. Preparing lessons and grading homework and tests can take an enormous amount of time, so it's a good idea to be as organized as possible.

Also consider what your expectations will be:

- Will you grade every homework assignment or just some of them?
- Will you give students an opportunity to earn extra credit?
- What kind of system will you use for grading tests?

Design Lesson Plans Early

Before you start planning, be aware of holidays off, assemblies, and similar interruptions. Design your lessons accordingly. Similarly, be sure you know your content, your state's standards, your school's expectations, and the ins and outs of child development. Be prepared with multiple learning styles and differentiated teaching strategies.

Try to develop time-saving strategies. Saving your lesson plan outline as a template on the computer can be very helpful—instead of rewriting the whole plan everyday, you can just fill in the blanks.

Establish Rules for Grading Homework

Along with establishing a consistent disciplinary policy early on, it's important to develop grading guidelines. Some teachers set the bar high at the beginning of the year by grading a little tougher than they normally would. Just as many students will underachieve if they think you are a soft grader, they will work hard to meet your expectations if your standards are high. However, it's important to assess your students' abilities and set realistic standards.

Grading every single assignment can get overwhelming; sometimes verbally assessing comprehension is enough. Rubrics are another useful tool for outlining expectations and scoring, as well as making sure you cater to the needs of all your students. They are also effective when students grade each other.

Returning graded assignments as soon as possible sets a good example, keeps your workload manageable, and prevents students' interest from waning. However, you should never use a student's work as an example of what not to do.

Consider sending grades home on a regular basis and getting them signed by a parent or guardian in order to keep everyone aware of students' progress. This prevents students and parents from being blindsided by poor grades.

Don't mistake quietness for comprehension. Check in with all students because some may be afraid to admit that they don't understand what's going on. If you feel there is a problem, don't wait to address a student's needs. If you believe that a student may have an undiagnosed disability, let your principal know and follow your school's procedure.

Finding tangible rewards for students' achievements is a great way to keep them motivated, particularly if you focus their efforts around gradually earning the rewards. These types of incentive systems work particularly well in the elementary grades.

DEAL WITH PARENTS EARLY ON

Establish a relationship with parents from the beginning—frequent, positive communication is essential to helping the children attain the best education possible. Here are a few tips for keeping in touch with parents:

- Make phone calls or email, even if you're just going to leave a message. Doing so will allow you to share good news and help guardians become more familiar with you.

- Give students homework folders that frequently travel between school and home.

- Be ready to deal with breakdowns in communication: it may be necessary to send multiple messages home.

- Send home a short newsletter of things to come.

SET UP PARENT–TEACHER CONFERENCES

Meeting with parents can often be intimidating for new teachers, particularly if a student is not performing well. It's a good idea to seek guidance from experienced teachers and to communicate with administrators if you encounter problems. In addition, try to follow these general guidelines when talking with parents:

- Remain professional. Choose your words carefully, have good things to say about the student, don't take heated words personally, keep examples of the student's work on hand, and document what is said during the meeting.

- Allow parents to ask the first question. This will help you understand their tone and their concerns.

- Be as thick skinned as possible when dealing with problems: some parents want to vent a little before getting to the crux of the issue. Let them vent, try to put them at ease, and then look for a solution or compromise.

- If a parent becomes excessively confrontational, inform an administrator.

- Be confident. Listen to what the parents suggest, but also stand up for what you believe is the best course of action.

BUILD STRONG RELATIONSHIPS WITH COLLEAGUES

Meet as many teachers in the building as you can: not only will you gain valuable insights about the inner workings of the school, but you'll also make new friends. Don't be afraid to step up and ask questions when information isn't offered. Veteran teachers are a tremendous resource for all kinds of information, from labor contracts to strategies for staying sane under pressure. Also, get to know the other new teachers. These people will be valuable sounding boards and will help you feel less alone.

Earn the respect of your colleagues by stepping up to committee work and by proving yourself to be a reliable, competent teacher. You should also be polite and friendly with the staff and custodians: you'll need their help for all sorts of reasons.

Finally, be professional, timely, and unafraid to calmly share your opinions or disagree with administrators. Your professionalism and enthusiasm will earn you their respect and ensure that your needs are met.

DEALING WITH PAPERWORK

Ah, paperwork! Be aware of what kinds of paperwork you need to fill out and file, including the school Improvement Plan, special education forms relating to Individualized Education Plans, budget requests, reading and math benchmarks, and permanent record cards. Try to sit with fellow teachers when filling out forms. Their companionship will make these tedious tasks more fun.

UNDERSTANDING UNIONS

Depending on your school district, you may be part of a teacher's union. It is important to gain a clear understanding of union requirements. You'll want to know the following:

- How much money will be deducted from your paycheck for union dues?

- How can you obtain a copy of the most recent union contract?

You may wish to contact the New York State United Teachers (nysut.org) or the United Federation of Teachers, which represents teachers in New York City.

ALLOW YOURSELF DOWNTIME

Finally, always give yourself time to wind down and distance yourself from the classroom. This is essential to prevent burnout or resentment over a lack of free time, and it will allow you to pursue other interests and personal relationships.

ADDITIONAL RESOURCES

BOOKS

Capel, Susan, Marilyn Leask, and Terry Turner. *Learning to Teach in the Secondary School: A Companion to School Experience.* 3rd ed. Oxford: Taylor & Francis, 2010.

Dillon, Justin. *Becoming a Teacher.* 3rd ed. Berkshire, England: Open University Press, 2007.

Goodnough, Abby. *Ms. Moffett's First Year: Becoming a Teacher in America.* New York: Public Affairs, 2006.

Howe, Randy. *Training Wheels for Teachers: What I Wish I Had Known My First 100 Days on the Job: Wisdom, Tips, and Warnings from Experienced Teachers.* Chicago: Kaplan, 2004.

Parkay, Forrest W., and Beverly Hardcastle Stanford. *Becoming a Teacher.* 8th ed. Boston: Allyn & Bacon, 2009.

Staff of U.S. News and World Report. *U.S. News Ultimate Guide to Becoming a Teacher.* Naperville, IL: Sourcebooks, 2004.

Wong, Harry K., and Rosemary T. Wong. *The First Days of School: How to Be an Effective Teacher.* 4th ed. Mountain View, CA: Harry K. Wong Publications, 2009.

MAGAZINES AND JOURNALS

American Educator

Harvard Educational Review

The New York Times Education Life

Phi Delta Kappan

INTERNET RESOURCES

teachernet.com/htm/becomingateacher.htm
Community for K–8 educators

pbs.org/firstyear/beaTeacher/
PBS: How to become a teacher

newsweekshowcase.com/education/id/graduate-programs/teacher-training/
Teacher education and recruitment; teaching as a second career

eric.ed.gov (Education Resources Information Center)
Large teaching and education database

aft.org
American Federation of Teachers

proudtoserveagain.com/index.html
Troops to Teachers program—gives former members of the U.S. military the opportunity to become public school teachers, providing help with certification, job searching, and more.

ed.gov
U.S. Department of Education

teach-nology.com
Free and easy-to-use resources for teachers

theteachersguide.com

behavioradvisor.com

kidsource.com

Sites with Tips from Teachers

ncrel.org/he/tot/teach.htm: Teachers' input on teaching, learning how to teach

teachingtips.com: Tips from an experienced teacher

atozteacherstuff.com: A teacher-created site listing online resources and tips

Lesson Plan Sites

education-world.com

theteacherscorner.net

lessonplansearch.com

teachnet.com

General Teaching Job Sites

schoolspring.com

teachers-teachers.com

job-hunt.com/academia.shtml

educationjobs.com

abcteachingjobs.com

k12jobs.com

jobs2teach.doded.mil/Jobs2Teach/J2TDefault.asp (part of the Troops to Teachers website)

wanttoteach.com/newsite/jobfairs.html (national teaching job fair website)

New York Resources

nysed.gov
New York State Education Department

uft.org
United Federation of Teachers—union in New York City

nysut.org
New York State United Teachers—state union

nysed.gov/teachers/teachers.html
Resources for teachers

Job Sites

nyeducationjobs.com

nyedjobs.org